THE
ULTIMATE
GUIDE TO
PRAYER

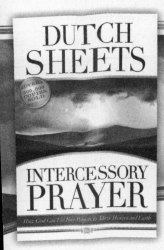

DUTCH
SHEETS

INTERCESSORY
PRAYER

How God Can Use Your Prayers to Move Heaven and Earth

How to Pray for
LOST
LOVED ONES
DUTCH SHEETS
Best-Selling Author of Intercessory Prayer

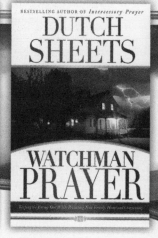

BESTSELLING AUTHOR OF *Intercessory Prayer*

DUTCH
SHEETS

WATCHMAN
PRAYER

Keeping the Enemy Out While Protecting Your Family, Home and Community

THREE BESTSELLERS IN ONE VOLUME

DUTCH SHEETS

Regal

For more information and
special offers from Regal Books, email us at
subscribe@regalbooks.com

Published by Regal
From Gospel Light
Ventura, California, U.S.A.
www.regalbooks.com
Printed in the U.S.A.

This work is a compilation of the following titles:
Intercessory Prayer © 1996 by Dutch Sheets
How to Pray for Lost Loved Ones © 2001 by Dutch Sheets
Watchman Prayer © 2000 by Dutch Sheets

Rights for publishing this book outside the U.S.A. or in non-English languages are
administered by Gospel Light Worldwide, an international not-for-profit ministry.
For additional information, please visit www.glww.org, email info@glww.org, or write to
Gospel Light Worldwide, 1957 Eastman Avenue, Ventura, CA 93003, U.S.A.

To order copies of this book and other Regal products in bulk quantities,
please contact us at 1-800-446-7735.

CONTENTS

BOOK ONE

INTERCESSORY
PRAYER

How God Can Use Your Prayers to Move Heaven and Earth

DUTCH
SHEETS

To the Sheets team—Ceci, my wife and best friend;
Sarah and Hannah, our two precious daughters;
and yours truly—lovingly dedicate this labor of love to Jesus.
"Thank You, Sir, for the price You paid and the
passion that still motivates You. You're our Hero.
It is fun and a great honor to serve and represent
You on the earth. We look forward to many more
wonderful times and days with You!"

P.S. "We hope You like the book—we did it for You!"

FOREWORD

The modern prayer movement began around 1970. True, it had been burning brightly in Korea for some decades previously, but it was around 1970 that it started to spread worldwide. In recent years the expansion of the prayer movement has been exponential. Quality of prayer is increasing along with quantity of prayer. Flames of prayer are being lit in virtually every church movement on every continent. Pastors are giving prayer a higher priority, children are praying fervently and effectively, prayer movements and prayer ministries are proliferating, theological seminaries are introducing courses on prayer, and even secular magazines have been featuring cover stories about prayer.

I am one of those who has been deeply touched by the contemporary prayer movement. For a good bit of my ministry career, prayer was boring to me. Oh, I knew the Bible taught that we must pray and that God answers prayer. I also knew prayer was included as a normal part of the day-by-day routine of Christian individuals, families and churches. But I would look forward to a prayer meeting with about as much enthusiasm as I look forward to visiting the dentist. No longer!

It was the sovereign hand of God that drew me into what would become an intense involvement with the worldwide prayer movement back in 1987. Since then, I have researched prayer diligently. I have improved my personal prayer life greatly. I have taught prayer seminars and seminary courses on prayer. I helped to coordinate prayer activities for the A.D. 2000 Movement and I have written several books on prayer. The reason I mention these things is not to blow myself up as some sort of spiritual giant, which I am not. It is rather to display some credentials as a backdrop to a statement I am about to make.

As a professional scholar, I accept the responsibility of keeping abreast of the literature relating to prayer to the best of my ability. My personal library currently includes many shelves of books about prayer, and the number continues to increase rapidly. Looking over that section of my library, which I can see from where I am now sitting, I see no book that compares to this one written by my good friend Dutch Sheets.

I know every book has its own unique features. But *Intercessory Prayer* is in a category by itself. In my opinion, Dutch Sheets has provided, more than any other contemporary author, what could be considered the standard biblical theology for the worldwide prayer movement. I was thrilled as I first read page after page of solid biblical teaching about the many facets of prayer. As I did, I was pleasantly surprised to come across concept after concept that I had not considered before. Few things I have read have turned on more lights than *Intercessory Prayer*. Others have agreed with me, since the book has sold hundreds of thousands of copies.

It is a danger, I realize, to classify anything as "theology." To many, reading theology is about as interesting as watching lawn bowling. But Dutch Sheets is one of those theologians who are also dynamic communicators. Instead of making simple things complicated, like some theologians, he knows how to make complicated things simple.

Sunday after Sunday, Pastor Dutch preaches to hundreds in Freedom Church, one of Colorado Springs's most dynamic churches. As he does in his sermons, Dutch brings to life every point he makes through real life stories, some about his own experiences and some about the experiences of others. Every one of them shows how God can be glorified through the prayers of any believer.

If you want new power in your prayer life and in the prayer life of your group, you have the guidebook you need in your hands. Your prayers will have more power to the degree they have more substance. You will not read far before you realize you are absorbing some of the most substantial teaching about prayer available today. As I have done, you will thank God and thank Dutch Sheets for this outstanding book.

C. Peter Wagner
Presiding Apostle
International Coalition of Apostles

1

THE QUESTION IS . . .

No Hope

I knew the person I was going to pray for was very ill. What I didn't know was that she was comatose with a tracheostomy in her throat, a feeding tube in her stomach and had been in that condition for a year and a half. Seeing her for the first time was like expecting a prescription and receiving brain surgery. Her sister, who had asked me to visit this young lady, had not given me the whole story for fear I wouldn't go at all. She knew if she could just get me there once, I'd probably go back. She was right!

The doctors gave Diane (not her real name) no hope for living, let alone coming out of the coma. Even if she did regain consciousness, she would basically be a vegetable because of her extensive brain damage, or so the doctors believed.

Have you ever stood beside someone in this kind of condition and asked God for a miracle? To stand beside death and ask for life can be intimidating. It can also teach us a lot—about life, about death, about ourselves and about our God. Especially when we stand beside the same person 60 to 70 times, for an hour or more each time, throughout the course of a year.

Confronted with the Unexpected

It didn't work out as I expected. Life rarely does, does it?

I expected the Lord to heal this young lady through our prayers in a dramatic, easy, quick way. After all, that's how it happened with Jesus.

- I didn't expect to invest three to four hours of my life each week for a year (including the travel time).
- I didn't expect humiliation and insults from the staff of the nursing home where she stayed.
- I didn't expect to cry so much.
- I didn't expect to be so bold at times.
- I didn't expect to be so intimidated at times.
- I didn't expect it to take so long.
- I didn't expect to learn so much!

The Miracle

Yes, God restored Diane! He healed her brain, the outer layer of which the doctors said had been totally destroyed by a virus. Every part of it was covered with infection. "No hope," they said.

The front page of the *Dayton Daily News* (not the real place or newspaper) read, "Woman Awake, Alive, Healthy After Two Years in Coma." The doctors called it a "medical miracle." "We have no explanation," they said, though they stopped short of giving God the glory.

It actually happened on a Saturday morning when she was all alone. Earlier that week Diane had been moved from the nursing home to a hospital for treatment of an infection. After administering more tests, the doctors determined her condition had grown worse and informed her family that she would probably die soon.

When Diane's sister relayed this information to me, I dashed off to the hospital.

Knowing comatose people can often hear and understand everything happening around them, I spoke much to her. As we later learned, because of the damage to her brain Diane was not hearing me. But on this Wednesday afternoon, I spoke to her as usual.

"This nightmare is almost over," I said with tears streaming down my face. "Nothing can keep us from receiving our miracle. Nothing!"

The memory is forever imprinted on my mind. As I exited the hospital weeping, I remember saying to myself again and again, "Nothing can keep us from our miracle. Nothing!"

It was not just a strong hope I had at this point but a great faith. I had turned to God many times throughout the course of that year asking Him if He had really sent me to this little girl. Each time I received His assurance: "I sent you. Don't quit."

The Power of Persistence

Now, I've been accused of being quite a stubborn fellow, and I suppose that's true. In fact, I've "stubborned" myself into a lot of trouble, including two major concussions playing football when a couple of fellows had more size and muscle behind their "stubborn" than I did.

Stubbornness, however, can be channeled into a righteous force called persistence or endurance. I've found it to be one of the most important spiritual attributes of the Christian life. Charles Spurgeon said, "By perseverance the snail reached the ark."[1]

A lack of endurance is one of the greatest causes of defeat, especially in prayer. We don't wait well. We're into microwaving; God, on the other hand, is usually into marinating. So I persisted for a year, and as I did my faith grew until I knew deep inside we were going to win. My motto had become Galatians 6:9: "Let us not lose heart in doing good, for in due time we shall reap if we do not grow weary."

My persistence was rewarded when, three days after that Wednesday in the hospital, Diane woke up with full restoration to her brain. News about the miracle spread to other nations. In fact, the nursing home where she had stayed received inquiries from Europe wanting to know about her incredible recovery.

Every hour and every tear I had invested became worth the wait when I saw Diane awake and heard her speak the words, "Praise the Lord."

What did I learn from that year-long endeavor? Much, plus a whole lot! And I'm still learning.

> In "The Last Days Newsletter," Leonard Ravenhill tells about a group of tourists visiting a picturesque village who walked by an old man sitting beside a fence. In a rather patronizing way, one tourist asked, "Were any great men born in this village?" The old man replied, "Nope, only babies."[2]

I've learned that no one is born a prayer hero. They are shaped and refined on the practice field of life.

A Hollywood talent judge said of Fred Astaire, one of the top singers, dancers and actors of all time: "Can't act. Can't sing. Can dance a little."[3] I'm sure Satan has passed his judgment on me at times in my life: "Can't preach. Can't lead. Can pray a little." Thank God for His grace, patience and commitment to me. I've stumbled forward more than backward in life.

So Many Questions

From this and other prayer journeys—from failures as well as victories—from hundreds of hours of study, I've formed some thoughts to share with you. I believe they will answer many questions, such as:

- Is prayer really necessary? If so, why? Isn't God sovereign? Doesn't that mean He accomplishes what He wants, when He wants? If so, why pray?

- Is God's will for a Christian automatically guaranteed or is it linked to prayer and other factors?

- Why does it often take so long to get a prayer answered? Why is persistence required? Jacob wrestled with God. Is that what we are to do in prayer? I don't like the thought of wrestling with God, do you?

- What about prayer for the lost? How can I be more effective? I get a little frustrated trying to think of new ways to ask God to save people, don't you? I thought He *wanted* to save them. Then why do I feel as though I'm trying to talk Him into it? Is there a better way? Do I ask for their salvation again and again or simply petition Him once and then just thank Him in faith?

- What about spiritual warfare? If Satan is defeated and Christ has all authority, shouldn't we just forget about the devil? Does God bind the devil or do we?

- What exactly is intercessory prayer? And don't just tell me it's "standing in the gap." Enough religious quotes and spiritual jargon. I know the thought is taken from the Bible, but what does it mean?

• What about protection? Is everything that happens to me or my family simply allowed by God? Or is there something I need to do to procure our safety?

• How do we "bear one another's burdens" (Gal. 6:2)?

• Is there a right time for answers to prayer or does the timing depend on me?

Are you getting tired of all these questions? I know I am—so I'll stop. You may even be tired of asking yourself some of them. I know I was. Many people stopped asking them long ago, and probably stopped praying, too.

Please don't do that!

Keep asking! I've discovered that the right answer begins with the right question. I've also discovered that God is not offended by a sincere question. He won't satisfy the skeptic and He is not pleased with unbelief, but He loves an honest seeker. Those who lack and ask for wisdom He does not rebuke (see Jas. 1:5). He is a good Dad. Will you pray this prayer with me?

Father, we need more understanding—not more knowledge. We have so much of it now that we are becoming confused. Yes, and even cynical at times because our knowledge has not always worked. In fact, Father, our Bibles often seem to contradict our experiences. We need some answers. We need a marriage of theology and experience.

We've been encouraged by the stories of other great prayer warriors—the praying Hydes, the David Brainerds, the Andrew Murrays and the apostle Pauls. But frankly, Lord, it gets a bit frustrating when our prayers don't seem to work. And intimidating as well because we don't know if we will ever be able to pray two to three hours a day, as these great intercessors did.

We need more than inspiration now. We need answers.

So, as Your disciples did, Lord, we say, "Teach us to pray."
We know it often requires hard work, but can't it also be fun? We
know there will be failures, but how about a few more successes? We
know "we walk by faith, not by sight" (2 Cor. 5:7), but
couldn't we see a few more victories? . . . Souls saved? . . .
Healings?

We are tired of cloaking our ignorance in robes of blind
obedience and calling it spirituality. We are tired of religious
exercises that make us feel better for a while but bear little last-
ing fruit. We are tired of a form of godliness without the power.

Help us, please. In Jesus' name we pray. Amen.

THE NECESSITY OF PRAYER

Because I Said So!

"Because I said so!"

Don't you just hate it when that's the reason given for doing something? Not only is it frustrating, but it's also a motivation killer. It's one thing when the question "Why?" stems from a rebellion-rooted resistance, but when one sincerely doesn't understand why, this answer can be a real bummer. I remember having my knuckles rapped with a ruler for asking the simple question, "Why?"

Whack! "Because I said so! Now be quiet and do it."

I still wish I could rap that teacher's knuckles with a yardstick and not tell her why! (Don't worry, we'll deal with forgiveness and inner healing another time.)

None of us wants to do something just because someone else said so. Oh, I know God requires things of us at times without the full knowledge of why, but they are usually occasional obedience and trust issues—not the way He expects us to live life on a regular basis. We are not programmed robots who never ask why. He does not require an ostrich mentality of us: head in the sand, blind to the truth, the issues, the facts.

I Wonder Why

God has given us a Bible full of answers to the *whys* of life. The one I'm interested in is: Why pray? I'm not speaking of why in the sense of needing this or that. Obviously we ask because we want or need something. I'm speaking of why in the context of God's sovereignty.

Do my prayers really matter all that much? Isn't God going to do what He wants anyway? Most people, even if only subconsciously, believe just that. The proof is in their prayer life, or lack thereof.

Can my prayers actually change things? Does God *need* me to pray or does He just *want* me to pray? Some would argue an omnipotent God doesn't "need" anything, including our prayers.

Can God's will on Earth be frustrated or not accomplished if I don't pray? Many would brand me a heretic for even raising the question.

But these and other questions deserve answers. I've discovered that understanding the why of doing something can be a great motivating force. The opposite is also true.

As a kid I wondered why the sign said "No diving" in the shallow end of the pool. Then one day I hit my head on the bottom. I don't do that anymore.

I used to wonder why I shouldn't touch the pretty red glow on the stove. I found out.

I wondered why a fellow in front of me in the woods said, "Duck."

I thought, *I don't want to duck. I don't have to duck.* Then the branch whopped me upside the head. Now I duck.

I Need to Know

Someone said, "To err is human, to repeat it is stupid." I'm sure I've even qualified for that once or twice, but not with these three *because now I know why!* However, we're not talking about bumps, burns and bruises here; we're talking about eternal destinies. We're talking about homes, marriages, the welfare of people we love, revival in our cities—the list continues.

When God says, "Pray," I want to know it will matter. I'm not into religious exercises and my time is valuable—so is yours. Was S. D. Gordon right or wrong when he said, "You can do more than pray *after* you have prayed, but you cannot do more than pray until you have prayed. . . . Prayer is striking the winning blow . . . service is gathering up the results"?[1]

If God is going to do something regardless of whether or not we pray, then He doesn't need us to ask and we don't need another waste of time. If it's all *que sera, sera,* then let's take a siesta and let it all just happen.

If, on the other hand, John Wesley was correct when he said, "God does nothing on the earth save in answer to believing prayer," I'll lose a little sleep for that. I'll change my lifestyle for that. I'll turn the TV off, and even miss a meal or two.

- I need to know if that cyst on my wife's ovary dissolved because I prayed.
- I need to know if I was spared in the earthquake because someone prayed.
- I need to know if Diane came out of her coma with a restored brain because we prayed.
- I need to know if my prayers can make a difference between heaven and hell for someone.

Is Prayer Really Necessary?

The real question is: Does a sovereign, all-powerful God need our involvement or not? Is prayer really necessary? If so, why? I believe it is necessary. Our prayers can bring revival. They can bring healing. We can change a nation. Strongholds can come down when and because we pray. I agree with E. M. Bounds when he said:

God shapes the world by prayer. The more praying there is in the world the better the world will be, the mightier the forces against evil. . . . The prayers of God's saints are the capital stock of heaven by which God carries on His great work upon earth. God conditions the very life and prosperity of His cause on prayer.[2]

I couldn't agree more—and want to share with you why I believe this is so. If you concur with me, you'll pray more. You will most likely pray with greater faith, too.

God's Original Plan

The answer to why prayer is necessary lies in God's original plan when He created Adam.

I used to think Adam had to be pretty awesome. I now know he was, as my kids would say, "way awesome." (For those who don't have teenagers or young kids, "way" means "very" or "totally.")

The name Adam means "man; human being."[3] In other words, God made man and called him "Man." He made a human and called him "Human." He made an adam and named him "Adam." In fact, oftentimes when the Bible uses the term "man" the actual Hebrew word is *adam*, spelled just like our English word. I share this simply to say that Adam represents all of us. What God intended for Adam, He intended for the entire human race.

What was God's intention? Initially, He gave Adam and Eve and their descendants dominion over the entire earth and all creation as we see in Genesis 1:26-28:

Then God said, "Let Us make man in Our image, according to Our likeness; and let them rule over the fish of the sea and over the birds of the sky and over the cattle and over all the earth, and over every creeping thing that creeps on the earth." And God created man in His own image, in the image of God He created him; male and female He created them. And God blessed them; and God said to them, "Be fruitful and multiply, and fill the earth, and subdue it; and rule over the fish of the sea and over the birds of the sky, and over every living thing that moves on the earth."

We see this also in Psalm 8:3-8:

When I consider Thy heavens, the work of Thy fingers, the moon and the stars, which Thou hast ordained; What is man, that Thou dost take thought of him? And the son of man, that Thou dost care for him? Yet Thou hast made him a little lower than God, and dost crown him with glory and majesty! Thou dost make him to rule over the works of Thy hands; Thou hast put all things under his feet, all sheep and oxen, and also the beasts of the field, the birds of the heavens, and the fish of the sea, whatever passes through the paths of the seas.

Adam, God's Re-Presenter on Earth

The Hebrew word *mashal*, translated "rule" in verse 6 of this passage, indicates that Adam (and eventually his descendants) was God's *manager* here, God's *steward* or *governor*. Adam was God's *mediator, go-between* or *representative*.

Psalm 115:16 also confirms this: "The heaven . . . the Eternal holds himself, the earth He has *assigned* to men" (*Moffatt Translation*, emphasis added). This translation communicates with greater accuracy the meaning of the Hebrew word *nathan*, otherwise frequently translated "given." God didn't give away ownership of the earth, but He did assign the responsibility of governing it to humanity.

Genesis 2:15 says, "Then the Lord God took the man and put him into the garden of Eden to cultivate it and keep it." The word "keep" is a translation of the Hebrew word *shamar*, which means "to guard or protect."[4] It is the primary word used for a watchman in the Scriptures. Adam literally was God's watchman or guardian on the earth.

No serious student of the Bible would argue that Adam was God's representative here. But what does it actually mean to represent someone? The dictionary defines "representation" as "to present again."[5] Another way to say it might be to "re-present" someone. A representative is one who re-presents the will of another. I, for example, am honored to represent Christ often throughout the world. I hope I *present* Him *again* as I speak in His name.

The dictionary also provided these meanings: "to exhibit the image and counterpart of; to speak and act with authority on the part of; to be a substitute or agent for."[6] Sounds very similar to what God told Adam, doesn't it?

Now, it's no small task to re-present God. Therefore to help us humans more adequately carry out this assignment, God made us so much the same as Himself that it was illusionary. "And God created man in His own image, in the image of God He created him; male and female He created them" (Gen. 1:27). The Hebrew word for "image" is *tselem*, which involves the concept of a *shadow*, a *phantom* or an *illusion*.[7]

An illusion is something you think you see, but on closer observation you discover that your eyes have tricked you. When the rest of creation saw Adam, they must have done a double take, probably thinking something along these lines: *For a moment I thought it was God, but it's only Adam.* How's that for re-presentation? It's pretty heavy theology, too!

We are also told that Adam was *similar* to or *comparable* to God. The Hebrew word *demuwth*, translated "likeness" in Genesis 1:26, comes from the root word *damah* meaning "to compare."[8] Adam was very much like God!

Psalm 8:5 actually says human beings were made just "a little lower than God." God even gave us the ability to create eternal spirits, something He had entrusted to no other creature! Later, the same verse says humanity was crowned with God's very own glory.

Speaking of heavy theology, the definition of the Hebrew word *kabowd*, which is translated "glory," literally means "heavy or weighty"![9] This, of course, is linked to the concept of authority. We still use the picture today when we refer to one who "carries a lot of weight." Adam carried the weight on the earth. I don't know what he weighed but he was heavy. He represented God with full authority! He was in charge!

The Greek word for "glory," *doxa*, is just as revelatory. It involves the concept of recognition. More precisely, it is that which causes something or someone to be recognized for what it really is.[10] When we read in Scripture that humankind is the glory of God (see 1 Cor. 11:7), it is telling us God was *recognized* in humans. Why? So that humans could accurately *represent* Him. When creation looked at Adam, they were supposed to see God. And they did! That is, until Adam sinned and fell short of the glory of God. God is no longer recognized in fallen humankind. We must be changed back into God's image "from glory to glory" (2 Cor. 3:18) for this recognition to be realized again.

My purpose is not to overwhelm or impress you with a lot of definitions, but rather to broaden your understanding of God's plan for humankind at the Creation. Therefore, let's summarize what we've said using a compilation of the preceding verses and definitions:

Adam was comparable to or similar to God—so much like God that it was illusionary. God was recognized in Adam, which meant that Adam "carried the weight" here on Earth. Adam represented God, presenting again His will on the earth. Adam was God's governor or manager here. The earth was Adam's assignment—it was under Adam's charge or care. Adam was the watchman or guardian. How things went on planet Earth, for better or worse, depended on Adam and his offspring.

Please think about that. If the earth remained a paradise, it would be because of humankind. If things became messed up, it would be because of humankind. If the serpent ever gained control, it would be because of humankind. Humanity really was in charge!

Why would God do it this way? Why would He take such a risk? From what I know about God in the Scriptures and from my personal walk with Him, I find only one conclusion: God wanted a family—sons and daughters who could personally relate to Him, and vice versa. So He made our original parents similar to Himself. He put His very life and Spirit into them, gave them a beautiful home with lots of pets, sat down and said, "This is good." Daily He communed with them, walked with them, taught them about Himself and their home. He said, "Give me some grandsons and granddaughters." God was now a dad, and He was thrilled!

Granted, this is the Sheets's paraphrase, but it doesn't really change the Scriptures—it is leading us to a conclusion about the necessity of prayer.

God Works Through the Prayers of His People

Let's move on to this conclusion. Because we are talking about "weighty" stuff, such as glory crowns, illusions and people creating eternal things, how is this for heavy? So complete and final was Adam's authority over the earth that he, not just God, had the ability to give it away to another! Listen to the words of Satan in Luke 4:6-7 as he tempted Jesus: "I will give You all this domain and its glory; for *it has been handed over to me, and I give it to whomever I wish.* Therefore, if You worship before me, it shall all be Yours" (emphasis added).

The part about the domain being handed over to him was true and Jesus knew it. He even called Satan "the ruler of this world" three times in the Gospels (see John 12:31; 14:30; 16:11).

And here comes heavy number two: So complete and final was God's decision to do things on Earth through human beings that it cost God the Incarnation to regain what Adam gave away. He had to become a part of the human race. I can't think of a more staggering truth. Certainly nothing could give weightier proof of the finality of this "through humans" decision God made. Without question, *humans were forever to be God's link to authority and activity on the earth.*

Here we have, I believe, the reason for the necessity of prayer. God chose, from the time of the Creation, to work on the earth through humans, not independent of them. He always has and always will, even at the cost of becoming one. Though God is sovereign and all-powerful, Scripture clearly tells us that He limited Himself, concerning the affairs of Earth, to working *through* human beings.

Is this not the reason the earth is in such a mess? Not because God wills it so, but because of His need to work and carry out His will through people.

Is this not the story woven throughout the Scriptures:

- God and humans, for better or worse, doing it together?
- God needing faithful men and women?
- God needing a race through whom to work?

- God needing prophets?
- God needing judges?
- God needing a human Messiah?
- God needing human hands to heal, human voices to speak and human feet to go?

Doesn't He need us to ask for His kingdom to come, His will to be done (see Matt. 6:10)? Surely He wouldn't want us to waste our time asking for something that was going to happen anyway, would He?

Didn't He tell us to ask for our daily bread (see Matt. 6:11)? And yet, He knows our needs before we even ask.

Didn't He tell us to ask that laborers be sent into the harvest (see Matt. 9:38)? But, doesn't the Lord of the harvest want that more than we do?

Didn't Paul say, "Pray for us that the word of the Lord may spread rapidly and be glorified" (2 Thess. 3:1)? Wasn't God already planning to do this?

Are not these things God's will? Why, then, am I supposed to ask Him for something He already wants to do if it's not that my asking somehow releases Him to do it? Let's look briefly at three more biblical passages that support this.

Elijah's Fervent Prayers

In 1 Kings 18, we find the story of God needing and using a person to accomplish His will through prayer. It is the account of Elijah praying for rain after three years of drought. James 5:17-18 also mentions this occasion, and we know from his account that not only did Elijah's prayers bring rain, but they also stopped the rain three years earlier. We know we're in trouble when the prophets are praying for drought!

In verse one of 1 Kings 18, after three years of this judgment, God spoke to Elijah and said, "Go, show yourself to Ahab, and

I will send rain on the face of the earth." Then at the end of this chapter, after several other events have occurred, Elijah prays seven times and finally the rain comes.

According to the statement in verse one, whose idea was it to send rain? . . . Whose will? . . . Whose initiation? Answer: God's, not Elijah's.

Then why, if it was God's will, idea and timing, did it take a human's prayers to "birth" the rain? (Elijah was in the posture of a woman in that culture giving birth, symbolizing the concept of travailing prayer.)

Why did Elijah have to ask seven times? Seven is the biblical number of completion, and I'm sure God was teaching us that we must pray until the task is accomplished. But why would this or any other prayer endeavor require perseverance, when it was God's will, idea and timing?

And finally, did Elijah's prayers really produce the rain or was it simply coincidental that he happened to be praying when God sent it?

James clarifies the answer to this last question. Yes, "the effectual fervent prayer" of this man stopped and brought the rain:

> Elijah was a man with a nature like ours, and he prayed
> earnestly that it might not rain; and it did not rain on
> the earth for three years and six months. And he prayed
> again, and the sky poured rain, and the earth produced
> its fruit (Jas. 5:17-18).

The only logical answer to the question of why Elijah needed to pray is simply that *God has chosen to work through people.* Even when it is the Lord Himself initiating something, earnestly desiring to do it, He still needs us to ask. Andrew Murray succinctly speaks of our need to ask: "God's giving is inseparably connected with our asking. . . . Only by intercession can that power be brought down from heaven which will enable the Church to conquer the world."[11]

As to Elijah's need for perseverance, I don't want to comment extensively at this time, but for now suffice it to say that I believe our prayers do more than just petition the Father. I've become convinced that in some situations they actually release cumulative amounts of God's power until enough has been released to accomplish His will.

Daniel, a Man of Prayer

Another example that supports our premise of the absolute need for prayer is found in the life of Daniel. In 606 B.C. Israel had been taken captive by another nation because of its sin. Years later in Daniel 9 we're told that while reading the prophet Jeremiah, Daniel discovered it was time for Israel's captivity to end. Jeremiah had not only prophesied the captivity of which Daniel was a part, but he also prophesied the duration: 70 years.

At this point Daniel did something very different from what most of us would do. When we receive a promise of revival, deliverance, healing, restoration, etc., we tend to passively wait for its fulfillment—but not Daniel. He knew better. Somehow he must have known that God needed his involvement because he said, "So I gave my attention to the Lord God to seek Him by prayer and supplications, with fasting, sackcloth, and ashes" (Dan. 9:3).

No verse in Daniel, as there is with Elijah, specifically says Israel was restored because of Daniel's prayers, but with the emphasis given to them, the insinuation is certainly there. We do know that the angel Gabriel was dispatched immediately after Daniel started praying. However, it took him 21 days to penetrate the warfare in the heavens with the message to inform Daniel that "Your words were heard, and I have come in response to your words" (Dan. 10:12). I can't help wondering how many promises from God have gone unfulfilled because He can't find the human involvement He needs. Paul E. Billheimer says:

> Daniel evidently realized that intercession had a part to play in bringing the prophecy to pass. God had made the prophecy. *When it was time for its fulfillment He did not fulfill it arbitrarily outside of His program of prayer. He sought for a man upon whose heart He could lay a burden of intercession. . . . As always, God made the decision in heaven. A man was called upon to enforce that decision on earth through intercession and faith.*[12]

God Needs Our Prayers

Another Scripture strongly supports our contention that even though God's existence and character are completely independent of any created thing (see Acts 17:24-25) and God already has all resources in His hands (see Job 41:11; Ps. 50:10-12), God needs our prayers:

> "And I searched for a man among them who should build up the wall and stand in the gap before Me for the land, that I should not destroy it; but I found no one. Thus I have poured out My indignation on them; I have consumed them with the fire of My wrath; their way I have brought upon their heads," declares the Lord God (Ezek. 22:30-31).

The implications of these verses are staggering. God's holiness, integrity and uncompromising truth prevent Him from simply excusing sin. It must be judged. On the other hand, not only is He holy, but He is also love and His love always desires to redeem, to restore and to show mercy. Scripture tells us that God takes no pleasure in the death of the wicked (see Ezek. 33:11).

The passage is clearly saying, "While My justice demanded judgment, My love wanted forgiveness. Had I been able to find a human to ask Me to spare this people, I could have. It would have allowed Me to show mercy. Because I found no one, however, I had to destroy them."

I don't like the implications of this passage any more than you do. I don't want the responsibility. I don't like to consider the ramifications of a God who has somehow limited Himself to us earthlings. But in light of these and other passages, as well as the condition of the world, I can come to no other conclusion.

Either God wants the earth in this condition or He doesn't. If He doesn't, which is certainly the case, then we must assume one of two things. Either He is powerless to do anything about it, or He needs and is waiting on something from us to bring about change. Peter Wagner agrees with this when he says:

We must understand that our sovereign God has for His own reasons so designed this world that much of what is truly His will He makes contingent on the attitudes and actions of human beings. He allows humans to make decisions that can influence history. . . . Human inaction does not *nullify* the atonement, but human inaction can make the atonement *ineffective* for lost people.[13]

This truth could intimidate us with the responsibility it implies, or even condemn us because of our lack of prayer. But another possibility exists as well. A responsibility can also be a privilege; a responsibility can be enjoyable. If allowed, this revelation can elevate us in our hearts to new positions of dignity alongside our heavenly Father and Lord Jesus. Jack Hayford said, "Prayer is essentially a partnership of the redeemed child of God working hand in hand with God toward the realization of His redemptive purposes on earth."[14]

Let's rise to the occasion and embrace the incredible invitation to be co-laborers with God . . . to be carriers of His awesome Holy Spirit and ambassadors for His great kingdom. Let's represent Him!

Awaken us to our destiny, Lord!

Questions for Reflection

1. How complete was Adam's (humankind's) dominion upon the earth? Can you explain how this relates to the necessity of prayer in order for God to work?

2. What did God mean when He said we were made in His image and likeness?

3. How does the story of Elijah's praying for rain (see 1 Kings 18) reinforce our assertion that God works through prayer? How about Daniel's prayer for the restoration of Israel?

4. What is the root meaning of "glory"? How does this relate to prayer and representation?

5. How does it feel to be a partner with God?

3

RE-PRESENTING JESUS

Looking for Answers

When you don't know what you're looking for, you'll probably never find it. When you don't know what you're doing, you probably won't do it well.

I remember sitting in English class one day during high school. I never was very good in English—too busy doing important things such as playing football and running track. It was Friday afternoon and we had a big game that night. You can probably guess where my mind was.

After I spiked the ball into the end zone, listening to the deafening roar of the crowd, my mind gradually drifted back to my English class. The teacher was saying something about a "present participle."

Now, I had no idea what a participle was, but it didn't sound good to me. And I knew the fact that it was "present" either meant it was a current situation or something present in the room.

"Dutch," my teacher said, probably realizing I had been elsewhere, "can you find the present participle for us?"

I didn't know whether to look on the floor, the ceiling or out the window. Trying to appear as innocent, intelligent and concerned as possible, I looked around the room for a few seconds before responding, "No, ma'am, I don't see that participle anywhere. But don't worry, I'm sure it will turn up somewhere."

I never did figure out what that present participle was, but it must not have been as bad or serious as I thought because when I said that everyone sort of laughed. I was relieved, having added a little peace of mind to an obviously troubled teacher and bluffed my way out of a potentially embarrassing situation.

What is intercession anyway?

No, it's not.

I know you said prayer or something similar. But technically speaking, intercession isn't prayer at all. Intercessory prayer is prayer. Intercession is something a person does that he or she can do in prayer. That's about as confusing as a present participle, isn't it?

Think of it this way: Agreement isn't prayer, but there is the prayer of agreement. Faith isn't prayer, but there is the prayer of faith. In the same way that a person can't intentionally pray a prayer of agreement until he or she understands the meaning of agreement, a person won't be very effective in intercessory prayer until he or she understands the concept of intercession.

Are you still with me?

Before we define intercession—so that we can define intercessory *prayer*—we're not only going to do so literally, but also in the context of (1) God's plan for humankind at the time of the Creation, (2) the disruption of that plan by the Fall and (3) God's solution. In other words, we're going to see the concept of intercession in these settings and allow them to help us define it. This will accomplish three things:

1. It will help you understand the concept of intercession so that you can understand intercessory prayer.

2. It will enable you to see Christ's role as THE intercessor. (Our intercessory *prayer* will always and only

be an extension of His intercessory *work*. This is crucial and will become clearer as we progress.)

3. With that kind of knowledge, it will make you the most spiritual person in your prayer group!

Defining Intercession

Let's look first at the literal concept of intercession; then we'll think about it in the context of the Fall.

According to Webster, "intercede" means "to go or pass between; to act between parties with a view to reconcile those who differ or contend; to interpose; to mediate or make intercession; mediation."[1]

Using the same source, "mediate" means "between two extremes; to interpose between parties as the equal friend of each; to negotiate between persons at variance with a view to reconciliation; to mediate a peace; intercession."[2]

Please notice that these terms are largely synonymous with some of the same words used to define each—"between," "interpose" and "reconcile." Notice also that one is used to define the other: "mediation" defines "intercession" and "intercession" defines "mediation."

As can be clearly seen from these definitions, the concept of intercession can be summarized as mediating, going between, pleading for another, representing one party to another for, but not limited to, legal situations.

Intercession happens in our courts daily with lawyers interceding for clients.

Intercession happens in contractual meetings daily with attorneys representing one party to another.

Intercession happens in offices and business meetings daily as secretaries or other associates "go between," representing one to another. Nothing spiritual about it.

It involves delegation.

It involves authority.

It boils down to representation. As we discussed in the previous chapter, to represent means to re-present, or present again.

Many years ago my dad hired an intercessor (we called him a lawyer) to represent him in court. Dad had been stopped by some policemen, beaten up quite badly and thrown in jail—all of this with my mother and then three-year-old sister watching. The policemen thought he was someone else! Dad was actually on his way home from a church service where he had preached that night, which added to the irony and injustice of the entire ordeal.

Our attorney went *between* Dad, the judge, the other lawyer and the policemen. He listened to the case, gathered proof, found out what Dad wanted and then *re-presented* it in court. He *mediated* well.

We won.

All intercession is not in the sense of an attorney. That's only one example. Any work of representation or mediation between is intercession.

Now, let's think about this concept in light of the Creation and the Fall. Adam was supposed to represent God on planet Earth—managing, governing or ruling for Him. God told Adam what He wanted and Adam re-presented Him to the rest of the earth. Adam was a go-between for God. Literally, Adam was God's intercessor or mediator on the earth.

Christ, the Ultimate Intercessor

Adam, of course, failed and God had to send another human, called the "last Adam," to do what the first Adam was supposed to do and fix what the first Adam messed up. So Christ came to re-present God on the earth. He became the intercessor or mediator, going between and re-presenting God to humanity.

According to John 1:18, Jesus exegeted God for us: "No man has seen God at any time; the only begotten God, who is in the bosom of the Father, He has explained Him." The Greek word translated "explained" is actually *exegeomai*, from which we get our English word "exegete."[3]

You have probably heard of the small child who "was drawing a picture and his teacher said, 'That's an interesting picture. Tell me about it.'

'It's a picture of God.'

'But nobody knows what God looks like.'

'They will when I get done,'" said the young artist.[4]

Jesus came and drew us a picture of God! Now we know what He looks like.

But that's not the only direction of His interceding. Great irony exists in the fact that Man who was meant to be God's intercessor, mediator or representative on Earth now needed someone to mediate *for him*. He who was made to represent God on the earth now needed someone to represent him *to* God. Christ, of course, became that representative, intercessor or mediator. Not only did He represent God to man, but He also represented man to God. This God-man was the attorney for both sides!

He is the ultimate, final and only go-between. He is "the Apostle [God to the human race] and High Priest [the human race to God] of our confession" (Heb. 3:1). He is Job's great go-between, hanging between heaven and Earth, placing one hand on God and the other on humans (see Job 9:32-33).

Are you getting the picture? Christ's intercession, in keeping with its literal meaning, was not a *prayer* He prayed, but a *work* of mediation He did.

And I hope you're ready for this: I don't believe the intercession attributed to Him now in heaven on our behalf is prayer either. I'm certain it refers to His work of mediation (see 1 Tim. 2:5), to His being our Advocate with the Father (see 1 John 2:1). He is now functioning as our representative, guaranteeing our access to the Father and to our benefits of redemption.

In fact, He tells us in John 16:26 that He is not doing our asking or petitioning of the Father for us: "In that day you will ask in My name, and I do not say to you that I will request the Father on your behalf." So what is He doing as He makes intercession for us? He is mediating, or going between, not to clear us of charges against us as He did to redeem us from sin, but to present each of us to the Father as righteous and one of His own.

When I approach the throne, He is always there saying something such as: "Father, Dutch is here to speak with You. He isn't coming on his own merits or righteousness; he is here based on Mine. He is here *in My name*. I am sure You remember that I've *gone between* You and Dutch and provided him with access to You. He has a few things to ask You."

Can't you just hear the Father say in response, *Of course I remember, Son. You've made him one of Ours. Because he came through You, Dutch is always welcome here.* He then looks at me and says, *Come boldly to My throne of grace, Son, and make your request known.*

Jesus isn't *praying* for us; He is *interceding* for us so that we can pray. This is what is meant by asking "in His name."

Let's look at one more aspect of Christ's intercession in the context of the Fall. Basically, humanity needed two things after the Fall. They needed someone to "go between" themselves and God to *reconcile* themselves to God; they also needed someone to "go between" themselves and Satan to *separate* themselves from him. One was a uniting, the other a disuniting. One reestablished headship, the other broke headship. It was a twofold work of intercession.

We needed both. Jesus did both. As the intercessor-mediator, He went between God and humanity, reconciling us to the Father; and between Satan and humanity, breaking Satan's hold.

This was the redemptive *work* of intercession and it is complete. Therefore, in the legal sense of humanity's redemption, Christ is the *one and only* intercessor. This is why the Scriptures say, "For there is one God, and one mediator also between God and men, the man Christ Jesus" (1 Tim. 2:5). The verse could just as easily read, "one intercessor."

This revelation is critical. It means our *prayers* of intercession are always and only an extension of His *work* of intercession.

Why is this so important? Because God won't honor any intercession except Christ's, and also because this understanding will make our *prayers* of intercession infinitely more powerful.

Let's return to our conversation in the throne room. I am there asking the Father to extend mercy and bring salvation to the people of Tibet. The Father could reply, "How can I do this? They are sinners. They worship false gods, which is really worshiping Satan. And besides, they don't even want Me to do this. They themselves have never asked."

I answer, "Because Jesus *interceded* or *mediated* for them, Father. I am asking based on what He did. And He needs a human on Earth to ask for Him because He is in heaven now. So, as He taught me, I'm asking for Your Kingdom to come and Your will to be done in Tibet. I'm asking for some laborers to be sent there. I'm asking these things for Christ and through Christ. And I am asking You to do it based entirely on the redemptive work He has already done."

The Father replies, "RIGHT ANSWER! You heard the man, Gabriel. What are you waiting for?"

Distributors for God

When I say our *prayers* of intercession are an extension of His *work* of intercession, the difference is in distributing versus producing. We don't have to produce anything—reconciliation, deliverance, victory, etc.—but rather we distribute, as the disciples did with the loaves and fishes (see Matt. 14:17-19). *Our calling and function is not to replace God, but to release Him.*[5] It liberates us from intimidation and emboldens us to know that:

- The Producer simply wants to distribute through us.
- The Intercessor wants to intercede through us.
- The Mediator wants to mediate through us.
- The Representative wants to represent through us.
- The Go-between wants to go between through us.
- The Victor wants His victory enforced[6] through us.
- The Minister of reconciliation has given to us the ministry of reconciliation (see 2 Cor. 5:18-19). We now represent Him in His representation ministry. *God continues to incarnate His redemptive purposes in human lives.*[7]

We don't deliver anyone, we don't reconcile anyone to God, we don't defeat the enemy. The work is already done. Reconciliation is complete. Deliverance and victory are complete. Salvation is complete. Intercession is complete! Finished! Done! WOW! What a relief. And yet . . .

We must ask for the release and application of these things. So, let me offer the following as a biblical definition of intercessory prayer: *Intercessory prayer is an extension of the ministry of Jesus through His Body, the Church, whereby we mediate between God and humanity for the purpose of reconciling the world to Him, or between Satan and humanity for the purpose of enforcing the victory of Calvary.*

Christ needs a human on the earth to represent Himself through just as the Father did. The Father's human was Jesus; Jesus' humans are us, the Church. He said, "As the Father has sent Me, I also send you" (John 20:21).

The concept of being sent is important and embodies the truths of which we have been speaking. A representative is a "sent" one. Sent ones have authority, as long as they represent the sender. And the importance or emphasis is not on the sent one but on the sender. The setting of conditions and the ability to carry out or enforce them is all the responsibility of the sender, not the sent one. For example, an ambassador representing one nation to another is a sent one. He has no authority of his own, but he is authorized to represent the authority of the nation sending him.

Jesus was a sent one. That is why He had authority. He received it from the Father who sent Him. Forty times in John's Gospel alone He mentions the important fact of being sent by the Father. The result of this arrangement was that, in essence, He wasn't doing the works, but the Father who sent Him (see John 14:10).

The same is true with us. Our authority comes from being sent ones, representing Jesus. As long as we function in that capacity, we function in Christ's authority. And, in essence, we're not really doing the works; He is.

Let me illustrate. In 1977, while praying about an upcoming journey to Guatemala, I heard the words: *On this trip, represent Jesus to the people.*

At first I rebuked the voice, thinking it was an evil spirit trying to deceive me. But the voice came again, this time adding the words: *Be His voice, be His hands, be His feet. Do what you know He would do if He were there in the flesh. Represent Him.*

Suddenly I understood. I was not going to represent myself or the ministry with which I was working. In the same way that Jesus represented the Father—speaking His words and doing His works—I was to represent Jesus. And if I really believed I was functioning as an ambassador or a sent one, then I could believe it wasn't my authority or ability that was an issue but Christ's—I was simply representing Him *and what He had already done.*

A Galilee Jesus Became a Guatemala Jesus

Once in Guatemala I traveled with a team to a remote village far from any modern city. There was no electrical power, no plumbing, no phones. Our purpose in being there was to build shelters for the villagers whose adobe homes had been destroyed in the devastating earthquake of 1976. It had killed 30,000 people and left 1,000,000 homeless. We had trucked in materials and were building small, one-room homes for them during the daylight hours. In the evenings we would hold services in the center of the village, preaching the gospel of Jesus Christ to them, explaining that His love was motivating us to spend our time, money and energies helping them.

We had been ministering for one week with very few people coming to Christ. The people were listening, but not responding.

I was to preach on the final night of our trip. Just as the service was about to begin, a team member told me about something he and others had found on the far side of the village—a little girl, six or seven years old, tied to a tree.

Not believing what they were seeing, they asked the family that lived there, "Why is this small girl tied to that tree?" It was obvious she lived there, much like a dog, in the back yard—nasty, filthy, helpless and alone.

"She is crazy," the parents replied. "We can't control her. She hurts herself and others and runs away if we turn her loose. There is nothing else we can do for her, so we just have to tie her up."

My heart broke as the member shared what he had seen. It was on my mind as we began the service. A few minutes into my message, standing on a folding table under the stars, the same voice that had spoken to me before the trip began speaking to me again.

Tell them you are going to pray for the little insane girl across the village tied to the tree. Tell them you are going to do it in the name of this Jesus you've been preaching about. Tell them that through Him you are going to break the evil powers controlling her—that when she is free and normal, they can then know that what you are preaching is true. They can believe that the Jesus you are preaching about is who you say He is.

I responded to the voice in my heart with fear and trembling. I believe the words were something like, *WHAT DID YOU SAY???*

Same instructions.

Being the man of faith that I am, I replied, *What is plan B?*

Rebellion and failure, came the response. *Remember what I said to you before the trip began? Represent Jesus.*

Faith began to rise. *The emphasis is not on me in this situation,* I thought, *but on the One who sent me. I am simply His spokesman. I merely release what He has already done. He has finished the work of delivering this little girl; my prayers release the work. I'm only a distributor of what He has already produced. Be bold, sent one. Enforce the victory!*

With new assurance I began informing the people about what I was planning to do. They nodded in recognition as I mentioned the girl. Expressions of intrigue turned to astonishment as they listened to my plans.

Then I prayed.

On a moonlit night in a tiny, remote village of Guatemala with a handful of people as my audience, my life changed forever.

Jesus came out of hiding. He became alive: relevant . . . sufficient . . . available! A "hidden" Jesus emerged from the cobwebs of theology. A yesterday Jesus became a today and forever Jesus. A Galilee Jesus became a Guatemala Jesus.

And a new plan unfolded to me. A new concept emerged—Jesus and me.

The Heavenly Pattern

For the first time I understood the heavenly pattern: Jesus is the Victor—we're the enforcers; Jesus is the Redeemer—we're the releasers; Jesus is the Head—we're the Body.

Yes, He set the little girl free.

Yes, the village turned to Christ.

Yes, Jesus prevailed through a sent one.

So the partnership goes on—God and humans. But the correct pattern is critical: My *prayers* of intercession release Christ's finished *work* of intercession.

His work empowers my prayers—my prayers release His work.

Mine extends His—His effectuates mine.

Mine activates His—His validates mine.

In Kingdom Enterprises we're not in the production department. We're in distribution . . . BIG difference. He's the generator. We're the distributors.

Awesomites Re-Presenting His Awesomeness

I think this makes us His co-laborers. What do you think? I think Christ is awesome and wants us to be "awesomites." Humble awesomites representing His awesomeness, but awesome nonetheless. More than conquerors! Christ and His Christians, changing things on the earth.

There are many wounded and hurting individuals "tied to trees" around the world. You work with some, others live across the street. One of them probably just served you in a checkout line, seated you in a restaurant or served you food. Their chains are alcohol, drugs, abuse, broken dreams, rejection, money, lust . . . well, you get the point.

Plan A is for supernatural but ordinary people like you and me to: (1) wholeheartedly believe in the victory of Calvary—to be convinced that it was complete and final, and (2) to rise up in our role as sent ones, ambassadors, authorized representatives of the Victor. Our challenge is not so much to liberate as to believe in the Liberator; to heal as to believe in the Healer.

Plan B is to waste the Cross; to leave the tormented in their torment; to scream with our silence, "There is no hope!"; to hear the Father say again, "I looked, but found no one"; to hear the Son cry once more, "The laborers! Where are the laborers?"

Come on Church! Let's untie some folks. Let's tell them there is a God who cares. Let's represent—let's mediate—let's intercede!

"Can anyone find the present participator?"

Questions for Reflection

1. Define intercession and intercessory prayer. What is the difference? Why is this important?

2. How are intercession and mediation related?

3. Can you explain what I meant when I said Christ was THE intercessor and that our *prayers* are an extension of His *work*?

4. Explain the two aspects of Christ's intercession—reconciling and separating—relating it to humankind's twofold need created by the Fall.

5. What is the significance of being a "sent one"?

6. Do you know anyone chained to a "tree"? Please help them.

4

MEETINGS: THE GOOD, THE BAD AND THE UGLY

Boy Meets Girl

"Dutch Sheets, I want you to *meet* Celia Merchant." The world suddenly stood still and my life changed forever.

The second most important *meeting* of my life was taking place—only my introduction to Jesus ranked higher. It was 1977 and I was a student in Bible college.

Having just enjoyed a time of private prayer, I emerged from the prayer room to see two individuals carrying a large folding table. One of them was a male friend of mine, the other was the most beautiful young lady I had ever laid eyes on.

Oh, it wasn't the first time I had seen her, but it was my first face-to-face encounter. Weak-kneed and tongue-tied, I nearly tripped over myself grabbing her end of the table. With a gallant demonstration of chivalry and muscle, I relieved her of her burden and nearly knocked the other guy off his feet showing how fast I could carry that table.

He then introduced me to what had to be my missing rib, and I knew life would never be right if I didn't marry this woman! I told God as much. Fortunately, He agreed and so did she. Life is good!

I sure am glad I spent that time in prayer. I would not have wanted to miss that *meeting*!

Boy Meets Baseball

I had another memorable *meeting* when I was in the sixth grade. This one wasn't so pleasant. It would also remain with me the rest of my life, however. A baseball *met* my front teeth. The baseball won—they usually do. I have two nice caps on my front teeth today as a result of that *meeting*.

I thought about revealing that I was trying to teach another kid to catch a baseball when it happened, but that would be too embarrassing. I won't mention that I was demonstrating what not to do when the accident happened. But I will say that when teaching your kids the fine points of baseball, show them what to do—not what not to do. Doing it backward leads to unpleasant *meetings* and cosmetic smiles.

God Meets a Mate, Satan Meets His Match

A figure hangs on a cross between heaven and Earth. Two *meetings* are about to take place—one good and pleasant, one ugly and violent. A Man is about to *meet* His bride and a serpent is about to *meet* a curveball to the teeth:

> For this cause a man shall leave his father and mother, and shall cleave to his wife; and the two shall become one flesh. This mystery is great; but I am speaking with reference to Christ and the church (Eph. 5:31-32).

> Arise, O Lord; save me, O my God! For Thou hast smitten all my enemies on the cheek; Thou hast shattered the teeth of the wicked (Ps. 3:7).

Such beauty, such ugliness . . . union, disunion . . . joining, breaking . . .

Actually, many other *meetings* could be mentioned as taking place through the Cross:

- Mercy *met* judgment.
- Righteousness *met* sin.
- Light *met* darkness.
- Humility *met* pride.
- Love *met* hate.
- Life *met* death.
- A cursed One on a tree *met* the curse that originated from a tree.
- The sting of death *met* the antidote of resurrection.

All the good guys won!

Only God could plan such an event—let alone have it turn out perfectly. Only He could marry such extremes in one occurrence. Who but He could shed blood to create life, use pain to bring healing, allow injustice to satisfy justice and accept rejection to restore acceptance?

Who could use such an evil act to accomplish so much good?

Who could transform an act of amazing love into such violence, and vice versa? Only God.

So many paradoxes. So much irony.

Don't you find it fascinating that the serpent who accomplished his greatest victory from a tree (of the knowledge of good and evil) suffered his greatest defeat from a tree (the Cross of Calvary)?

Don't you find it ironic that the first Adam succumbed to temptation in a garden (Eden) and the last Adam overcame His greatest temptation in a garden (Gethsemane)?

Can God ever write a script!

Perhaps you have guessed by now that hidden somewhere in these three stories—my wife, the baseball and the Cross—are pictures of intercession. In fact, I've actually used one of the definitions of the Hebrew word for "intercession," *paga*, 23 times thus far. I'll continue to use it more than 30 additional times by the end of this chapter. How's that for redundancy?!

Intercession Creates a Meeting

The Hebrew word for "intercession," *paga*, means "to meet."[1] As we have already seen by studying the English word, intercession is not primarily a prayer a person prays, but something a person does that can be done through prayer. This is also true in the Hebrew language. Although the word "intercession" has come to mean "prayer" in our minds, its Hebrew word does not necessarily mean "prayer" at all. It has many shades of meaning, all of which can be done through prayer.

Throughout the remainder of the book, we will look at several of these meanings, and then put them into the context of prayer. As we do, our understanding will increase of what Christ did for us through His intercession and what our re-presenting of it on the earth through prayer really entails. As the opening stories imply, the first usage of *paga* we will explore is "to meet."

Intercession creates a *meeting*. Intercessors *meet* with God; they also *meet* the powers of darkness. "Prayer meetings" are aptly named!

A Meeting for Reconciliation

Similar to Christ's, often our *meeting* with God is to effect another *meeting*—a reconciliation. We *meet* with Him asking Him to *meet* with someone else. We become the *go-between*: "Heavenly Father, I come to you today (a *meeting*) asking You to touch Tom (another *meeting*)." On the opposite end of the spectrum, as Christ did through spiritual warfare, our *meeting* with the enemy is to undo a *meeting*—a breaking, a severing, a disuniting. All of our praying intercession will involve one or both of these facets: reconciliation or breaking; uniting or disuniting.

First, we will look at a couple of Scriptures that describe what Christ did when He *met* the Father to create a *meeting* between God and humanity. Then we will look at the warfare aspect. Psalm 85:10 states, "Lovingkindness and truth have met together; righteousness and peace have kissed each other." Let's examine more fully this beautiful description of the Cross.

God had a dilemma seen through four words in this verse. He not only is a God of *lovingkindness* (which represents His mercy, kindness, love and forgiveness), but He is also a God of *truth* (which represents His integrity and justice). He does not merely represent *peace* (safety, wholeness and rest), but also *righteousness* (holiness and purity), without which there can be no peace.

The dilemma is this: A truly holy, righteous, just and true God cannot simply forgive, grant mercy to or bestow peace on a fallen humanity without compromising His character. Sin cannot be excused. It must be judged and with it the sinner. So, how can this holy, yet loving, God marry the two? THE CROSS!

On the Cross lovingkindness and truth *met*. Righteousness and peace kissed each other. And when they did, so did God and humanity! We kissed the Father through the Son! We *met* Him through the blood of Christ! Jesus grabbed our end of the table and was introduced to His bride.

In one sovereign, unsearchable act of wisdom, God satisfied both His love and His justice. He established righteousness as well as peace. *Who is like unto You, O Lord? Who can describe Your great mercy, Your awesome power, Your infinite wisdom?*

When this took place, Christ's ministry of reconciliation was being accomplished: "Who reconciled us to Himself through Christ . . . namely, that God was in Christ reconciling the world to Himself" (2 Cor. 5:18-19).

Because we now represent Christ in His intercession, let's apply these verses to ourselves. Verse 18 says He "gave us the ministry of reconciliation." In other words, through our praying intercession, we release the fruit of what He did through His act of intercession. We bring individuals to God in prayer, asking the Father to *meet* with them. We, too, have been given the ministry of reconciliation. Whether for a person or a nation, regardless of the reason, when we're used to create a *meeting* between God and humans, releasing the fruit of Christ's work, *paga* has happened.

It might be as you are prayer-walking through your neighborhood, asking God to *meet* with families and save them.

It could be a prayer journey into another nation. Our church has sent teams of intercessors into some of the darkest countries upon the earth for the sole purpose of prayer—creating *meetings* between God and humanity—divine connections through human conduits.

Meetings that Heal

I have witnessed miracles of healing as God *met* with people. In 1980 I was on another of my many journeys into Guatemala. On one occasion my wife, another couple and I were ministering to an elderly lady who had recently been saved. We had gone to her home to share some teaching with her.

Approximately six months earlier this lady had fallen from a stool and severely broken her ankle. As is often the case with the elderly, the fracture was not healing well. Her ankle was still badly swollen and she was in much pain. While we visited with her, the other gentleman and I both sensed that God wanted to heal her ankle—right then.

After sharing this with her and obtaining her agreement, we asked her to prop her leg on a stool. I began to pray, sort of.

Has God ever interrupted you? He did me on this occasion. (Oh, that He would always be so "unmannerly"!) When I stepped *between* her and God to effect a *meeting*, the presence of God came so powerfully into the room that I stopped in mid-stride and mid-sentence. I had taken one step toward her and uttered one word, "Father."

That's all He needed!

It's as though He was so eager to touch this dear lady that He couldn't wait any longer. I realize that what I'm about to say may sound overly dramatic, but it's exactly what took place.

The presence of the Holy Spirit filled the room so strongly that I froze in my tracks, stopped speaking and began to weep. My wife and the other couple also began to weep. The lady we were ministering to began to weep. Her foot began to bounce up and down on the stool, shaking uncontrollably for several minutes as she had a powerful encounter with the Holy Spirit— a *meeting*! The Lord healed her and filled her with His Spirit.

On the same visit to Guatemala, my wife and I, along with the couple previously mentioned, were asked to pray for a woman hospitalized with tuberculosis. We found her in a ward with approximately 40 other women, the beds being only about three feet apart. It was simply an area in the hospital where the doctors and nurses could attend the very poor. Not even partitions separated the women. And yes, this woman was coughing her tuberculosis all over those around her.

As we talked and prayed with her, we noticed the lady in the next bed observing us closely. When we finished she asked if we would be willing to pray for her. Of course we were glad to and inquired about her need. She pulled her arms out from under the covers and showed us her two hands, curled back toward her body, somewhat frozen in that position. They were totally unusable. Her feet were also the same way.

While in the hospital for back surgery, the doctor had accidentally cut a nerve in her spinal cord, leaving her in this condition. There was nothing they could do to correct the problem.

Compassion filled our hearts as we asked the Lord to *meet* her need. Nothing noticeable happened, but we encouraged her to trust the Lord and drifted across the room to see if we could share Jesus with anyone else. No hospital employees were present, so we had relative freedom to do as we pleased.

Just as we began to visit with another lady across the room, we heard a sudden commotion and someone screaming, "Milagro! Milagro! Milagro!" We turned to look and saw the lady moving her hands wildly, opening and closing them, wiggling her fingers, kicking her feet under the covers and shouting the Spanish word for miracle. A *meeting* had taken place!

I don't know who was more surprised—the lady who was healed, the other ladies in the room or me. I hoped for a miracle but I don't think I believed for one. I remember thinking, *This sort of thing only happened during Bible days.*

The next thing we knew, every woman in the room was begging us to minister to them. We went from bed to bed—just like we knew what we were doing—leading women to Christ and praying for their recoveries. I remember thinking, *This is wild. Is it real or am I dreaming? We're having revival in a hospital ward!* Several were saved, the lady with tuberculosis was also healed and another lady who had been scheduled for exploratory surgery the following morning was instead sent home healed. In general, we just had a good time! We even sang a song or two. Probably shouldn't have because a hospital employee heard us, came to the room and asked us to leave. She left but we didn't. Too many women were begging for prayer. A few minutes later she returned and "graciously" escorted us out of the hospital.

What on earth can turn a sad, hopeless, disease-filled ward into a church service? God! God *meeting* with people. And prayer *meetings* create God *meetings*!

I don't want to mislead you into thinking that miracles will always happen as easily as they did on these two occasions.

However, we can bring individuals into contact with God and that is the very meaning of the word "intercession." It often requires much intercession; but whether it takes days or minutes, it's always worth the effort. The important thing is that we do it.

She-Bear Meetings

Let's progress in our thinking to the breaking aspect of intercession *meetings*—enforcing the victory of Calvary. I call this "the bear anointing" because of Proverbs 17:12: "Let a man *meet* a bear robbed of her cubs, rather than a fool in his folly."

I've never met a she-bear in the wild with or without her cubs, and I hope I never do. But a wise old woodsman, instructing me in the art of surviving bear encounters, gave me the following piece of wisdom: "Son, try to avoid them, if possible! But if you can't and it's a female you run into, don't ever get between mama and her cubs. Because if you do there's fixin' to be a *meeting*, and you're gonna be on the receiving end!"

Now, before I'm lynched for contextual murder of the Scriptures, let me say I am not insinuating that this verse is talking about prayer. I am saying, however, that the word for "meet" is our Hebrew word translated "intercession," *paga*. Other Hebrew words could have been used, but this one was chosen partly because it often has a very violent connotation. In fact, *paga* is frequently a battlefield term (for examples, see Judg. 8:21; 15:12; 1 Sam. 22:17-18; 2 Sam. 1:15; 1 Kings 2:25-46).

Intercession can be violent!

Meetings can be unpleasant! Some can be downright ugly!

Such as the one Satan had with Jesus at Calvary when Christ interceded for us. Satan had come between God and His "cubs." He ought not to have done that! Satan's worst nightmare came true when, with 4,000 years of pent-up fury, Jesus *met* him at Calvary. The earth rocked, and I do mean literally, with the force of the battle (see Matt. 27:51). The very sun grew dark as the war raged (see v. 45). At the moment of what Satan thought was his greatest triumph, he and all his forces heard the most terrifying sound they had ever heard: God's laugh of derision (see Ps. 2:4)!

The laughter was followed by the voice of the Son of man crying with a loud voice, "*Tetelestai.*" This Greek word is translated "It is finished" in John 19:30. Please don't think Jesus was talking about death when He spoke that word. No way! *Tetelestai* means to fully accomplish something or bring it to its completed state,[2] as the word "finished" would imply, but it was also the word stamped on invoices in that day meaning "Paid in full."[3] Jesus was shouting, "The debt is paid in full!" Hallelujah!

Christ was quoting from Psalm 22:31 when He chose this statement. Three of His seven sayings on the cross come from this psalm. The Hebrew word He quoted from this verse is *asah*. He may have actually been speaking Hebrew, using this very word, even though John recorded it in Greek. The word means, among other things, "to create."[4] It is used in Genesis, for example, when God created the earth. I believe that not only was Christ saying, "The debt is paid in full," but also, "Come forth, new creation!" No wonder the earth shook, the sun reappeared, the centurion was terrified (see Matt. 27:54) and Old Testament saints were resurrected (see Matt. 27:52-53). Don't tell me God doesn't have a flare for the dramatic. The Cross defines drama.

And yes, behind the scenes it was violent. Captives were rescued (see 1 Pet. 3:19; 4:6; Isa. 61:1), bruises were inflicted (see Gen. 3:15; Isa. 53:5; 1 Pet. 2:24), keys were exchanged, authority was transferred (see Matt. 28:18).

An interesting word is used in 1 John 3:8 that adds insight to what happened at the Cross. The verse reads, "For this purpose the Son of God was manifested, that he might destroy the works of the devil" (*KJV*). "Destroy" is the Greek word *luo*, which has both a legal and a physical meaning. Understanding its full definition will greatly enhance our knowledge of what Jesus did to Satan and his works.

The legal meaning of *luo* is (1) to pronounce or determine that something or someone is no longer bound; (2) to dissolve or void a contract or anything that legally binds.[5] Jesus came to dissolve the legal hold Satan had over us and to pronounce that we were no longer bound by his works. He "voided the contract," breaking Satan's dominion over us.

The physical meaning of *luo* is to dissolve or melt, break, beat something to pieces or untie something that is bound.[6] In Acts 27:41, the boat Paul traveled on was broken to pieces (*luo*) by the force of a storm. In 2 Peter 3:10,12, we're told that one day the elements of the earth will melt or dissolve (*luo*) from a great heat. Jesus not only delivered us legally, but He also made certain that the literal consequences of that deliverance were manifested: He brought healing, set captives free, lifted oppression and liberated those under demonic control.

Enforcing the Victory

Our responsibility is to enforce the victory as we also *meet* the powers of darkness. It is interesting to know that Jesus used the same word, *luo*, to describe what we, the Church, are to do through spiritual warfare. Matthew 16:19 tells us, "I will give you the keys of the kingdom of heaven; and whatever you shall bind on earth shall be bound in heaven, and whatever you shall loose on earth shall be loosed in heaven." The word "loose" in this verse is *luo*.

Now, the question is, "Did Christ *luo* the works of the devil or do we *luo* the works of the devil?" The answer is yes. Although Jesus fully accomplished the task of breaking the authority of Satan and voiding his legal hold upon the human race, someone on Earth must represent Him in that victory and enforce it.

With this in mind and remembering that the Hebrew word for "intercession," *paga*, means to *meet*, let's state it this way:

> We, through *prayers* of intercession, *meet* the powers of darkness, enforcing the victory Christ accomplished when He *met* them in His *work* of intercession.

This is exactly what took place in Guatemala when we prayed for the little girl tied to a tree, mentioned in the previous chapter. We *met* the powers of darkness and enforced the victory of the Cross.

Several years ago in Guatemala, a friend of mine pointed out a vibrant, healthy young woman and told me the following story. When he first saw her just a few months prior to this time, she was paralyzed from the neck down. She could move her head slightly, but could not speak. "The young lady has been this way for two years," my friend was informed by her pastor. "And the puzzling thing is that the doctors can find nothing physically wrong with her to create such a problem."

My friend, who was visiting the church as a guest speaker, discerned that the cause was demonic. Not knowing the church's position about such matters, he discreetly approached this wheelchair-bound young lady, knelt next to her and whispered in her ear. As he did, he was *going between* (intercession) her and the powers of darkness, *meeting* them with the power of Christ. He prayed, "Satan, I break (*luo*) your hold over this young lady in the name of Jesus. I command you to loose (*luo*) your hold over her and let her go." (Parenthetical words are mine.)

No manifestation or immediate change occurred. A week later, however, she was able to move her arms a little. The following week she was moving her arms normally and her legs slightly. The recovery continued for a month until she was totally free and well.

She then told my friend the following details about the cause of her condition and why the doctors could find no reasonable explanation. "A teacher in my school who was also a witch doctor made a sexual advance toward me, which I refused. He grew angry and told me that if I didn't have sex with him, he would place a curse on me."

She knew nothing about such things and didn't think much about it. A short time later, however, this condition of paralysis came upon her. Her inability to speak prevented her from communicating with anyone about what had taken place.

What happened to bring about this girl's freedom? An individual stepped *between* this young lady and the powers of darkness, *meeting* them in the name of Jesus, enforcing His victory. That . . . is intercession!

A *meeting* can be a good and pleasant experience or it can be a violent confrontation between opposing forces. The intercessor is either going to *meet* with God for the purpose of reconciling the world to the Father and His wonderful blessings, or he is going to *meet* Satanic forces of opposition to enforce the victory of Calvary. The purpose will vary, but one thing is certain:

The prayers of an understanding intercessor WILL create a *meeting*. And when the *meeting* comes to a close, something will have changed.

Don't be intimidated by the size of the giant. Jesus has qualified you to represent Him. And don't be intimidated by past failures. Be like the small boy playing in the backyard with his bat and ball:

"I'm the greatest baseball player in the world," he said proudly. Then he tossed the ball in the air, swung and missed. Undaunted, he picked up the ball, threw it into the air and said to himself, "I'm the greatest player ever!" He swung at the ball again, and again he missed.

He paused a moment to examine bat and ball carefully. Then once again he threw the ball into the air and said, "I'm the greatest baseball player who ever lived." He swung the bat hard and again missed the ball.

"Wow!" he exclaimed. "What a pitcher!"[7]

Deny unbelief access. You can do it!
Let's have a prayer *meeting*!

Questions for Reflection

1. In what way does a meeting picture intercession? How does *paga* establish the correlation between the two?

2. Explain the two opposite kinds of meetings discussed in this chapter. How does each one represent Calvary?

3. Define *luo* and comment on Christ doing it and the Church doing it.

4. Think of someone you know who needs a meeting with God. How and when can you help facilitate this?

5. Don't you think God will be thrilled when you do number 4?

CHEEK TO CHEEK

※▒※

Lean on Me

Charlie Brown was pitching and doing a lousy job. Lucy was giving him grief, as usual. Finally, he could bear the misery and humiliation no longer. In an expression of exasperation that only Charlie Brown could think of, he stood on his head right there on the pitcher's mound.

As Lucy's degrading mockery continued, the ever-loyal Snoopy did the unexpected. He walked onto the pitcher's mound and stood on his head beside Charlie Brown, sharing his humiliation.

Sound biblical? The Bible says, "Weep with those who weep" (Rom. 12:15) and "Bear one another's burdens" (Gal. 6:2). Although this involves "standing on our heads" together—sharing each other's pain, it does NOT convey the full scope of these verses. We're not merely to *carry* burdens for our brothers and sisters in Christ; we're to *carry them away* . . . Big difference! One involves sharing a load; the other involves removing a load.

Actually, two words are used for "bearing" in the New Testament. One word could be construed to mean standing beside a brother or sister in times of need to strengthen and comfort. The other, however, means something entirely different.

The first one, *anechomai*, means "to sustain, bear or hold up against a thing,"[1] much as a person would tie a stake to a tomato plant to sustain it from the weight it carries. The strength of the stake is transferred to the plant and thus "bears it up." When the Lord commands us to bear with one another in Colossians 3:13 and Ephesians 4:2, He isn't simply saying, "Put up with one another."

Although He is telling us to do that, He is also saying, "Stake yourselves to one another." In other words, we're to come alongside a weak brother or sister who is "weighted down" and say, "You're not going to fall and be broken or destroyed, because I'm staking myself to you. My strength is now yours. Go ahead, lean on me. As long as I can stand, you will."

What a wonderful picture for the Body of Christ. Fruit will result.

Jackie Robinson was the first black to play major league baseball. While breaking baseball's color barrier, he faced jeering crowds in every stadium. While playing one day in his home stadium in Brooklyn, he committed an error. His own fans began to ridicule him. He stood at second base, humiliated, while the fans jeered. Then shortstop "Pee Wee" Reese came over and stood next to him. He put his arm around Jackie Robinson and faced the crowd. The fans grew quiet. Robinson later said that arm around his shoulder saved his career.[2]

Sometimes the world is more biblical than we are!

Carry the Burden Away

The second word is *bastazo*, meaning "to bear, lift or carry" something, with the idea being to carry it *away* or *remove* it.[3] It is used in Romans 15:1-3 and Galatians 6:2, which we will look at shortly.

An amazing and little-understood aspect of intercession is exemplified by Christ in which He performed both of these bearing concepts. We have already established that His intercession for us was not a *prayer* He prayed, but a *work* He did. It was a work of "going between" to *reconcile* us to the Father and *break* Satan's dominion. And, of course, understanding His work in this area paves the way for an understanding of ours.

The intercessory work of Christ reached its fullest and most profound expression when our sins were "laid on" Him and He "bore" them away:

> All we like sheep have gone astray; we have turned every one to his own way; and the LORD hath *laid on* him the iniquity of us all . . . he hath poured out his soul unto death: and he was numbered with the transgressors; and he *bare* the sin of many, and made *intercession* for the transgressors (Isa. 53:6,12, *KJV*, emphasis added).

The Hebrew word *paga* is used twice in these two verses. Isaiah 53 is one of the most graphic Old Testament prophecies of Christ's cross. *Paga* is translated "laid on" once and "intercession" once. Both instances refer to when our sins, iniquities, diseases, etc., were placed upon Him. The New Testament describes this identification accordingly: "He made Him who knew no sin to be sin on our behalf, that we might become the righteousness of God in Him" (2 Cor. 5:21).

Christ then "bore" our sins and weaknesses away, "as far as the east is from the west" (Ps. 103:12). He is not still carrying them—somewhere, somehow, He disposed of them. The Hebrew word for "bore" or "bare" in this chapter is *nasa*, meaning "to bear away"[4] or "remove to a distance."[5] (We would spell the *KJV* "bare" today "bear.")

As already mentioned, the Greek counterpart, *bastazo*, means essentially the same. This connotation of bearing something to get rid of it becomes increasingly significant as we discuss our role in this facet of Christ's ministry of intercession. It is imperative to know that we don't simply carry someone's burden. We *stake* (*anechomai*) ourselves to the person and *carry the burden away* (*bastazo*), helping them *get rid of it*!

The Scapegoat

The concept of a scapegoat comes from this redemptive intercessional work of Christ and illustrates well our concept of carrying something away.

A scapegoat takes someone else's blame and resulting consequences. My older brother, Tim, who is now a pastor in Ohio, was an expert at diverting blame to me when we were kids. I was always perfectly innocent as a child, never doing anything wrong. He was always the troublemaker.

Mom and Dad were forever taking his side—they could never see through his falsities and manipulation nor believe that I was so perfect. My entire childhood was one of enduring false accusation—being Tim's scapegoat! I've spent the last 20 years as an adult seeking inner healing for this injustice.

Of course you know that none of that is true—I was only almost perfect. But at least it allows me to get even with Tim for the few times he did successfully divert blame my way and it also illustrates my point. (By the way, I never did this to him.)

In the Old Testament, two animals were used on the Day of Atonement. One was sacrificed; the other was used for the scapegoat. After the high priest placed his hands on the scapegoat's head, confessing the sins of the nation, it was released into the wilderness never to be seen again. It symbolized Christ the scapegoat crucified outside the city *bearing away* our curse.

Christ the scapegoat bearing our curse is well illustrated by a story I read in the book *What It Will Take to Change the World* by S. D. Gordon. The following is my paraphrase of this story about a couple who discovered that their 14-year-old son had lied to them. The young boy, whom we'll refer to as Steven, had skipped school three consecutive days. He was found out when his teacher called his parents to inquire about his well-being.

The parents were more upset by Steven's lies than his missing school. After praying with him about what he had done, they decided on a very unusual and severe form of punishment. Their conversation with him went something like this:

"Steven, do you know how important it is that we be able to trust one another?"

"Yes."

"How can we ever trust each other if we don't always tell the truth? That's why lying is such a terrible thing. Not only is it sin, but it also destroys our ability to trust one another. Do you understand that?"

"Yes, sir."

"Your mother and I must make you understand the seriousness, not so much of skipping school, but of the lies you told. Your discipline will be that for the next three days, one for each day of your sin, you must go to the attic and stay there by yourself. You will even eat and sleep there."

So young Steven headed off to the attic and the bed prepared for him there. It was a long evening for Steven and perhaps longer for Mom and Dad. Neither could eat, and for some reason when Dad tried to read the paper the words seemed foggy. Mom tried to sew but couldn't see to thread the needle. Finally it was bedtime. About midnight as the father lay in bed thinking about how lonely and afraid Steven must be, he finally spoke to his wife, "Are you awake?"

"Yes. I can't sleep for thinking about Steven."

"Neither can I," answered Dad.

An hour later he queried again, "Are you asleep yet?"

"No," answered Mom, "I just can't sleep for thinking about Steven all alone up in the attic."

"Me neither."

Another hour passed. It was now 2:00 A.M. "I can't stand this any longer!" murmured Dad as he climbed out of bed grabbing his pillow and a blanket. "I'm going to the attic."

He found Steven much as he expected: wide awake with tears in his eyes.

"Steven," said his father, "I can't take away the punishment for your lies because you must know the seriousness of what you have done. You must realize that sin, especially lying, has severe consequences. But your mother and I can't bear the thought of you being all alone here in the attic, so I'm going to share your punishment with you."

Father lay down next to his son and the two put their arms around each other's necks. The tears on their cheeks mingled as they shared the same pillow and the same punishment . . . for three nights.[6]

What a picture! Two thousand years ago God crawled "out of bed" with His blanket and pillow—actually three spikes and a cross of crucifixion—"staked" His tear-stained cheek next to ours and "bore" our punishment for sin. His attic was a tomb, His bed a slab of rock and the cheek next to His was yours—yours and mine.

That's right. Christ was not alone on the cross. We were with Him. He was actually there to join us in our sentence of death. No, we may not have been there physically, but we were there spiritually (see Rom. 6:4,6). And of course, as He hung there He was "bearing" some things. Our sins were being "laid on" Him and He was carrying them away.

Christ didn't quite finish the job, however.

Wait! Before you "stone" me with letters and phone calls, please look at Colossians 1:24: "Now I rejoice in my sufferings for your sake, and in my flesh I do my share on behalf of His Body (which is the church) in filling up that which is lacking in Christ's afflictions."

Our Part

What could possibly be lacking in Christ's afflictions? Our part. In fact, the *Amplified Bible* actually adds those words: "And in my own person I am making up whatever is still lacking and remains to be completed [on our part] of Christ's afflictions, for the sake of His body, which is the church." Ours isn't exactly the same as His was, of course: carrying another's sin, curse or blame. "But He, having offered one sacrifice for sins for all time" (Heb. 10:12) took the sins of the world upon Himself. Nonetheless, there is a "sharing" and "a filling up that which is lacking in Christ's afflictions."

That which is lacking is really the point of this entire book, not just this chapter. It's the "re-presenting" of which we have spoken. It's the mediating, the going between, the distributing, the enforcing. It's our part.

Let's look, then, at our part in this *bearing* aspect of Christ's work of intercession. We have already mentioned the "staking" facet in Colossians 3:13 and Ephesians 4:2. Let's examine the other aspect in Romans 15:1-3 and Galatians 6:2, then we will see how the two work together in our intercession:

> Now we who are strong ought to *bear* the weaknesses of those without strength and not just please ourselves. Let each of us please his neighbor for his good, to his edification. For even Christ did not please Himself; but as it is written, "The reproaches of those who reproached Thee fell upon Me" (Rom. 15:1-3, emphasis added).

Bear one another's burdens, and thus fulfill the law of
Christ (Gal. 6:2, emphasis added).

As mentioned earlier, the Greek word for "bear" in both verses is *bastazo*, which, synonymous with the Hebrew *nasa*, means
"to lift or carry," conveying the idea of removing or carrying
away. In implementing Christ's priestly ministry of intercession,
we're not simply to carry burdens *for* others; we're to carry them
away from others—just as Jesus did.

Please remember, however, we're not literally *re-doing* what
Christ did; we're *re-presenting* what He did. There's a big difference between the two. We're representing Him, extending His
work—He who bore our infirmities, diseases, sins, reproaches
and rejection when they were "laid on" (*paga*) Him.

He is the balm of Gilead (see Jer. 8:22), but we apply this
healing salve.

He is the fountain of life (see Jer. 2:13; 17:13), but we are
dispensers of His living water.

His is the comforting shepherd's staff (see Ps. 23:4), but He
allows us the privilege of extending it.

Yes, not only did He bear our weaknesses, but He's also still
"touched with the feeling of our infirmities" (Heb. 4:15, *KJV*).
And He wants to touch us with the same compassion that we,
too, might be bearers.

Think about it: the great Healer "healing" through us; the
great High Priest "priesting" through us; the great Lover "loving" through us.

He inaugurated the new covenant with His blood (see Heb.
12:24), but in reference to *our part*, He has "made us able ministers of the new testament" (2 Cor. 3:6, *KJV*—"testament" is just a
KJV word for "covenant").

Yes, Christ has made us "able ministers." And if I understand
the word correctly, ministers administer something. What do we

administer? The blessings and provisions of the new covenant.

And who secured and guarantees those benefits? Jesus, of course. Then this verse is just another way of saying that we have been made able distributors of what Christ already accomplished.

Released Through Others Coming to Your Aid

This verse came alive for me when my friend Mike Anderson made the following statement: "Sometimes the covenant of the Lord is released to you through others coming to your aid." At the time, Mike and his wife were missionaries in Jamaica. The statement was made on the heels of a life and death struggle they had just experienced with their son who had contracted a critical illness. The young child, two or three years old, had regressed for several days to a point of near death. That's when Mike called me and a few other individuals in the United States.

I knew something fairly serious had to be occurring when the prayer meeting I was leading was interrupted to inform me about an emergency phone call from Jamaica.

"I'm sorry to interrupt your meeting, Dutch," my friend Mike began, "but I desperately need your help."

"What is it?" I asked.

"It's my son, Toby," Mike replied. "He is deathly ill with a raging fever. The doctors haven't been able to find the cause. They've done all they know to do, but nothing seems to help. It is questionable whether or not he can survive another night in his condition. I have been praying and praying for him but can't seem to break this attack. The Lord has now revealed to me that his condition is being caused by a strong spirit of infirmity, which He actually allowed me to see as I was praying. I have not been able to break its power over my son, however, even though I've warred against it for hours. But I feel the Lord has shown me that if some strong intercessors join me, we can break this attack."

Mike and his wife, Pam, are strong in the Lord. They pray. They have faith. They understand authority. They were not in sin. Why then, you might ask, could they not get the breakthrough they needed on their own?

I don't know. But I suspect the Lord wanted to teach them (and those of us praying with them) the principle I'm now sharing with you.

The people I was meeting with and a few others Mike had called went into prayer. We asked God to meet (*paga*) with this child. We said essentially, "Father, allow us to move into our priestly role as intercessors (*paga*), enforcing the victory of Jesus in this situation, re-presenting or administering the blessings of the new covenant. Stake us to Toby and allow us, along with Christ, to be touched with the feeling of this infirmity. Lay on (*paga*) us this burden that we might bear (*nasa, bastazo*) it away. We ask this in Jesus' name—based on who He is and what He has done, Father."

We then bound the power of Satan over this child's life—in Christ's name, of course, because it was His victory we were "administering." Then we growled with "the bear anointing" (see chapter 4). No, we didn't really, but lighten up and enjoy the symbolism. Besides, I think maybe there was a growl in the Spirit! Perhaps a roar would be more accurate because the Lion of the tribe of Judah roared through us. He does "roar out of Zion," you know (see Joel 3:16; Amos 1:2). And we are certain He did because Mike called back a few hours later and said, "Almost immediately after I contacted several of you to pray with me, the fever broke and my son began to improve. Within a few hours he was well and released from the hospital."

Praise God! The Body of Christ had functioned as the Lord intended, and Jesus was glorified.

Mike continued, "I asked the Lord why I needed others to help me break this attack against my son. He reminded me of the story of Joshua and the army of Israel coming to the aid of the Gibeonites, who were helplessly outnumbered by five armies." Mike then recounted the story from Joshua 9 and 10 for me, which I'll briefly summarize for you.

The Gibeonites were one of the Canaanite tribes that Joshua and Israel were supposed to destroy. They had deceived the Israelites, however, into believing they had come from a far country in order to enter a covenant with them. Joshua and the Israelites neglected to pray about this and were therefore deceived into a binding, covenantal agreement. (Have you ever "forgotten" to pray about something and gotten into trouble?)

Even though it was born of deceit, the covenant was still valid and made Israel an ally of Gibeon. Therefore, a few days later when five armies marched against Gibeon, they called upon Joshua for help—based on the strength of covenant. Even though the agreement was conceived in deception, Joshua and his army traveled all night to arrive in time and rescue the Gibeonites. The entire story is an incredible demonstration of the power of covenant.

After calling my attention to this story, Mike then spoke these words to me: "Dutch, after reminding me of this story, the Lord planted the following thought in my heart as to why I needed help overcoming this spirit: 'Sometimes the covenant of the Lord is released to you through others coming to your aid!'"

Isn't that profound? The Almighty administering the blessings of the covenant through us. That's what intercession is all about. *Paga*: He "lays on" us someone else's need. *Anechomai*: We "stake" ourselves to that person. *Bastazo*: We "carry away" the weakness or burden.

Enforcing and Treading upon the Enemy

A further profound picture of this partnership between Christ and the Church is exemplified in this same story of Israel and the Gibeonites. It's found in Joshua 10:22-27. Joshua is an Old Testament picture or type of Christ, and Israel pictures the Church. Joshua's name, which is actually the Hebrew equivalent to the name Jesus, had been changed earlier in his life to paint this picture. It had formerly been Hoshea.

After Joshua and the army of Israel defeated the five Canaanite armies in defense of the Gibeonites, the kings of these armies fled to hide in a cave.

Upon discovering them, Joshua ordered the kings to be brought to him and made them lie down on the ground. He was about to enact a very familiar custom, which was to place his foot on their necks or heads to display his conquest. Oftentimes the defeated army, or armies in this case, would then be paraded before the conquering king or general, observing him as he "displayed" his conquest. This is what Colossians 2:15 is referring to when it says of Christ, "When He had disarmed the rulers and authorities, He made a public display of them, having triumphed over them through Him."

Joshua, however, is about to do something very different and very prophetic. Rather than place his foot on the necks of these kings, as was the typical custom, Joshua summoned some of his soldiers and had them do it. No more literal picture of Christ and the Church, His army, could have been given to us. In fulfillment of this prophetic picture, when Jesus defeated Satan and his principalities and powers, the rulers of the darkness of this world, He, too, called His army to Him and said, "You put your feet on the necks of these enemies."

When Ephesians 2:6 says that He "raised us up with Him," Christ is saying, "It's not only My victory, but it's also yours."

He is also saying, "What I have done, you must enforce. I have put them under My feet legally—under My authority—but you must exercise that authority in individual situations, causing the literal fulfillment of it."

That is why Romans 16 says, "And the God of peace will soon crush Satan under *your* feet" (v. 20, emphasis added). And Luke 10:19 tells us, "Behold, I have given *you* authority to tread upon serpents and scorpions, and over all the power of the enemy, and nothing shall injure you" (emphasis added). This is what happened when we helped Mike: an enforcing and a treading.

Sometimes a "laying on" requires a "treading upon"!

Psalm 110, a futuristic Messianic psalm relating to Christ, also pictures our partnership with Him. It foretells that Christ would, after His resurrection, ascend to the right hand of the Father. According to the New Testament, at the time of His ascension and enthronement, He had *already* placed all other authorities under His feet:

And He put all things in subjection under His feet, and gave Him as head over all things to the church (Eph. 1:22).

For He has put all things in subjection under His feet. But when He says, "All things are put in subjection," it is evident that He is excepted who put all things in subjection to Him (1 Cor. 15:27).

But Psalm 110 informs us that He would still be *waiting* for them to become His footstool: "Sit at My right hand, *until* I make Thine enemies a footstool for Thy feet" (Ps. 110:1, emphasis added).

Wait a minute. Do we have a contradiction between this Messianic prophecy and the New Testament verses that say after He ascended to the Father's right hand they were *already* under His feet? No. Then why the seeming inconsistency? *Are* they under His feet or *will* they be placed there? The answer is YES! They are *legally* through the Cross. They will be *literally* as we do "our part." Verses 2 and 3 of Psalm 110 describe our part:

> The Lord will stretch forth Thy strong scepter from Zion, saying, "Rule in the midst of Thine enemies." Thy people will volunteer freely in the day of Thy power; in holy array, from the womb of the dawn, Thy youth are to Thee as the dew.

The word "power" in this passage, *chayil*, is also translated "army."[7] Christ is looking for a volunteer army that will stretch forth His strong scepter of authority, ruling in the midst of their enemies, enforcing His great victory. So, once again, did He place all other authorities under foot or do we? YES! He did; we enforce. He conquered Satan and his kingdom; we enforce the victory.

As we stated, sometimes a "laying on" results in a "treading upon."

In other words, at times when Christ lays a prayer mission or burden on us (*paga*) that we might bear it away (*nasa, bastazo*), the task involves warfare. No serious Bible student could study the word "intercession" (*paga*) and separate it from the concept of warfare. This will be obvious as we focus more directly on spiritual warfare in upcoming chapters.

Both the Hebrew and Greek words used for "tread," *darak* (Hebrew)[8] and *pateo* (Greek),[9] involve the concept of violence or war. The Hebrew word *darak* actually came to be used for "bending the bow"[10] when about to shoot an arrow and is still used today in Israel for the command, "Load your weapons." Both words are used for treading or trampling in a wine press, a fittingly used symbolism of Christ overcoming His enemies in Isaiah 63:3 and Revelation 19:15.

The verse in Revelation says, "And from His mouth comes a sharp sword, so that with it He may smite the nations; and He will rule them with a rod of iron; and He treads the wine press of the fierce wrath of God, the Almighty." We in America even have a verse from the famous hymn "The Battle Hymn of the Republic" taken from these two verses of Scripture: "He is trampling out the vintage where the grapes of wrath are stored, He has loosed the fateful lightning of His terrible swift sword."[11]

It's amazing to me that these same two words are used to describe not only Christ at war, but also our warfare. Let me give you one such reference. In Joshua 1:3, the Lord said to Joshua, "Every place on which the sole of your foot treads, I have given it to you, just as I spoke to Moses." The word "tread," of course, is *darak*. God wasn't telling Israel that everywhere they walked or stepped was theirs. He had already marked off the perimeters of the inheritance. He was saying symbolically, "Every place that you are willing to load your weapons and take, I'm going to give to you."

So, one more time, was God giving or were they taking? YES! And just to prove my point, remember that the previous generation under Moses was afraid and wouldn't *darak* (load their weapons and fight) and God wouldn't give.

Please don't think for a moment that it's any different for us today. These things happened to Israel as types or shadows for us (see 1 Cor. 10:6,11). That which our Joshua-Jesus has and is giving to us won't automatically come to us either, just because we belong to Him. We, too, must take "the weapons of our warfare" (2 Cor. 10:4) and *darak*!

This is intercession, as it was through Christ and is through us. Oftentimes it is to be done for our brothers and sisters as we, like Christ, climb into their attics of despair, place our cheeks next to theirs and carry away the burdens or weaknesses.

- May Christ live *through you*!
- May that which is lacking in Christ's afflictions—our part—be lacking no more!
- May the scepter be extended from us as we rule in the midst of our enemies, making them His footstool!
- May the terrifying roar of the Lion of Judah resound from the Church!
- May the covenant of the Lord be administered in the earth!

I read the following father-and-son story which serves as a fitting end to this chapter:

In spite of repeated warnings, a small boy continued coming home late after school. One morning his parents informed him that there was no more grace—he must arrive on time that evening. He was late again.

At dinner that night the young man discovered his punishment. On his plate was only a piece of bread. The boy was shocked and dismayed. After waiting a few moments for the full impact to do its work, the father took the boy's plate and gave him his fill of meat and potatoes.

When the boy was grown to manhood he said, "All my life I've known what God is like by what my father did that night."[12]

To be like Christ will cost us. Our cause is costly. The work of intercession has a price. Let's pay it. Let's push back from our bountiful table once in a while and show someone what God is like.

Questions for Reflection

1. Explain the two types of bearing in the Scriptures. How do they pertain to intercession? What does *paga* have to do with bearing?

2. Can you explain how the scapegoat is a picture of intercession?

3. How does the account of Joshua and the Israelites in Joshua 10:22-27 picture the partnership between Christ and the Church?

4. In what way does Psalm 110 picture the relationship between Jesus and the Church?

5. Have you told Jesus yet today that you love Him?

NO TRESPASSING

Protective Boundaries

"No dumping allowed. Trespassers will be violated."

I used to laugh every time I drove by the sign. This wasn't a homemade sign. It was a professionally made metal sign posted by a city in Oklahoma (I won't tell you which one). It was even the fancy kind with fluorescent letters that could be easily seen at night. But those who made it were confused and instead of saying "Trespassers (or Violators) will be prosecuted," they worded it "Trespassers will be violated."

I hope they were merely confused. Perhaps they weren't. Maybe in that town the law violated lawbreakers instead of prosecuting them. I decided I didn't want to find out.

There is an aspect of intercession that relates to protection: protective boundaries—posting signs in the spirit, if you please: "No dumping allowed, Satan. Trespassers will be violated."

In the nineteenth chapter of Joshua, the word *paga* (intercession) is used several times. The passage is describing the dimensions or boundaries of each of the tribes of Israel. It is translated several ways in different translations, including "reached to," "touched," "bordered," "boundary." *The Spirit-Filled Bible* says *paga*, when used in this context, is the extent to which a boundary reaches.[1]

Does it surprise you that the word used for "intercession," *paga*, is also translated "boundary"? It really shouldn't. It only seems logical to me that perimeters of protection be linked to prayer. I want to state emphatically: We CAN build boundaries of protection[2] around ourselves and others through intercession. What a comfort to know that this truth is inherent in the very meaning of the word.

Many Christians believe that protection from accidents, destruction, satanic traps and assaults, etc., is automatic for the Christian—that we do nothing to cause it—that it is based on the sovereignty of God alone. In other words, when God wants to protect us from these things, He does; when He chooses not to, He allows them to happen.

This belief simply means that whether or not we are delivered from destructive things is based entirely on God, not us. Those who adhere to this teaching usually believe nothing can happen to a Christian that is not allowed by God. Others go so far as to say this is true for everyone, not just Christians. They believe God is in control of everything that happens on Earth.

That God is not directly in control of *everything* that takes place on Earth can be seen in the simple facts:

· He would never decide a person should be raped or abused.
· He would never desire that the innocent suffer.
· He would never will murder, pillage, racial genocide and a thousand other things.

Governing Principles

Whether or not God directly controls every event in the life of a Christian can be answered by stating that the basic laws of sowing and reaping, cause and effect, individual responsibility and the free will aren't negated when we come to Christ. *All* promises from God are attached to conditions—governing principles. Most, if not all, of these conditions involve responsibility on our part. Protection is no exception.

Most of us don't like that. It threatens us and somehow weakens God in our minds to imply He's not in total control of everything. And the majority are greatly offended if anything is taught implying that a failure to receive protection, provision, healing, an answer to prayer, or anything else from God could be our fault.

I can understand how it might threaten us—I'm threatened by me—but I don't understand why it offends. Are any of us claiming perfection? Aren't all of us going to fail once in a while? Then why are we offended when a teaching suggests that these imperfections and failures might hinder us?

Why are we offended and opposed to a teaching that says our unbelief kept us from receiving something when so often the Bible says if we believe and do not doubt or waver we'll receive (see Matt. 17:20; 21:21; Mark 11:22-24; Jas. 1:6-7)?

Why are we offended when it is implied that our inability to persevere created lack when the Bible says that we "through faith *and patience* inherit the promises" (Heb. 6:12, emphasis added)?

Why are we confused or angry when it is suggested that our not doing something caused failure when the Bible says if we're "willing *and obedient*" we'll eat the good of the land (Isa. 1:19, *KJV*, emphasis added)?

As many as 80 percent of those who consider themselves born again don't tithe, thereby opening themselves to a curse. Yet they are offended when someone implies that their lack of provision might be their own fault (see Mal. 3:8-12).

We don't forgive and still have the gall to think God will hear and answer our prayers (see Mark 11:25-26).

Often, we eat poorly, don't exercise and abuse our bodies in other ways. Then we blame our sicknesses on God's will.

We don't properly train our children, yet we're offended with the suggestion that their rebellion might be our fault (see Deut. 6:7; Prov. 22:6).

We don't abide in Christ and His Word. Still we blame it on "God's will" when we "ask what we will" and it isn't done (John 15:7).

We know faith comes through hearing and meditating on God's Word (see Rom. 10:17), and most of us do very little of that. But let someone imply that we didn't receive a promise because of unbelief and we're irate.

The Scriptures teach that "He that dwelleth in the secret place of the most High" (*KJV*) receives the protective promises of the remainder of Psalm 91 . . . that I have an armor I must wear and carry, including the shield of faith, to ward off Satan's fiery darts (see Eph. 6:13-18) . . . that Satan goes about like a roaring lion seeking whom he may devour and that I am to resist him (see 1 Pet. 5:8; Jas. 4:7) . . . and yet, let someone suggest that my lack of protection from some destructive happening could be my own fault and I'm offended. How about you?

I'm certainly not implying that God *never* allows us to walk through difficulties, that *all* our problems are because of disobedience or that *all* unanswered prayer is because of unbelief. I'm simply saying that many of our failures and difficulties are our fault, not "God's will"; we have a part to play in the securing of protection and other heavenly provisions.

Let's try to lay down our fears, insecurities and tendencies toward offense. Let's accept the fact that the Scriptures are filled with principles that put responsibility on us, which must be met to receive God's promises. Let's realize this doesn't cancel grace and promote salvation by works. Grace does not imply "no responsibility" on our part. Let's realize the love of God is unconditional, but His favor and blessing are not.

Let's cast off all laziness, complacency and apathy. Let's realize we will fall short at times and not feel condemned when we do. *Let's!*

Building Boundaries Through Prayer

If you're still willing to finish this book after such a dissertation—back to protection. You've probably guessed by now that I don't believe it is automatically ours just because we are Christians. We must do things to secure it, one of which is building boundaries (*paga*) of protection through prayer.

I heard a minister in Fort Worth, Texas, tell the story of another pastor who years ago received divine protection as a result of prayer-building walls or boundaries of protection (*paga*). This pastor had developed the discipline of beginning every day with an hour of prayer.

One particular day, however, he felt a strong leading of the Holy Spirit to pray longer, so he continued for a second hour. After two hours he still felt the need to keep on praying, so he persevered for a third hour, asking for God's protection and blessing on his day, as well as for other things. He then felt released from the need to pray longer, so he stopped.

That evening as he was mowing his lawn, he felt something repeatedly brush up against his leg. He looked down and saw a coiled rattlesnake trying to strike him, but it just couldn't hit him. Instead, it kept brushing either side of his leg.

Why had the man felt the need to pray longer that morning? What was he doing? Among other things he was building "boundaries" of protection through prayer—*paga*.

Some would say, of course, that God doesn't need three hours of prayer to protect one from a rattlesnake. I would agree. He didn't "need" seven days of marching around Jericho to tear it down either, but He chose to do it that way. He doesn't "need" to spit in a person's eye to heal them, but He did once. Why He requires things to be done certain ways, we don't always know, but we do know that for us *obedience is the key*. If He says "three hours" then three hours is exactly what it will take.

Dwelling in the Secret Place

Consistency is also a key when it comes to prayer for protection. We must "dwell" in the secret place to "abide" under the Almighty's protective shadow: "He that dwelleth in the secret place of the most High shall abide under the shadow of the Almighty" (Ps. 91:1, *KJV*). Jesus equated the "secret" place to the prayer closet in Matthew 6:6. The word "dwell" in Psalm 91:1 is *yashab*, which means "to remain or abide; to dwell in or inhabit."[3] The point is that it must be a lifestyle, not a once in a while activity. We must make the secret place our habitation or "dwelling" place. Many believers' prayer lives are too sporadic to build solid walls of protection.

The word "abide" in this same verse is *luwn*, which means, among other things, "to spend the night."[4] Let's read it with that meaning: "He that dwelleth in the secret place of the most High, shall *spend the night* under the shadow of the Almighty." In other words, prayer is like the Word of God—we don't read enough today for the entire week. We must have "daily bread" or manna. Likewise, we must go to the secret place daily and when we do we can "spend the night" there. Tomorrow, however, we must go again. Consistency is a key.

I heard a visiting minister in Eaton, Ohio, share this testimony of God's protection in World War II. He served on a ship and every day he and a few other sailors would have a prayer time, seeking God for protection for themselves and the ship. What were they doing? Building boundaries (*paga*) of protection.

"In one battle," he related, "an enemy plane dropped a bomb onto the deck of our ship. Instead of exploding, however, to everyone's astonishment the bomb bounced off the deck and into the water, just like a rubber ball would!" This minister went on to say that in battle after battle they and the ship were miraculously spared.

Well-Timed Times to Pray

Boundaries of protection! No trespassing! Life in the secret place!

This facet of intercession is not only to be something we do on a *general* regular basis for our family and loved ones. There are also *specific* times when the Holy Spirit will alert us to particular situations that need protective prayer. These are what the Scriptures call *kairos* times.

There are two Greek words for "time." One is *chronos*, which is time in general, the general "time in which anything *is* done."[5] The other word, *kairos*, is the strategic or "right time; the opportune point of time at which something *should be* done."[6]

A window of opportunity would be *kairos* time.

A well-timed attack in war would be *kairos* time.

When someone is in danger or about to be attacked by Satan, that is a *kairos* time.

What time it is would be *chronos* time.

The Bible speaks of well-timed (*kairos*) temptations (see Luke 4:13; 8:13). No doubt coincidental temptations occur—a person just happening to be in the wrong place at the wrong time—but there are also well-planned, well-timed temptations. It pays to be alert, both for ourselves and for others. I've had the Holy Spirit prompt me to pray for individuals, especially young believers, with the thought, *It's a* kairos *time of temptation for them.* This is what took place in Luke 22:31-32 when Jesus interceded for Peter, praying that his faith not fail him after he denied Christ. It worked.

Is it possible that some who have fallen away from Christ would not have if someone had interceded for them?

The Scriptures also inform us of strategically timed persecution (see Acts 12:1; 19:23). This is usually to discourage, to distract or, in extreme cases, to destroy us. In these references, during times of renewal and success in the Early Church, Satan launched orchestrated attacks of persecution. They failed.

Is it possible that much successful persecution against the Church could be stopped or rendered unfruitful if we were alert and interceded against it?

Often we forget the instruction to not lean on our own understanding, and fail to acknowledge Him in our intercession (see Prov. 3:5-6). We do not wait for or listen to the promptings of the Holy Spirit, usually to our own hurt. We forget that "we wrestle not against flesh and blood" (Eph. 6:12, *KJV*) and that the "weapons of our warfare are not carnal" (2 Cor. 10:4, *KJV*). We are so afraid of becoming demon conscious (putting an overemphasis on them) that we become demon unconscious. Sometimes our quest for balance gets us out of balance.

Ephesians 6:18, the context of which is spiritual warfare, says that we are to "be on the alert . . . for all the saints" and "pray at all times [*kairos*] in the Spirit." He is not telling us here to pray all the time, which would be *chronos*, but to pray at all strategic times (*kairos*). In other words, we are in a war and if we are alert He will warn us of the well-timed attacks (*kairos*) of the enemy so that we can create a boundary (*paga*) of protection by praying.

Kairos, a Time to *Paga*

One morning several years ago as I was praying, the Lord gave me a mental picture. Some might call it a vision. Whatever it is called, I saw something: a rattlesnake coiled at my dad's feet. Seemed like a *kairos* time to me! I spent about 15 minutes praying earnestly for his protection until I felt released from the urgency.

The next day he called me—he was in Florida, I was in Texas—and said, "You'll never guess what happened yesterday. Jodie [my stepmother] went out back to the shed. Before walking in as she normally would, she pushed the door open, stopped and looked down. There where she was about to step was a coiled rattlesnake. She backed away carefully, came and got me and I killed it."

I said to Dad, "Yeah, I know."

Surprised, he asked, "How did you know?"

"I saw it in the spirit," I responded, "and prayed for your protection. You owe me." (No, I didn't really say the part about owing me. I acted real humble and said something like, "Praise God" or "Praise Jesus." You know how we do it!)

What was I doing as I prayed for him? Setting boundaries (*paga*) of protection around him and Jodie.

How did I pray? I asked the Father to protect them. I bound any attempt of Satan to harm them. I quoted a verse or two of Scripture promising protection. Then I prayed in the Spirit.

Gail Mummert, a member of our fellowship in Colorado Springs, shared this remarkable testimony of protection during a *kairos* moment in Lancaster, Texas:

As we were driving home in threatening weather, my husband, Gene, turned on the radio for a local report. Funnel clouds had indeed been spotted nearby. After arriving home, things grew strangely calm.

In a short while, the wind started to blow fiercely. Trees were bent over and the very walls of the house began to flutter. Windows rattled and hail beat on the car port.

"Get into the hall and close the doors," my husband shouted. "Get pillows, blankets and a flashlight."

"Nana, I'm scared," cried our five-year-old grand-son, William.

"Jesus will take care of us. Don't be afraid," I told him.

Suddenly sirens began to go off in our small town. The walls moved as though they weren't anchored to anything. "If we're not in a tornado, we're close," shouted Gene as he ran into the hall.

"Link arms and sit on the floor," I said.

"I love you," Gene said to us as he surrounded us with blankets and pillows, covered us with his body and enveloped us with his arms.

A mighty rushing wind was all around us and sucked us together into a ball. "Pray! Keep praying," he said.

"God Almighty, help us!" we screamed.

Explosion!

Windows shattered, glass flew everywhere. Another explosion. The walls caved in. Debris shot everywhere like arrows toward their target.

"Jesus, help us! You are our Savior! You are our King!" my voice cried. I looked up—the roof was falling on us. A ladder crashed down on my husband's back.

"Now start praising Him," Gene shouted through the wind. The next blast was the worst. There was nothing we could do. Only He could help us. Everything was out of control, but we knew the sovereignty of God. We knew we were at the point of death, but we shouted, "Thank You, Jesus! Thank You, Lord!"

Suddenly, peace filled me like a flood. A sweet voice filled my heart, "I've heard your cry for help. I've bent the heavens for you. No matter what happens around you, I'm here protecting you." Tears flooded my face and I knew Jesus was protecting us. It seemed His arms had surrounded us. I knew we would be safe.

The tornado was over. The rain beat down on us with a force I had never felt before. We were safe. "Mama, I see the sky," little William said.

"William, that's because the roof is gone. We probably won't have any walls, either," Gene informed him.

"I'm so thankful we're okay," our daughter Wendy cried. "Jesus protected us, didn't He?" Though buried under tons of debris, our hair covered with insulation and glass, we were okay. Just a few minor injuries.

Talk about walls of protection! Several people were killed and many injured in that devastating tornado, but the everlasting arms of the Lord protected the Mummert family. Gail was privileged to share her entire story with *The Dallas Morning News*. The newspaper even printed her testimony about the protection of the Lord.

I had a friend in Dallas several years ago who experienced an interesting answer to prayer in a *kairos* situation. She had gone early one morning to visit her son and daughter-in-law. The son worked an all-night shift, so, awaiting his return from work, his wife and mother visited for a while. As time wore on and the son didn't arrive, Mom began to feel uneasy. Something didn't seem right.

Thinking that perhaps he was still at work, they called his place of employment, "No," they were told, "he has already left."

Becoming more alarmed the mother said, "I'm concerned. Let's drive toward his place of work."

She had assumed her son had left work at his normal time and should have been home by then when, in fact, he had left just moments before their call. But the Lord was directing even in that because, though he was not in any danger yet, the Holy Spirit knew a *kairos* moment was coming for this young man, and He wanted this praying mother there when it happened.

As Mom and daughter-in-law drove toward his workplace on a busy Dallas parkway, they saw him coming from the other direction on his motorcycle, traveling around 40 to 50 miles per hour. As they watched, he fell asleep and veered off the road, hit the curb and flew 40 or 50 feet through the air. He was not even wearing a helmet.

As the boy was moving through the air, Mom was praying, *"Jesus, protect my son!"* She continued to pray as they turned around and drove back to him. A crowd had already gathered around him, and they ran to the scene, wondering what they would find.

They found a miracle! No injuries—no bones broken, no lacerations, no internal injuries. Just a dazed young man wondering what had happened.

Paga happened . . . *Kairos paga* happened! Boundaries happened. A mother picked up on the warning from the Holy Spirit and was therefore in the right place at the right time.

Does this mean that if you weren't there praying when someone you loved had an accident, you're to blame for their injury or death? Of course not. If we all played that guessing game, it would drive us insane. It simply means we must be alert, and when warnings do come from the Holy Spirit, we must respond by praying—building some boundaries.

I heard a guest lecturer at Christ for the Nations in Dallas, Texas, tell another interesting story involving not a *kairos moment*, but a *kairos season* of building boundaries (*paga*) of protection.

He had a vivid reoccurring dream, which he felt strongly was a warning from the Lord, of his married daughter dying. In the dream he was not shown how her death happened, but he felt strongly that Satan had a well-laid plan to take his daughter's life. So as not to alarm her, he told only his son-in-law and the two of them began to intercede (*paga*) daily for her safety. They were building boundaries (*paga*) of protection around her.

This minister related how several times a day—while he worked, drove his car, walked, whenever it came to mind—he would bind Satan's plan to take his daughter's life. "How would he do this?" some might ask. "What did he say?" He probably said things like:

- "Father, I bring my daughter to You." That is creating a "meeting" (*paga*) with God.

- "I ask You to protect her from any trap Satan has set for her. You said You would deliver us from the snare of the trapper" (see Ps. 91:3). That is building "boundaries" (*paga*) of protection.

- "Thank You for laying this prayer burden on me that I might lift off and carry away from her (*nasa*) this assignment of death." That's having someone else's burden or weakness "laid on" (*paga*) us.

- "Satan, I bind this plan of yours and break any hold you may have gained in this situation. Your weapons against her won't prosper and you're not going to take her life." That is "meeting" (*paga*) the enemy to break.

- "I do this in the name of Jesus!" That's basing all our *prayers* on the *work* Christ has already done. It's *representing* Him . . . administering what He has already accomplished . . . *enforcing* His victory.

About a month later—remember, I said this was a *kairos season* and I said he prayed *daily*—his daughter received a promotion at work. With the promotion came a life insurance policy that mandated a physical exam.

At one point in the process, after a blood sample had been taken, a doctor addressed her in a near panic with the question and comments, "Lady, what have you been doing in your diet? We can find no potassium in you at all! You should be dead. There is no reasonable explanation as to why you're alive. When this deficiency occurs, a person normally feels fine but suddenly drops dead. We must get you to the hospital immediately and begin to replenish the potassium."

She lived, of course. She had been on a strange diet for several weeks, during which she had eaten only one or two kinds of food. Though there was no reasonable explanation as to why she lived, we know the spiritual explanation: a boundary (*paga*) of protection built in the spirit through prayer.

Under the Shadow of the Most High. Keep Out!

Perhaps the most amazing example of *kairos*-timed intercession in my life happened on one of my journeys to Guatemala. I was one of 40 to 45 individuals traveling to a remote place on the Passion River in the Peten Jungle. Our mission was to build a combination clinic and outreach station on the river. We were to be constructing two buildings as well as doing a little preaching in the nearby villages.

It was an amazing trip. We ate monkey meat and boa constrictor. We killed huge tarantulas, a nine-inch scorpion and a coral snake in our camp. I was attacked by ants that, unbeknownst to us, had taken refuge in the lumber we were hauling and sleeping on as we traveled all night up the river. We flew in old, rickety army planes and landed on fields from which goats had to be cleared prior to our arrival. (None of this has anything to do with prayer, but it lets you know how incredibly brave I am and how much I've suffered for the cause of Christ.)

Our leader, Hap Brooks, had me leading songs from the front of our long dugout canoe as we journeyed up and down the river. His favorite was "It's a Good Life Livin' for the Lord." He also made me utter my famous Tarzan call, which was incredibly good and would reverberate across the river and into the jungle. Natives from the villages would stand on the banks and listen. Having never seen or heard of Tarzan, of course, they were not terribly impressed—in fact they sort of had that "who is that idiot?" look on their faces. That is, until the animals in the jungle began to come to me! They had the same expression. (This has nothing to do with prayer, either, but it lets you know how incredibly talented I am.)

Back to the purpose of the story. Prior to leaving for the jungle, we spent our first night (Friday) in Guatemala City, the capital of Guatemala. We had arranged months earlier for the Guatemalan airlines to fly us the following day into the jungle. On our arrival at the airport Saturday afternoon, we were informed that they had changed their plans and would fly us to our destination not that day but the next.

Feeling an urgency to go as scheduled due to the limited amount of time to accomplish our mission, our leaders pressed the airlines for three hours to honor their original agreement.

"No," the manager said in his broken English, "we take you tomorrow."

"But you agreed months ago to take us today," we argued.

"We have no pilot available," they countered.

"Find one," we pleaded.

"What is your hurry? Enjoy the city," they encouraged us.

And so it went for three hours, in and out of offices, meeting with one official, then another. Finally, in exasperation, one of them threw up his hands and said, "Okay, we take you now! Get on that plane—quickly!"

We all ran to the plane, throwing our bags and tools into the baggage area ourselves. We wanted to leave before they changed their minds.

That night, while we were 250 miles away, an earthquake hit Guatemala City and killed 30,000 people in 34 seconds! Had we stayed in the city one more night—as the airlines wanted us to—some of our team would have been killed and others injured. We know this for certain because on our return to the city we saw the building we had stayed in the night before the earthquake—and would have been staying in again had we not left on Saturday—with huge beams lying across the beds.

The connection between all this and our subject is that an intercessor from our home church back in Ohio had received a strong burden to pray for us on the second day of our journey. For *three hours* she was in intense intercession for us. Can you guess which three hours? Yes. The three hours that our leaders were negotiating with the airline officials.

We didn't know that our lives would have been in jeopardy had we stayed another night in Guatemala City, but God did. This intercessor didn't know it either. She only knew that for some reason she had a strong burden to pray for us. She was alert, as Ephesians 6:18 instructs us, and perceived the *kairos* time. There isn't a doubt in my mind that she helped create the protection and intervention we experienced.

There is a life in the secret place, but it's not automatic for believers. Although we are promised protection from our enemy, we have a definite part to play in the securing of it for ourselves and for others. The intercessor knows this and leaves nothing to chance, posting signs for all the forces of hell to see: "Under the shadow of the Most High. Keep out!"

Questions for Reflection

1. How is the connection between *paga* and protection made?

2. Is all protection automatic for Christians? Is everything that happens to us allowed by God, or do our actions and prayers have a part in it? Explain.

3. Comment on consistency in prayer as it relates to protection.

4. Explain the difference between *chronos* and *kairos* and how this relates to intercession.

5. Have you posted any "No Trespassing" signs lately?

BUTTERFLIES, MICE, ELEPHANTS AND BULL'S-EYES

A Happening by Chance

I was riding high, literally. About 200 feet high, as a matter of fact. I was parasailing in Acapulco.

My wife, Ceci, and I were on the last day of our three-day vacation in this tourist hot spot. I had been watching this activity all week, seeing the boats pull individuals from off the beach, up into the air and across the beautiful waters. These airborne sailors would soar effortlessly for 5 to 10 minutes, enjoying their freedom from the bonds of the earth, and then be swung back onto the beach. To the amazement and cheers of us less-adventurous earthlings, they would land softly and accept our applause. They didn't even get wet.

For two days I watched this. Now I've always wanted to parachute—actually, wondered what it would be like is closer to the truth—but was smart enough to not do it before I married. My wife has since asked me not to, which is now my face-saving excuse. *But maybe this would satisfy my curiosity*, I thought as I watched this activity. Finally, I decided I wasn't quite that curious.

We men have a constant need to impress the ladies in our lives, demonstrating our fearlessness and ability to rise to any challenge.

"Wow, that looks pretty awesome," my wife said.

"Aw, it doesn't look that difficult," I replied in my best matter-of-fact "any guy could do it" voice. "All you do is run off the beach and let the boat do the rest. I'd do it, but you probably wouldn't want me to. Besides, it's not worth the money."

To my absolute horror, she responded excitedly, "Oh, I wouldn't mind. In fact, I'd love to see you do it and it's not really that expensive. Give it a try!"

Oh, my dear heavenly Father, I cried inwardly, *get me out of this!*

Get yourself out of it, I heard in my heart. *You got yourself into it.*

"Oh, you're just saying that for me, dear," I responded to her. "I know you would really be terrified if I did this, but thanks for thinking of me. I won't put you through it, though."

"No, really, I *want* you to. It would make a great picture and, besides, what could go wrong?" she asked. "Go for it."

"Okay," I said foolishly. "Yeah, what could go wrong?"

There are times in your life when the thing to do is fake an injury, come up with an unexplainable headache or simply humble yourself, admit you're an egotistical male liar and repent of your sin. But I decided to save face. Now tell me, with God's sense of justice and humor, do you really think He was going to allow that?

It was the final morning of our stay. We were to leave in an hour or so. I was in my street clothes, shoes and all. Even kept my watch on. After all, you didn't even touch the water. I should have known this didn't always go as planned when they made me sign that release form but . . .

I was the first of the day. Takeoff was fairly routine and within seconds I was 200 feet high, enjoying a bird's eye view of the beach. Being the first of the day, they were pulling me along the beach, only about 50 or so yards out from the shoreline so that they could advertise for their day's business.

I actually began to enjoy it. It was a real high (pun intended). People along the shore began to wave at me and cheer me on. I was the center of attention for everyone. I, of course, waved back in a "not too demonstrative, this is no big deal" sort of way. Just being cool.

Suddenly, I had the strange sensation the water was getting closer. A second later I knew it was getting closer. Another second and I *lighted upon* the water with a great splash. "How the mighty have fallen!"

This is impossible, I thought. *This is a dream. A BAD dream.* Remembering that I had never tasted salt water in a dream, it didn't take me long to realize that it wasn't a dream at all and that it was very possible. I swam to the boat, which had experienced engine failure, and climbed aboard. Now I was totally cool—wet and cool!

The driver of the boat finally got it started again and we drove back to the starting point. With my best "it's no big deal, in fact, it was kinda fun" swagger, I waded back onto the beach. To this day I don't think my wife knows how I really felt. Like most women she never picks up on it when my male ego is asserting itself. Why, just the other day when she thought we needed to stop and ask for directions . . .

I can hear the wheels of your mind turning. You are wondering what part of this story could possibly have anything to do with intercession, except for a couple of fleeting seconds when I was in SERIOUS prayer. Actually, another of our definitions of *paga* is used, which is "to light upon."[1] The concept, of course, is landing on or coming to a certain place, and the inference is that it is happening by chance. We might, therefore, use the phrase "chance upon" or "happen upon." I'll give you the reference for this shortly and explain its connection to prayer, but first let's look at a couple of other introductory points.

Our Helper

This chapter is about our Helper, the Holy Spirit. Without any doubt the greatest single key to successful intercession is learning to cooperate with the Holy Spirit, allowing Him to be all He was sent to be in us. Jesus called Him our "Helper" in John 14:26: "But the Helper, the Holy Spirit, whom the Father will send in My name, He will teach you all things, and bring to your remembrance all that I said to you."

Some translations use the word "Comforter" instead of "Helper," but the word is *Parakletos* and means "one called alongside to aid, help or support."[2] It is such a powerful word that the *Amplified* version uses seven words to communicate its rich meaning: "Comforter (Counselor, Helper, Intercessor, Advocate, Strengthener, Standby), the Holy Spirit." I want to focus on Him as our "Helper" and "Intercessor."

We read in Romans 8:26-28 that He wants to help us in our prayer lives:

> And in the same way the Spirit also helps our weakness; for we do not know how to pray as we should, but the Spirit Himself intercedes for us with groanings too deep for words; and He who searches the hearts knows what the mind of the Spirit is, because He intercedes for the saints according to the will of God. And we know that God causes all things to work together for good to those who love God, to those who are called according to His purpose.

Notice that verse 28 begins with the word "and," which is a conjunction connecting verse 28 to verses 26 and 27, making it dependent on what is said there. In other words, all things DON'T work together for good in the lives of Christians unless certain conditions are met. All things CAN work together for our good, and God's will is for all things to work together for our good, but this isn't automatic. We have a part to play. It happens as verses 26 and 27 are being implemented.

I don't believe the intercession of the Holy Spirit spoken of in these verses refers only to "tongues." However, most of us in Pentecostal and charismatic circles believe it has to include this gift, which we believe allows the Holy Spirit to literally pray through us. It is not my intention in this book to prove this, nor am I implying that those who do not practice it are second rate in their praying.

If you do not pray in this way, it is my strong desire not to offend you. I have great love and respect for my non-charismatic brothers and sisters in Christ. Yet, it is impossible for me to share what I believe the Lord has taught me concerning this passage without referring to praying in tongues, or as the Scriptures also word it, "praying in the Spirit."

I will, therefore, be saying a good bit about this. From this point on, however, in an effort to be as inclusive and inoffensive as possible, I will only use the phrase "praying in the Spirit." To charismatic readers, when you see this phrase, please know that I am including "tongues." To the rest of you, please interpret with your belief of what it means to "pray in the Spirit."

This passage says that the Holy Spirit wants to help us in our "weakness." The word in Greek is *astheneia* and means literally "without strength" or ability.[3] An "inability to produce results" is the concept communicated by the word.

Have you ever felt an inability in your prayer life to produce results? Have you ever come up against a "mountain" you couldn't move? I recall that happening to me a few years ago, or was that a few hours ago? It's a fact of life.

The Lord then says in this verse that one of the reasons we have this "inability to produce results" is because we don't always "know how to pray as we should." The word "should" here is a very important word. *Dei* is primarily a legal term meaning "that which is necessary, right or proper in the nature of a case; what one must do; that which is legally binding for someone."[4]

For example, Luke 18:1 tells us, "Men *ought* always to pray, and not to faint" (*KJV*, emphasis added). The verse does not mean, "It would be a good idea to pray." It is declaring, "It is absolutely necessary—binding upon you—that you pray."

Jesus used the word when He said of the woman bent over from a spirit of infirmity, "And ought not this woman, being a daughter of Abraham, whom Satan hath bound, lo, these eighteen years, be loosed from this bond on the sabbath day?" (Luke 13:16, *KJV*). His reason that she should be loosed from this spirit was her being "a daughter of Abraham." In other words, she had a covenantal right to it. Because He had the ability to give her what she had a covenantal right to, He said in essence, "Is it not necessary and binding upon me that I deliver this daughter of Abraham from this infirmity?"

Now that we understand the strength of the word, let's put it back into Romans 8:26. The Lord is saying that we don't always know what needs to happen in a given situation. We don't always know what is necessary or right.

I find myself wondering at times, *How do I pray for this person or situation, Lord? What needs to happen?*

At other times I have felt led by the Holy Spirit to pray for someone, yet had no way at that moment of knowing why the person needed prayer.

Sometimes mature intercessors are prompted by the Lord to pray, and not only do they not know what they are praying for, but they also don't know for whom they are praying. They just feel a burden to pray. Talk about a weakness—an inability to produce results. Talk about not knowing what is "necessary, right or proper" in a situation.

What do we do in these circumstances? This is when the Holy Spirit wants to help us. He will lead us as we pray, perhaps revealing things about the situation to us, or bringing Scriptures to our minds so that we can pray them in the situation. He will certainly help us by empowering our prayers. But another way He wants to help us is by literally praying through us as we pray in the Spirit.

The Right Place at the Right Time

This now brings us to *paga* and the definition mentioned earlier: "light upon" or "light on *by chance.*" The setting where the word is used this way is in Genesis 28:10-17.[5] The passage is describing Jacob's flight from Esau after conniving from him his birthright. After traveling all day Jacob needed a place to spend the night "because the sun was set." Verse 11 says he "lighted upon" (*KJV*) a particular place and there he spent the night. Notice that Jacob had not predetermined to spend the night there, he didn't choose the place in advance, but was guided *by chance*—"because the sun was set."

The place as it turns out was a very special place, Bethel, which means "house of God." Jacob actually referred to it as a "gate of heaven." Even though most translations say Jacob lighted on "a" place, the literal Hebrew wording is "the" place. What was simply *a* place to Jacob, chosen by chance, was *the* place to the Lord and sovereignly chosen by Him. It was there that Jacob had a mighty, life-changing encounter with God.

It was there that he saw the angels ascending and descending from heaven. It was at that time that God extended to him the same covenant He had made with Abraham, and informed Jacob that through his lineage He would save the world. He also promised great blessing to Jacob, to protect him and bring him back to his homeland safely. In short, it was a place where

Jacob's entire destiny was foretold and his history shaped.

Nice story but how does that relate to intercession and to Romans 8:26-28? I'm glad you asked!

Like Jacob, who was not guided to this special place by his own reasoning or understanding, we are not always able to be directed in prayer by ours either. Consequently we often feel weak and anemic in our ability to produce results. At times it seems the process is hit and miss, as though we have to land or "light upon" the situation correctly "by chance."

That's okay. It's one of the primary meanings of *paga*.

And it isn't really hit and miss because what is by chance for us is not to our Helper, the Holy Spirit. In fact, *paga* also means "bull's-eye."[6] They still use the word this way in Israel today. Close your eyes and fire! When we allow Him to intercede through us, just as He sovereignly guided Jacob to the right place at the right time, He will cause our prayers to light upon (*paga*) the right person or place, in the right way, at the right time, bringing forth the will of God in situations. And that's right good!

- Bethels will occur!
- Meetings with God will occur!
- Heaven's gates will open!
- Destinies will be written!
- History will be shaped!

"Too dramatic," you say? If you said that, you don't know God well enough. Or perhaps you don't believe strongly enough that we can involve the miracle worker in our praying. I submit to you that one of the reasons we don't see more miracles is because we don't expect more miracles. Our Bible—on both sides of the Cross—presents a lot of them. They come from God, however, and the way to see more of them is to involve Him in more situations. Praying in the Spirit does this.

The Butterfly Anointing

At times when I'm praying in the Spirit I feel like a butterfly looks. Have you ever observed a butterfly flying from one location to another? They flutter this way and that, up and down, "herky-jerky." It appears they do not have the slightest idea where they are going. They almost look drunk. When I begin to pray in the Spirit, not knowing what I'm saying, sometimes with my mind wandering this way and that, I feel as though I'm trying to move in the "butterfly anointing."

Where am I going?

What am I doing?

Will I land in the right place, on the right person?

Is this really accomplishing anything?

But just as surely as that butterfly knows exactly where it's going, so too the Holy Spirit directs my prayers precisely! They WILL "light upon" correctly.

This truth is profoundly illustrated by a story I heard a minister from Cleveland, Tennessee, relate that happened in one of his meetings. He was ministering in a small church in Canada. He did not know anyone in the church well, as it was his first time there. About 15 minutes into his message, he heard the Holy Spirit speak inwardly to him, *Stop your message and begin to pray in the Spirit.*

I'm sure you can imagine the awkwardness of such a thing, especially since he really didn't know these people. The leading of the Holy Spirit was so strong, however, that he obeyed. "You'll have to excuse me," he said, "but the Lord has just instructed me to stop my message and pray in the Spirit." He began to pace the platform, praying in the Spirit audibly.

Five minutes went by. Nothing.

Ten minutes went by. Nothing.

Fifteen minutes went by. Still nothing.

I don't know about you, but I would be feeling pretty nervous by that time. I would have been looking for that button on the podium I've longed for a time or two that I could push to disappear through a trap door! Talk about a weakness—an inability to produce results (*anaideia*). He hadn't even the slightest idea what this was all about.

Talk about not knowing how to pray as he should—what was necessary, right or proper (*dei*)!

Talk about needing to light upon by chance. Talk about the butterfly anointing!

Twenty minutes.

The people had simply sat and watched and listened. Suddenly a woman in the back began to scream, leaped to her feet and ran to the front of the church.

"What is happening?" the minister asked.

"My daughter is a missionary deep in Africa," the lady began. "So deep, in fact, that it takes 3 weeks to get where she is. You have to travel by automobile, then a boat, ride an animal and walk for a total of 21 days. My husband and I just yesterday received a telegram from the people she works with informing us that she had contracted a fatal disease that runs its course in 3 days. If she was in civilization it could be treated, but it would take too long to get her there. 'She'll probably die within 3 days,' they told me, 'and all we can do is send you her body as soon as possible.'"

"The last time my daughter was home," the lady continued, "she taught me some of the dialect of the people with whom she works. And you just said, in that dialect, 'You can rejoice, your daughter is healed. You can rejoice, your daughter is healed.'"

And she was!

WOW! Now that is *PAGA*! That is lighting upon the right person at the right time in the right way. That is Holy Spirit help. That is the butterfly anointing.

Why did it take 20 minutes? Because it's a long way from Canada to Africa and it took the Holy Spirit awhile to flutter like a butterfly all that way?! Well, maybe not. I'm not sure why it took 20 minutes. There are several reasons why I believe perseverance is often necessary in prayer, but that is for another chapter. (Persevere and you will come to it.)

Taking Hold of Together with Against

Another tremendous way the Holy Spirit aids us in our intercession is hidden in the meaning of the word "helps." "And in the same way the Spirit also *helps* our weakness" (Rom. 8:26, emphasis added). The Greek word is *sunantilambanomai*. I think you have to speak in tongues just to say this word. There must be a revelation in it somewhere. It is a compound word made up of three words. *Sun* means "together with," *anti* means "against," and *lambano* means "to take hold of."[7] Putting them together, a very literal meaning of the word would be "take hold of together with against."

How's that for help?

In situations where we're experiencing an inability to get results, the Holy Spirit not only wants to direct our prayers precisely, causing them to light upon correctly, but He also wants to take hold of the situation together with us, adding His strength to ours. "'Not by [your] might not by [your] power, but by My Spirit,' says the Lord of hosts" (Zech. 4:6) will the mountain be moved.

Although the context of 2 Corinthians 12:9 is not prayer, praying in the Spirit is perhaps the greatest example of when His strength is made complete in our weaknesses. When we realize our weaknesses, our inability to produce results, it causes us to look to Him for help. If we allow Him to pray through us, He will take hold together with us. We just have to believe that when the Holy Spirit takes hold, something is going to move!

Please notice that both the word "helps" and its literal definition "takes hold *together* with against" implies not that He is doing it *for* us, but *with* us. In other words, this isn't something the Holy Spirit is simply doing in us, with or without our participation. No, we involve Him by praying in the Spirit, which is actually allowing Him to pray through us.

Several years ago my wife, Ceci, developed a troubling pain in her abdomen. It began as a minor discomfort and grew in intensity over the course of a year, at which time she went to have it checked. The doctor found an ovarian cyst about the size of a large egg. He informed us that surgery was necessary to remove it and possibly the ovary as well.

The doctor was a believer and understood spiritual principles, so I talked with him about giving us a little time to pray for healing. "Doc," I said, "if you can give us some time I think we can get rid of it by prayer."

Being fairly confident that the cyst was not malignant or life threatening, he replied, "I'll give you two months. If you don't get it your way, we'll get it mine."

"Fair enough," I agreed.

We prayed for Ceci with every biblical method we knew of: laying on of hands, elders anointing her with oil, the prayer of agreement, speaking the Scriptures, binding, loosing, casting out and, like good charismatics, we even knocked her on the floor and let her lay there awhile—sometimes you just have to try everything! The next time you speak with someone who insinuates they always know exactly what needs to happen in prayer and spiritual warfare, tell them Dutch Sheets doesn't believe it. (They will then ask you who Dutch Sheets is, but don't be intimidated by that.)

No change in her condition occurred, and I realized we were going to have to obtain this healing through perseverance and laying hold by faith (see 1 Tim. 6:12). That, by the way, is the way most answers to prayer come—not as instant miracles, but through fighting the fight of faith and patience.

I felt I needed to spend an hour a day praying for Ceci. I began my prayer times by stating my reason for approaching the Father. Then I referred to the Scriptures on which I was basing my petition. I would quote them, thanking the Father for His Word and Jesus for providing healing. This usually took no more than five or six minutes. I prayed in the Spirit for the remainder of the hour. This went on for a month.

Some would believe that to be an unreasonable amount of time to pray for something—an hour a day for a month. Others would say God doesn't need that long to heal someone. I'm only telling you what worked for me. And I've discovered that He does not have only one way of doing things, even the same things. His creative varieties never seem to end. The key for us is always obedience.

After a couple of weeks of this, one afternoon the Lord showed me a picture as I was praying in the Spirit. I saw myself holding this cyst in my hand squeezing the life out of it. I did not yet know that the literal meaning of "helps" in Romans 8 was "taking hold of together with against," but the Holy Spirit was teaching me a wonderful truth.

I knew, of course, that I couldn't really get my hands on the cyst, but He was showing me that as I allowed Him to pray through me, HE was "lighting on" and "taking hold with me against" the thing. Obviously, it was His power making the difference.

It sort of reminds me of the mouse and elephant who were best friends. They hung out together all the time, the mouse riding on the elephant's back. One day they crossed a wooden bridge, causing it to bow, creak and sway under their combined weight. After they were across, the mouse, impressed over their ability to make such an impact, said to the elephant, "We sure shook up that bridge, didn't we?"

Kind of reminds me of some of our advertisements and testimonials. You'd think He was the mouse and we were the elephant. (Maybe that's why we don't shake many bridges.)

After seeing the picture of myself squeezing the life out of the cyst, I asked Ceci if there was any change in her condition. "Yes, the pain is decreasing," she informed me.

The doctor's response was, "If the pain is decreasing, the cyst must be shrinking. Keep doing whatever it is you're doing."

I tried hard to make sure I wasn't conjuring up any mental images, but twice more the Holy Spirit showed me this same picture. Each time the cyst was smaller. The last of them, which was the third time overall, was about a month into the process. In the picture the cyst was about the size of a quarter and as I prayed it vanished in my hand. I knew the Lord was letting me know the work was finished. Even though Ceci said there was still a very small amount of discomfort, I could not bring myself to pray about it any further. I knew it was done.

Three days later she informed me that all the pain and discomfort was gone. The subsequent ultrasound confirmed what we already knew in our hearts—no more cyst!

You know what happened, don't you? *PAGA!*

- A "taking hold of together with against" happened.
- A "Bethel" happened.
- A "lighting on" happened.
- A "laying on" and "bearing away" happened.
- A "meeting" happened.
- An "enforcing" happened.
- A "representation" happened.

Intercession happened! And it can happen through you!

The butterfly anointing combined with the bear anointing and a serpent was defeated again. (Please don't give this book to any super-religious people or any of the ministries called to fix all of us "crazimatics." They'd put my bear into hibernation and transform my butterfly into a worm again.)

The most important point I want to communicate to you through this book is that God wants to use YOU. You don't have to be a pastor or prophet. You don't have to be Brother or Sister Well Known. You don't have to know Greek from Swahili. You simply have to be a believer in Jesus—one of His chosen representatives—one called and authorized to administer the blessings of the new covenant—a Christian.

God the Father wants to release the *work* of Jesus through your *prayers*. The Holy Spirit wants to help you. Bethels are waiting to be discovered. Histories are waiting to be written, destinies shaped.

Don't be intimidated by your ignorance, "not knowing what is necessary, right or proper." Don't allow your weaknesses to paralyze you into inactivity. Rise up! Better still, allow your Helper to rise up in you! Together, you can shake any bridge!

Just make sure you know who the mouse is.

Questions for Reflection

1. Can you explain the connection between Genesis 28:10-17 and Romans 8:26-27? Be sure to include comments on *paga*, the butterfly anointing and praying in the Spirit.

2. What does the Holy Spirit do to "help" us in our weaknesses?

3. Think of situations where you don't know how to pray as you should. Make a decision to allow the

Holy Spirit to help you. Decide when you're going to give Him the opportunity to do so.

4. If you had it to do over again, would you still choose Jesus? (What a dumb question!)

8

SUPERNATURAL CHILDBIRTH

———⟡———

(Warning: This chapter could drastically alter the population of the kingdom of darkness and increase the need for new-convert classes.)

The Coach

I coached my wife, Ceci, through 65 hours of labor during the births of our two daughters, Sarah and Hannah. Told her exactly what to do and when—for about the first 10 minutes. She then assumed the roles of coach, player, umpire, referee and any other position that presented itself. Being the intelligent man I am and loving life as I do, it didn't take me long to discern that the only way to survive this "bonding" effort was compliance—quick and without questions.

It was an education. I had no idea she was such a capable instructor. We have it all on video, which can be ordered through Dutch Sheets Ministries, P.O. Box . . . just kidding!

I learned all about how to do what I did in those first 10 minutes from several weeks of classes on "natural childbirth." After the first 10 minutes, I didn't need the training. Everything came quite naturally.

This chapter is about "*super*natural childbirth." My success rate was poor in praying for the lost, as was everyone else's I knew. So I thought I'd see what the Bible had to say about it: not much! At least not directly. Nowhere does it say to ask God to save someone. This puzzled me. How could something so important have so little said about it? It seemed that general principles of prayer would have to be applied to intercession for the lost.

I did find one verse that said, "Ask of me, and I shall give thee the heathen for thine inheritance" (Ps. 2:8, *KJV*). But I knew this was a prophetic Old Testament verse referring to the Father telling Jesus to ask. I figured Christ had already done this and the Father had probably said yes.

I found that we were to ask for laborers to be sent into the harvest (see Matt. 9:38). But that wasn't asking God to save anyone; it was asking for workers. I also discovered some things concerning spiritual warfare, which we will look at in a later chapter, and I found a few Scriptures concerning travail.

Travail, What Is It?

Travail, what was it, anyway? What did it do? I knew what I thought it was, but I wasn't satisfied. *Is it a valid form of prayer?* I wondered. *Is there really a prayer that births?*

Yes, I now believe, although it is not easy to define and explain. And it is controversial. How can a mere human have a part in birthing spiritual life? What do groaning, weeping and hard work have to do with it?

One segment of the Body of Christ probably believes they already have an adequate understanding of what it is. Another has likely heard enough to think they don't want to know any more about it. And there's probably a group who have heard nothing about it. I appeal to all three: Read on with an open mind.

This chapter becomes quite theological and perhaps requires deeper thinking than others. But please realize that the word "theology," contrary to popular belief, is not a swearword, nor does it mean "boring." It actually means "the science or study of God."[1] And I'm sure I've read somewhere in the Bible, "*Study* to show yourself approved unto God." So don't be hesitant to do some. "He who studieth this chapter, yea verily, shall be truly awesome" (Additions 1:1).

This prayer called travail always puzzled me. I was raised in a stream of the Body of Christ that believed in it, although it didn't occur often. The few times I did see what I was informed was travailing intercession, it involved a little old lady who was also one of the few prayer warriors in the church. It seemed to me that it was treated as a sort of mystical thing no one really understood (such as where babies came from), very few ever did (and those only rarely), but everyone revered.

It Happened to Me

It actually happened to me once, although I didn't make the kind of noise I'd heard others make. (Those I had heard sounded a lot like my wife when she was in labor.) I was probably 9 or 10 years old and it occurred while praying for an unsaved aunt.

One night as I lay in bed, I felt a strong burden to pray for her salvation. I remember getting out of my bed, onto my knees and weeping uncontrollably, asking God to save her. I was so young and it was so long ago that I can't remember how long it lasted—probably 30 minutes to an hour. Finally, the burden lifted and I went to sleep.

My aunt lived about an hour and a half away from us. For some "unknown" reason, however, she called us later that week and said she wanted to come to our church that Sunday morning. We did not know at the time that she was actually coming to the service planning to give her life to Christ, and did. I was amazed. I had travailed for her, and that very same week she drove the long distance to give her heart to the Lord.

Travail was wonderful but I didn't understand it. And I only did it once. I couldn't help wondering why something that helped people get saved happened so infrequently. But the truth was, this sort of intense and anguishing prayer just didn't seem to "come upon" anyone very often. Because that defined travail to us, we just had to wait and be patient—like the troubling of the pool of Bethesda in John 5.

I didn't question the concept—I knew that would be irreverent. *God forbid that anyone would have questions about something so spiritual!* The things we couldn't explain, we treated as too holy to question. We were supposed to act as if the questions weren't there—admitting them might be too disrespectful. So we didn't let God or anyone else know we had them. (I still think I can fool God once in a while!)

The Thomas Anointing

Then one day I discovered that the disciples asked Jesus a lot of questions when they didn't understand things. Sometimes the questions even seemed a little irreverent, implying that His teaching skills weren't all that great. They would ask about His parables and question some of His difficult sayings. Oh, they couched their words in nice language, calling Him "Master" and such, but you know as well as I that they were really saying, "What in the world are you talking about?"

Once when He told them to eat His flesh and drink His blood, a group of them told Him it was "a hard saying." We know what they really meant: "This is weird stuff." That bunch finally left Him.

On another occasion Christ was waxing eloquent about the disciples not being troubled because there were lots of houses where His Father lived. He was going to go there, build a few more for them, then come back and take them there. And of course, they knew the way to this place . . . (see John 14:1-4). About this time Thomas—thank God for Thomas—said what all of them were thinking: "Time out, Jesus. We don't have the foggiest idea what You're talking about. We don't even know *where* You're going, let alone *how to get there.*" I'm sure Christ's answer really helped, "I'm the way, You go through Me." I don't think the disciples understood a lot of what Jesus said until later.

As the Twelve usually did, I still most often do the safe, reverent and spiritual thing: I act like I understand, even when I don't. It keeps me ignorant but I look good, which is what really matters! Once in a while, however, the Thomas anointing comes and I just go ahead and tell God He has done a poor job of explaining something . . . such as travail.

As I thought about this subject of travail, I decided to allow some of the nagging questions I had buried to go ahead and surface: *If travailing intercession really helps get people saved, then why is it so hard to do and why does it happen so seldom and why do only a few do it and why does it have to be so loud and strange and why didn't You say more about what it is and how to do it?*

That's lousy English, but it's a great question!

Spiritual Experiences Versus Physical Façades

I would like to suggest two things at this point. First, I believe biblical travail is an important, if not essential, part of intercession for the lost. Second, I don't believe it is defined by groaning, wailing, weeping and hard work. Natural travail certainly is, and spiritual travail *can* include these things. I do not believe, however, that it *must* include them, and I'm convinced it is not defined by them. In fact, I believe a person can travail while doing the dishes, mowing the lawn, driving a car—anything a person can do and still pray.

We in the Church have done with this subject what we do with many. By our very natures we have a need to see or feel something in order to believe in it. Thus, *we tend even to judge what is happening in the spirit by what we see naturally.*

For example, if we pray with someone for salvation or repentance, we tend to believe the person who weeps is probably receiving more than the one who doesn't. We even say things such as, "The Holy Spirit really touched him or her." This is because we see his or her reaction.

In actuality, however, I have observed some who did not cry or show any emotion while praying who were totally transformed. On the other hand, I have witnessed some who sobbed and wept in seeming repentance, much like Judas (see Matt. 27:3-5), but experienced no change whatsoever. Again, the point is, *you cannot judge what is happening in the realm of the spirit by what takes place in the natural realm.*

We in charismatic and Pentecostal circles have a phenomenon we call being "slain in the Spirit." Although this is not a biblical term and the practice is certainly abused, I believe people can and do fall under the power of God. We have, however, done a similar thing with this experience. During a meeting where this particular phenomenon is happening, we tend to believe those who fall down are receiving more from the Lord than those who do not. At times we even judge whether anything at all is happening by whether or not people fall down.

I have been in meetings where I have observed this happening to the degree that I am certain the emphasis and goal became getting people to fall down, rather than a faith that allowed the Holy Spirit to do whatever He wanted, however He wanted. In other words, *we began to judge what was happening in the spirit realm by what we saw naturally.* This is dangerous. It leads to extremes, imbalanced teaching, wrong expectations and striving after the flesh.

In any spiritual release of power and anointing, the possibility of a physical manifestation always exists—that is biblical. People may weep. People may at times fall down under the power of God. People may laugh, perhaps hilariously. They may even appear drunk. Sometimes when God moves there is a physical manifestation; oftentimes there is not. But *we can never ever judge what is happening in the spirit by what we see in the natural.*

Travail, a Spiritual Happening

This is also true with travail. When choosing the term, the Holy Spirit uses a *physical* phenomenon—childbirth—to describe a *spiritual* happening or truth. In doing so, His emphasis is not on the physical realm but the spiritual. And the comparison is not meant to be literal or exact. In other words, the Holy Spirit is not trying to describe what is happening *physically* but rather *spiritually* when He uses the word "travail." It isn't a natural birth, but a spiritual one.

The emphasis is meant to be on the *spiritual* power released to give birth *spiritually*, not the *physical* phenomenon that might accompany it (groanings, weepings, crying out, etc.). Most of us who have been associated with travailing prayer have made what happens physically the focal point, thereby missing the spiritual point that something is being born of the Spirit.

It's easy to find out if you have made this mistake. Ask yourself the question and answer it honestly: When you hear the word "travail" in the context of prayer, do you think first of *what* is taking place in the spirit (a birthing), or *how* it is happening outwardly (in the body)? Most of you probably answered with the latter—how. The rest of you—well, I'm suspicious. You most likely relied on the theology of the little boy in Sunday School who was asked what a lie was. "It is an abomination unto God," he replied, "and a very present help in time of trouble."

Most of us have unconsciously defined a work of the Spirit by a work of the body. It would probably be wise to use different verbiage, perhaps "birthing through prayer," rather than the word "travail" to aid in changing this. This phrase would be acceptable biblically because, as we will see later, the Hebrew words for "travail" actually mean "give birth" or "bring forth." The translators, not necessarily the Holy Spirit, decided when to use the term "travail."

In defining travail outwardly we have not only missed the real issue, but we have also unconsciously accepted what I believe is a lie of Satan: Only a few people can really travail, and then only rarely. I do not believe this is true. In fact, I believe all of us can involve ourselves in travailing (birthing) intercession, and do so regularly. The key is to realize that the emphasis is on birthing something spiritually, not on what happens to us as we do it. (Please remember, I have said travailing intercession can include strong physical manifestations, but it doesn't have to and isn't defined by them.)

The Birthing Prayer

For the sake of changing our mindset, from this point on in the chapter, I will use the words "birthing prayer" interchangeably with "travail" in referring to this type of intercession.

Having said all that, let me say plainly and emphatically: There is an aspect of prayer that births things in the Spirit. We are "birthers" for God. The Holy Spirit wants to "bring forth" through us. Jesus said in John 7:38, "From his *innermost being* shall flow rivers of living water" (emphasis added). "Innermost being" is the word *koilia*, which means "womb."[2] We are the womb of God upon the earth. We are not the source of life, but we are carriers of the source of life. We do not generate life, but we release, through prayer, Him who does.

David and Polly Simchen, members of our church in Colorado Springs, recently received the answer to more than four years of prayer for the salvation of their son, Jonathan. Polly, and a few of her friends, demonstrated throughout this course of time one of the most tenacious and thorough examples of intercession I have ever witnessed, including this concept of birthing. The following are some excerpts from Polly's testimony. They are somewhat lengthy but filled with pertinent illustrations of things I intend to discuss in this and other chapters (emphasis added):

> We gave Jonathan to God before he was ever born and raised him in church, but at 17 years of age, through a combination of several well-laid plans of the enemy, he began to wander away from God. It wasn't long before he was living a life of total rebellion, characterized by drugs and all the things that accompany such a lifestyle. Through these things, his diabetes became a greater problem, and at times he would end up in the hospital, only to get out and go back to running and doing drugs.
>
> About that time Pastor Dutch began teaching the church about intercession. Though initially devastated and at times frozen with fear, we began to learn more and more. As my friends and I would intercede together, God gave instructions of how to pray, along with many uplifting promises and words of encouragement.
>
> We would *paga*, asking the Holy Spirit to *hover*—around his bed as he slept, in his car, wherever he was—and *birth life* into him. I did this daily.
>
> Many times, for seasons almost daily, we anointed his room, his doors and windows, his bed, his car, his clothing and anything else he came in contact with. Many times I would go into his room and sing in the Spirit for

an hour or more. I sang things like, "The name of Jesus is exalted in this place—over this bed, over these things, these clothes, everything!" I sang, "Jonathan has a destiny I know he will fulfill." My friends Shirley and Patty and I would sometimes pray four to six hours late at night.

On one occasion Pastor Dutch taught about prayer cloths. Immediately I thought, *We can do that for Jonathan!* Pastor Dutch, David and I together laid hands on a prayer cloth, releasing God's power and anointing into it, agreeing that the anointing would break the yoke of drugs, sin, ungodly friends, perversion and anything else that needed breaking. We cut the cloth into about 12 pieces and put them under his sheets, inside his pillow, hidden in the flaps of his wallet, sewed into the cuff of his pants, under his pocket, inside holes in his walls and inside the tag on the tongue of his shoes. With each one we would *declare*, "The anointing breaks the yoke."

At times it seemed things would get worse; it was like Jonathan was on a mission to destroy his life. But we stood fast in loving him, speaking God's plan over his life, anointing and singing over his room and car, interceding daily and declaring Scripture after Scripture. We also declared and called forth every word and promise God had ever given to us about Jonathan. The more we declared the Scriptures, the more our faith grew. Every few months we would take a new prayer cloth to Pastor Dutch and repeat the process.

We also involved ourselves in *spiritual warfare* for Jonathan. We cursed the power of drugs and asked God to remove every ungodly influence in his life—although we always prayed for the salvation of his friends, three of whom have also come to Christ. God took our fears and converted them into fighting!

In January of this year, 1996, we received a word from a friend, saying God was about to *"tip the bowl"* of our prayers. Pastor Dutch had taught us about that, and we could hardly wait.

In February 1996, after more than four years, we could see God was dealing with Jonathan. He wanted his life to be straight. He started to read his Bible and became concerned about the salvation of his girlfriend. He began to hate the power drugs had over his friends. Then one night at one of our prayer meetings, he prayed a prayer of re-commitment to Christ. We watched in amazement as the things of the world began to fall away from Jonathan and the things of the kingdom of God became clear and appealing. Just last week (May 1996), his girlfriend also gave her life to Christ. Does God answer prayer? You bet He does!

Throughout four years of intercession, the Lord taught us much about prayer and gave us great encouragement along the way—a pastor who cared and taught us, friends who cared and prayed, prophetic words concerning Jonathan's call and God's hand on him. He even allowed my husband, David, to see the angel that would ride in Jonathan's car everywhere he went, even twice when he spent the night in jail. All fear left and we were able to fully trust God.

Thank you, Pastor Dutch, and Ceci too, for everything you have done. We are so thankful to God for the miracle that has taken place in our precious son. No one could ever convince us prayer doesn't work! God is faithful and we are forever grateful!

As stated earlier, I will examine more fully many of the ways in which Polly prayed, which I italicized, throughout the remainder of this book. At this point, however, let's examine this amazing facet of prayer—travail. May the Holy Spirit give us ears to hear.

Can we de-mystify this subject of travail? I believe we can. The following passages either directly mention travailing (birthing) prayer or the context and wording implies it:

1 Kings 18:41-45: "Now Elijah said to Ahab, 'Go up, eat and drink; for there is the sound of the roar of a heavy shower.' So Ahab went up to eat and drink. But Elijah went up to the top of Carmel; and he crouched down on the earth, and put his face between his knees. And he said to his servant, 'Go up now, look toward the sea.' So he went up and looked and said, 'There is nothing.' And he said, 'Go back' seven times. And it came about at the seventh time, that he said, 'Behold, a cloud as small as a man's hand is coming up from the sea.' And he said, 'Go up, say to Ahab, "Prepare your chariot and go down, so that the heavy shower does not stop you." So it came about in a little while, that the sky grew black with clouds and wind, and there was a heavy shower. And Ahab rode and went to Jezreel.'" (The posture of Elijah in this passage is that of a woman in his day while giving birth. We are meant to see that Elijah was actually in travailing [birthing] prayer. James 5:16 also refers to this event and calls it "fervent" prayer.)

Psalm 126:5-6: "Those who sow in tears shall reap with joyful shouting. He who goes to and fro weeping, carrying his bag of seed, shall indeed come again with a shout of joy, bringing his sheaves with him."

Isaiah 66:7-8: "Before she travailed, she brought forth; before her pain came, she gave birth to a boy. Who has heard such a thing? Who has seen such things? Can a land be born in one day? Can a nation be brought forth all at once? As soon as Zion travailed, she also brought forth her sons."

John 11:33,35,38,41-43: "When Jesus therefore saw her weeping, and the Jews who came with her, also weeping, He was deeply moved in spirit, and was troubled. . . . Jesus wept. . . . Jesus therefore again being deeply moved within, came to the tomb. Now it was a cave, and a stone was lying against it. . . . And so they removed the stone. And Jesus raised His eyes, and said, 'Father, I thank Thee that Thou heardest Me. And I knew that Thou hearest Me always; but because of the people standing around I said it, that they may believe that Thou didst send Me.' And when He had said these things, He cried out with a loud voice, 'Lazarus, come forth.'"

Matthew 26:36-39: "Then Jesus came with them to a place called Gethsemane, and said to His disciples, 'Sit here while I go over there and pray.' And He took with Him Peter and the two sons of Zebedee, and began to be grieved and distressed. Then He said to them, 'My soul is deeply grieved, to the point of death; remain here and keep watch with Me.' And He went a little beyond them, and fell on His face and prayed, saying, 'My Father, if it is possible, let this cup pass from Me; yet not as I will, but as Thou wilt.'"

Romans 8:26-27: "And in the same way the Spirit also helps our weakness; for we do not know how to pray as we should, but the Spirit Himself intercedes for us with groanings too deep for words; and He who searches the hearts knows what the mind of the Spirit is, because He intercedes for the saints according to the will of God." (The context of this passage is travail—see Romans 8:22-25. The Lord speaks of all creation and us groaning and travailing, then speaks of the Holy Spirit doing it in us.)

Galatians 4:19: "My little children, of whom I travail in birth again until Christ be formed in you" (*KJV*).

Although these passages do not fully explain *what* it is or *how* it is done, some things are clear:

- The Holy Spirit is involved.
- It is associated with spiritual reproduction.
- It aids in the maturing process of believers.
- It can be very intense, involving fervency, tears and even groaning.
- Assuming Christ was in travail at Lazarus's tomb and Elijah was in birthing prayer on the mountain, it is involved in producing physical miracles, not just the new birth.

The Holy Spirit, God's Birthing Agent

It will help to keep us from error and alleviate some of your concerns if I state clearly up front, we don't birth anything spiritually; the Holy Spirit does. He is the birthing agent of the Godhead (see Luke 1:34-35; John 3:3-8). He is the power source of the Godhead (see Acts 1:8; 10:38; Luke 4:14,18). He is the power behind Creation, which, as we will see, is likened to a birthing (see Gen. 1). He is the one who supplies power to God's will, giving it life and substance. He gives birth to the will of God. He is the one who breathes God's life into people, bringing physical and spiritual life (see Gen. 2:7; Ezek. 37:9-10,14; Acts 2:1-4). Concerning salvation, we call this the new birth or the new creation.

Therefore, anything we might accomplish in intercession that results in a birthing would have to be something that causes or releases the Holy Spirit to do it.

For example, Elijah as a human being couldn't birth or produce rain. Yet, James tells us his prayers did. Paul couldn't create the new birth or maturity in the Galatians, yet Galatians 4:19 implies that his intercession did. We cannot produce spiritual sons and daughters through our human abilities, yet Isaiah 66:7-8 tells us that our travail can. If we cannot create or birth these and other things through our own power or ability, then it seems fairly obvious that our prayers must in some way cause or release the Holy Spirit to do so.

Understanding, then, that it is the Holy Spirit's power actually doing the work, I want to say unequivocally that *there is a prayer that births.*

If this is indeed so, we should be able to find some references that use the same words to describe what the Holy Spirit does in birthing or bringing forth life as are used to describe what our prayers accomplish. Can we? Yes! And the contexts make very clear what the Holy Spirit actually does to release this life-giving power.

Genesis 1:1-2 says, "In the beginning . . . the earth was without form, and void" (*KJV*). The words "without form" are the Hebrew word *tohuw*, which means "a desolation; to lie waste; a desert; a worthless thing";[3] "confusion";[4] "empty (barren); a formless, lifeless mass."[5] The basic concept is lifelessness or sterility; no order, no life. Verse two goes on to tell us "the Spirit of God moved upon the face of the waters." What does it mean when it says the Holy Spirit moved?

We use the term today in Christian circles when we speak of the Holy Spirit moving in a service. We say things such as, "The Lord really moved today," or "The Holy Spirit was moving mightily." But what do these and similar statements mean? We have an ethereal concept of what it means to us: We are implying that He was doing something; He was active. But what was He doing? Was He moving from one place to another? Was He moving upon the hearts of people? What does the word "move" mean in these contexts?

Actually, this usage of the word finds its roots here in Genesis. The Hebrew word used for "moving," *rachaph*, literally means "to brood over."[6] The *Amplified* translation actually uses the words "was moving, hovering, brooding over." The margin of the *New American Standard* also uses the word "hovering." So, *rachaph* is a hovering or brooding over something.

Webster's Dictionary defines "brood" as "offspring; progeny; that which is bred or produced."[7] A hen's brood, for example, is her chicks that she has produced. It comes from the root word "breed," which we know means giving birth to something.

In using this term to describe Creation, the Holy Spirit is using the analogy of "birthing" something. He was "bringing forth" life. A Hebrew scholar informed me that *rachaph* is, indeed, a reproductive term in the Hebrew language that can be used to describe a husband hovering over his bride. Pretty graphic, but it confirms that *rachaph* is literally a reproductive term. One lexicon defined it as "brooding and fertilizing."[8]

We know from the New Testament that Jesus was calling forth life in this Genesis setting. We are told that all things were created by His Word (see John 1:1-3; Col. 1:16). But it was the Holy Spirit that brooded or hovered over the earth, releasing His creative energies or power at the words of Jesus, giving birth to what Christ spoke.

Psalm 90:2 confirms this, actually calling what the Holy Spirit did at Creation a birthing. The verse uses two important Hebrew words, *yalad* [9] and *chuwl*. [10] It reads, "Before the mountains were born [*yalad*], or Thou didst give birth to [*chuwl*] the earth and the world, even from everlasting to everlasting, Thou art God."

Although the words are not translated as such in this verse, they are the primary Hebrew words for travail. Each one is translated variously in the Old Testament: "bring forth," "born," "give birth to," "travail," and others (see Deut. 32:18; Job 15:7; 39:1 for examples). Regardless of how they are translated, the concept is that of giving birth to something. It is not always referring to a literal, physical birth, but is often used in creating. We do the same thing in our vocabulary. We might say an idea, vision or nation was "born" or "conceived." We're obviously not speaking of a physical birth, but of something new coming into being. In much the same way, Psalm 90:2 likens the Genesis Creation to a birthing.

Hovering Over and Bringing Forth

Now, let's make the prayer connection. These are the very same words used in Isaiah 66:8: "As soon as Zion *travailed* [*chuwl*] she also *brought forth* [*yalad*] her sons." This is extremely important! *What the Holy Spirit was doing in Genesis when He "brought forth" or "gave birth to" the earth and the world is exactly what He wants to do through our prayers in bringing forth sons and daughters.* He wants to go forth and hover around individuals, releasing His awesome power to convict, break bondages, bring revelation and draw them to Himself in order to cause the new birth or new creation in them. Yes, *the Holy Spirit wants to birth through us.*

Marlena O'Hern, of Maple Valley, Washington, tells of doing this for her brother. We'll share more details about this in chapter 10, but Marlena had been praying for her brother, Kevin, for

about 12 years. Not realizing how to pray scripturally and specifically, she often grew frustrated and made the mistake of trying
to pressure him into doing what was right, which would only
make things worse.

Early in 1995 she heard me teach about intercession for the
lost. She, her husband, Patrick, and their children all began to
pray for Kevin. One of the things they prayed was that the Holy
Spirit would hover over him. In about two weeks, Kevin was
born again and is serving the Lord today.

The second example of the Holy Spirit hovering and bringing forth life out of lifelessness is in Deuteronomy 32:10-18. All
four of the previously mentioned Hebrew words are used in
this passage: *tohuw, rachaph, yalad* and *chuwl*. In this passage
Moses is recounting to the Israelites their history and speaks of
Israel as an individual, obviously referring back to Abraham,
the father of the nation. In verse 10, Moses says God found him
in a *tohuw* situation—in other words, lifeless or barren.

Abraham was in the same barren condition the earth was in
prior to the Creation. Neither he nor Sarah had the ability at
this point to produce life. They were sterile, lifeless. We are then
told in verse 11 that like an eagle hovers (*rachaphs*) over its
young, the Lord hovered over them. The Holy Spirit brooded
over Abraham and Sarah, releasing His life and power, giving
them the ability to conceive!

We read in Hebrews 11:11 that by faith Sarah received
dunamis (the miraculous power of the Holy Spirit)[11] to conceive.
As He hovered, God was actually birthing a nation in them. The
renewing the Holy Spirit did to their bodies as He hovered was
so real that it was after this point that a king wanted Sarah as
his own wife because she was so beautiful. Also, Abraham
received a lasting change and had other children after this.

Later in the passage (Deuteronomy 32:18) *yalad* and *chuwl*,
the primary Hebrew words for "travail" or "giving birth," are

used: "You neglected the Rock who *begot* you and forgot the God who *gave you birth*" (emphasis added). The identical words are chosen in this passage to describe the Holy Spirit's hovering over Abraham and Sarah to bring forth life as were used in the Genesis Creation and in Isaiah 66:8. *The hovering that brought forth natural Israel will also bring forth spiritual Israel.*

Our third example of the Holy Spirit's bringing forth life as He hovered or brooded over is found in Luke 1:35, the conception of Christ in Mary. The angel of the Lord came to Mary telling her that she would bear a child. She responded by asking, "How can this be, since I am a virgin?" (v. 34).

The answer was, "The Holy Spirit will come upon you, and the power of the Most High will overshadow you." "Overshadow" is the Greek word *episkiazo*, which means "to cast a shade upon; to envelope in a haze of brilliancy; to invest with supernatural influence."[12] It is in some ways a counterpart for the Hebrew word *rachaph*. Thayer says it is used "of the Holy Spirit exerting creative energy upon the womb of the Virgin Mary and impregnating it."[13]

The word is only used three times in the New Testament. At the transfiguration of Jesus in Matthew 17:5, the passage says the cloud of the Lord "overshadowed" them. It is also used in Acts 5:15 when people were trying to get close to Peter—in his shadow—that they might be healed. Have you ever wondered how Peter's shadow could heal anyone? It didn't. What was actually happening was that the Holy Spirit was "moving" out from Peter—hovering—and when individuals stepped into the cloud or overshadowing, they were healed.

Perhaps you have seen this phenomenon. I have. I've been in services where God was moving in such a strong way that before people were ever prayed for or touched by anyone, they were saved, healed or delivered. They came under the *episkiazo* or hovering of the Holy Spirit.

Maybe you've been in a meeting where the Spirit of the Lord began to hover over the whole room and move in a particular way. At times God has even done this over entire communities. In many of the classic revivals of the past, stories are told of an individual driving close to a church where God has been moving in mighty ways and the person begins to weep, goes to the church, walks inside and says, "Something drew me here and I want to get saved."

What happened? The moving or hovering of the Holy Spirit became so great that He brooded over an entire geographical area to bring forth life. I believe this will even happen over nations as more and more prayer is generated for the unreached people of the earth. There has never been a time in history with the amount of prayer that is currently being offered for the lost. The Spirit of the Lord is being released through this intercession to hover over not only cities, but entire nations. We will see dramatic revivals as this hovering continues and intensifies through the prayers of the saints.

Can a Land Be Born in One Day?

I was preaching in Ohio in 1990, shortly after the fall of the Berlin Wall and some of the Communist nations in Europe. This was the season, you will recall, when governments were falling like dominoes and events were happening weekly that would normally have taken decades to occur. It was indeed extraordinary.

As I preached under a very strong anointing, the Holy Spirit came upon me and I began to prophesy. In the course of my message, I said, "Just as you have seen nations fall politically in a day, so you will see nations fall before Me spiritually and be born again in a day." Even as I said this, I found myself wondering if it could really happen. After the service I went to the Lord in prayer, saying, "Father, I do not want to speak in Your name when it is not You. Nor do I want to hype Your people with sensational statements. I need to know if that was You speaking through me."

The Lord's answer to me was surprising. He gave me the reference Isaiah 66:7-8 in which I knew verse 8 said, "As soon as Zion travailed she also brought forth her sons." What I did not realize until looking up the reference was that the preceding verse is a question: "Can a land be born in one day? Can a nation be brought forth all at once?" "As soon as Zion travailed she also brought forth her sons" is actually an answer to this question.

I knew the Lord was assuring me that He was, indeed, declaring through me that nations would be born again in a day. There would come such a move of the Spirit, such a hovering and brooding, such a power released by the Spirit of God over areas that entire nations would come to Christ overnight. I don't know if overnight is literal or figurative, but I'll accept either, won't you?

The passage in verse 8 informs us that this will be through the travail of Zion. If Zion includes the Church, which it certainly does (see Ps. 87; Heb. 12:12; 1 Pet. 2:4-10), and those being born are sons and daughters of Zion, this is a promise that not only pertains to Israel, but also to us, the Body of Christ. *We can birth sons and daughters through travail.*

A Sense of Birthing

Carol Millspaugh, also of our fellowship in Colorado Springs, tells of an experience she had in Germany several years ago. At the time, she worked in counseling, first as a psychotherapist, then in full-time ministry as a Christian counselor. Carol would spend time interceding for her clients' situations and for their salvation.

One particular couple she counseled had many problems: addictions, eating disorders, family problems, and others. Neither were believers; in fact the wife was an atheist. Carol said she felt as though she were pregnant with them, that she was carrying them in her spirit. She would intercede for them daily, often moaning and crying for hours. This went on for several months.

During her times of intercession, the Lord would reveal things about them to Carol and she would share this information with them on an individual basis. Carol wasn't aware of it initially, but the Lord was preparing them for salvation.

Then one day the Spirit powerfully hovered over them during their session, enabling them to be able to hear and understand as Carol shared Scriptures with them. The next time she met with them, both of them received the Lord together. Carol said a strong sense of a birthing was happening. Then began the time of growing and maturing as Carol nurtured them and helped them find solid biblical teaching and Christian relationships.

Based on these examples from the Scriptures—Creation, the birth of Israel and Christ's conception—I would like to offer the following as a definition of spiritual travail: "Releasing the creative power or energy of the Holy Spirit into a situation to produce, create or give birth to something." Travailing intercession would simply be prayer that causes this. At the risk of redundancy, I want to restate this phrase, using it to offer a formal definition of travailing intercession: *"A form of intercession that releases the creative power or energy of the Holy Spirit into a situation to produce, create or give birth to something."*

I use the words "produce" and "create" because travail is spoken of in the Scriptures not only in the context of someone being born again, but also of bringing forth other things. For example, when the Holy Spirit was hovering through Peter, He was bringing forth healing (see Acts 5:15). Through Elijah it was rain (see 1 Kings 18:45); through Paul it included maturity (see Gal. 4:19).

Christ's Travail

Let's look at the two previously mentioned examples from Christ's ministry where He was involved in travail or birthing prayer. The first is John 11:33-44, the resurrection of Lazarus. Just before going to the tomb, verse 33 says Jesus "was deeply moved in spirit, and was troubled." A more literal translation of this phrase is that Jesus "was moved with indignation in His spirit and deeply troubled Himself."[14]

The word "troubled" is *tarasso*. It means "to stir up or agitate," like an agitator in a washing machine. Jesus was stirring up the anointing within Himself. Verse 38 literally says He again was moved with indignation.

According to these verses, the tears Christ shed were not merely tears of sympathy, but of indignation and the stirrings of His spirit. We also know they were taking place in the context of prayer because verse 41 informs us that before raising Lazarus from the dead, Jesus said to the Father, "I thank Thee that Thou heardest Me." He then gave the command, "Lazarus, come forth."

Although it cannot be conclusively proven, I believe Christ was in strong travail, releasing the life-giving power of the Holy Spirit before He ever gave the command, "Lazarus, come forth." As I stated earlier, I do not believe it is *necessary* to weep and groan, etc., in order to release the birthing power of the Holy Spirit (travail). It *can* and *will* happen at times, however, when we move into deep intercession, as it did in this circumstance with Jesus.

This is what took place when I interceded for my aunt. I was involved in a form of travail. Although not groaning, I was weeping heavily. It was obviously not the emotion that caused her salvation, but my response to the prompting of the Holy

Spirit, allowing Him to move through me. This released Him to go hover around my aunt, enveloping her with His power and life, convicting her of sin and possibly breaking some strongholds.

It doesn't always happen quickly. Occasions do occur when we move into a time of intercession and almost immediately see the results, as was the case with my aunt. However, as with Polly and her son, a season of prayer is usually necessary when, on a regular basis, we allow the Spirit of God to intercede through us. This releases Him to go hover around an individual with His life-giving power, doing what is necessary to cause the person to be born again.

Another occasion when Jesus was involved in travail was in the Garden of Gethsemane. Without any question, Christ's redemption of humanity—the work of intercession—began with His travail in the Garden. Isaiah prophesied of Him, "He shall see of the *travail* of His soul and shall be satisfied" (Isa. 53:11, *KJV*, emphasis added).

In fulfillment of this, Jesus cried out in Gethsemane, saying, "My soul is exceeding sorrowful, even unto death" (Matt. 26:38, *KJV*). It was in the Garden of Gethsemane that redemption began and the victory of the entire ordeal was won.

We know that redemption was beginning in this travail for a couple of reasons. Luke tells us Jesus began to shed great drops of blood. Jesus was not simply sweating so profusely that it was like a person bleeding. He was literally bleeding through the pores of His skin, a medical condition known as hematidrosis. We must understand that when the blood of Christ began to flow, redemption was beginning, for it is through the shedding of His blood that we have the cleansing from sin (see Heb. 9:22).

We also know that redemption was beginning in the Garden because when Jesus said, "My soul is exceeding sorrowful, even unto death," the word used for "death" is *thanatos*. This word is often used for death as the result and penalty of sin.[15] This is the death Adam experienced when he fell.

Two other words could have been used that mean simply physical death. When *thanatos* is used, however, it frequently implies death as a result of sin. For Christ to use this word quite possibly meant that the sin of the world was already being laid upon Him.

Through these two occurrences, we see that the redemption that ended at the cross most likely began in the Garden travail. I believe the term "travail" was used, not so much because He was working hard, but because He was bringing forth the new birth. It also seems logical that because our intercession releases the fruit of this birthing, it too is called travail.

Bringing Forth the Fruit of Calvary

In summary, the Holy Spirit desperately wants to release His creative, birthing powers through us, bringing forth the fruit of Calvary. He wants to use us in *tohuw* (lifeless, fruitless, desolate, barren) situations, releasing His life into them:

- As He did at Creation. But through our intercession, He wants to bring forth "new creations" in Christ Jesus.

- As with Israel when He hovered over the barren bodies of Abraham and Sarah, bringing forth a nation, He wants to bring forth "spiritual Israel" from us.

- As with Mary when He hovered, bringing forth or conceiving the Christ in her, He desires to bring forth Christ in people through our intercession.

- As happened with Lazarus's resurrection, through our intercession He wants to bring forth spiritual life from death.

• As in Gethsemane when the fruit of our redemption was pressed from the vine, Christ Jesus, He wants the fruit of that work to be pressed forth again through our intercession.

• As through Peter people were healed, He wants to heal people through our intercession. He wants to hover around them, releasing His life.

Not only does He want to do this for salvation and healing, but travail is also to be done for maturing and developing believers. Paul said in Galatians 4:19, "My little children, of whom I travail in birth again until Christ be formed in you" (*KJV*). He called them his children because he had travailed once until they were born again. Then he said he was in travail "again" until Christ was formed in them. These people were already born again. Paul was obviously referring to their maturing process. This is an aspect of intercession we can involve ourselves in to help believers mature.

Hospitals have intensive care units where the staff is able to keep a close eye on patients who have undergone organ transplants. Even when the operations are successful, it is routine procedure to classify these patients as being in "critical, but stable condition" and keep them in ICU until they gain strength.

Spiritual organ transplants occur as people become Christians and receive new hearts. To grow strong in the Lord, they must receive intensive nurturing. It is exciting to be part of the birthing process—praying them into the kingdom of God. However, it is also necessary to intercede for them through their critical but stable condition stage.[16]

When the Lord first taught me this truth, I was counseling with four or five people who were in very difficult situations. Three of them were extremely suicidal. I was spending hours each day with these people, trying to help them through their situations. There were times when they would call me saying they were going to take their lives right then. I remember one of these people calling at 2:00 A.M., saying, "I have a gun to my head right now and I'm going to blow my brains out." It was a stressful season, to say the least.

It was at that time the Lord revealed to me this concept of our prayers releasing the Holy Spirit to hover around individuals, birthing life in them. He clearly spoke these words to my heart: *If you spent a fraction of the time releasing My Holy Spirit to go and hover around them bringing life as you do talking to them, you would see many times the results.*

I know a good deal when I hear it! I began to spend a couple of hours every day praying for them. Most of my prayer was in the Spirit. I would simply say, "Father, I bring so and so before You now, asking that as I pray the Holy Spirit would be released to go hover around so and so, bringing forth Christ." Then I would usually just begin to pray in the Spirit. I saw immediate results. Maturity came quickly. Almost overnight bondages began to fall off. Victories occurred in their lives. It was remarkable.

What was taking place? The Holy Spirit was being released through my prayers to go hover—*rachaph, episkiazo*—around these individuals, releasing His power and life.

Releasing the Rain of the Spirit

The Bible speaks of travailing for other things as well. In 1 Kings 18, Elijah prayed fervently seven times for rain. We are told in this passage that the posture he maintained while praying was the position of a woman in that day giving birth.

The symbolism is clear. Elijah was in travail. He was birthing something. Without any question, the posture of Elijah is to symbolize this for us. Why else would God give us the position he was in while praying? And please don't miss the implication of this passage. *Even though it was God's will to bring the rain and it was also God's time for the rain, someone on Earth still had to birth it through prayer.*

In this example, travail released literal rain. We could take the story to its fullest symbolic picture and say that our travail releases the rain of the Spirit. I'm sure that would be valid because the physical drought pictured Israel's spiritual dryness, and the rain pictured God's ability to bless again after the purging of the idolatry earlier in the chapter.

Our prayers can and do cause the Holy Spirit to move into situations where He then releases His power to bring life. We do have a part in producing the hovering of the Holy Spirit. The power that created the universe through His *"rachaph-*ing" has been deposited in the Church—while untold millions await their births into the kingdom of God.

Like Elijah, we must take up our position, believing that the prayers of mere men can accomplish much. We must release the power of the Holy Spirit through our intercession to hover, bringing forth the fruit of what Christ has already done. We are an integral part of the Father's birthing process into the kingdom of God.

As I said while coaching my wife, "Come on, Church, *push!*"

Questions for Reflection

1. How have we defined travail improperly and how has this hindered intercession?

2. Explain the connection between Genesis 1:1-2; Deuteronomy 32:10-18; Luke 1:35 and travail.

3. What do we mean when we speak of the "moving" of the Holy Spirit?

4. When and where can one travail? For what can one travail? Can you think of a situation in which God might want to do some birthing through your prayers?

5. Does God answer prayer?

9

PRO WRESTLERS

Brother Wonderful and His Interpreter

"Resist the devil and he will flee from you! How many of you talk to the kingdom of darkness once in a while?" I asked in my most anointed preaching voice.

I was on a roll. Preaching up a storm, as we said back in Ohio where I was raised. I was fresh out of Bible school and feeling like God's latest edition to the Brother Wonderful Fraternity of World Changers International. Had those people right where I wanted them—hanging on every word. If Mom could have seen me then! She and God would probably have found a place for me at the Lord's right hand—next to James and John.

The only problem was that I was in Guatemala preaching through an interpreter.

"So," you might ask, "why should that be a problem?"

Because my interpreter didn't seem to share my theology, and her convictions ran deep. She looked at me indignantly and said in no uncertain terms, "I won't say that!"

Her words kind of interrupted my eloquent flow. "Huh?" I replied.

"I won't say that."

"What do you mean you won't say it? You're supposed to say what I say."

"Well, I won't say it."

"Why not?"

"I don't believe in it."

"Well, the Bible says to do it."

"Where?"

"James 4:7."

Now, keep in mind that we were standing in front of a church full of people who were watching this obviously unpleasant verbal exchange between Brother Wonderful and his interpreter.

They hadn't prepared me for this in Bible school. As I stood wondering what to do next, she began to look for James 4:7 . . . Took her forever to find it. She then read it to the audience, I think. She may have been telling them how stupid I was for all I know.

We tried to continue. She wouldn't allow me to quote any other verses, though. As I would mention one, she would take her time finding it and read it, I think . . . Didn't take me long to figure out she didn't know her Bible very well, however, so I started paraphrasing verses so that she wouldn't recognize them as Scripture. After she had unknowingly said the verse, I would look at her with a smug smile and say, "That was found in . . ." At which time she would bore into me with very unspiritual eyes.

We just never did seem to get that flow back.

Laying Hold of the Victory

Intercession, according to our definition, involves two very different activities. One is a *reconciling*, the other is a *separating*. One is a *tearing away*—a disuniting, the other a *joining to*—a uniting. This is what Christ did through His work of intercession, and it's what we do in our continuation of it. In light of this, it is important to realize that much of our intercession must be a combination of the two.

It is often not enough to simply ask the Father to do something, although this is most Christians' total concept of prayer. Many times it is necessary to accompany asking with a spiritual "warfare" or "wrestling," enforcing the victory of Calvary. As Arthur Mathews said, "Victory is an accomplished fact, but it does need a man to lay hold of that victory and precipitate a confrontation with the enemy, and resist him."[1]

Jack Hayford, in his book *Prayer Is Invading the Impossible*, says:

> To see both sides of Jesus is to see both sides of prayer. It is to see the need for compassion, for care, for concern, for weeping with those that weep, for sympathy, for groaning, for aching deeply because of what you sense transpiring in human lives. And it is to learn the place and time for anger, when we see Satan's wiles successfully destroying; for indignation, when the adversary's program violates territory that is rightfully Christ's; for boldness, when demonic hordes announce their presence; for attack, when the Holy Spirit prompts an advance.[2]

As with my interpreter in Guatemala, many don't believe in spiritual warfare. They believe Jesus took care of the devil and we don't need to concern ourselves with him. Others believe our actions, holy lifestyles, obedience and, I suppose, other things bind the devil, but we don't address him or his demons. Still others believe we can deal with or address evil spirits, but only in people. We cannot, they would say, command or rebuke demons in places or situations.

This book is not meant to offend those who disagree, nor is it to defend my position on this subject. It would take an entire book—perhaps several—to adequately prove the validity and demonstrate the how-tos of spiritual warfare. Several wonderful books are available that thoroughly defend and explain the subject. I have listed several in the bibliography at the end of this book. My intent in this book is to establish the absolute connection between spiritual warfare and intercession, especially for—but not limited to—warfare for the unsaved.

Paga Involves Warfare

To be sure, extremes do exist. I heard someone recently describe a cartoon. It portrayed the devil with 40 to 50 strands of rope around him and several individuals next to him discussing the situation.

"What do we do now?" one asked.

"I say we bind him again!" was the response of another.

Although imbalances occur, nonetheless, it is impossible to separate the word "intercession," *paga*, from warfare. Fifteen times it is used in this context.[3] I tell you emphatically, *violence and war are rooted in the very meaning of the word*. It is translated in various ways when speaking of warfare: "attack," "fall upon," "strike down," "impinge," as well as others (see Judg. 8:21; 1 Sam. 22:11-19; 2 Sam. 1:11-16; the essence is the same in all of them—people in battle attacking one another). Hear me clearly: *Paga* involves warfare!

Again, Jack Hayford says, "But there is a way to face impossibility. *Invade it!* Not with a glib speech of high hopes. Not in anger. Not with resignation. Not through stoical self-control. But with violence. And prayer provides the vehicle for this kind of violence."[4]

When we try to separate warfare from intercession, we do so to our own detriment. Much time and energy is wasted dealing with symptoms, when in many situations the real cause of the problem is spiritual or demonic: "For we wrestle not against flesh and blood, but against principalities, against powers, against the rulers of the darkness of this world, against spiritual wickedness in high places" (Eph. 6:12, *KJV*). We must guard against an overemphasis upon Satan and demons, but we in America err in the other direction. Most people stop in Ephesians 6:12 after the words "we wrestle not."

Ignorance Is Costly

Our ignorance of Satan and his tactics, as well as how to deal with them, is costly for us. Second Corinthians 2:11 tells us, "In order that no advantage be taken of us by Satan; for we are not ignorant of his schemes." The context is forgiveness, but a general principle is also revealed in this verse.

The word "ignorant" is the Greek word *agnoeo*. It means "without knowledge or understanding of."[5] Our English word "agnostic" is derived from it. Technically, an agnostic is not a person who is unsure if he or she believes in God. We now use the word this way; but in actuality, an agnostic is a person who does not know or understand, regardless of the subject. We also get the word "ignore" from the same root. In this verse we're urged not to ignore or be an agnostic—without understanding—where the devil is concerned.

"Schemes" is the word *noema*. It literally means "thought."[6] The verse is essentially saying, "Don't be without understanding of the way Satan thinks." *Noema* came to also mean "plans, schemes, plots, devices" because these things are born in the thoughts of the mind. For greater insight, let's insert all of them into the verse: "Don't be without understanding of the way your enemy thinks and operates—of his plans, plots, schemes and devices." Is there not also a subtle promise here? If God suggests we are not to be ignorant of Satan's schemes, He must be willing to reveal them to us.

What if we are unaware of his schemes? He'll take "advantage" of us. The word is *pleonekteo*, which is a compound word meaning literally "to have or hold the greater portion" (*pleon*— "the greater part"; *echo*—"have or hold").[7] It is easy to see why this is a word for "covet." It also means "overreach."[8]

In boxing, the person who has the longer reach has the "advantage" and usually gets in more blows. The word is also translated "make a gain"; Satan makes a lot of gains on those who are unaware of his ways. Bullinger says it means "to make a prey of, to defraud."[9]

Let's put all these definitions together: "To the degree we are ignorant of the way our adversary thinks and operates—of his plans, plots, schemes and devices—to that degree he will gain on us, prey on us, defraud us of what is ours and have or hold the greater portion."

The greater portion of what? Whatever! Our homes, marriages, families, communities, money, government, nation, and more.

Twenty-five years ago the Church in America was without understanding of what Satan was planning, and he got the greater portion of our schools. The same could be said of our government.

Have you ever been taken advantage of? Have you ever received the smaller portion? In my Bible college days, we had a way of enlightening the superspiritual who thought it necessary to intercede for the world while giving thanks for a meal. They were ignorant of our scheme when we asked them to pray over the food. While they traversed the globe, we enjoyed the greater portion of their meals! It was a real test of their true spirituality. (I am deeply embarrassed by this abominable practice in my past and would never do it today. But for those of you who feel you must intercede over your food, save it for your prayer closet!)

Paul was taken advantage of in 1 Thessalonians 2:18. Satan gained on him (*pleonekteo*) in the ongoing war over spreading the gospel: "For we wanted to come to you—I, Paul, more than once—and yet Satan thwarted us." We know Paul won more battles than he lost. But he was human and at times Satan succeeded in thwarting his plans. Please notice it doesn't say God changed His mind about where Paul was to go. It clearly says that Satan hindered him. Those people who would have us think Satan can do nothing except what God allows, and that we are to ignore him, should reread these two verses. God doesn't ignore the devil and neither should we. And he certainly does a lot of things God doesn't "allow" him to do.

The only sense in which it can be said that God allows everything that happens on Earth is that He created the laws and principles—sowing and reaping, cause and effect, and the free will of humans—that govern the earth. We, however, implement these principles and determine much of what we reap and experience. Satan, too, understands these laws and uses them to his advantage whenever possible.

Satan's Hidden Schemes Prevail

I heard a minister in Tulsa, Oklahoma, tell of the deliverance of a person for whom he had prayed at length. It seems this person could never achieve any stability in life or in his walk with the Lord. He would find a job, then quickly lose it; then walk with the Lord for a while, then turn away. This cycle repeated itself again and again with no amount of prayer seeming to make a difference.

One day as the minister prayed for this young man, the Lord showed him a picture of three demons that were following the fellow everywhere he went. They were not in him, but always there to influence him. The minister saw names over each demon, describing what they did. One at a time he bound them in Jesus' name and commanded them to leave the young man alone.

From that moment on, everything changed. Stability came. Success followed. Eventually the young man became a wealthy businessman as well as a minister. And he is still walking with God today. It is always good and right to ask the Father to strengthen and mature individuals, but this man needed something more: someone to exercise authority and enact a deliverance. His instability was the symptom of demonic influence that he was not strong enough in himself to overcome. Satan had the advantage and as long as his schemes remained hidden, he prevailed.

Although some issues concerning spiritual warfare are open for debate—certainly it is a subjective area—others are a certainty:

- We are in a very real war (see 2 Cor. 10:4; 1 Tim. 1:18).
- We are soldiers in this war (see Ps. 110:2-3; 2 Tim. 2:3-4).
- We are to wrestle against all levels of the kingdom of darkness (see Eph. 6:12).
- We are to resist the devil (which would in most situations be his demons) and he will flee from us (see Jas. 4:7; 1 Pet. 5:9).
- We are to tread on Satan and his demons (i.e., exercise authority over them—see Luke 10:19; Rom. 16:20).
- We are to cast out demons (see Mark 16:17).
- We have authority to bind (forbid) and loose (permit) when dealing with the agents and gates of hell (see Matt. 16:19).
- We have powerful weapons designed to overcome the kingdom of darkness (see 2 Cor. 10:4; Eph. 6:10-20).

This is by no means an exhaustive list of warfare Scriptures. To be sure, God doesn't give us detailed formulas for doing all the previously mentioned warfare acts. God is not into formulas in any area of biblical truth. He is concerned with relationship and He gives us principles that must be applied as the Holy Spirit leads us.

For example, the Lord does not give us a particular formula for a worship service. It is not important that we worship in exactly the same way, but that we worship. He does not give exact formulas for church government or placing pastors. Every stream of the Body of Christ seems to do it differently. What matters is not that we all govern the same, but that we have godly government.

I'm not implying absolutes don't exist in Scripture; I am simply saying that rarely do they appear in the area of method. There is nothing sacred or unsacred about the method. What is important is that we walk according to the revelation of the Scriptures we have been given, and that we do this by the direction of the Holy Spirit. He alone knows exactly what is needed in each situation.

Be a Pro Wrestler

Likewise, in spiritual warfare the point is not so much how we wrestle, but that we wrestle. None of these assertions from Scripture about warfare are defensive in nature. They are all offensive. We are to aggressively deal with the forces of darkness whenever the challenge or opportunity arises. Five times the word "against" is used in Ephesians 6. The word in Greek is *pros*, which is a strengthened form of *pro*.

Pro means "in front of,"[10] either literally or figuratively (in the sense of superior to). We use the concept today in the word "professional," or in its shortened form "pro." A pro athlete is one who is "in front of" or "superior to" others. *Pros* also has the connotation of stepping forward and facing toward something or someone.[11] The symbolism in this Ephesians passage is of a wrestler stepping forward and facing his opponent. God is saying to us, "Step forward and face the powers of darkness. Be a pro wrestler!"

Don't be like the bodybuilder visiting Africa, who was asked by a village chief what he did with all his muscles. The bodybuilder thought an exhibition might better serve to explain it, so he proceeded to flex his bulging calves, thighs, biceps and triceps, demonstrating how he performed in competition. After admiring this amazing specimen for a few moments, the chief inquired, "What else do you use them for?"

"That's about it," answered the muscular man.

"That's all you use those huge muscles for?" reiterated the chief.

"Yes."

"What a waste," muttered the chief in disgust. "What a waste."

So many of us are like this bodybuilder. We're strong in the Lord, well equipped to deal with our adversary, but we never use our strength or our weapons. Step into the ring!

As we wait upon the Lord, He will show us which strategy or method of warfare to use. God is a God of relationship. He is a Father who is passionately in love with His family and He prioritizes love over labor. It is our relational aspect of our walk with Christ that prepares us for the warring aspect.

Devotion to Christ, the Springboard for Everything

It is interesting, even paradoxical, but true, that warfare is often born from worship. *Out of our waiting often comes warring.* It is the simplicity and purity of devotion to Christ that must be the springboard for everything we do. "But I am afraid, lest as the serpent deceived Eve by his craftiness, your minds should be

led astray from the simplicity and purity of devotion to Christ"
(2 Cor. 11:3).

Our depth of revelation in any other area of truth does not
diminish the need for simple, pure devotion to Christ. In fact,
it increases it. The larger the tree, the deeper must go the roots.
Likewise, the more we spread ourselves upward and outward
into the multidimensional aspects of the Kingdom, the more
we must allow the decomplicating effect of our relationship
with Christ to go downward.

The context of 2 Corinthians 11:3 is deception. To whatever degree Satan can distract us from our relationship with Christ,
to that degree we are walking in deception, regardless of how
much other revelation we may be walking in.

I want to mention three of the Old Testament words for
"waiting" upon the Lord, each of which has a different shade of
meaning. The first one is *dumiyah*, which means "silently waiting
with a quiet trust."[12] The thought conveyed is a strong, calm,
quiet trust in the Lord. David said in Psalm 62:1-2, "My soul
waits in silence for God only; from Him is my salvation. He only
is my rock and my salvation, my stronghold; I shall not be greatly shaken."

The second word, *chakah*, means "adhere to" or "long for."[13]
"Our soul waits for the Lord; He is our help and our shield" (Ps.
33:20). This is what David felt when he said, "My soul thirsts for
God" (see 42:2; 63:1). He was *chakah*—longing for God's company.

The third word, *qavah*, means "to wait for . . . with eager
expectation."[14] It also means "to bind something together by
twisting" or braiding.[15] The main thought, then, for *qavah* is
"eager expectation and oneness; a joining, a braiding together."
The following verses are examples of this:

Wait for the Lord; be strong, and let your heart take
courage; Yes, wait for the Lord (Ps. 27:14).

Yet those who wait for the Lord will gain new strength; they will mount up with wings like eagles, they will run and not get tired, they will walk and not become weary (Isa. 40:31).

Let's summarize the three meanings, putting them all together: "Silently waiting with a strong, calm trust, longing for His presence and eagerly expecting Him—for you know He'll show up—anticipating and then experiencing the oneness that results as your hearts become entwined." Hallelujah!

Psalm 37:7,9,34 demonstrates how waiting upon the Lord can relate to warfare:

Rest in the Lord and wait patiently for Him; do not fret because of him who prospers in his way, because of the man who carries out wicked schemes. . . . For evildoers will be cut off, but those who wait for the Lord, they will inherit the land. . . . Wait for the Lord, and keep His way, and He will exalt you to inherit the land; when the wicked are cut off, you will see it.

Waiting upon the Lord brings with it the ability to possess our inheritance. "Inherit" is the word *yaresh*, also translated "possess," and means "legally an heir; military invasion in order to seize."[16] Those who wait upon the Lord inherit and possess—worship and warfare! It's like David waiting upon the Lord, longing for Him, worshiping Him, writing songs to Him, and the next minute rising up, grabbing a lion by the mane and ripping his head off! Warring and winning were born from worshiping and waiting.

Looking Good, Lacking Anointing

When Mary was seated at the feet of the Lord and Martha was busy in the kitchen (see Luke 10:40), the passage says Martha was distracted with all her preparations. The word "distraction" is the word *perispao*. It means literally "drag around in circles."[17] The word for "preparations" is the New Testament word for "ministry"—the same word we would use for a person in the ministry. Even pure ministry for Jesus can become a weight we drag around.

Spiritual warfare and prayer in general can also become a weight we drag around. It often loses its life, becomes legalistic and a chore—something required and endured. We become so busy *for* Him that we don't have time to be *with* Him. We're dragging our ministry around in circles, going nowhere and accomplishing nothing for the kingdom of God.

Several years ago I was going through a difficult place in my life. Al Straarup, a dear friend of mine, called me and said, "I was praying for you with a friend this morning and God gave him a picture."

I thought, *Thank You, Jesus. Here comes my answer.*

Al continued, "There was a circle on the ground." (I was ready for a great revelation—the wheel in the middle of a wheel or something!) "You were walking on that circle."

I replied, "Yeah? Yeah?"

He said, "That's it. You were just walking in circles."

"That's my word from God?" I asked.

He responded, "Yeah, that's it. Sorry."

I hung up the phone and said, "I guess it's true. That's what I'm doing, Lord—walking in circles . . . busy, but going nowhere." I stepped off that treadmill and into the presence of the Lord. I stopped walking and started waiting.

Jesus looked at Martha and said, "Mary has chosen the good part, which shall not be taken away from her" (Luke 10:42). "Good part" is the word *agathos*. It's contrasted to another word for "good" in Greek—*kalos*, which means something is "constitutionally good"[18] or, in other words, is made well. But *kalos* doesn't necessarily imply any practical usefulness or benefit. It may simply look good. Nothing is wrong with it, but it may not have any practical purpose.

On the other hand, *agathos*—the word for "good part" that Mary chose—is a word that means "good and profitable; useful; beneficial."[19] It is often translated "good works." The Lord is saying, "If you spend time waiting upon Me, seated at My feet, it puts something in you. You will not only look good, but you'll also be good for something." We often look good, but lack anointing. We must wait in His presence and allow all ministry, including our warfare, to be born of relationship.

God's Timing, God's Terms, God's Method

Waiting upon the Lord will keep us from becoming reactionary to the devil. Our response is not to the devil. We do nothing on his terms, nor are we to do anything in his timing. God chooses the times and the terms of battle. He told Joshua at Jericho (see Josh. 6), as he was on his face in worship, "Seven days, Joshua. Not a moment before. Don't do anything until I tell you." He was saying, "I choose the timing of battle."

God chose the terms, also. "Take no prisoners—only Rahab escapes. The spoils are to be given to Me. I choose the terms—you don't, Satan doesn't, no one else does. If you do it My way, you'll always win. Do it the devil's way and you will find yourself walking in circles." God chose the timing, the terms and the method. Warfare is not a responsive reaction but responsible action. It must be born from obedience, not necessity. We follow our Captain, not our foe.

The Lord told David to go to battle when the wind blew in the treetops, not until then (see 2 Sam. 5:24). He told Saul to wait seven days for Samuel to come and offer the sacrifice (see 1 Sam. 13:8-14). The enemy was encamped about them and the people were getting nervous, so Saul finally said, "I'm going to have to offer this sacrifice myself—do it my way—because we've got to get on with the battle here." Samuel showed up immediately after the sacrifice and gave him God's perspective: "You blew it, Saul, and the kingdom is going to be taken from you and given to someone after my heart. I can't have a warrior or leader who is reactionary—who leads the people according to his own wisdom and ideas. It has to be My way. You wait on Me!"

At times, God may say that worship is the key, as it was for Jehoshaphat on the battlefield (see 2 Chron. 20:1-30) and for Paul and Silas in the jail (see Acts 16:16-36). As we ministered on the streets of the Mardi Gras several years ago, the Lord led us on one occasion, 200 strong, to march silently down the street. An awesome fear of the Lord and presence of God began to hover over the entire area. The Lord had established His awesome presence and silenced His foes. A literal hush came to the streets.

On another occasion, however, He led us to march down the middle of Bourbon Street singing the poignant worshipful song "Emmanuel" by Bob McGee. This time a spirit of conviction began to hover over the street as we sang this powerful song that speaks of humanity's true destiny. As before, a silence came. It seemed as though the Lord had totally taken charge. At one intersection, which was blocked off for foot traffic, we gathered in a circle on our knees and continued to sing. As we knelt worshiping, a man literally ran into our circle, crying out that he wanted to know God.

That's praise warfare! It's also intercession (*paga*)—attacking the enemy. As Christ is enthroned in worship, Satan is dethroned in the heavenlies (see Pss. 22:3; 149:5-9). As we lift up the Son, we pull down the serpent.

The strategy of the Holy Spirit at other times might be love—acts of kindness, giving, forgiving. I was part of a reconciliation ceremony at Confluence Park in Denver, Colorado, on November 12, 1992, between Native Americans and several European Americans. I emceed the gathering, in fact, which was sponsored by Reconciliation Coalition, a ministry led by Jean Stephenson.

The strategy was really quite simple: repent and ask their forgiveness for stealing their land, breaking covenants and killing their ancestors. When one of them, on behalf of his people, extended forgiveness to us and welcomed us to this land, *something broke in the spirit realm*. It was a cold, dreary day, but the moment he spoke those words the sun broke through the clouds and shone upon us. That day marked the beginning of a major work of reconciliation between these two people groups. Why? Our act of humility and love, along with theirs, was also an act of warfare that tore down strongholds in the spirit realm. . . . Warfare through humility. . . . Violent love. Paradoxical, isn't it?

On other occasions the Holy Spirit may lead a person to join with others in agreement to break the back of the enemy. John G. Lake, a missionary to South Africa in the first half of this century, tells the story of a fever epidemic that in a single night struck a portion of South Africa. The devastation was such that in one month a fourth of the entire population of that region died. There were not caskets enough to meet the need and people were being buried in blankets, so great was the devastation.

Lake tells of a powerful intercessor who began to pray. For days—all day long and into the night—he stationed himself under a tree and prayed against the plague. Several times Lake asked the man, "Are you getting through?"

He would reply, "Not yet." But one day he said to Lake, "I feel today that if I had just a little help in faith my spirit would go through." Lake got on his knees and joined the man in prayer. What happened next is amazing. It is recorded in Lake's own words:

As we prayed, the Spirit of the Lord overwhelmed our souls and presently I found myself, not kneeling under the tree, but moving gradually away from the tree. . . . My eyes gradually opened, and I witnessed such a scene as I never witnessed before—a multitude of demons like a flock of sheep! The Spirit had come upon him also, and he rushed ahead of me, cursing that army of demons, and they were driven back to hell, or the place from whence they came. Beloved, the next morning when we awoke, that epidemic of fever was gone.[20]

A Time to Shout

Truly, there is a time for aggressive, violent spiritual warfare in intercession. I realize many would shrink from such extreme action in prayer—running and shouting at the enemy. There is, however, a time for such spiritual intensity. More than once I have found myself shouting at spiritual powers or mountains of adversity while in intercession. I'm not spiritually ignorant enough to believe a certain volume level is required to rebuke evil forces, but the Scriptures do allow for it and even suggest that, at times, it unleashes something in the Spirit:

- Zerubbabel shouted grace to a mountain (see Zech. 4:7).
- Israel shouted at Jericho (see Josh. 6:16).
- Gideon's army shouted before the battle (see Judg. 7:20).
- Jesus shouted on the cross (see Matt. 27:50).
- Israel shouted when the Ark of the Covenant would lead them to a new place: Let God arise, let His enemies be scattered (see Num. 10:35; Ps. 68:1).

I'm not trying to start the First Church of the Screaming Warriors, but I am trying to demonstrate that warfare, even intense and sometimes loud warfare, is valid. Joash, the king of Israel, was rebuked and suffered defeat because of his lack of spiritual intensity in striking with the arrows (see 2 Kings 13:14-19).

At other times, the strategy of the Lord may be to simply speak the Word as a sword or make biblically based declarations into the situation. When led by the Holy Spirit, this strategy is devastating to the enemy.

On one occasion I was trying to mediate a peace between three parties. The circumstance had reached a potentially violent point, and I had been assured by one party that on the following morning he was going to get physical. I knew he meant it and that someone would be hurt and others would be in jail. I was up quite late praying, pleading with God to stop this when, at around 2:00 A.M., the Lord shocked me with these words: *Why are you begging Me to do this? You know My will in this situation. And the problem is being caused by a spirit of anger and violence. Bind it! Declare My Word and will into the situation.*

I did and went to bed. The next morning, for some "unexplainable" reason, without any discussion, everyone had a change of heart. Peace and harmony ruled where the night before violence and anger had reigned. What had happened?

Paga happened.

Calvary happened.

Psalm 110:2 happened: "The Lord will stretch forth Thy strong scepter from Zion, saying, 'Rule in the midst of Thine enemies.'"

Seizing and Securing Our Inheritance

A word of caution is necessary at this point. As we involve ourselves in spiritual warfare, it is imperative that we remember we are not trying to defeat the devil. He is already defeated. We do not re-defeat, we re-present, the victory of the Cross. All that we do in our praying intercession must be an extension of what Christ did through His work of intercession.

Christ *paga'*ed the devil. He attacked him and crushed his headship over the earth (see Gen. 3:15). The Hebrew word for "head" in this verse, *rosh*, is actually speaking of headship or authority.[21]

Psalm 2:9, speaking prophetically of Christ, says, "Thou shalt break them with a rod of iron, Thou shalt shatter them like earthenware." The crushing of Genesis 3:15 and the breaking and shattering of Psalm 2:9 all have essentially the same meaning: to break something into pieces and scatter it. Christ shattered and scattered the headship of the serpent like a broken piece of glass. It was a total defeat.

But what Christ did, we must release and enforce. What He provided for us, we must seize by faith with spiritual weapons. Timothy was told in 1 Timothy 6:12, "Fight the good fight of faith; take hold of the eternal life to which you were called, and you made the good confession in the presence of many witnesses." Timothy already had eternal life, yet he was told to "take hold of" it.

Is that interesting to you? You can have it and not have it. You can own it and not possess it. The word is *epilambanomai* and means "to seize"[22] something. Like Israel in the Old Testament, who had been given their inheritance by God yet still had to take it, so it is with us. Their inheritance was not necessarily their possession. Ours won't automatically fall into our laps either, just as theirs didn't.

Moffatt translates the verse as "Fight in the good fight of the faith, *secure* that life eternal to which you were called" (emphasis added). Wuest's translation reads, "Take possession of the eternal life into a participation of which you were called."

As one would seize and secure territory in war, so we must seize and secure our inheritance in Christ. Who are we to seize it from? Certainly not God! We must take it from the world, the flesh and the devil.

Jack Hayford gives an enlightening amplification of Matthew 16:18-19, based on what the Greek literally says:

> Whatever you may at any time encounter (of hell's counsels which I'm declaring my church shall prevail against), you will then face a decision as to whether you will or won't bind it. What transpires will be conditional upon your response. If you do personally and consciously involve yourself in the act of binding the issue on earth, you will discover that at that future moment when you do, that it has already been bound in heaven![23]

Amazing! So much depends on our obedience and responsible action. Our inheritance in Christ is not guaranteed or automatic.

She Stepped Forward

Sue Doty shared the following testimony regarding doing spiritual warfare in her city. She stepped forward!

> I sensed the Lord wanted me, along with a team of intercessors, to go on a prayer walk over a specific route, but that some preparation was necessary. First, I talked with my pastor about this and then went to drive along the route I knew we were to prayer-walk. As I approached a theater (X-rated movie house, video shop and bookstore), the Holy Spirit started to give me specific instructions. He told me to cast out the spirits of pornography and lust, and I did so. He also told me to pray in the Spirit. After a short time I was released from praying, and I continued on the rest of the route before going home.

On that Friday the Lord revealed to me what had
actually happened. I turned on the local news to hear
that this particular theater had been ordered by the city
to close its doors. The day after I had been there to pray,
the city conducted a surprise inspection. The theater
was cited for several violations and its doors were immediately closed and locked.

What was so remarkable was that the city had
already inspected the building a short time before and
it had passed inspection. But without warning, and for
no apparent reason, it was being inspected again. God
had really moved! The theater did meet code violations
and was re-opened for a short period of time before a
judge ordered it to close for one year. Now the property is up for sale.

I had taken the course "Intercessory Prayer—The
Lightning of God" by Dutch Sheets and I knew many
charges had been placed in the wall, but this was the
kairos time and the wall fell under the power of God. [By
"charges" she is referring to the *dunamis*—dynamite—of
the Holy Spirit that I teach about in the previously mentioned course.]

A Legal Breaking of Headship

"But why would warfare ever be necessary if Christ defeated
Satan and his demons?" many ask. "Didn't Christ take away his
power, disarm him and destroy his works? Didn't He deliver us
from Satan's power?"

The answer to these questions lies in an accurate understanding of what Christ actually did when He defeated Satan.
Satan's destruction wasn't a literal one, but rather a legal breaking of his headship or authority. Nowhere does the Bible say

Christ delivered us from Satan's power. It says He delivered us from his *exousia*—authority—or in other words, the right to use his power on us:

> Colossians 1:13: "For He delivered us from the domain [*exousia*] of darkness, and transferred us to the kingdom of His beloved Son."

> Luke 10:19: "Behold, I have given you authority [*exousia*] to tread upon serpents and scorpions, and over all the power [*dunamis*] of the enemy, and nothing shall injure you."

> Colossians 2:15: "When He had disarmed the rulers and authorities, He made a public display of them, having triumphed over them through Him." The word "disarmed" is the Greek word *apekduomai* and means Christ divested Himself of the rulers and authorities.[24] That's theological jargon for, "He whipped them!"

Power never was and never will be the issue between God and Satan. Authority was the issue—the authority Satan had obtained through Adam. Jesus did not come to get back any power, nor to remove Satan's power. He came to regain the authority Adam lost to the serpent and break his headship over the earth.

Satan still has all the inherent powers and abilities he has always had. He "prowls about like a roaring lion" (1 Pet. 5:8). And, contrary to what some teach, he still has his teeth. He still has "fiery darts" (Eph. 6:16, *KJV*). If you don't believe this, try going without your armor. What he lost was the right (authority) to use his power on those who make Jesus Lord. However, Satan is a thief and a lawbreaker and will use his power or abilities on us anyway if we don't understand that through Christ we now have authority over him and his power. *Authority is the issue.* Power does the work, but authority controls the power.

This truth is well illustrated in the battle between Israel and Amalek in Exodus 17:8-13. In this famous passage Moses went to the top of a hill with the staff of God in his hand while Joshua led the army on the battlefield below. As long as Moses held up the rod of God, Israel prevailed; when he lowered it, Amalek prevailed.

The victory was not decided by the strength or power of Israel's army. If this had been the case, they would not have faltered when the staff was lowered. Nor was it a morale thing—they weren't watching Moses for inspiration while in hand-to-hand conflict! An unseen battle in the heavenlies actually decided the outcome on the battlefield. And when the rod, representing the rule or authority of God, was lifted by the authorized leader of Israel, Joshua and the army prevailed. In other words, it was not power on the battlefield—though it was necessary—that was the deciding factor, but authority on the mountain. *Authority is the key issue; power never has been.*

Approaching the Father

One final thought in introducing this subject of warfare: It is important to know that in our wrestling we are not to wrestle with God. I don't know about you, but the very thought terrifies me! The verses most often used to teach that we should are from Genesis 32:22-32, where Jacob wrestled all night with the angel of the Lord. Many a dynamic message has been preached using the words of Jacob as an example for what we should do in prayer: "I won't let you go until you bless me" (see v. 26). I've done it myself.

However, Scripture does not present this wrestling match as an example of how we are to pray. The reason it lasted so long is (1) God allowed it—the angel could have flipped Jacob into orbit had he wanted to. He once sent one angel to destroy an army (see 2 Chron. 32:21); (2) God and Jacob were after different things. Jacob wanted protection from Esau; God desired a nature change in Jacob.

Notice what, on the surface, seemed like a ridiculous question the angel asked Jacob: "What is your name?" Doesn't it seem strange to you that in the midst of this wrestling match they began to have a nice little conversation trying to get acquainted? That is not really what was happening. God was trying to get Jacob to acknowledge the truth about his nature, which was described by his name. The *Amplified* translation demonstrates this clearly: "[The Man] asked him, What is your name? And [in shock of realization, whispering] he said, Jacob [supplanter, schemer, trickster, swindler]!" (Gen. 32:27).

That's all the Lord needed: revelation and confession. Immediately grace was released and a nature change occurred. His name was also changed to Israel. A study of Jacob from this point on shows the great difference in his nature.

"But Jacob prevailed," some might say.

Only by losing. The only way to win a wrestling match with God is to lose. If you win, you lose; if you lose, you win. The only way to find our lives is to lose them (see Matt. 16:24-26; Luke 9:23-25). Jacob lost Jacob and found Israel. Such sweet defeat!

The point of our study, however, is to reveal that this story is not an example of how we are to petition our heavenly Father. We are to approach Him with bold confidence (see Heb. 4:16), knowing He is our Friend and Father. We are to ask "according to His will" (1 John 5:14), not try to wrestle from Him something He might not want to give. We are laborers together with Him (see 2 Cor. 6:1), not warring against Him. We storm the gates of hell (see Isa. 28:6; Matt. 16:18), not the gates of heaven.

Persistence in prayer is necessary, but it is not to overcome God's reluctance. This is vital to know and remember. It is impossible to ask in faith, which is a requirement, if a person does not believe it is God's will to do what he or she is asking. Why then, is persistence necessary? That is for another chapter. He who persists will find it!

The purpose of this chapter, however, is to say: *There is a warfare or wrestling necessary at times in our intercession. Paga* includes the concept and the Scriptures teach it. We must do it with balance and understanding, but *we must do it!* To ignore Satan is to abdicate to Satan.

In the next chapter, we will apply this concept of warfare to doing it for the lost. We have a vital role to play in setting the captives free. Let's make a gain on the kingdom of darkness!

Questions for Reflection

1. What are the two opposite activities usually needed in intercession? Why are both necessary? Does the meaning and use of *paga* reinforce this?

2. Explain 2 Corinthians 2:11. How does it reinforce the fact that we're not to ignore Satan?

3. Can you explain the connection between worship, waiting and warfare? How does Joshua picture this? Similarly, what insights can be gleaned from Mary and Martha concerning this?

4. Why would spiritual warfare ever be necessary if Christ defeated and destroyed the powers of darkness? Include comments on the difference between authority and power.

5. Are we supposed to wrestle with God in prayer? Explain.

6. Define the word *pro* from Ephesians 6, commenting on its connection to spiritual warfare.

7. Why is it important to choose preaching interpreters carefully? (Hint: "I won't say that.")

MOST HIGH MAN

Peeling Off the Veils

I watched the cesarean section delivery of a baby on television once. It was on one of those educational channels that enlighten us to some of the things we need to know to survive in life. Thank God for cable!

I also saw a face-lift on the same channel. They peeled the skin right off the face! Then they sucked up a bunch of cellulite. I don't know what kind of cells those are, but they also sucked up some fat—I knew what that was. Seemed to me they should have left the "lite" cells and sucked up the fat cells, but I reckon they had some reason for doing what they did. The things we do to look better. Believe me, now I know why they say beauty is only skin deep.

The delivery of the baby fascinated me the most. I always figured they just cut the skin and out plopped the baby. No way! They pert-near (that's Texan for nearly) turned that poor woman inside out. Pulled out and pointed out things I didn't even know I had (!)—ovaries and stuff like that. When they finally got to the baby, it was all they could do to pull it out. I don't know why it held on like it did. If it had been seeing what I was seeing, it would have wanted out of there fast.

Anyway, all of us need to be educated on the finer points of C-sections and face-lifts. And if you're gonna read a book by someone, you probably want to know that person is well versed in many areas of life. We don't need no more dumb authors!

Hopefully by now you know there is a method to my madness and somehow—perhaps minutely—but somehow, this relates to intercession.

The Bible says there is a veil that keeps unbelievers from clearly seeing the gospel:

> And even if our gospel is veiled, it is veiled to those who are perishing, in whose case the god of this world has blinded the minds of the unbelieving, that they might not see the light of the gospel of the glory of Christ, who is the image of God (2 Cor. 4:3-4).

My lexicons told me the word "veil" means "to hide, cover up, wrap around."[1] The Greek word is *kalupsis*. They said the inside of a tree is veiled by bark; the inside of a human body is veiled by skin. I understood immediately!

The New Testament word for a "revelation" is simply *kalupsis* with the prefix *apo* added—*apokalusis*. *Apo* means "off or away,"[2] so literally a revelation is an unveiling, an uncovering. As I watched those surgeries, I received a revelation of the inside of a human body—at least some of it.

The Veil in the Unbeliever

This chapter is all about spiritual warfare for the lost. It is perhaps the most important in the book. The primary purpose of the previous chapter was to prepare us for this one. We have a part to play in lifting the veil off the mind of the unbeliever. Second Corinthians 10:4, which we will elaborate on later, speaks of strongholds that are a part of this veil. We participate in the destruction of these fortresses. Strongholds are not demons; they are places from which demons rule.

We will look closely at several words from these two passages to gain a more thorough understanding of what is being said. The passage in 2 Corinthians 4:3-4 tells us there is a veil or covering over the minds of unbelievers that keeps them from clearly seeing the light of the gospel. It is important to know *they don't see the gospel because they can't see it. They don't understand it because they can't understand it.* They must have an unveiling—a revelation.

Recently, I was visiting with a brother in Alaska who was telling me about a friend to whom he has been witnessing. He said, "It's just like you teach, Dutch. The man actually said to me, 'I know there is something to what you're saying because it's obvious what it has done for you. *But I can't yet fully see it*'" (emphasis added).

In times past it always seemed difficult for me to understand how some people could hear and reject powerful gospel presentations. Now I know. When "hearing" it, they didn't hear what I heard, see what I saw or understand what I understood. What the unbelievers heard was filtered through a belief system—a veil—that caused them to hear something totally different. The fourth verse of 2 Corinthians 4 clearly states this: "that they might not *see* the light of the gospel of the glory of Christ, who is the *image* of God" (emphasis added). They simply do not see the same "image" of Christ that we do. To clearly see Him is to love and want Him. We'll describe some of the components of this "stronghold" in more detail later in the chapter. At this point it is imperative to establish that it exists.

A Distorted Perspective

This distorted perception of the unbeliever is well illustrated by the story of a woman driving home alone one evening when she noticed a man in a large truck following her. Growing increasingly fearful, she sped up, trying to lose her pursuer, but it was futile. She then exited the freeway and drove up a main street, but the truck stayed with her, even running red lights to do so.

In a panic, the woman wheeled into a service station, jumped from her car and ran inside screaming. The truck driver ran to her car, jerked the back door open and pulled from the floor behind her seat a man that was hiding there.[3]

The lady was fleeing from the wrong person. *She was running from her savior!* The truck driver, perched high enough to see into her back seat, had spied the would-be rapist and was pursuing her to save her, even at his own peril.

As was this lady's, the perspective of unbelievers is distorted. People run from the pursuit of a God who is desiring to save them from destruction. Those of us who know Him realize we love God because He first loved us. When sinners, however, hear of a loving God who wants only their best and died to provide it, they often see instead only the promise of loss and a lack of fulfillment.

Letting in the Light

The word "light" in 2 Corinthians 4:4 is *photismos*, which means "illumination."[4] It is similar to another word in Ephesians 1:18, "enlightened," which is the word *photizo*—"to let in light."[5] We can almost see the English words "photo" or "photograph" in these Greek words; they are, indeed, derived from them. What happens when one takes a photo? The shutter on the camera opens, letting in light, which brings an image. If the shutter on the camera does not open, there will be no image or picture, regardless of how beautiful the scenery or elaborate the setting.

The same is true in the souls of human beings. And this is exactly what is being said in these two verses in 2 Corinthians 4. It sounds like photography language. It makes no difference how glorious our Jesus or how wonderful our message—if the veil (shutter) is not removed, there will be no true image (picture) of Christ.

Oh, sometimes we talk people into a salvation prayer without a true revelation (unveiling), but there is usually no real change. That is why fewer than 10 percent—I've heard figures as low as 3 percent—of people who "get saved" in America become true followers of Christ. The reason is that there is not true biblical repentance, which only comes from biblical revelation.

Repentance does not mean to "turn and go another way"— a change of direction. That's the Greek word *epistrepho*, often translated "converted" or "turn," and is the *result* of repentance. Repentance—*metanoia*—means to have "a new knowledge or understanding"—a change of mind.

In biblical contexts, repentance is a new understanding that comes from God through an unveiling (revelation). It is the reversing of the effects of the Fall through Adam. Humanity chose their own wisdom, their own knowledge of good and evil, right and wrong. Humanity now needs a new knowledge—from God. Paul said in Acts 26:18 that he was called "to open their eyes"—enlightenment, unveiling, revelation, repentance—"*so that* they may turn [*epistrepho*][6] from darkness to light."

Information Versus Revelation

We need to understand—and I'm afraid most do not—the difference between *information* and *revelation*. Information is of the mind; biblical revelation, however, involves and affects the mind, but originates from the heart. Spiritual power is only released through revelation knowledge. The written word (*graphe*)[7] must become the living word (*logos*).[8] This is why even we believers must not just read but also abide or meditate in the

Word, praying as the psalmist: "Open my eyes, that I may behold wonderful things from Thy law" (Ps. 119:18). The word "open," *galah*, also means "unveil or uncover"[9]—revelation.

Information can come immediately, but revelation is normally a process. As the parable of the sower demonstrates, all biblical truth comes in seed form. Early in my walk with the Lord, I was frustrated because the wonderful truths I had heard from some outstanding teachers were not working for me. When I heard the teachings, they had seemed powerful to me. I left the meetings saying, "I will never be the same!" But a few weeks and months later, I was the same.

As I complained to God and questioned the truth of what I had heard, the Lord spoke words to me that have radically changed my life: *Son, all truth comes to you in seed form. It may be fruit in the person sharing it, but it is seed to you. Whether or not it bears fruit depends on what you do with it.* Spiritual information seeds must grow into fruit-producing revelation.

Knowledge or information alone, which is what humans have glorified and where they have begun their quest for meaning ever since the Fall, does not produce salvation. It does not necessarily lead to a true knowledge of God. Jesus said to the Pharisees, "You search the Scriptures, because you think that in them you have eternal life; and it is these that bear witness of Me" (John 5:39).

The Pharisees knew the Scriptures (*graphe*) probably better than you or I, but they did not know God. Many theologians today know the Scriptures thoroughly but don't know God well. Some, perhaps, do not know Him at all. They couldn't sit quietly in His presence for two hours without being bored silly. They have much information, but little or no revelation. Revelation makes the Scriptures "spirit and life" (John 6:63). It makes them live.

Why is this so important? Because we are forever short-circuiting God's process and, in so doing, short-circuiting the results. It is revelation that leads to biblical faith and true change. Without it we are simply appealing to a fallen, selfish, humanistic mind that is always asking, "What's in it for me?" When we appeal to this mentality through human wisdom and intellect alone, we often preach a humanistic, "What's in it for them" gospel, and we produce—at best—humanistic, self-centered converts.

If, on the other hand, we preach a pure gospel, including repentance and the laying down of a person's own life (lordship of Christ), unbelievers are sure to reject it unless they receive a biblical revelation. In fact, our gospel is often ridiculous or moronic to them: "But a natural man does not accept the things of the Spirit of God; for they are foolishness to him, and he cannot understand them, because they are spiritually appraised" (1 Cor. 2:14). The word "foolishness" is *moria*, from which we get the word "moron."

Birthing True Repentance

What is the solution? We must allow the Holy Spirit time to birth true repentance in them through God-given revelation. This produces God-centered Christians, not self-centered ones. God knows we could use some of those, especially in America.

Two or three years ago, a lady we'll call Sarah related to me a testimony of praying for her sister and brother-in-law. Although generally nice people, "they were very anti-Christian, and were my husband's and my greatest persecutors spiritually, mocking and making fun of us."

Sarah had been praying for them *for 20 years*, but they had shown no interest in the gospel. "Because of their attitude toward God and the gospel," Sarah admits, "I had developed a hard heart toward them. I was religiously proud against them and praying out of a wrong motive."

After listening to me teach on intercession, Sarah's hope was renewed and the Holy Spirit prompted her with the question, *When are you going to do this for your family?* She repented of her attitude, got her heart right and forgave them for their attitude toward God. Then she began to pray as I had instructed.

Sarah's need to repent personally and change her own attitude is a valuable lesson for us. Attitudes in our own hearts often keep God from being able to answer our prayers. Isn't it ironic and tragic that our own sin might hinder our prayers for another sinner? Jesus said, "First take the log out of your own eye, and then you will see clearly to take the speck out of your brother's eye" (Matt. 7:5). You may need to forgive your spouse, child or loved one before God can use you to deliver him or her.

Sarah prayed several things and remembers praying specifically "for the veil to be lifted off of their eyes so that they can see and understand the truth of the gospel." Also, she prayed "that they would come to Christ together so that one would not persecute the other."

A couple of months later—remember, before applying these principles and dealing with her own heart she had prayed for *20 years*—Sarah called to speak with her sister. She heard this amazing report: Earlier that day her brother-in-law had awakened and felt they should go to church. (They *never* went to church.) So they found a small church and, during the altar call, *both of them gave their lives to Christ.* She then apologized to Sarah for the way they had treated her—their attitudes totally changed. They are still walking with the Lord. About nine months later, Sarah's father also came to the Lord.

This will work for you, too!

Blinded by Pride

How does Satan blind the mind of the unbeliever? What gives place to this veil? I believe the Lord has shown me a valuable clue. The word "blinded" in 2 Corinthians 4:4 (*KJV*) is *tuphloo*, which means "to dull the intellect; to make blind."[10] The root word, *tupho*, has the meaning of making smoke,[11] and the blindness in this passage is like a smoke screen that clouds or darkens the air in such a way as to prohibit a person from seeing. This made sense to me, but it didn't seem to fully answer how he did it. Then I made a fascinating discovery.

From this same root comes a word (*tuphoo*) that is used for being high-minded, proud or inflated with self-conceit.[12] The picture is of one who is "puffed up," much like smoke puffs up or billows. When I saw the connection between the words "blindness" and "pride," a major missing link was supplied for me. I realized immediately it was the sin of pride, passed on from Lucifer to humankind in the Garden, that Satan uses to blind them. I realized that most rejection of Christ, whether from the works motivation of most false religions or the simple fact most people just don't want to give lordship of their lives to another, is due to pride. It is the ultimate enemy of Christ and will ultimately be dealt with in finality when every knee bows and every tongue confesses that Christ is Lord. Pride will be dealt its final blow!

The captain of a ship on a dark night saw faint lights in the distance. He told his signalman to send the message: "Change your course 10 degrees south."

Immediately he received the response: "Change your direction 10 degrees north."

The proud captain was angry that he was being challenged, so he sent a further message: "Change your course 10 degrees south. This is the captain speaking!"

He received the response: "Change your direction 10 degrees north. I'm Seaman Third Class Jones."

The captain, thinking he would terrify this insubordinate sailor, wired a third message: "Change your direction 10 degrees south. I am a battleship."

The final reply came: "Change your course 10 degrees north. I am a lighthouse."[13]

The Male Pride Factor

God, the light of the world, is forever trying to get fallen humanity to alter their course. Arrogant humans, who have chosen to captain their own lives, usually charge on to their own destruction.

This pride factor also answered my question of why, regardless of where I went in the world, I found more women saved than men. I knew it couldn't be because they were smarter! The reason is that this root of pride is stronger in men than in women—most men at least. Some of us in the ultra-humble class no longer have a problem with it.

The reason pride is stronger in men is *that which was strongest in us in a pure form before the Fall became strongest in a perverted form after the Fall*. The motivation in men that found its greatest fulfillment in covering, nurturing, protecting and caring for—leading from a servant motivation—turned inward at the time of the Fall.

The desire to lead became a desire to dominate or lord over, a giving nature turned into a getting nature and a secure humility was transformed into an insecure pride. To see how we men were supposed to cover and lead, we need only to look at Jesus, who led and walked in amazing authority and power, yet from a pure serving motivation.

Counselors will counsel many more women than men because it is so difficult for a man to say, "I need help." Women are usually the first to say, "I'm sorry" or "I was wrong." Men are usually more competitive. Women are usually more giving and selfless. Why are these things true? The pride factor in men.

Praying for the Lost

This understanding of the blinding ability of pride is a tremendous clue in how to pray for the lost. It is mentioned again, along with several other important insights, in 2 Corinthians 10:3-5:

> For though we walk in the flesh, we do not war according to the flesh, for the weapons of our warfare are not of the flesh, but divinely powerful for the destruction of fortresses. We are destroying speculations and every lofty thing raised up against the knowledge of God, and we are taking every thought captive to the obedience of Christ.

Most Christians have interpreted these verses, especially verse five, as something we are to do for ourselves. Although I have no problem with doing it for ourselves, the context is certainly that of spiritual warfare for others. *The Living Bible* makes this very clear. As you read it in this paraphrase, notice also the references and inferences to the root of pride we saw in 2 Corinthians 4:4.

> It is true that I am an ordinary, weak human being, but I don't use human plans and methods to win my battles. I use God's mighty weapons, not those made by men, to knock down the devil's strongholds. These weapons can break down every proud argument against God and every wall that can be built to keep men from finding Him. With these weapons I can capture rebels and bring them back to God, and change them into men whose hearts' desire is obedience to Christ.

As we observe these verses more closely, we'll see that the Lord gives us not only a solution for the pride problem, but also identifies and offers God's remedy for other aspects of the stronghold. This passage is both fascinating and enlightening.

Notice first that God tells us what should be obvious: The weapons of our warfare are not carnal or fleshly. This simply means they aren't human. God knows we often overlook the obvious, so He states it clearly. We will never win people on an intellectual basis, nor will we do it through innovative techniques or methods alone. We certainly won't do it by nagging them, putting notes in their sandwiches or berating them with statements such as "When are you going to get right with God?"

When we approach people on a human basis, especially if they feel we are pressuring them, we generally make things worse. This is because the root of pride in them that says, *I don't want anyone else controlling me or telling me what to do*, rises up and defends itself. If we attack this pride on a human level, we will only strengthen it.

God's Holy Detonators

On the other hand, we have weapons that are "divinely powerful" to pull down strongholds, if we would only realize it. God says, "Instead of using yours, I'll let you use Mine. Yours won't work, Mine will." The word "powerful" is *dunatos*[14] and is actually one of the New Testament words for a miracle. These weapons empowered by God will work miracles. The word is also translated "possible." I like that. Do you have anyone that seems impossible? Will it take a miracle? With this power, they become possible. And, of course, this is the Greek word from which we get the word "dynamite." This stuff is explosive!

This dynamite is explosive for the "destruction of fortresses" or, as the *King James* translation says, is capable of "pulling down strongholds." "Destruction" and "pull down" are the word *kathairesis*. This important and powerful word has a couple of pertinent meanings. One of them is "to bring down with violence or demolish" something.[15] With this powerful, miracle-working dynamite behind our weapons, we can become demolition agents violently tearing down Satan's strongholds.

I remember as a small child watching the destruction of an old brick school. I was fascinated as the huge cement ball, attached to a gigantic crane, was swung time after time into the building, crashing through walls and ceilings, bringing incredible destruction. I suppose this would be, in one sense, a viable picture of our warfare as we systematically—one divine blow at a time—work destruction on the strongholds of darkness. It truly does usually happen this way—a systematic, ongoing, one-blow-at-a-time war against Satan's stronghold.

Yet, I saw another huge building in Dallas, Texas, demolished several years ago. This edifice was much larger than the school I had seen destroyed as a child. This one covered nearly an entire city block, or at least it seemed that way to me. The demolition crew didn't use a wrecking ball for this one. And it didn't take days—it took seconds. They used dynamite, strategically placed by experts to demolish this major structure in less than 10 seconds.

I like to think that this in some ways can also be a picture of our intercession. Unlike this physical building, we don't usually see the answer in seconds—we may be strategically placing the dynamite of the Spirit for days, weeks or months. But every time we take up our spiritual weapons and use them against the strongholds of the enemy, we are placing our explosive charges in strategic places. And sooner or later the Holy Detonator of heaven is going to say, "Enough!" There will be a mighty explosion in the spirit, a stronghold will crumble to the ground, and a person will fall to his knees.

Mary's *Paga*

Eva Popham from Ohio shared the following testimony with me of this very thing happening to a lady to whom she ministered:

> When Sandra Sims and I first saw Mary in the nursing home, she was demon possessed. Whenever we would come down the hall toward her, she would begin to shake, make violent noises and say things such as, "I know who you are. I know who you represent. I don't want you here." She would use a lot of profanity and disgusting, vile language.
>
> Everyone at the nursing home was afraid of Mary. No one, from the cleaning staff to nurses, would enter her room alone and no one wanted to take care of her because of her violent nature. Thus, she did not receive very good care. When it was absolutely necessary to enter her room, several of the staff would go together. Mary would not allow anyone to touch her or get near to her.
>
> We prayed and fasted for Mary on a consistent, regular basis. It was a couple of months before Mary would even allow us to enter her room. We prayed that God would remove all calluses and pain from her heart [*logismos*] so that the demons would no longer have anything to hang on to.
>
> God showed us that Mary had been severely abused as a child. We would bind Satan from exercising power over Mary and declare that he could not speak to her [*noema*]. We asked for a hedge of protection to be around her and for God to give her dreams and visions as well as for angels to minister to her. We bound up the evil forces that were already in her so that they could no longer operate.

For approximately eight months after we were first able to enter her room, we consistently prayed and fasted for her as well as ministered to her. At this time I gave a testimony at our church, Love and Faith Christian Fellowship in Cincinnati, Ohio, about reaching out to Mary. I asked everyone to please pray for her. We joined together in prayer for Mary during that service, and many continued to pray for her. Pastor Mike Murray was given a picture of her to pray over. We continued to pray for God's perfect will to be done in Mary's life. We bound Satan and prayed for all of his doors to be closed in her life.

Sandra and I ministered to Mary's hurts and she eventually let her anger go by an act of faith [another *logismos*]. She willed for her life to be changed. There was nothing left for the enemy to have as a stronghold in her.

About two weeks later Mary gave her life to the Lord! Today she is dramatically different: She lets people love her and touch her; her voice is becoming more and more soft and gentle; there is even a marked difference in her before-and-after pictures. It's like the real Mary is just now finally appearing. The presence of God is on her now.

The head nurse of the nursing home called Sandra and me into her office to give us a thank-you gift for what we have done with Mary. She told us the staff had all been asking, "What have they been doing with Mary? She is so different!" Because she is no longer violent, the staff is no longer frightened of her, so they are beginning to properly care for her.

Hallelujah! That's *paga*! That's a demolition!
I will be explaining the italicized words *logismos* and *noema* as we progress—they are specific components of the strong-

hold. But first . . . along with demolish, there's another interesting meaning to *kathairesis*. It was used figuratively of
"removal from office."[16] Wow! Is that ever what we're after! . . .
A new Lordship . . . A different ruler. Our weapons, charged
with God's authority, can enforce the breaking of the headship
of the serpent. Jesus legally broke it; we can see it become literal through our prayers. Hallelujah!

The Stronghold, Satan's Prison Within

But just what does this word "stronghold" that we throw
around so pervasively in the Body of Christ actually mean? The
word is *ochuroma*, coming from the root word *echo*, which
means "to have or hold."[17] This word for "stronghold" (*KJV*) or
"fortress" (*NASB*) is literally a place from which to *hold* something *strongly*. It is also the word for a fort, a castle or a prison.

I've seen pictures of foxholes and trenches hastily dug in
times of war to maintain a position. That's a hold. On the other
hand, I toured a huge castle on top of a mountain in Salzburg,
Austria, several years ago. From this seeming impregnable fortress
on a hill, someone had ruled the territory. That's a stronghold!

In essence, Satan has a place of strength *within* unbelievers
from which he can hold on to them strongly. They are prisoners, captives, slaves. Christ was sent "to proclaim release to the
captives" (Luke 4:18). I can guarantee you, however, that as His
proclamation goes forth now, it will be through the mouth of
the Church!

Now we come to verse five of 2 Corinthians 10, an extremely important verse. Let's read it again: "We are destroying speculations and every lofty thing raised up against the knowledge
of God, and we are taking every thought captive to the obedience of Christ." It is important to know that "destruction"
in verse four and "destroying" in this verse are the same words.

The *KJV* does a most unfortunate thing in using two totally different words, "pulling down" and "casting down." It is necessary to know these are the same words in order to realize the Holy Spirit is carrying on the same thought. Verse four says our divinely empowered weapons can demolish strongholds, and verse five is going to elaborate more fully just what the strongholds are that we're going to demolish. In other words, *He describes for us exactly what comprises the stronghold or prison!* This is critical information as we begin to war for the lost.

Specifically, He shares with us three major components of the fortress. These are the things we will begin to call out and demolish as we war over individuals with our divinely empowered weapons. I believe this can be done over people groups as well, but the context here seems to indicate that it is speaking primarily of individuals.

Mindsets

The first aspect of the stronghold He mentions is "speculations"—*logismos*. This word speaks not of the scattered individual thoughts of humans, but of their calculative reasoning, their wisdom or logic.[18] Our word "logic" is actually derived from this Greek root. *Logismos* is the sum total of the accumulated wisdom and information learned over time. It becomes *what one really believes*—the person's mindset. Moffatt calls them "theories." Humanity, before the Fall, got their wisdom and logic—their beliefs—from God. Now, James 3:15 tells us they come from the earth, the soul or intellect, and demons.

These *logismos* would include philosophies (whether formally identified or unnamed personal ones), religions, humanism, atheism, Hinduism, Buddhism, Islam, racism, intellectualism, Judaism, materialism, roots of rejection, perversions—anything that causes a person to think a certain way.

How do these *logismos* blind individuals? How do they veil truth? The way the human mind functions dictates that when people hear the gospel, *before they even have time to think or reason about it*, it is filtered through the subconscious where all other information—including these *logismos*—is stored. This means that unbelievers don't hear what we are saying; they hear what we are saying *plus* what they already believe.

For example, I was sharing the gospel with a girl who had been horribly abused. "God is love," I said. "He loves you so much He sent His Son to die for you."

She did not hear only what I said. She also heard in her mind—I know because she said to me—"Oh? If He is love, why would He have allowed me to have been so abused? Doesn't sound like a loving God to me." That is a *logismos*—a belief, a philosophy, her wisdom, her logic. Someone will need to intercede for her and help tear it down.

On another occasion I was sharing the gospel with a fellow who had a *logismos* I call "good-ole-boy-ism." He was just too nice a guy to think he needed saving. "I'm a pretty good guy," he said. "I don't cheat on my wife, beat my kids, lie, curse or steal. I don't think God would send me to hell."

How does the gospel break through these arguments? Certainly the gospel of truth itself has power to break down some of this when anointed by the Holy Spirit. But it usually takes a long period of time—*if* you can get them to listen. It is much wiser to plow the ground ahead of time, preparing for the reception of the seed by pulling down these strongholds.

Perhaps you already know what these *logismos* are in the person for whom you are praying. If not, ask the Holy Spirit to reveal them to you. He will. And when He does, call them by name, quoting 2 Corinthians 10:3-5. Say, "In the name of the Lord Jesus Christ I am destroying you, stronghold of . . ." Do it daily until the person comes to Christ.

All Pride That Rises Up

The second part of the stronghold we must demolish is "every *lofty thing* raised up against the knowledge of God" (v. 5, emphasis added). I like using the *KJV* for this verse because it uses "high thing" to translate the Greek word *hupsoma*, which is actually the same root word for "Most High" God. It actually means "any elevated place or thing."[19] This is referring to the same root of pride we discovered hidden in the word "blinded" in 2 Corinthians 4:3-4. It is the "most highness" that came to humanity at the Fall when Adam and Eve bought the lie "You too shall be as God" (see Gen. 3:5).

Humankind, like Satan, attempted to exalt themselves to a place of equality with the Most High. We became not the Most High, but our own most high, filled with pride. One leading lexicon even defined *hupsoma* as "all pride that rises up."[20] The word would then encompass all mindsets that exalt themselves against the knowledge of God.

The good news is that we can also tear down this stronghold in people through spiritual warfare so that they can humble themselves and bow their knees to Christ. Listen to this entire verse again in *The Living Bible*:

> These weapons *can* break down *every* proud argument against God and *every* wall that can be built to keep men from finding Him. With these weapons I *can* capture rebels and bring them back to God, and change them into men whose hearts' desire is obedience to Christ (emphasis added).

I like the "cans" and "everys" in the verse. The Lord doesn't wish us luck or tell us that we will win a few once in a while. He lets us know we *can* break down *every* proud argument and *every* wall; we *can* capture rebels! And we must!

Thoughts and Temptations

Considering the third aspect of strongholds, the Lord tells us we can "take every thought captive to the obedience of Christ." The word "thought" is *noema*, which also means plans, schemes, devices or plots. It refers to the spontaneous thoughts and temptations Satan uses to assault the unbelievers, as well as the schemes and plans he uses to keep them in darkness. In intercession we must declare boldly that no weapon of Satan's will prosper. We must bind his plans and stand against them through prayer. We can and should pray that the unbeliever be shielded from Satan's thoughts and temptations.

Marlena O'Hern, of Maple Valley, Washington, had been praying for her brother, Kevin, to be saved for approximately 12 years, with no seeming results. She basically prayed things such as "Lord, come into his life," or "Lord, reveal Yourself to him." As with many of us, she didn't realize there were more specific biblical ways to pray.

Also, similar to the rest of us, she sometimes grew frustrated and tried to take things into her own hands, saying things such as, "You just need to give your life to the Lord" or "You have to quit doing the stuff you're doing." Predictably, this would only result in her seeing the pride and rebellion in Kevin rise up, actually making things worse. "Then I would really feel like I had blown it," she said.

"Kevin was heading down a rocky road. He had major problems, including drugs, depression and extreme anger," Marlena relates.

Early in 1995 she took a class of mine in which I taught these principles about praying for the lost. Marlena shared them with her husband, Patrick, and their children. They began to pray the principles over Kevin. They specifically prayed the following (all parenthetical remarks are mine):

- That God would lift the veil over him (revelation and enlightenment)
- For the Holy Spirit to hover over him and protect him
- For godly people to be in his pathway each day
- To cast down anything that would exalt itself against the knowledge of God, specifically pride and rebellion (This would include the *hupsoma* aspect of the stronghold.)
- To take down all known strongholds—thought patterns, opinions on religion, materialism, fear (This is the *logismos* dimension of the stronghold.)
- To bind Satan from taking Kevin captive; to bind all wicked thoughts and lies Satan would try to place in Kevin's mind (These would be the *noema* aspect of the stronghold.)
- That the armor of God would be placed on him

After two weeks of praying in this way, Kevin overdosed on drugs and, in his time of need, cried out to God. "The Lord met him in a powerful way. The veil was definitely lifted and he had a revelation of God. He now has an understanding of the Word and responds to it. The confusion is gone! Kevin separated himself from the world and his former friends. He is now pursuing God and Christian relationships. His focus is on pleasing God, knowing Him more and more. He is even considering missions."

"We know that we are of God, and the whole world lies in the power of the evil one" (1 John 5:19). Yet we have been given authority! We can turn unbelievers "from darkness to light and from the dominion of Satan to God" (Acts 26:18). We are called to enforce and make effectual the freedom Christ procured.

The unbeliever cannot war for himself. He cannot and will not overcome the strongholds of darkness, and he will not understand the gospel until the veil lifts. We must take our divinely dynamic weapons and fight. The powers of darkness will resist, but "do not be afraid of them; remember the Lord who is great and awesome, and fight for your brothers, your sons, your daughters, your wives, and your houses" (Neh. 4:14).

Questions for Reflection

1. What is meant by the word "veil" in 2 Corinthians 4:3? How does this apply to unsaved people? Can you explain how this is related to a biblical revelation?

2. What is meant by Satan's "blinding" the minds of unbelievers? How is this connected to the Fall of humanity? How is this significant where men (versus women) are concerned?

3. Explain the meaning of enlightenment. Can you describe the analogy to this and photography?

4. What is the true meaning of repentance? How is this connected to biblical revelation?

5. Define a stronghold. Now describe the three aspects of the stronghold in unbelievers and how intercession can be applied to each.

6. Who are you going to do this for? Will it work for them? Hallelujah!

THE LIGHTNING OF GOD

Strike the Mark

This was about the coolest thing I had discovered since baseball. I was in the fifth grade, and in that ornery, but not mean, "can't stand baths," "all girls have cooties" stage of life. I had recently procured my first magnifying glass.

I'm not sure how I discovered I could hold a magnifying glass at just the right angle to the sun and catch a piece of paper on fire. I didn't do anything majorly bad, like the time I nearly burned the science classroom down with my volcanic exhibition. Never did figure out why that teacher gave me a C just because he had to run to the window with a burning volcano and throw it outside. Looked pretty real to me. Nor was it like the time I burned the kitchen cabinets because I forgot about the french-fry grease. I didn't get a grade on that endeavor, although my mom's response was very educational.

This was nothing like those incidents. I just burned a piece of paper on the playground. Then this brilliant idea leaped up from my fallen Adamic psyche. I called my friends over, assuring them I had a really cool demonstration to show them. Looking at Duncan, one of the mean guys in the class, I said to him in my best "you're the lucky guy" tone of voice, "Duncan, hold your hand out. I want to show you something."

Duncan didn't leave his hand there very long. He chased me all around that playground! Some guys just can't take a joke.

Is there a picture of intercession hidden anywhere in this? Yes. One of the ways *paga* is translated is "strike the mark." The reference is Job 36:32: "He covers His hands with the lightning, and commands it to *strike the mark*" (emphasis added). When God releases His light, causing it to flash forth from His presence like lightning, its striking the desired target is likened to intercession.

Although the word *paga* is not used, Habakkuk 3:4 also speaks of light flashing forth from the hand of God: "His radiance is like the sunlight; He has rays flashing from His hand, and there is the hiding of His power." The *Amplified* translation is also very descriptive: "And His brightness was like the sunlight; rays streamed from His hand, and there [in the sunlike splendor] was the hiding place of His power."

We are like a magnifying glass in one sense—no, we don't add to or magnify God's power—but we do let the "Son" shine forth through us, directing His light to desired situations, allowing it to "strike the mark."

Have you ever seen a tree struck by lightning? If so, you've seen a picture of intercession. I do lots of praying in a woods nearby. At times I come across trees struck by lightning. The lightning is so hot it literally changes the molecular structure of the trees and twists the trunks until they look like the stripes on a candy cane. The temperature in a lightning bolt can reach 30,000 degrees Celsius (45,000 degrees Fahrenheit), hotter than the surface of the sun. That's hot stuff! And God uses this to picture His judgments!

If I have my theology straight, the Creator must be greater than the creation. That means the power or energy in God is greater than a lightning bolt. No wonder the Scriptures say, "As wax melts before the fire, so let the wicked perish before

God. . . . The mountains melted like wax at the presence of the Lord. . . . He raised His voice, the earth melted" (Pss. 68:2; 97:5; 46:6).

"For our God IS a consuming fire!" (Heb. 12:29).

To explain this chapter adequately, I need to lay a good foundation. Therefore, I want us to look at quite a few Scriptures that associate God with light or lightning. One of the purposes of looking at so many is to demonstrate the consistency and prevalency of this theme. I hope you don't get bored with the Bible. If you do, you probably should skip this chapter. Better yet, repent and read on!

God Is Light

The following verses associate God with light or lightning, and there are numerous others that could be given. I have italicized various words or phrases to call your attention to the theme of light:

1 John 1:5: "And this is the message we have heard from Him and announce to you, that *God is light*, and in Him there is no darkness at all."

Hebrews 1:3 (*AMP*): "He is the sole expression of the glory of God [*the Light-being, the outraying or radiance of the divine*], and He is the perfect imprint and very image of [God's] nature, upholding and maintaining and guiding and propelling the universe by His mighty word of power. When He had by offering Himself accomplished our cleansing of sins and riddance of guilt, He sat down at the right hand of the divine Majesty on high."

1 Timothy 6:16: "Who alone possesses immortality and *dwells in unapproachable light*; whom no man has seen or can see. To Him be honor and eternal dominion! Amen."

(See also Jas. 1:17; Exod. 19:16; Ezek. 1:14; Rev. 4:5.)

At times His light, or the release of it, is associated with His glory. The following verses are examples of this:

Luke 2:9: "And an angel of the Lord suddenly stood before them, and *the glory of the Lord shone* around them; and they were terribly frightened."

Luke 9:29,32: "And while He was praying, the appearance of His face became different, and *His clothing became white and gleaming.* . . . Now Peter and his companions had been overcome with sleep; but when they were fully awake, they saw His glory and the two men standing with Him." (We read in the margin of the *NASB* that the word "gleaming" means literally *"flashing like lightning."* Wuest also translates it this way. No wonder Peter wanted to build tabernacles there!)

Revelation 21:23: "And the city has no need of the sun or of the moon to shine upon it, *for the glory of God has illumined it, and its lamp is the Lamb.*"

(See also 2 Cor. 3:7.)

Sometimes this light, lightning or glory of God is released from His mouth and often called a sword. The first four verses identify God's words or mouth as His sword. The remaining verses make the connection to light or lightning:

Ephesians 6:17: "And take the helmet of salvation, and the *sword* of the Spirit, which is the *word* of God."

Revelation 2:16: "Repent therefore; or else I am coming to you quickly, and I will make war against them with the *sword of My mouth*."

Revelation 19:15: "And *from His mouth comes a sharp sword*, so that with it He may smite the nations; and He will rule them with a rod of iron; and He treads the wine press of the fierce wrath of God, the Almighty."

(See also Heb. 4:12.)

Psalm 29:7 (*AMP*): "*The voice of the Lord splits and flashes forth forked lightning*."

Ezekiel 21:9-10,15,28: "Son of man, prophesy and say, 'Thus says the Lord,' Say, '*A sword, a sword* sharpened and also polished! Sharpened to make a slaughter, polished to *flash like lightning*! . . . I have given *the glittering sword*. Ah! It is made for *striking like lightning*, it is wrapped up in readiness for slaughter. . . . And you, son of man, prophesy and say, 'Thus says the Lord God concerning the sons of Ammon and concerning their reproach,' and say: '*A sword, a sword* is drawn, polished for the slaughter, to cause it to consume, that it may be *like lightning*."

Deuteronomy 32:41 (*AMP*): "If I whet My *lightning sword* and My hand takes hold on judgment, I will wreak vengeance on My foes and recompense those who hate Me." (Sometimes movies can have interesting parallels to Scripture. Luke Skywalker from *Star Wars* isn't the only one who overcomes evil with a sword of light. God has the real one!)

(See also Ps. 18:13-14; Hos. 6:5, *NIV*.)

Thus far, we have God associated with light or lightning, which sometimes shines forth as His glory. It is released from His mouth at times, becoming a powerful weapon. The following Scriptures speak of God's light in the context of Him dealing with His enemies:

Psalm 97:3-4: "Fire goes before Him, and burns up His adversaries round about. *His lightnings lit up the world*; the earth saw and trembled."

Revelation 8:5: "And the angel took the censer; and he filled it with the fire of the altar and threw it to the earth; and there followed peals of thunder and sounds and *flashes of lightning* and an earthquake."

Revelation 16:18: "And there were *flashes of lightning* and sounds and peals of thunder; and there was a great earthquake, such as there had not been since man came to be upon the earth, so great an earthquake was it, and so mighty."

(See also Ps. 78:48; Rev. 11:19.)

These last few Scriptures associate the release of God's light in the context of deliverance of His people:

Psalm 18:14: "And He sent out His arrows, and scattered them, and *lightning flashes* in abundance, and routed them."

Psalm 77:17-18: "The clouds poured out water; the skies gave forth a sound; Thy arrows flashed here and there.

The sound of Thy thunder was in the whirlwind; The *lightnings* lit up the world; the earth trembled and shook."

Psalm 144:6: "*Flash forth lightning* and scatter them; send out Thine arrows and confuse them."

(See also Ps. 27:1.)

According to all these and other fascinating Scriptures, God is light and at times this light or glory flashes forth from Him as bolts of lightning. Many times the Bible says that in order to deal with His enemies—whether for Himself or His people—God simply releases this glory or light into the situation. It flashes forth like lightning and *PAGA* HAPPENS! God's power "strikes the mark."

This happened once several thousand years ago when there was a coup attempt in heaven. Lucifer, inflated with pride, decided he would exalt himself to God's position. "Not!" as my kids would say.

Bad idea, Satan.

This war didn't last long—about as long as it takes for a lightning bolt to flash its brilliant light across the sky. Jesus said it this way in Luke 10:18-20 (Sheets's paraphrase): "Don't get excited, guys, just because demons are subject to you in My name. That's no big deal. I watched Satan cast from heaven. It didn't take long—lightning flashed and he was gone. Get excited because you have a relationship with God."

Light Overcomes Darkness

We don't know that lightning literally flashed when Satan was ousted, but for some reason Jesus used this picture. He said it was "like lightning" (v. 18). I believe it actually flashed. It doesn't really matter, however, because whether or not it literally flashed, the analogy is certainly given of light overcoming darkness.

In fact, I don't necessarily think that in all of the previously mentioned references, literal lightning bolts were observable in the natural realm of sight. At times there certainly were, as when Christ's clothes were glowing and flashing at His transfiguration or when His glory lights the throne room of heaven.

The point, however, is not what can be seen with the human eye, but what happens in the spiritual realm: Light overcomes darkness. And the light is more than a symbolic representation of God's goodness or purity; it represents His power or energy. So whether the lightning itself is literal or symbolic, the results are the same: God's power overcoming the kingdom of darkness.

This analogy of darkness and light is prevalent throughout Scripture. Another powerful example of God's light prevailing over the darkness of Satan is at the Cross. John 1:4-5 says, "In Him was life and the life was the light of men. And the light shines in the darkness, and the darkness did not comprehend it."

The word "comprehend" is the Greek word *katalambano*, which can mean either "comprehend" or "apprehend."[1] Many scholars believe it should be translated with the latter word in this passage because the powers of darkness were not trying to comprehend or understand Christ. They were trying to apprehend or overpower Him, much like a policeman would apprehend a criminal. This makes much more sense to me.

Wuest translates verse 5 accordingly: "And the light in the darkness is constantly shining. And the darkness did not overwhelm it." Moffatt says it this way: "Amid the darkness the light shone, but the darkness did not master it." The Cross was a war—light overcoming darkness. God arose and His enemies were scattered.

Bob Woods, in *Pulpit Digest*, tells the story of a couple who took their son, 11, and daughter, 7, to Carlsbad Caverns. As always, when the tour reached the deepest point in the cavern, the guide turned off all the lights to dramatize how completely dark and silent it is below the earth's surface. The little girl, suddenly enveloped in utter darkness, was frightened and began to cry. Immediately was heard the voice of her brother: "Don't cry. Somebody here knows how to turn on the lights."[2]

All creation was terrified, groping in the darkness of sin. Two thousand years ago, God announced to His groping and frightened humans, "Don't cry. Somebody here knows how to turn on the lights."

I believe Satan has some reoccurring nightmares. One of them is when the light—lightning—flashed in heaven and kicked him out. He probably hates thunderstorms. Why, they even sound like the majestic voice of God!

"The Lord also *thundered* in the heavens, and the Most High uttered His *voice*, hailstones and coals of fire. And He sent out His arrows, and scattered them, and *lightning flashes* in abundance, and routed them" (Ps. 18:13-14, emphasis added).

"The *voice* of the Lord is upon the waters; the God of glory *thunders*, the Lord is over many waters" (Ps. 29:3, emphasis added).

Imagine Satan's horror when the light of God flashed forth at the Cross, the same light that had expelled him from heaven. I can just hear him screaming, "Oh, no. Hear it comes again! He wouldn't let me have heaven and He won't let me have Earth either."

The Lightning Anointing

Yes, at the Cross the counterfeit "angel of light" met Mr. Light Himself and nothing has been the same since! The great "light" being even reproduced Himself into a bunch of little lights—"For you were formerly darkness, but now you are light in the Lord; walk as children of light" (Eph. 5:8)—filling them with His very glory!

For the first time Satan understood Isaiah 60:1-3:

Arise, shine; for your light has come, and the glory of
the Lord has risen upon you. For behold, darkness will
cover the earth, and deep darkness the peoples; but the
Lord will rise upon you, and His glory will appear upon
you. And nations will come to your light, and kings to
the brightness of your rising.

Bummer! he must have thought.

For the first time he understood that the Old Testament temple was a picture of us, this new race of people called Christians
("little Christs"), and that the glory of God was in every one of
them. *"Major bummer!"*

Which brings things back to us. Please read the following
statements carefully, making each connection. If intercession is
pictured by God's lightning striking the mark . . . and if
Christ's work of intercession when He met Satan, breaking his
headship, was light overcoming darkness . . . and if our praying intercession simply releases or re-presents Christ's . . . then
I think it safe to say that our intercession releases the lightning
of God to flash forth into situations, bringing devastation to
the powers of darkness:

- Calvary flashing forth again
- The light of the world shining again
- The royal priesthood proclaiming the excellencies of
  Him who called them out of darkness into His mar-
  velous light (see 1 Pet. 2:9)
- The laser of prayer burning intensely
- The lightning sword of the Spirit flashing brightly
- Jesus and the Father are glorified in the Church (see
  Eph. 3:21)!

We have looked at the "bear anointing" and the "butterfly anointing"—maybe this is the "lightning anointing"!

In John 1:5, which we quoted earlier, the phrase "the light shines in the darkness" could just as accurately read "the light is constantly shining," due to the tense and mood of the verb. Some translations actually do translate it this way. The light that overcame darkness is still shining—the victory lives on. Yet it must be released through the Church!

In his first All-Star game, Roger Clemens, the great pitcher for the Boston Red Sox, came to bat for the first time in years due to the American League's designated hitter rule. After watching a blazing fastball by Dwight Gooden whiz past him, Clemens turned and asked the catcher, Gary Carter, "Is that what my pitches look like?"

"You bet it is!" responded Carter.

From then on Clemens pitched with far greater boldness, having been reminded of how a good fastball can be so overpowering to a hitter.[3]

We often forget how powerful the Holy Spirit in us is . . . how destructive to darkness is His lightning sword. It has supernatural power to overcome the works of darkness—when we release it with confidence.

Dutch Meets Goliath on Bourbon Street

I led an outreach of 200 students from Christ for the Nations Institute to Mardi Gras in 1979. We focused most of our ministry on Bourbon Street, where the biggest portion of the partying occurs. I have seen few places where darkness rules so dominantly as it does at this continuous celebration of evil.

We had many hours of prayer and preparation before going on this outreach, and were assured in our hearts that we had established victory in the Spirit. The light had preceded us. We

felt we were going physically only to reap the spoils. We saw
dozens of people come to Christ and experienced many dramatic events as time and time again light triumphed over
darkness. It was not without its tests, however. One of the
events that impacted me greatly was an encounter we had
with a demonized man who intended to do some of us bodily
harm—kill us.

I spent most of my time walking the length of Bourbon
Street interceding for the "troops" as they witnessed and prayed
with folks. One evening my partner and I crossed the street to
speak with two of our students, who happened to be carrying a
sign that read, "God Loves You!"

As we stood talking, a giant of a man, whom we'll call
Goliath, came at us seemingly out of nowhere. He was about 10
feet tall (at least 6′ 6″) and weighed 500 pounds (at least 260
pounds). He was dressed from head to toe as a Roman soldier—
or maybe as a Philistine soldier—and carried a long whip he was
cracking as he came up to us. His lips were covered with bloody
froth and blood was trickling out of the corners of his mouth.

He approached us, cracking the whip and growling like a
mad dog. The area around us cleared as people backed off and
watched. Goliath then began to shout in a deep, raspy voice,
"God is love, huh? I'm gonna kill you!"

This is not good, I perceived quickly, being the astute man I
am. I wanted to speak some powerful Scripture as a sword, but
the only verse that came to mind was, *To live is Christ; to die is gain*.
It just didn't seem like the one I wanted!

As I stood wondering why one of the other three team members didn't do something, the reason suddenly occurred to me—
I was the leader! Being the wise leader that I am, I shouted,
"Every man for himself." Then to myself I added, *Legs, don't fail
me now!* I felt more like the butterfly anointing than the lightning anointing.

Of course, I didn't really say and do those things, but there was a strong fear that tried to rise up in me. What did I actually do? I PAGA'ed—big time *paga*! And when I glanced at the other three, their lips were silently moving. They were *paga*'n too!

It was *paga* times four. Magnifying glass, don't fail me now!

As we stood and bound the powers of darkness in this man in the name of Jesus, within seconds he began to change. His countenance changed, his voice changed and his attitude changed. The demons controlling him had been overcome. Light prevailed. The man actually appeared confused. He looked at us with a strange expression, muttered something about going ahead with what we were doing and walked away slowly as the crowd watched in amazement.

Light overcame darkness. God's power "struck the mark" (*paga*), quieting the evil spirits and saving us from embarrassment and probable injury.

Later that night as we all gathered and shared our war stories of the day, all were amazed as we related how fearless, confident and in control we were as "Goliath" confronted us. "Never a doubt," we all assured the group. "Never a doubt." May God forgive us!

Living Temples That Carry Glory

My father, Dean Sheets, who pastors in Ohio, saw light overcome darkness while he was on a missions trip to Haiti. He was preaching the gospel and praying for the sick according to Mark 16:15-18. As you are probably aware, the national religion of Haiti is voodoo; consequently, demon activity is prominent and strong. The powers of darkness have been given free reign.

Dad felt specifically led by the Holy Spirit to pray for blind individuals, so he invited them forward. Twenty people responded. As he stood before them one at a time, waiting for direction from the Holy Spirit, he was given the same instruction for 19 of the 20: "Cast out the spirit causing the blindness." Each time he did they were healed instantly, seeing perfectly.

Paga! Light striking the mark, penetrating darkened eyes, bringing sight.

What many believers are not aware of is that we are filled with the very glory and light of God. When the apostle Paul, inspired by the Holy Spirit, said, "Do you not know that you are a temple of God, and that the Spirit of God dwells in you?" (1 Cor. 3:16), he used the Greek word *naos* for "temple,"[4] which always referred to the holy of holies. He was literally saying, "Don't you know you are the holy of holies?"

The word "dwells" is taken from the Old Testament word *shakan*, which means "dwelling or abiding."[5] The *"shekinah* glory" was the abiding or dwelling glory found in the holy of holies. Paul was saying that in Christ the *shekinah* glory of God now *shakans* in us (see 1 Sam. 4:4; 2 Sam. 6:12-19). We are the new holy of holies, a temple of living stones not made with hands, but by God Himself. Second Corinthians 4:6-7 says it this way:

> For God, who commanded the light to shine out of darkness, hath shined in our hearts, to give the light of the knowledge of the glory of God in the face of Jesus Christ. But we have this treasure in earthen vessels, that the excellency of the power may be of God, and not of us (*KJV*).

Israel carried the Ark of the Covenant, representing the presence and glory of God, into battle (see Josh. 6:6). When the Ark set out, the shout would go up, "Rise up, O Lord! And let Thine enemies be scattered, and let those who hate Thee flee before Thee" (Num. 10:35). Psalm 68:1, a warfare verse, is a quote of this verse in Numbers. That same presence and glory now abides in us. The message we are to understand is that the key to victory is carrying this presence of God into battle with us. He rises and scatters His enemies *through us*! We are now His carriers!

Release the Light

Arise, shine, Church, for your light has come and the glory of the Lord has risen upon you. Darkness, indeed, does cover the earth and deep darkness the peoples, but it is a defeated darkness. Nations are looking for the light, kings for the brightness of our rising (see Isa. 60:1-3). We are soldiers of the light. We must boldly release the power of the Most High into situations, allowing the victory of Christ access. He has given us His light, He has given us His sword, He has given us His name. Use them!

Position yourself toward the Son and allow Him to shine through you, striking the mark! Wield the laser sword of the Spirit. We often forget how powerful the Holy Spirit in us is—how destructive to darkness is His lightning sword. It has supernatural power to overcome the works of darkness—when we release it with confidence.

Station yourself spiritually in front of your rebellious children and ask God to send a bolt of meekness to them. Aim the light of liberty at their addictions, whether they be drugs, sex, alcohol, or whatever. Be aggressive in the spirit.

Spouses, ask God to shine forth into the lives of your mates, breaking through the darkness of deception and liberating them.

Pastors, call upon the Holy Spirit to flash, breaking strife, division and complacency over your congregations. While you are waiting for God to do something, He may be waiting on you. Release the light! Call it forth in Jesus' name.

As the Israelites carried the presence and glory of God into battle, so must we. All that was in the Ark of the Covenant is in us: the Bread of Life, the rod of priestly authority and the law of God. And the glory that was upon it now shines through us. Act like it! Strike with the sword—speak the Word! "Let God arise" through your intercession "and His enemies be scattered."

Questions for Reflection

1. How is *paga* related to lightning?

2. Explain the connection between God's light/lightning and His judgments. Can you explain how this happened at the Cross?

3. What is the relationship between God, light, His sword and our intercession?

4. Where is the holy of holies? How does this relate to intercession?

5. Think of a situation where light overcame darkness. How did God do it? Now, think of a current situation in which intercession can be used to see the same results.

6. Do you like representing Jesus?!

THE SUBSTANCE OF PRAYER

Two frogs fell into a can of cream,
or so it has been told.
The sides of the can were shiny and steep,
the cream was deep and cold.
"Oh, what's the use," said number one,
"It's plain no help's around.
"Good-bye, my friend, good-bye, sad world"
and weeping still he drowned.

But number two, of sterner stuff,
dog paddled in surprise.
The while he licked his creamy lips
and blinked his creamy eyes.
"I'll swim at least a while," he thought,
or so it has been said.
It really wouldn't help the world
if one more frog were dead.

An hour or more he kicked and swam,
not once he stopped to mutter.
Then hopped out from the island he had
made of fresh churned butter.
(Author unknown)

Dutch Sheets

Lessons from Three Men and a Frog

I first heard this witty poem 20 years ago in a message by John Garlock, one of my professors at Christ for the Nations Institute, on the subject of tenacity. There aren't many messages that a person remembers 20 years later, but John Garlock has a knack and an anointing for preaching "rememberable" sermons. Others, of course, have a similar gift of preaching very forgettable messages. I've heard lots of them, and even preached my share.

Brother Garlock mentioned the story found in 2 Samuel 23:8-12 about three of David's mighty men: Shammah, Adino and Eleazar. Shammah had tenacity in the face of a humble assignment, defending a small plot of lentils from a bunch of Philistines. Adino personified tenacity in the face of overwhelming odds as he killed 800 Philistines single-handedly. Eleazar pictured tenacity in the face of incredible overwhelming fatigue as, after fighting for several hours, his hand had to be pried from his sword.

Thanks, Professor Garlock, for teaching me through three men and a frog the importance of perseverance and endurance. I rank it near the top of my list of most important spiritual traits. And the longer I live, the higher it rises. "Hang in there" didn't make it into the Ten Commandments, but it did into the nine fruits of the Spirit.

The word *makrothumia*, translated "long-suffering" in Galatians 5:22 (*KJV*), is defined by *Strong's Concordance* as "longanimity or fortitude."[1] That's what I said, "Hang in there."

In this day of instant everything—from "fast foods" to "get-rich-quick schemes" to "how to have the biggest church in town overnight" conferences to "four easy steps to answered prayer" seminars—we are rapidly losing the character trait of hanging in there. We cook faster, travel faster, produce faster and spend faster . . . and we expect God to keep pace with us, especially in prayer.

Dick Eastman, in his book *No Easy Road*, states:

> Much of society has forgotten to persevere. . . . Few have a striving spirit like the artist Raphael. Once he was questioned, "What is your greatest painting?" He smiled, saying, "My next one." One finds Raphael always striving to do better. This is what we need in prayer, an attitude of persistence.[2]

We are much like the African cheetah that must run down its prey to eat. It is well suited for the task, as it can run at speeds of 70 miles per hour. The cheetah has only one problem, however, in that it has a disproportionately small heart, which causes it to tire quickly. If it doesn't catch its prey quickly, it must end the chase.

How often we have the cheetah's approach in prayer. We speed into our closets with great energy, we speed to the front of the church, or we speed to someone else for prayer. But lacking the heart for a sustained effort, we often falter before we accomplish what is needed. For our next prayer excursion, we decide to pray harder and faster, when what is needed may not be more explosive power, but more staying power—stamina that comes only from a bigger prayer heart.[3]

George Müller was a "stayer." One example of his persistence is related by Dick Eastman in the previously mentioned book:

> "The great point is never to give up until the answer comes. I have been praying for sixty-three years and eight months for one man's conversion. He is not saved yet, but he will be. How can it be otherwise. . . . I am

praying." The day came when Müller's friend received Christ. It did not come until Müller's casket was lowered in the ground. There, near an open grave, this friend gave his heart to God. Prayers of perseverance had won another battle. Müller's success may be summarized in four powerful words: He did not quit.[4]

Easy Doesn't Do It in Prayer

The very Son of God spent many entire nights praying in order to fulfill His ministry. It took Him three arduous hours in Gethsemane to find strength to face the cross: "He offered up both prayers and supplications with loud crying and tears" (Heb. 5:7).

We, on the other hand, have mastered the art of one-liners in prayer, and think if we give God a two-hour service once a week we're fairly spiritual. "Easy does it" might be good advice in a few situations, but for most of life, including prayer, easy *doesn't* do it.

A pilot early in a flight went to the back of the plane to check on the reason for a warning light. The problem was a door ajar, which flew open as he approached it. The pilot was immediately sucked from the aircraft.

The copilot, seeing by his panel that a door was open, turned back toward the airport immediately and radioed for a helicopter to search the area. "I believe I have a pilot sucked from the plane," he said. After landing the plane, everyone was astonished to find the pilot holding on to the rung of a ladder, which he had miraculously managed to grab. He had held on for 15 minutes and, still more amazing, had managed to keep his head from hitting the runway, though it was only six inches away!

Upon finding the pilot, they had to pry his fingers from the ladder! That's perseverance![5]

Anyone long associated with the Church of this century, especially in America, knows that our problems do not result from a lack of information or material strength. If we fail in achieving what God asks from us as we run our race, it will be a failure of heart and spirit.

Like the frog, I have kicked and swum my way over time to more victories than I have accomplished quickly and easily. I have fought until my hand clove to the sword. I have found that a tenacious endurance is often the key to victory in prayer.

But WHY?

Why is persistence required in prayer? This I have labored about for years. Does God have a certain amount of prayers required for certain situations? Do we talk Him into things? Does God ever "finally decide" to do something? Do we earn answers through hard work or perseverance?

The answer to all these questions is no.

"What about the prayer of importunity in Luke 11:5-13?" some will ask. "Doesn't it teach that we importune or persist with God until He decides to give us what we need?"

The answer is an emphatic no! We don't persist against God.

The word "importunity" in Luke 11:8 (*KJV*) is an unfortunate translation of the word *anaideia*, which actually means "shame-lessness"[6] or "bold unashamedness."[7] *Aidos*, the root word, means "modesty or shame"[8] and is translated as such in 1 Timothy 2:9. Here in Luke 11, it is in its negative form, making it "without modesty or shame."

The point of this story is the same as Hebrews 4:16, which is to approach the throne of grace boldly, not with a sense of unworthiness or shame. As the petitioner in the story, we can approach our friend, God, at any time knowing we are accepted.

Is God using the waiting period to teach us? I think at times this is certainly the case, and yet, if this is the reason for a delay, we shouldn't need to pray for the same thing again and again—once and then a waiting in faith would be adequate.

In other situations the delay might be that God has the right time for an answer to prayer. "And let us not lose heart in doing good, for in due time we shall reap if we do not grow weary" (Gal. 6:9). But, again, if this is the reason, asking once and waiting in faith should be sufficient.

So why is a persistence or perseverance necessary in prayer? Why did it take me 30 hours of praying to get the cyst dissolved on my wife's ovary? Why did it take a year to obtain a miracle for the little girl in the coma? Why does it sometimes demand several years of intercession to see someone saved? Why did Elijah have to pray seven times before the rain came? Why did Daniel have to pray 21 days before the angel broke through with his answer?

His Throne in Our Hearts

There are probably reasons I am not aware of for the need for persistence in prayer. I certainly don't have all the prayer answers, but I want to submit one explanation for your consideration. I believe our prayers do more than simply motivate the Father to action. I have become convinced of something Gordon Lindsay, a great man of prayer and the founder of Christ for the Nations, called the "substance" of prayer.[9] In fairness, I must say I don't believe it can be conclusively proven, but there is great weight of evidence suggesting it, and I have embraced it as truth.

The concept is that our prayers do more than just motivate the Father to action. They actually release the power of the Holy Spirit from us to accomplish things. Certain types of praying would of course do this more than others.

For example, in our chapter on travail we spoke of this happening as we pray in the Spirit. Another powerful way this occurs would be through speaking the Word of God as a sword into situations (see Eph. 6:17). General declarations or commands are other activities that release the power of the Holy Spirit (see Matt. 17:20; Mark 11:23). The practice of the laying on of hands is another scriptural method of imparting power (see Mark 16:18; Heb. 6:2).

That there is literal power from the Holy Spirit that can be released from us is absolute. The power of God that brings life, healing and wholeness to the earth flows out from us—the Church.

Please don't picture some throne in heaven and feel like it's all there. He has now made His throne in our hearts and we are the temple of the Holy Spirit. We are the *naos* of God. In 1 Corinthians 3:16 and 6:19, this word means "holy of holies."[10] We are now the holy of holies, the dwelling place of God upon the earth. When He moves to release power upon the earth, it doesn't have to shoot out of the sky somewhere—it comes from His people where His Spirit dwells upon the earth.

The Church, God's Womb upon the Earth

Whether through speaking, touching, laying hands on the sick, declaration or worship, when God's power starts flowing upon the earth, it is flowing through human vessels. We, the Body of Christ, are God's womb from which His life is birthed or released upon the earth. The life that Christ produces flows from the womb of the Church.

In John 7:38, Jesus said, "He who believes in Me, as the Scripture said, 'From his innermost being shall flow rivers of living water.'" The innermost being, or belly (*KJV*), is the word *koilia*, which literally means "womb." Translating it literally, we would say, "Out of his womb shall flow rivers of living water." The word "womb" speaks of reproduction. It speaks of birthing. It speaks of the bringing forth of life.

A similar phrase is found in Revelation 22:1-2:

And he showed me a river of the water of life, clear as crystal, coming from the throne of God and of the Lamb, in the middle of its street. And on either side of the river was the tree of life, bearing twelve kinds of fruit, yielding its fruit every month; and the leaves of the tree were for the healing of the nations.

The picture here is of Jesus as the source of life. Out of Him flows the river with trees on either side. Leaves are produced by the trees, which are fed by the river, which is fed by Jesus. People—the nations—eat the leaves and are made whole.

What I want to point out is that the phrase "river of the water of life" in this passage is the same phrase in Greek as the "rivers of living water" in John 7. There is no difference between the river of life flowing out of the Lamb bringing healing and wholeness to the earth, and the rivers of living water that are to be flowing from the womb of the Church. We are His birthing vessels, His incubation chambers. Why should that surprise us? Is it not supposed to be the very life of Jesus in us that we are ministering to the earth?

John 7:39 tells us, "But this He spoke of the Spirit." It is the Spirit of God flowing from us. He doesn't lay hands on the sick—we lay hands on the sick. He doesn't lay hands on a person and ordain—He tells us to do it for Him. He, inside of us, releases a river to flow into that person, and they are now anointed and appointed by God. When He wants to bring forth the gospel, which is the power of God unto salvation and life, He does not echo it from the heavens. He speaks it through us. God's life, the literal power and energy of God, flows out of our mouths and penetrates the hearts of unbelievers, and they are born again.

We are the ones who wield the sword of the Spirit—the spoken Word of God. When the Spirit of God wants to cut and bring judgment into situations, He doesn't just speak from the clouds. He speaks from His people—out of our spirits. When I speak His Word into a situation at the direction of the Holy Spirit, it is as if the Lamb of God Himself spoke the Word. It releases God's life! We are the womb of God from which the river is supposed to flow.

Measurable Power

It is important to realize that this power is measurable. There are cumulative amounts of it. That there are measurable levels of almost any spiritual substance is easily proven.

There are measurable levels of faith. Romans 12:3 says, "as God has allotted to each a measure of faith." The word "measure" here is *metron* from which we get the word "meter." In other words, God has "metered out" to each a portion of faith; from there it must grow. There are levels of faith. There are measurable portions of righteousness. There are even measurable portions or degrees of sin.

In Genesis 15:16, God told Abraham He was going to give the land to his descendants in four generations. The reason He could not give it to him yet was because "the iniquity of the Amorite is not yet complete."

There are measurable levels of grace. Second Corinthians 9:8 says, "And God is able to make all grace abound to you." In fact, in Acts 4:33, we are told that "with great power gave the apostles witness of the resurrection of the Lord Jesus, and great grace was upon them all" (*KJV*). The Greek word for "great" is *megas*, from which we get "mega." There is grace, there is mega grace and there is all grace!

There are measurable degrees of love. John 15:13 speaks of greater love. Matthew 24:12 talks of love that has grown cold. Philippians 1:9 refers to love abounding more and more.

There are measurable degrees of the power of God. In Mark 6:5, there was a measurable degree of the power of God missing.

The verse says that because of the unbelief of the people in Nazareth, "He could do no miracle there." The Greek does not say, "He chose not to" or "He didn't." It says literally, "He could not" because their level of faith or unbelief had hindered the flow of the power of God. Although He was able to heal a few sick people, He could not work a miracle.

The same verse that talks about a "mega" grace talks about "mega" power (see Acts 4:33, *KJV*). They had mega power because they had mega grace! My point is simply that the aspects of the spirit realm are very tangible and real. The anointing is real. Power is real. We do not see it, but it is there. There are measurable, cumulative amounts that exist in the realm of the spirit.

Certain amounts of this power or river or life must be released in the realm of the spirit to accomplish certain things. Different amounts are required for different things. Just as in the natural you need different levels of power for different things, so it is in the spirit realm. It is like the difference between the amount of power it takes to light a flashlight versus a building, or a building as opposed to a city. The same thing is true in the spirit. Different amounts of God's power are needed to accomplish certain things.

Differing Measures of Power

Let's look again at Mark 6 where Jesus could not get enough power flowing in Nazareth to work a miracle. Enough power was flowing to get some healings, the implication being that they were minor, because the verse differentiates between the healings and miracles. Enough power was flowing for one, but not the other. This implies that differing amounts are needed for different things. Jesus could release enough to get a few healings, but He couldn't get enough flowing, because of their unbelief, to work a miracle.

The disciples in Matthew 17:14-21 had been casting out demons and healing the sick because Jesus had given them authority and power to do so. A lunatic boy was brought to them, however, and they couldn't get the job done. Jesus came along, and it was no problem for Him to exorcise the demon causing the lunacy.

The disciples had enough power flowing in their ministry to deal with most demons and diseases, but they came up against one that required more faith and power—and they didn't have enough to overcome that one! Again, the obvious implication is that different measurable levels are needed to accomplish different things.

I'm thoroughly convinced this principle is a reason it takes awhile to get most prayers answered. Receiving an instant miracle is far and away the exception. Usually it is not just a matter of asking the Father to do something, but rather a matter of releasing enough power in the spirit to get the job done. Most Christians are not aware of this. After asking, we tend to sit back and wait on God when He is often waiting on us. We have failed to understand that there are prayers that do more than just ask Him.

Sometimes, when it appears God has finally "gotten around to it" or when we think something just suddenly happened, the truth is that enough power has finally been released through prayer to accomplish it.

Prophets Who Persevered for the Power

When the prophet Elijah came to the widow's son who had died, he spread himself out on the corpse face to face and prayed three times (see 1 Kings 17:21). Why did it take three times? Because the man of God wasn't where he needed to be spiritually? Because he didn't have enough faith? Because he didn't do it right the first two times?

We are not told the reason, nor is it insinuated that any of those things are true. I believe the reason was that he was releasing a little more life out of his spiritual womb or spirit each time. It takes a good bit of life to raise the dead!

In previous chapters we have looked at 1 Kings 18, where Elijah prayed for rain, and discussed the significance of God choosing to work through man and man travailing to bring forth God's will. Let's look at this passage again.

In 1 Kings 18:1, the Lord said to Elijah, "Go, show yourself to Ahab, and I will send rain on the face of the earth." God didn't say, "I might." He didn't say, "If you pray hard enough." He didn't say, "I'm thinking about it." He just said, "I'm going to do it." It was God's timing, God's idea, God's will.

Yet, we are told at the end of this chapter that Elijah labored in prayer diligently seven times in the posture of a woman in travail before clouds appeared and the rain came. He didn't casually walk to the top of the mountain and say, "Lord, send the rain," and immediately it was done. That's not the "effectual, fervent prayer" James 5:16-18 tells us Elijah did to first stop and then bring the rain.

The question we must ask ourselves is: If it was God's will, timing and idea, then why did Elijah have to pray seven different times until the rain came? The most reasonable explanation to me is that it was necessary to persevere until he had completed enough prayer—until enough power had been released through his intercession to go up into the heavens and get the job done.

Why did it take Daniel 21 days to get his answer when God sent an angel to him the very first day he started praying? I would think if God wanted to send an angelic messenger, He could get it through immediately if He wanted. He has enough power, doesn't He? Then why was this angel detained for 21 days?

I believe Daniel's faithful praying every day was releasing power into the realm of the spirit. Not until enough power was released to break through the demonic opposition in the spirit could God get the angel through with the answer!

Please understand that I am not limiting God's power. I am fully aware that one word from God could rout every demon in hell. What must be factored in is God's decision to work on the earth through man. It seems reasonable to me that if a man's prayers were responsible for the angel being dispatched, they would also be the key to breaking through with the message. As Billheimer said, "Although the answer to his prayer was granted and already on the way, if Daniel had given up it presumably would never have arrived."[11]

Releasing the River of Power

Why did it take Jesus three hours in the Garden of Gethsemane to break through? Why didn't the angels come immediately and comfort Him? Surely God was not holding out on this righteous, sinless man! Power was being released in the spirit to cause the breakthrough.

I am not speaking to you about vain repetition. I am not talking about asking God again and again and again. I am talking about understanding the ways and principles of God enough to know how to release the river in order to give birth to things out of your spiritual womb. When we intercede, cooperating with the Spirit of God, it releases Him to go out from us and hover over a situation, releasing His life-birthing energies until that which we are asking for comes forth.

Why did it take a month to get rid of the cyst on my wife's ovary? What was I doing as I prayed for her an hour every day during that time? I was releasing the river from my womb!

Some would say that God finally did it after I had persevered enough. No. Throughout the entire month, her pain was decreasing, which according to our doctor had to mean the cyst was shrinking. It didn't just suddenly happen. Power being released in the realm of the spirit was accomplishing something physically inside of her. Every day when that power was released, it was destroying the cyst just a little bit more . . . and more . . . and more.

Why did I have to pray for more than a year for the comatose young lady I told you about at the beginning of this book? I went to see her at least once a week for a year, speaking the Word of God, weeping, calling forth a new brain inside of her head and fighting the good fight of faith. Why did it take a year? Because it takes a lot of power to form a new brain. Why didn't God do it instantly? I don't know. I tried everything I knew to get Him to do so.

I said, "Damsel, I say unto you, 'Arise!' " She arose not! I did all the things I'd read about the heroes of faith doing. In faith, I even sat her up in the bed and commanded her to wake up, but like a limp rag doll she flopped back down on her pillow. I do not know why God chose not to do it as an instant miracle, but because He didn't I'm relatively certain of this: A measurable amount of the river had to flow until there was enough of it to produce that miracle.

Ephesians 3:20-21 says:

> Now to Him who is able to do exceeding abundantly beyond all that we ask or think, according to the power that works within us, to Him be the glory in the church and in Christ Jesus to all generations forever and forever, Amen.

The word for "exceeding abundantly beyond" is the same word for the abundant grace of God in Romans 5:20. The word is *huperperissos*. *Perissos* means "superabundant";[12] *huper* means "beyond" or "more than."[13] Together, they would mean super-abundantly with more added to that. That's like saying more than more than.

Ephesians 3:20 says He has enough power to do more than we can ask or think with more added to that—more than more than.

So, why are we often deficient?

Operative Power

The power source is not the problem. The rest of Ephesians 3:20 gives us a clue. It tells us He is going to do this more than more than enough "according to the power that works within us." Wuest translates the phrase "in the measure of the power which is operative in us." The word "measure" is *kata*, which not only has this implication of that which is measured in us, but Strong says it is also used at times with the connotation of "distribution."[14] He is going to do this superabundantly more than we can ask or think in the measure of the power that is distributed from us. Are you distributing power? Are you distributing the river?

Please don't think you are releasing enough power to accomplish the miraculous by sporadic or casual praying. You are not! You must release the power of God inside of you on a consistent basis. James 5:16 says, "The *effectual fervent* prayer of a righteous man availeth much" (*KJV*, emphasis added). Wuest translates it this way: "A prayer of a righteous person is able to do much as it operates." Notice the verse doesn't say, "A prayer of a righteous person is able to do much because it causes God to operate."

It certainly does this, but that's not what this verse is telling us. It says, "A prayer of a righteous person is able to do much as it [*the prayer*] operates." The *Amplified* translation reads, "The earnest (heartfelt, continued) prayer of a righteous man makes tremendous power available [dynamic in its working]." Wow! Our prayers go to work. Notice the word "continued." The *Amplified* captures the present tense meaning of the verb. We have the power inside of us that created the world. We have the same power in us that went into the depths of the earth and took the keys from the kingdom of darkness. We must release it. Release the river! Release the power! Release it and release it and release it and release it some more! Again and again and again!

Tipping the Prayer Bowls of Heaven

As we do, the Scriptures indicate that our prayers accumulate. There are bowls in heaven in which our prayers are stored. Not one bowl for all of them but "bowls." We don't know how many but I think it very likely that each of us has our own bowl in heaven. I don't know if it's literal or symbolic. It doesn't matter. The principle is still the same. God has something in which He stores our prayers for use at the proper time:

> Revelation 5:8: "And when He had taken the book, the four living creatures and the twenty-four elders fell down before the Lamb, having each one a harp, and golden bowls full of incense which are the prayers of the saints."

> Revelation 8:3-5: "And another angel came and stood at the altar, holding a golden censer; and much incense was given to him, that he might add it to the prayers of all the saints upon the golden altar which was before the throne. And the smoke of the incense, with the prayers of the saints, went up before God out of the angel's hand. And the angel took the censer; and he filled it with the fire of the altar and threw it to the earth; and there followed peals of thunder and sounds and flashes of lightning and an earthquake."

According to these verses, either when He knows it is the right time to do something or when enough prayer has accumulated to get the job done, He releases power. He takes the bowl and mixes it with fire from the altar.

I want you to picture this. He takes the same fire that fell on Sinai, the same fire that burned the sacrifice consuming the rocks and water and everything else when Elijah was on the mountain, the same fire that fell at Pentecost, the same fire that destroys His enemies, the very fire of almighty God, and He mixes your bowl of prayers with His fire! Then He pours it upon the earth . . . lightning starts to flash, thunder crashes, the earth quakes. Something awesome happens in the realm of the spirit, which then affects the natural realm.

This must be what happened when Paul and Silas were in jail and began to sing praises late in the night. Worship started ascending, God was anointing it, the bowls filled and God poured it out. The earth literally started quaking, the jail door opened and their shackles fell off. As a result, the first convert in Asia was born again in Philippi. The gospel made its first penetration into a new continent on Earth.

Recently, I believe the Lord showed me what sometimes happens when we come to Him with a need, asking Him to accomplish what He says in His Word. In answer to our requests, He sends His angels to get our bowls of prayer to mix with the fire of the altar. *But there isn't enough in our bowls to meet the need!* We might blame God or think it's not His will or that His Word must not really mean what it says. The reality of it is that sometimes He cannot do what we've asked because we have not given Him enough power in our prayer times to get it done. He has poured out all there was to pour and it wasn't enough! It's not just a faith issue, but also a power issue.

I hope this doesn't alarm you. I get excited when I think about it. I didn't know it at the time, but when I was standing over the comatose girl, every time I spoke the name above every name, every time I prayed in the Spirit, every time I laid hold of His Word and promises, every tear I shed was put in a bottle (see Ps. 56:8)—or a bowl—and God was just watching until finally it was full.

Get Radical—Pour on the Power

And on a Saturday morning in 1986, the Almighty looked over at one of the angels and said, "See the little girl over there whose brain is no longer functioning that has to be fed through her stomach and breathe through a hole in her throat and is lying there like a living dead person and the doctors say there's no hope and that she's going to die? Do you see her? Take this bowl that's been filled, mix it with My fire, and go dump it on her head." The rest is history.

Go into your child's room if he or she is not born again and, preferably when they're not there, put prayer power—substance—in everything they touch. This power can go into clothing or handkerchiefs and minister to people. Enough anointing and power from the river flowed out of Paul's innermost being and went into his handkerchief that notable miracles took place when people touched those handkerchiefs. Enough of it was in Jesus' clothes that when they reached out and grabbed the very bottom edge of it, something flashed out of Him.

You will recall the testimony of Polly Simchen who came to me with a handkerchief and said, "Would you pray over this? We're going to cut it up and put a piece everywhere our son goes. We're going to hide it everywhere we can." As she shared earlier, Polly would come to me every once in a while and say, "I've run out of them. I need another one." So we would pray and douse another one in the anointing of God.

She hid one piece under the insole in her son Jonathan's shoe and he loaned his shoes to a friend. This was the most radical,

drunk, burned-out freak I'd seen in a long time. The friend
made a mistake! He wore the wrong person's shoes! No, actually his life was saved—radically saved, filled with the Spirit of
God and turned on for Jesus. Jonathan lost a rowdy friend because the friend became so filled with the presence of God that
Jonathan couldn't stand to be around him anymore. As we
mentioned earlier, Jonathan is now also living for the Lord.

Smear everything your children have with the anointing!
The Old Testament word "anoint" means "to pour or smear with
oil." It's okay to get a bit radical. Jesus liked it when people tore
roofs off, crawled on hands and knees pressing through crowds,
climbed trees, shouted obnoxiously crying out for mercy, bathed
His feet with tears and hair—He simply loves wholeheartedness.

John Killinger tells about an interesting method used in the
past to break a wild steed by harnessing it to a burro. The powerful steed would take off across the range, twisting and buck-
ing, causing the burro to be tossed about wildly. What a sight!
The steed would run away, pulling the burro alongside, and
they would drop out of sight—sometimes for days. Then they
would return, with the proud little burro in charge. The steed
had worn himself out, fighting the presence of the burro. When
he became too tired to fight anymore, the burro assumed the
position of leader. And that's the way it is many times with
prayer. Victory goes to the persistent, not to the angry; to the
dedicated, not to those who can provide great demonstrations
of emotion and energy. We need committed, determined, systematic prayer, not once in a while fireworks.[15]

Forgive Us, Father

*Father, why is the thing we need the most, the thing we do the least?
Why are most of us so busy we don't have time? You must have
many frustrated days when Your eyes roam to and fro throughout
the earth in search of someone whose heart is completely Yours.*

You must weep often when You seek for a man or woman to stand in the gap to fill the breech and find no one. Your heart must ache at times for us, Your people, to rise up and be what You've called us to be.

We humble ourselves before Your throne and ask You to forgive us for our lack of prayer. And forgive us as leaders, Lord, who have not told Your people the truth. Forgive us as a church—the Body of Christ—for allowing evil to rule in this land when You have more than enough power in our wombs to change it.

Forgive us, for it is not Your fault that we have a generation marked X. It is not Your will that we kill the next generation before it takes its first breath. It is not Your plan that we still have not overcome the principality of hatred that divides this land.

Forgive us, Lord. Cleanse us now and break the curses we have allowed to rule over us. Forgive us and cleanse us from the sin of apathy, complacency, ignorance and unbelief. Wash us with the water of Your Word. Break off of us this lethargic prayerlessness, which we justify a thousand different ways. It really boils down to disobedience, unbelief and sin.

Father, please forgive us and deliver us. Set us free from being hearers of the Word only, and not doers. Give us homes and churches that are founded on the rock of obedience to Your Word. Rise up in Your people with the stubborn tenacity that Jesus had, that the Early Church walked in. Cause us to cast off everything that would oppose Your Spirit, and move us into a realm that pays a price and lays hold of the kingdom of God.

Fill us with Your Spirit. Baptize us in fire. Let there be an impartation of the Spirit of grace and supplication. Let there be an anointing that comes from Your throne to hungry people who are tired of status quo, of mediocrity, of death and destruction. We are tired of it, God. We are tired of being defeated by a defeated enemy. We are tired of being held back from our destiny, both individually and as a nation. We are tired of lack and

disease. We are tired of sin. We are hungry for something—the
God of the Bible!

Questions for Reflection

1. Can you explain the real lesson being taught by the
    story in Luke 11:5-13? Is "the prayer of importunity"
    a good phrase to use in summarizing this passage?

2. What is meant by "the substance" of prayer? How
    does this relate to perseverance?

3. Provide some Scriptures demonstrating that spiri-
    tual things are measurable. Now apply this truth to
    prayer using Ephesians 3:20-21 and James 5:16.

4. Can you think of any situations where you may have
    stopped praying before your "bowl" was filled? Are
    there any current situations in your life that might
    need more power released to receive an answer?

5. Do you love Jesus?

13

ACTIONS THAT SPEAK AND WORDS THAT PERFORM

A Most Amazing Prayer Meeting

In 1988 I was invited to England with a dear friend of mine, Michael Massa, to teach for a week. Two intercessor friends of ours from England, Derek Brant and Lew Sunderland, had invited us to minister to a group of about 40, representing the four British Isles (England, Scotland, Wales and Ireland).

I didn't realize several things going into that week. First, I didn't factor in the combined *years* of intercession represented by the group—Lew alone had been interceding for England nearly 30 years. This small, insignificant detail meant simply that *anything could happen.*

Second, I didn't know the Holy Spirit was going to show up with such intensity that on the final evening I wouldn't be able to finish my message. When I paused and said, "The presence of God is so strong, I just cannot continue," a spirit of repentance and intercession for England came upon everyone and lasted all night.

Without question, it became one of the most amazing prayer experiences of my life. The prophetic actions and declarations that went forth—terms that I'll explain shortly—were incredible. We spoke Ezekiel 37:1-10 over the land in the same way Ezekiel himself prophesied to the dry bones of Israel and to the breath of God. We sat silently for over an hour—no one moving or uttering a word—in deep repentance and the fear of the Lord. The men among us walked the grounds all night in repentance and prophetic intercession, standing in the gap for the men of the land. It was truly an amazing night.

Third, I wasn't aware at the time that God was calling me to and giving me spiritual authority for the nation of England. I had received prophetic words and Scriptures from individuals speaking of a call to the nations. And I had certainly felt this was true, but I wasn't aware of a particular call for England, nor of the divine authority accompanying it.

I had been given Jeremiah 1:10 on more than one occasion: "See, I have appointed you this day over the nations and over the kingdoms, to pluck up and to break down, to destroy and to overthrow, to build and to plant." However, I wasn't sure I wanted such a calling, and must admit I didn't fully embrace it.

England's Call to a Reluctant Prophet

In May 1994 this same group invited me back to England, along with a worship team from the States, led by a close friend and associate, David Morris.

"It is time to follow up our last meeting by marrying the Spirit and the Word through anointed prophetic worship, followed by you, Dutch, speaking a prophetic message over the nation," they told me. "We're going to rent some of the old cathedrals around England and have the services in them. We feel this will release some things in the spirit and further pave the way for God to move."

"I don't have a prophetic message for England and besides, I'm too busy," was my response. I maintained this position for months, up until several weeks before the meetings were to take place. At that time three different intercessors told me within the span of one week that I had missed God's leading and was supposed to go to England.

Oh, they were nice about it and very respectful, but the Holy Spirit was a little more blunt in interpreting for them: *Wake up, Sheets!*

Being the spiritually astute man that I am, three independent words of correction were enough. After the last one, I immediately picked up the phone and instructed my secretary to call England, informing them that I had missed God and would come if they had no one else.

"No, we don't have anyone else," they told her. "We knew he was supposed to do it. We've just been waiting for him to hear."

It makes you feel terribly unspiritual when everyone in the world knows God's will for your life, but you!

Lest you begin to mistake this book for an autobiography, I'll get to the point. In the last of our meetings in England, all of which were very powerful, we were ministering in Westminster Chapel.

As I was preparing myself to preach in this well-known church laced with a rich and wonderful heritage, located just a block or two from Buckingham Palace, I heard these words deep in my spirit (I trust you're ready for this. You probably know by now that I can be a bit on the radical side.): *You are not preaching to the people in attendance tonight. You are preaching to this nation. You are to declare My Word to it, calling it back to righteousness, to holiness, to repentance, to Me. Call forth My anointing, My fire and My presence to this land again.*

Not wanting my hosts to think me too strange, I informed them as to what I intended to do. Then I did it!

I preached to the air.

I preached to the government.

I preached to the sinners of England.

I preached to the entire Body of Christ of England.

And I've never worked harder in my life. I felt as though I was warring against and trying to push through hordes of demons. At the conclusion of my message, I sat down behind the platform totally exhausted, drenched with perspiration and almost in a daze. I had no sense of victory or defeat, only of exhaustion from the battle.

Lew Sunderland, the matriarchal intercessor responsible for inviting and praying me there, a true mother in the faith, approached me with a sweet and understanding smile. Placing my cheeks in her hands, she assured me, "It's all right, darling, you made it through. You accomplished what was needed." She then said to me later, "You have accepted now, haven't you, darling"—to Lew everyone is darling—"that God has called you to this nation and has given you authority here?"

"Yes, ma'am," I said meekly and submissively, as would a small child to its mother after having just learned a valuable lesson.

"You won't question it any longer, now, will you?"

"No, ma'am."

"That's good. We'll just have you back when the Lord says it's time. Okay?"

"Yes, ma'am."

I returned the next month!

We received a call from England the week following our ministry. The message was, "Revival has broken out in London." Renewal had, indeed, hit the nation, with many people coming to Christ and thousands receiving a renewing touch of the Holy Spirit.

The Boomerang Anointing: Action and Declaration

I would never presume that revival came solely because of our ministry. The years of intercession by many and the countless hours of selfless labor by hundreds of godly men and women had much more to do with it than anything our team ever could have done. What part did we play? Prophetic worship—declaring through pageantry and song the splendor, greatness, rule and authority of God, and prophetic declaration—proclaiming the will and Word of the Lord into the spirit realm.

There is an interesting aspect of intercession few people understand and still fewer do. It is *prophetic action and declaration.* What do we mean by this? When we say something is "prophetic," we mean it's foretelling (speaking about or predicting future things) or forthtelling (actions or words that declare something for God). In the latter case it may not be futuristic at all. Something that is prophetic in nature can be one or both—foretelling or forthtelling.

Either of them can have a forerunning or preparatory purpose. Prophetic words or actions prepare a way, in the same sense that John the Baptist, the prophet, prepared the way with his words and actions for the Messiah to come and for the glory of the Lord to be revealed (see Isa. 40:1-5). Prophetic ministry releases the way for the glory of the Lord and the ministry of Jesus to follow. Prophetic actions and declarations prepare the way for God to work upon the earth.

In a sense, they release God to do something, as they become the implemented means or method through which He has chosen to work. They do not release Him in the sense that He is bound—God obviously is not bound. But they release Him in the sense that:

1. Obedience to God brings a response from God. As we shall see later in the chapter, prophetic actions and declarations mean nothing if they are not directed by God. In the same sense, when He gives instruction, it must be obeyed. He chooses to do things a certain way and when that way is implemented, it

releases God to do what He wants to do. He doesn't always explain why we must do it a particular way. Being God, He has that right. But when His chosen way is implemented, He does what He needs to do.

2. Faith releases God. When He says, "Do this," faith and obedience release Him.

3. They release Him in the sense that His creative and effectual Word is released upon the earth. God's creative power, energy and ability that come forth through His Words are released upon the earth through prophetic declaration! If you are not open to revelation, you'll never be able to embrace this. Open your heart to enlightenment.

A more complete definition would be: Prophetic action or declaration is something said or done in the natural realm at the direction of God that prepares the way for Him to move in the spiritual realm, which then consequently effects change in the natural realm. How's that for God and man partnering? God says to do or say something. We obey. Our words or actions impact the heavenly realm, which then impacts the natural realm. Maybe this is the "boomerang anointing"!

I'm sure by now you could use some biblical examples of this, so let me give you several. First, I want to give you biblical examples of prophetic action that preceded and/or released literal action in the earth. Then we'll examine some prophetic declarations.

Prophetic Action
Moses stretching forth his rod over the Red Sea is an example of prophetic action (see Exod. 14:21). Why did he have to stretch forth his rod? Because God said to. He wanted the symbolic rod of authority to be stretched over the Red Sea. If there had been

no extending of the rod over the sea, there would not have been a rolling back of the sea. God essentially said, "I want a prophetic act to release Me to do this!"

Another example of prophetic action is Moses' holding up the rod of authority at Rephidim where Israel was battling with Amalek (see Exod. 17:9-13). I shared the story in chapter 9 to point out the difference between authority and power, but it is also a vivid demonstration of prophetic action.

Moses was up on the mountain with the rod of authority lifted. When he held it up, Israel prevailed. When he let it down because of fatigue, Amalek prevailed. Morale wasn't the issue. Do you think those soldiers on the battlefield, instead of fighting, were watching Moses? It had nothing to do with morale—they probably didn't even see the rod going up and down.

It had to do with something happening in the realm of the spirit. This prophetic action was releasing something in the heavenlies. As it did, the authority of God was bouncing back to earth and giving victory to the Israelites. I can't explain it any more than that. Some things, when dealing with God, simply cannot be explained.

God's Way, Even When It Makes No Sense

Moses' hitting the rock in Exodus 17:6 is another example of prophetic action. He took the rod of authority, struck the rock and water came out. Why? Because God wanted it done that way. We could elaborate on all the symbolism of these actions and possibly understand why God did them, but the bottom line is: When He chose to do it a certain way, someone had to perform an act upon the earth that often made no sense, but when performed, released something in the spirit, which released something upon Earth. A person doesn't normally get water out of rocks when he or she hits them with a rod . . . unless God says to do it. Again, when He tells us to act, it impacts the spirit, affects the earth and produces results—like bringing water out of rocks. That's prophetic action!

Many of these examples appear in Scripture. In 2 Kings 13:14-19, Elisha was about to die and King Joash came to him for advice. The Assyrians were camped around Israel and he wanted some instruction from the prophet. Elisha said, "Take your arrow and shoot it out the window toward the enemy camp!" It was a declaration of war. The king and the prophet put their hands on the bow together, shooting the arrow. Elisha then said, "That's the arrow of the Lord's deliverance, King. Now take these arrows and strike the ground."

The king was about to be tested. His actions were going to be prophetic. Not knowing what the prophet was up to, he took the arrows and struck the ground three times.

The prophet was grieved and angry. "Three times you will have victory over your enemies, and then they will conquer you," he said. "You should have struck with the arrows at least five or six times, then you would have conquered them!"

This story doesn't seem fair to me. How was the king supposed to know he should keep striking? I think the point is that if God says to hit it three times, then you hit it three times. But if God simply says hit it, you hit it until He says stop! God was after prophetic action, but He didn't get what He wanted. Neither did the king!

People were healed in Scripture through prophetic action. Jesus made clay with saliva, rubbed it in a blind man's eyes and told him to go wash in the pool of Siloam (see John 9:6-7). Naaman the leper had to dip in the Jordan River seven times (see 2 Kings 5:10-14).

"I don't want to," he said.

"Then you won't get healed," replied Naaman's servants. Why? Because God chose to work in that way. And when God chooses to do it by a certain method, no other means will work.

Cindy Jacobs describes prophetic acts in her book *The Voice of God*:

> At other times, God would ask His people as a whole to do something that not only was prophetic, but also had great power as a form of intercession to bring profound change when obeyed. . . . In 1990, a team from Women's Aglow went to Russia to intercede for that nation. We were led to perform several prophetic acts. Our trip came before the fall of Soviet communism and several things happened that led us to believe we were being monitored. Before we left, my friend Beth Alves had a dream that we had actually buried the Word of God in the ground. This was to result in a critical prophetic act later in the trip.
>
> One strategy we used for intercession was to take a bus tour around the city. City tours are great because they take the visitors to all the historical sites. One place the tour visited was Moscow State University, a bastion of communist teaching. As we sat on a wall near the school, I suddenly remembered Beth's dream and thought of the "Four Spiritual Laws" tract I had in my purse. In a flash, I knew this was the place to do what Beth had dreamed about.
>
> I quickly jumped up (we had just a few minutes before the bus was leaving) and said, "Come on, let's plant the Word in the ground!" Several of the ladies came after me. Huffing and puffing as we ran, I reminded them of Beth's dream and told them of the tract. I glanced around to find the shelter of some trees in which to do the prophetic act. (We had encountered a person in Red Square that day whom we were pretty sure was a KGB agent, and since we weren't interested

in a premature prison ministry we had to be careful!)

Finding a sheltered place, I knelt and started to dig. This was a dismal failure as I only succeeded in breaking my fingernails. Finally, I found a stick and dug a hole. Dropping the tract into the ground, I quickly covered it up while the ladies prayed. Pointing toward the university, I began to prophesy, "The seed from this tract will grow schools of evangelism, and theology will be taught here."

Later on, after the fall of Russian communism, Billy Graham did start schools of evangelism there. Sister Violet Kitely, a friend of mine, told me that a church has been planted in Moscow State University by Shiloh Christian Center (a large church in Oakland, California).

What happens through these prophetic acts? They are intercessory in nature. In fact, they might be called intercessory acts. Certain aspects of what happens might seem speculative in nature. We cannot prove a correlation between obedience in doing a prophetic act and, say, the starting of schools of evangelism. Time and time again in Scripture, however, we see where God spoke to His children to perform an intercessory, prophetic act, and He powerfully moved as a result.[1]

Prophetic Declaration

Let's look at some biblical examples of prophetic words that precede God's doing something. In Jeremiah 6:18-19, Jeremiah prophesied and said, "Therefore hear, O nations . . . Hear, O earth." Similarly, in Jeremiah 22:29, he again prophesied, saying, "O earth, earth, earth, hear the word of the Lord" (KJV).

Many would think I was an utter fool if I walked out of my house and said, "All the earth, hear me now! And all the nations, I'm speaking to you." But that's what Jeremiah did. It was prophetic declaration that made no sense naturally.

We must understand that it is not an issue of what our words would normally do. It is rather speaking *for God*, which releases His power to accomplish something. Isn't this what happens as we preach or declare the gospel, which is the power of God for salvation (see Rom. 1:16)?

Our mouths, speaking God's Word, release the power of those words. Is this not also what occurs when we speak His Word as a sword in spiritual warfare? He infuses our words with divine power. Why then would He not in other situations allow us to be His voice? When Jeremiah said, "O Earth! Earth! Earth! Hear the Word of the Lord!" it was exactly the same as if God Himself were saying, "O Earth! Earth! Earth! Hear My Words!"

God told Jeremiah earlier that He was going to use him "to pluck up and to break down, to destroy and to overthrow, to build and to plant" (Jer. 1:10). Notice, then, in Jeremiah 31:28 He says He has done just that: plucked up, broken down, overthrown and destroyed. It is imperative to see that God did these things through the words of His prophet.

In Micah 1:2, the prophet said, "Hear, O peoples, all of you; listen, O earth and all it contains."

Wouldn't you feel rather foolish saying, "O earth and everything in it, God wants me to talk to you. Are you listening?" Micah did just that, however. Obviously all the earth didn't hear him . . . no more than the storm heard Jesus tell it to be still or the fig tree heard Him command it to die. Whether anything hears us isn't the point. What we are to understand is the power of Holy Spirit-inspired declaration—it releases the power of God into situations.

We Become His Voice

"But those were the prophets and Jesus," some might argue. Yes, but after rebuking the storm, Jesus rebuked the disciples for their fear and unbelief, implying that they should have rebuked it. He also followed up His cursing of the fig tree with a promise that we could speak to mountains and cast them into the sea. He is describing the power of Holy Spirit-inspired declaration. We become the voice of God upon the earth.

In her book *The Praying Church*, Sue Curran quotes S. D. Gordon:

> Prayer surely does influence God. It does not influence His *purpose*. It does influence His *action*. Everything that ever has been prayed for, of course I mean every right thing, God has already purposed to do. But He does nothing without our consent. He has been hindered in His purposes by our lack of willingness. When we learn His purposes and make them our prayers we are giving Him the opportunity to act.[2]

Hosea 6:5 is a powerful verse about God bringing judgment: "Therefore I have hewn them in pieces by the prophets; I have slain them by the words of My mouth." How did He do this? Through His words spoken by the prophets. God's words, released for Him by humans.

It is important to state clearly that to be effective, declarations must be the words or actions God commands. "So shall *My* word be which goes forth from *My* mouth; it shall not return to Me empty, without accomplishing what *I* desire, and without succeeding in the matter for which *I* sent it" (Isa. 55:11, emphasis added).

Please realize that when God said this, He was not talking about speaking from the clouds. He was referring to what He had been saying and was still saying to them through the prophet Isaiah. In essence He was declaring, "This man's words are My words. He is My voice. The words won't return to Me void, but will do exactly what I send them to do through this man!" That's pretty awesome!

Of course, there are some who say God doesn't speak anything directly to us today—He only uses the Bible—which would
mean the only thing we can declare for Him is Scripture. I have
great respect for my brothers and sisters who believe this, and
would encourage them to speak the words of the Bible into situations. To others of you who believe the Holy Spirit does
speak in our spirits, listen for His direction as you pray and,
when so led, boldly speak and do as He instructs. Of course, all
that we do must be judged by and never violate the Scriptures.

Beth Alves, in her outstanding prayer guide, *Becoming a Prayer
Warrior*, gives excellent and thorough instruction about hearing the voice of God.[3] It would be wise to study this or a similar
book to ensure accuracy in learning to hear God's voice. Also,
check with godly and mature leaders before doing anything of
a public nature or something that seems extremely strange.
Don't take your cue from the prophet Isaiah and run around
town naked (he probably wore a loincloth). Use wisdom and,
when in doubt, always check it out. If that isn't possible, when
in doubt, don't. Never do anything that contradicts Scripture
or might bring a reproach on the name of the Lord.

Saying What God Says

The word in the New Testament for "confession" is *homologia*,
which means "say the same thing."[4] Biblical confession is saying what God says—no more, no less. If it isn't what God is
saying about a situation, it does nothing. But if it is what He
says, it accomplishes much.

The Word of God is called a "seed" in the Scriptures. The
root word in Greek is *speiro*. *Spora* and *sperma* are variations of
the word, both of which are translated "seed" in the New Testament. It is easy to see the English words "spore" and "sperm"
in them.

God's method of reproducing or bringing forth life is His Word by which we are born again (see 1 Pet. 1:23), cleansed (see John 15:3), matured (see Matt. 13:23), freed (see John 8:31-32), healed (see Ps. 107:20)—as well as many other results. When God speaks His word, He is sprinkling seeds that will bring forth. The Word of God is never ineffective; it will always produce. When we speak God's Words into situations, as the Holy Spirit directs, we are sprinkling the seeds of God, which then give Him the ability to cause life to come forth!

Job 22:28 declares, "You will also decree a thing, and it will be established for you." The word "decree" means literally "decide and decree"[5]—determine something and then decree it. The actual meaning of *omer*, the word translated "thing" is "a word; a command; a promise."[6]

A more precise wording would be, "You shall decree or declare a word." Then He says it will be established for you. "Establish" is the word *qum*, meaning not only to establish, but also to "arise or stand up."[7] Here's what I believe God is saying: "You shall decree a word and it will rise up. You shall sprinkle My seed. It will arise (grow) and establish something in the earth."

Why don't you establish some salvation upon the earth by decreeing salvation seeds? Establish freedom for someone by declaring freedom seeds. Establish unity over your church or city by commanding unity seeds. Establish God's destiny over your children by sowing destiny seeds. Plant your own personal garden. Tend it well. See if God's Word won't produce a harvest. Re-present the victory of Calvary from your mouth!

Job 6:25 reads: "How forcible are right words!" (*KJV*). "Forcible" is the word *marats*, which also means "to press."[8] As the signet ring of a king presses a document with his seal, our words also seal things. They seal our salvation, the promises of God, our destinies and many other things.[9]

Ecclesiastes 12:11 tells us, "The words of the wise are as goads, and as nails fastened by the masters of assemblies" (*KJV*). Our words act as nails constructing things in the spirit. Just as a nail is used to keep a board in place, words are used to keep God's promises in place, allowing them to build or construct things in the spirit.[10]

Prophesying to Bones and Breath

Ezekiel and the Valley of Dry Bones is another example of prophetic declaration. "Speak to the bones!" God said to the prophet.

Can you imagine what Ezekiel thought? *Speak to them? God, if You want something said to skeletons, why don't You just do it?* But Ezekiel obeyed and said, "O dry bones, hear the word of the Lord." And they did! Bone came to bone, flesh came on them.

There was no life in them, however, and Ezekiel's next assignment amazes me more than prophesying to the bones. The Lord said, "Prophesy to the breath." Later in the passage we're told that the breath he was prophesying to was the Holy Spirit. God didn't say, "Prophesy *by* the Holy Spirit," nor did He say, "Prophesy *for* the Holy Spirit." God said, "I want you to prophesy *to* the Holy Spirit." Ezekiel did and the Spirit of God did what a man told Him to. Incredible!

Did the prophet actually command the Holy Spirit? Not really. He wasn't commanding God; He was commanding *for* God. As has been God's plan and heart from the Creation, He was partnering with man. Father and Sons, Inc. managing the planet! God working through the prophetic declaration of a human being. Who can fully understand such a thing?

Talking to the Wall

Several years ago the Lord sent Dick Eastman, president of Every Home for Christ, to Berlin. How would you like to get this assignment from God? The Berlin Wall was still up, and Dick felt the Holy Spirit prompting him with these instructions: *I want you to get on an airplane, fly to Germany, go to the Berlin Wall, lay your hands upon it and say five words to it: "In Jesus' name, come down!"* That was it—end of assignment! Five words and he could go home.[11]

How would you like to go to your spouse and say, "Uh, honey, the Lord has told me to do something."

"Yes, what is it?"

"Well, He wants me to go to Germany."

"Okay, what are you going to do over there?"

"Go to the Berlin Wall."

"Oh? What are you going to do at the Wall?"

"I'm going to put my hands on it and say, 'In Jesus' name, come down!' and then I'm going to come home."

Wouldn't that make for an interesting discussion?

That's exactly what Dick did, because he understood the power of prophetic action and declaration. Dick would never claim to be the only person used by God to bring down the Berlin Wall. However, shortly thereafter the Wall was torn down.

A Vision for the Youth

A few years ago I was in Washington, D.C., for the National Day of Prayer with the Master's Commission, a group of young people from Spokane, Washington. My wife, Ceci, and I accompanied them because, while I had been ministering to them a couple of months prior, I had an incredible picture—I believe it was a vision. The picture was of a stadium filled with young people who were radically committed to God. As I watched, this multitude of young people filed out of the stadium and flooded the nation, taking revival with them.

I shared the picture with these young people and a spirit of intercession came upon us that lasted for about 30 minutes. It was truly an awesome time of prayer for the youth of America.

As we finished praying, I felt I was to join these youths on their upcoming trip to Washington, D.C.

Shortly after we arrived in Washington, D.C., I sensed the Lord speak to me: *I'm going to confirm to you on this trip that I am sending revival to this nation. I'm also going to demonstrate to you that the youth will play a major role in it.*

The Vision Confirmed

My first confirmation came on The National Day of Prayer. There were probably 400 to 500 people gathered for the primary prayer meeting that morning—senators, congressmen, statesmen and spiritual leaders of the nation. I wasn't part of the program but was there to agree in prayer, as were most of the attendees. The Master's Commission had somehow received permission to be in the program, which was a miracle in itself. When these young people were invited up for their 15 minutes, they walked down the aisle singing, "Heal Our Land."

As they sang, the Spirit of God fell over the room like a blanket. Perhaps hovered would be a better way to phrase it. At no other point was the presence of God felt as strongly. I didn't see anyone present who wasn't weeping. Dr. James Dobson, who spoke after the Master's Commission, commented through tears that it is not often we get to witness history in the making. I'm sure everyone in attendance believed that day impacted the history of our nation.

These young people then rendezvoused with Norm Stone, a man from their church, Harvest Christian Fellowship. God called Norm several years ago to walk across America seven times as a prophetic act of repentance and intercession for the babies murdered in America through abortion. That is prophetic action! The Master's Commission, most of whom were from the same church, walked behind him, 20 miles a day for two weeks, praying.

The night before these young people were to join Norm, I heard these words from the Lord: *This is a prophetic declaration by Me that the generation that Satan tried to annihilate through abortion— My next generation of warriors in the earth—have not and will not be destroyed. I'm sending these young people to march behind Norm as a prophetic message saying, "No! This is My generation, Satan, and you will not have them!"*

Later that evening I heard the words, *I'm going to confirm to you once more that I'm sending revival to this nation in which the youth will have a major role. I'll do it through the Bible reading you're to do tonight.*

I was scheduled to be part of a three-day read-a-thon, the entire Bible being read by individuals while facing the Capitol building. Each person participating was allowed to read for 15 minutes, no more. We were required to read from wherever the progression happened to be in the Bible when our turn came. I didn't pick my reading time—someone else had signed me up the previous day and informed me I was supposed to be there at midnight the following night.

Due to the nature of the Lord's dealings with me at that time, I told Him, "Lord, there is only one way I could know of a certainty that You are confirming these things to me through my Bible reading. When I arrive, they must tell me that I can either read the book of Habakkuk or Haggai." This was not a fleece, nor was I testing God. It was because of the things I had already sensed Him saying to me through these two books.

Do you know the size of these books? They consist of *eight pages* in my Bible. What would the odds be, when not choosing my own reading—nor even the time of my reading, of my showing up and being told, "Here, read from these eight pages."

I walked up to the lady in charge.

"Are you Dutch Sheets?"

"Yes, I am."

"You are on in 15 minutes, after this person. You have your choice. You can either read the book of Haggai or the book of Habakkuk."

I nearly passed out! You can believe I read the Word of the Lord with authority, making prophetic declaration over the government of this nation with absolute faith that revival is coming.

Whatever He Says, Do It!

God is calling the Church to a new understanding of prophetic action and declaration, functioning as His voice and Body upon the earth. When He speaks His plan to us, however foolish it may seem—to hold up a rod, speak to the spiritually dead, walk our neighborhoods, march through our streets, hit rocks, decree to the earth, lay hands on and speak to oppressive walls, walk across America, read the Bible toward the Capitol, speak to a nation that isn't listening—He needs us to DO IT!

The Lord may lead you to go to the bedroom of a rebellious child and anoint things with oil, pray over clothing, speak over the child's bed, or some other symbolic act. Others of you will be called to make declarations over your cities and governments. Some will be told to march on land, claiming it for the kingdom of God. Whatever He says to you, do it. Be bold to declare the Word of the Lord over and into situations. Sprinkle the seed of His Word into the earth and expect a harvest. It will be established. It will arise! Life will come!

"You do know now that you're called to do this, don't you, darling?"

Questions for Reflection

1. Define prophetic action and declaration. Explain how they "release" God. Now give some biblical examples.

2. Can you explain the connection between God's Word, seeds and our Holy Spirit-inspired declarations?

3. Can you find some verses of Scripture that would be good to decree for an individual's salvation? . . . Healing? How about Scriptures to decree over your city?

4. Isn't God good?

THE WATCHMAN ANOINTING

The Genetic Plague

The only thing worse than shopping is watching someone shop. Except for my wife, of course. I don't mind at all following her around a mall for two or three hours. I show my interest periodically with pleasant little grunts—"Umph"; "Un-huh"; "Ahh-hum." Sometimes I get downright wordy—"Yes"; "No"; "Sure"; "HOW MUCH?!" I've gotten pretty quick at correcting that one: "Wow, what a deal!" I hastily add. About the closest thing I can compare "shopper watching" to would be watching a sewing match.

Which is why I'm sitting in the food court writing while my wife and youngest daughter, Hannah, shop. It's one of those outlet malls where they sell you the flawed stuff "on sale." My oldest daughter, Sarah, is with me, reading. She doesn't like shopping, either—yet. I informed her on the way to our "food court refuge" of the gene in her—which God gave all women—that simply hasn't kicked in yet. Told her not to worry, it'll happen.

In my studies of this genetic plague—most of them done through conversing with other men in food courts—I have discovered that no one knows for sure when the gene kicks in or what triggers it. It can hit anytime between the ages of 6 and 13. Sometimes it happens in the middle of the night; they just wake up with the shakes—flu-like symptoms. When it happened with

Hannah, I was ready to anoint her with oil, until Ceci informed me it wouldn't help.

"What do you mean it won't help?" I asked in surprise. "Of course it will."

"No," she said, "it's her shopping gene kicking in. We've got to get her to a mall—fast."

Mom was right, of course. She usually is. Hannah came home proudly holding her shopping bag, looking like she'd just caught her first fish. Women! Who can figure?

To prove my point, I just counted the men and women in the food court and surrounding stores—26 females and 9 males. Half the males were kids that had been dragged there against their wills. Another was writing—yours truly—and the rest were grunting, "Uh-huh." I felt sorry for one guy; he actually looked like a zombie. I think he finally cracked under the stress.

Ceci and Hannah are back now, getting something to drink and showing us their "deals." I'm grunting. Ceci is merely dropping Hannah off so that she can run back for one more thing. Seven-year-olds—apprentice shoppers—can't always keep up with the pros. They haven't had enough aerobics classes, for which the real motivation is shopping conditioning.

Watching What You Watch

Why couldn't God have made women to like normal things, such as sitting in a woods for days in sub-zero weather, waiting for a deer or elk to walk by? Now that's my idea of exciting watching! . . . Or watching a football game! I'm not into TV too much—unless it's a good sporting event. Ceci doesn't always understand me in this area, but she is kind about it. "Who are you rooting for?" she sometimes asks.

"I don't care who wins," I often reply.

"Are these any of your favorite teams?"

"No, not really."

"A favorite player or two, perhaps?"

"Naw, I don't know much about these guys at all."

"Then why are you watching the game?" she asks with a quizzical expression.

"Because it's football," I reply as patiently as I possibly can. Sometimes people can't figure out the obvious. I'll tell you what puzzles me—why she and my two daughters like to watch stuff that makes them cry. Go figure!

Many kinds of watching take place: TV watching, parade watching, watching the clock, stock market watching, bird watching (ranks right up there with sewing matches to me), and a thousand other things. I like to watch kids laugh. I hate to watch people cry. I've watched individuals born; I've watched others die.

I once watched a lady in San Pedro, Guatemala, look for a watch. It was her husband's—he died in the earthquake of 1976. So did three of her kids. All she and her surviving infant had left were the clothes on their backs. Their small adobe home was a mound of dirt.

When our interpreter asked her what she was digging for, she replied, "A bag of beans we had and my husband's watch. He was sleeping about here when he was killed," she said, pointing at an area of approximately 10 square feet. "It would mean so much to me if I could find his watch."

We started digging.

Although it was like looking for a needle in a haystack, we asked God to help us and waded into the three-feet-deep dirt. Right then I'd have charged hell for that watch. We found it an hour or so later.

"Muchas gracias," she repeated through tears, as she clutched the watch to her breast.

"Treasure" is such a relative term, I thought as I wiped my eyes. *I wish the world could see this. Maybe some priorities would change.*

I watched another lady, holding her three-year-old daughter, walk away from a food line in which I was serving. She was the last in line for the soup. As she held out the jar she had found, we looked at her and said, "No mas" (which means "No more"). Then I watched her walk away, holding her hungry child.

Things got all messed up at that point in my life. Neat little lists of needs disappeared. Certain important goals became strangely irrelevant. Things that mattered suddenly didn't. Bank accounts were looked at differently; success was redefined. Funny how one glance into four eyes can bring such chaos. In many ways, order has never been restored.

Be careful what you watch.

Be on the Alert

The Bible talks about watching—in various ways and for different reasons, not the least of which is watching in prayer. This chapter is about the "watchman anointing"—our calling and equipping as intercessors to be forewarned of and to pray against Satan's schemes and plans. It is a vital aspect of our intercession. Ephesians 6:18 says, "With all prayer and petition pray at all times in the Spirit, and with this in view, *be on the alert* with all perseverance and petition for all the saints" (emphasis added). The *KJV* version uses the word "watching" for the phrase "be on the alert."

First Peter 5:8, in warning us about our enemy, says, "Be of sober spirit, *be on the alert.* Your adversary, the devil, prowls about like a roaring lion, seeking someone to devour" (emphasis added). Again, other translations use the word "watchful." The context of both verses is spiritual warfare. Each mentions our adversary and challenges us to alertness or watchfulness, both for ourselves and for our brothers and sisters in Christ.

Another related verse, which we discussed in great detail in chapter 9, is 2 Corinthians 2:11: "In order that no advantage be taken of us by Satan; for we are not ignorant of his schemes."

So as not to duplicate the material, I will simply summarize the deducted meaning we gave of the verse based on the Greek words used: "To the degree that we are ignorant of the way our adversary thinks and operates—of his plans, plots, schemes and devices—to that degree he will gain on us, prey on us, defraud us of what is ours and have or hold the greater portion."

I want to draw four conclusions from these three verses—Ephesians 6:18, 1 Peter 5:8 and 2 Corinthians 2:11—as an introduction for this teaching:

1. *Protection from the attacks of our enemy—even for believers—is not automatic.* There is a part for us to play. Though God is sovereign, this does not mean He is in control of everything that happens. He has left much to the decisions and actions of humankind. If God were going to protect or safeguard us from Satan's attacks regardless of what we did, these verses would be totally irrelevant to Christians. Somewhere in our theology, we must find a place for human responsibility. At some point we must begin to believe that we matter, that we're relevant, for ourselves and for others.

2. *God's plan is to warn or alert us to Satan's tactics.* This is deduced from the simple fact that since God says not to be unaware of Satan's tactics, He must be willing to make us aware of them. If He says to be on the alert, this must mean that if we are, He will alert us. God wouldn't ask of us something that He wasn't also enabling us to accomplish.

3. *We must be alert—remain watchful—or we won't pick up on God's attempts to warn us of Satan's attacks and plans.*

If these attacks were always going to be obvious, alertness wouldn't be necessary. Isaiah 56:10 speaks of blind watchmen. What a picture! I'm afraid it has been a fairly good description of many of us in our watching roles. We're often like the disciples of old: We have eyes, but we do not see (see Mark 8:18). It's time we do more than gaze; we must alertly watch!

4. *If we are not alert and watchful, if we are ignorant of Satan's schemes, he will take the bigger portion.* He will gain on us, taking advantage of our ignorance. Contrary to popular belief, we really can be destroyed due to ignorance (see Hos. 4:6). We may not like to admit it, but Satan really has gained a lot of territory in America. Don't be like the desert nomad who awakened hungrily one night and decided he'd have a midnight snack. Lighting a candle, he grabbed a date and took a bite. Holding the date to the candle, he saw a worm, whereupon he threw the date out of the tent. Biting into the second date, he found another worm and threw it away, also. Deciding he might not get anything to eat if this continued, he blew out the candle and ate the dates.[1]

Sometimes we, too, prefer the darkness of denial to the light of truth. Though the truth really does hurt at times, it is still truth. Denial doesn't change it. Where Satan has made gains, let's admit it and determine to take them back!

Two New Testament words for "watching" make the connection to the Old Testament concept of watchmen: *gregoreuo* and *agrupneo*. Both mean essentially to stay awake, in the sense that a sentry would need to refrain from sleep. Some of the verses where they're found are the following:

Devote yourselves to prayer, keeping alert in it with an attitude of thanksgiving (Col. 4:2).

And He said to them, "My soul is deeply grieved to the point of death; remain here and keep watch. . . . Keep watching and praying, that you may not come into temptation; the spirit is willing, but the flesh is weak" (Mark 14:34,38).

Be of sober spirit, be on the alert. Your adversary, the devil, prowls about like a roaring lion, seeking someone to devour (1 Pet. 5:8).

Be on the alert, stand firm in the faith, act like men, be strong (1 Cor. 16:13).

With all prayer and petition pray at all times in the Spirit, and with this in view, be on the alert with all perseverance and petition for all the saints (Eph. 6:18).

But keep on the alert at all times, praying in order that you may have strength to escape all these things that are about to take place, and to stand before the Son of Man (Luke 21:36).

The last two verses combine *agrupneo* with *kairos*, the strategic time (discussed in chapter 6), challenging us to be on the alert for the *kairos* times and pray accordingly. Again, so as not to be repetitive, we won't repeat the teaching. However, another look at the full definitions of *paga* and *kairos* in chapter 6 will enable you to make the obvious connection between the watchmen and setting boundaries of protection.

The Trophies of Intercession

I will share one story, however, to illustrate. Cindy Jacobs, in her book *Possessing the Gates of the Enemy*, tells of walking in the watchman anointing at a *kairos* time. While attending a prayer gathering in 1990, she was awakened one night at 2:00 A.M. with a sense of alarm. As she waited on the Lord, He brought to her mind the picture of a couple and their three children, a family she knew was traveling in their van to the meeting. In this vision she saw a wheel on their van come off, causing a terrible accident.

Cindy began to pray fervently for their safety and continued throughout the night. Upon their arrival the following day, she asked if they had had any problems with the right wheel. Though they had not, Cindy insisted they go to a garage and get it checked. The mechanic who inspected the van was amazed. He said there was no way they should have been able to drive the van without the wheel coming off.

Upon returning from the mechanic, Cindy's husband, Mike, who had accompanied the brother to the garage, held up a bag and declared, "The trophies of intercession." It held the old bearings from the right front wheel.[2]

That is the watchman anointing in operation, sensing the danger at a *kairos* time and establishing boundaries (*paga*) of protection through intercession.

Biblical Watchmen

Let's broaden our understanding of biblical watchmen. What was their purpose? The term "watchmen" comes from the Old Testament and was used to describe what we would today call "sentries," "guards" or "lookouts." These individuals were responsible for protecting primarily two things: vineyards or fields from thieves and animals, and cities from invading forces.

Those watching crops were stationed on rocks, buildings or towers to provide a better range of vision. Towers or outposts in the fields usually had sleeping quarters because it was necessary to keep watch day and night during harvest. The watchmen would take shifts—one working, one sleeping—and thereby watch 24 hours a day.

This has great symbolism for us. In seasons of harvest, there is a more urgent need for watchmen, as the "thief" is going to do all he can to steal it, keeping the greater portion. It is little wonder that God has preceded the greatest harvest of souls the world has ever known—which is now happening—with the greatest prayer awakening in history. The Lord of the harvest is wise. I can assure you He has 24-hour sentries "watching" the harvest. May we be able to say with our Lord: Of those You have given me, not one of them perished (see John 17:12).

These watchmen were also posted on the city walls, where they would function as sentries. The following are a few Old Testament references:

> For thus the Lord says to me, "Go, station the lookout, let him report what he sees. When he sees riders, horsemen in pairs, a train of donkeys, a train of camels, let him pay close attention, very close attention." Then the lookout called, "O Lord, I stand continually by day on the watchtower, and I am stationed every night at my guard post" (Isa. 21:6-8).

> Lift up a signal against the walls of Babylon; post a strong guard, station sentries, place men in ambush! For the Lord has both purposed and performed what He spoke concerning the inhabitants of Babylon (Jer. 51:12).

On your walls, O Jerusalem, I have appointed watchmen;
all day and all night they will never keep silent. You who
remind the Lord, take no rest for yourselves (Isa. 62:6).

From the walls of the cities they would watch for two things:
messengers and enemies.

Watching for Messengers

They watched for messengers to inform the gatekeepers about
when to open the gates and when not to. In those days runners
were used to carry messages from city to city, and the watchmen would cry out when a friendly messenger was coming.
Skilled watchmen could sometimes even recognize the runners
by their stride before ever seeing their faces. In 2 Samuel 18:27,
the watchman said, "The running . . . is like the running of
Ahimaaz." Do you see any important symbolism here?

Seasoned watchmen are often alerted by the Holy Spirit,
before they ever have any concrete evidence, that certain "messengers" are not to be trusted. They recognize "wolves" sent to
devour the flock, or "hirelings" with improper motives. They
bring warnings to those in leadership. They recognize them
"by their stride," as it were—something just doesn't seem right.
They sense and discern. To be sure, we must guard against
human suspicion and judging after the flesh. But I have learned
to listen to my trusted watchmen (one of whom is my wife)
when they tell me they are uneasy about so and so. They are
usually right.

At times, they are unable to give me specific reasons, which
is difficult for my analytical mind, but I have learned to trust
them. Most false doctrine, division and general destruction in
the Body of Christ could be averted if the watchmen would
watch and the leaders would listen! Peter speaks of this need in
2 Peter 2:1-2:

But false prophets also arose among the people, just as there will also be false teachers among you, who will secretly introduce destructive heresies, even denying the Master who bought them, bringing swift destruction upon themselves. And many will follow their sensuality, and because of them the way of the truth will be maligned.

Paul warned the Ephesians of it in Acts 20:28-31:

Be on the guard for yourselves and for all the flock, among which the Holy Spirit has made you overseers, to shepherd the church of God which He purchased with His own blood. I know that after my departure savage wolves will come in among you, not sparing the flock; and from among your own selves men will arise, speaking perverse things, to draw away the disciples after them. Therefore be on the alert, remembering that night and day for a period of three years I did not cease to admonish each one with tears.

Evidently they heeded Paul's advice, for the Lord commended them in Revelation 2:2:

I know your deeds and your toil and perseverance, and that you cannot endure evil men, and you put to the test those who call themselves apostles, and they are not, and you found them to be false.

Watching for the Enemy

The watchmen on the wall also looked for the enemy. When they saw the potential danger approaching, they sounded an alarm, either by a shout or a trumpet blast. Soldiers could then prepare themselves for battle and defend the city. Watchmen do this today, in a spiritual sense. They alert the Body of Christ to attacks of the enemy, sounding the alarm. When the watchmen are functioning properly, we need never be caught off-guard by Satan and his forces.

As watchmen we do not live in fear of our adversary, nor do we live in "ignore - ance" of him. Contrary to what some would teach, alertness and vigilance are not synonymous with preoccupation. I must warn you, it is a common tactic of the enemy to dissuade Christians from watching for him by accusing them of a wrong emphasis.

Sadly enough, this message is often purported by well-meaning Christians. They teach that Satan is to be ignored or that little attention is to be paid him. No passage in the Bible supports this. Certainly we are not to become infatuated with Satan, but a good soldier is a well-informed soldier concerning his enemy. Be infatuated with and in awe of Jesus—be aware of the enemy. Love worship, not warfare, but when necessary, go to war.

In their book *How to Pray for Your Family and Friends*, Quin Sherrer and Ruthanne Garlock tell of a friend's pastor who had this attitude. "I don't think you should teach on spiritual warfare," the pastor told Hilda one day. "Concentrate on Jesus and not the devil."

Her response showed her wisdom and experience. " 'Pastor, I do concentrate on Jesus and his victory,' she answered respectfully. 'Jesus taught that we have authority over the evil one. Until I began to use Christ's authority in spiritual warfare, I had four children going to hell. I've learned to bind the enemy's work in my family members' lives. Today *all* my children and grandchildren serve the Lord. I've seen the results of spiritual warfare, and I want to help others.' "[3]

The Watchman Looks Ahead

Watchmen did not only guard cities and fields in Scripture. The Hebrew words translated "watchman" are *natsar, shamar* and *tsaphah*. They mean to guard or protect by watching over, but also by "hedging around something"[4] as with thorns. They even have the connotation of hiding or concealing something.[5] The watchman—through intercession—creates the secret place of protection (see Ps. 91).

Another interesting meaning of *tsaphah* is to "lean forward and peer into the distance." The connection to prayer should be obvious. The watchman looks ahead, "peering into the distance,"[6] to foresee the attacks of the enemy. He is pro-active, not re-active. This is prophetic intercession!

Let's look at several references where these words are used, with each usage referring to guarding or protecting something different. The first is in Genesis 2:15, which also happens to be the first time one of these words is used in the Bible. "Then the Lord God took the man and put him into the garden of Eden to cultivate it and *keep* it" (emphasis added).

Theologians have what is known as "the law of first mention." This refers to the general rule that the first time a major subject is mentioned in the Bible, significant facts are given concerning it that will remain consistent and relevant throughout the Scriptures.

For example, the first mention of the serpent—Satan—is in Genesis 3:1: "Now the serpent was more crafty than any beast of the field which the Lord God had made. And he said to the woman, 'Indeed, has God said, "You shall not eat from any tree of the garden"?'" It is easy to see this law at work here, as the verse speaks of Satan's subtlety or craftiness. God is informing us of one of the most important things we must remember about Satan: He is far more dangerous to us as the crafty serpent than as a roaring lion.

Be Defensive—Keep the Serpent Out!

Adam was told in Genesis 2:15 to guard or "keep" the garden. From what? It had to be the serpent! I assert this because first of all, it is much in keeping with the nature of God to have warned him. To have done otherwise would not have been consistent with God's character. Second, neither Adam nor Eve seemed shocked when a snake talked to them. It evidently didn't come as a total surprise. Third, what else could there have been (before the Fall) to guard, keep or protect from in the garden? Only the serpent.

I want to emphasize an important point—the first mention of this term in Scripture gives us one of the primary responsibilities of the watchman: *Keep the serpent out!* Guard or protect that which God has entrusted to your care from the subtle encroachment of the serpent. Keep him out of your garden! . . . your home, family, church, city, nation! . . . Keep him out!

The word is used again in Genesis 3:24 when God stationed a cherubim at the entrance of the garden to keep man from the tree of life. Adam didn't keep the serpent out, so an angel had to keep man out.

In Genesis 30:31, the watchman concept is used in guarding a flock. It doesn't take much insight to see the correlation here. We can guard the flock of God through intercession. Ecclesiastes 12:3 refers to protecting a house. Psalm 127:1 uses the concept in reference to guarding a city. And 1 Samuel 26:15 and 28:2 speak of doing it for a person. Proverbs 4:23 instructs us to do it for our hearts.

These three Hebrew words are also translated in several other ways. I'm going to list a few of them, elaborating briefly, to provide a more well-rounded understanding of the concept. As you will plainly see, pages could be written commenting on the symbolism and connection to prayer. For brevity's sake I have not done so, but I would encourage you to think and meditate on each one, allowing the Holy Spirit to bring insight to you personally.

1. Keep or Keeper
This is by far the most frequent usage of these words—at least 250 times. Watchmen keep things, places and individuals safe. They ensure against loss, theft or damage. They keep things intact, in possession.

2. Guard
Watchmen are guards. This word is obviously similar to the next one.

3. Bodyguard
Watchmen guard individuals, protecting them from danger and harm. They are shields—the secret service agents of the kingdom, guarding and protecting others. Watchmen represent Jesus by watching over others.

Often, intercessors in our fellowship inform me of times they have spent covering me in prayer. More than once I've been told, "Pastor, I was up most of the night praying for you." Occasionally they ask, "Was something wrong?"

"No," I usually respond, "and that's probably why." Often my problems and distractions are "laid upon" others and they "carry them away from me." I am grateful and wise enough to realize that much of my success is due to their faithfulness. What a comfort to know I have bodyguards in the spirit! There would be fewer casualties in our ranks if we had more faithful watchmen.

Peter Wagner, in his book *Prayer Shield*, offers five reasons pastors and other Christian leaders are in such great need of watchmen interceding for them:

1. *Pastors Have More Responsibility and Accountability.*
   James 3:1, "My brethren, let not many of you become
   teachers, knowing that we shall receive a stricter
   judgment."

2. *Pastors Are More Subject to Temptation.* Make no mistake about it, the higher up you go on the ladder of
   Christian leadership, the higher you go on Satan's
   hit list.

3. *Pastors Are More Targeted by Spiritual Warfare.* It has
   now become known that over the last several years,
   satanists, witches, New Agers, occult practitioners,
   shamans, spiritists and other servants of darkness
   have entered into an evil covenant to pray to Satan for
   the breakdown of marriages of pastors and Christian
   leaders. The spiritual warfare has intensified.

4. *Pastors Have More Influence on Others.* The fourth reason why pastors need intercession more than other
   Christians is that by the very nature of their ministry they have more influence on others.

5. *Pastors Have More Visibility.* Because pastors are up
   front, they are constantly subject to gossip and
   criticism.[7]

In the book, Wagner elaborates more thoroughly on each
reason. Elsewhere he says, "To the degree the intercessors pray,
the leaders gain protection against the fiery darts of the wicked
one, over and above the whole armor of God they are responsible for using."[8] This excellent book provides outstanding guidance about intercession for Christian leaders.

In the excellent training resource, *Becoming a Prayer Warrior*, Beth Alves offers a suggested daily guide to praying for spiritual leaders, which Wagner summarized as follows:

Sunday: Favor with God (spiritual revelation, anointing, holiness).

Monday: Favor with others (congregations, ministry staff, unsaved).

Tuesday: Increased vision (wisdom and enlightenment, motives, guidance).

Wednesday: Spirit, Soul, Body (health, appearance, attitudes, spiritual and physical wholeness).

Thursday: Protection (temptation, deception, enemies).

Friday: Finances (priorities, blessings).

Saturday: Family (general, spouse, children).[9]

4. Doorkeeper

Obviously similar to the next, so I will comment on both of them together.

5. Gatekeeper

Watchmen have the ability spiritually—in the prayer closet—to determine who or what goes in and out of their homes, their families' lives, their churches, their cities, etc. They discern by the Holy Spirit what to allow in, and through prayer, open and close the door. They invite in the work of the Holy Spirit and reject the works of darkness. They set boundaries, keeping enemies out. At times, when informed or confronted by an intercessor with the information that something improper has crept into our fellowship, I respond by asking, "What happened? Weren't you on the job?" I would simply say to the Body of Christ, "Don't blame it all on the pastors. You, too, are responsible for gatekeeping."

6. Preserve or Preserver

Watchmen preserve or keep things from ruin and destruction. They preserve lives, anointings, moves of God and a host of other things by covering them in prayer. Sherrer and Garlock tell of four ladies who functioned as watchmen for their farms. These women walked the perimeters of the fields while the husbands worked, sometimes covering as much as six miles in a day.

They prayed for protection from insects, crop diseases, hail and drought. They asked God to give their husbands wisdom in farming and marketing and prayed for angels to be assigned to the efforts.

The results were amazing. It turned out to be one of their better years. No storm or insect damage, no unwise decisions and a good profit—while others around them had a difficult year with little profit.

We simply aren't practical enough at times with our intercession tactics. These ladies, watching in intercession, opened the way for God's blessing upon their families' financial endeavors.[10]

7. Pay attention

Watchmen must be on the alert. They must pay attention. Though obvious, it is important enough to emphasize. As soldiers, God "calls us to attention." Lives are at stake. The harvest must be guarded. Pay attention, watchmen!

8. Observe

This embodies the same concept as paying attention, yet adds the emphasis of contemplativeness and sharpness. Don't just look—see. Be observant. Quite simply, watchmen watch! They observe what others fail to see. We can observe much in prayer, often even before it happens.

9. Behold

This one is similar to observe, of course, but I list it because it reemphasizes the need for seeing clearly.

10. Beware

Watchmen must be vigilant, aware, on the alert. Again, 1 Peter 5:8 warns us to be of sober spirit. Always beware, intercessor! Watch for the lion and when you see him at work immediately "meet" him, enforcing Calvary's victory with the "bear anointing."

11. Protect

In the same sense as guarding and keeping, watchmen protect. They build walls or boundaries of protection from the attacks of the devil. They distribute this blessing of the Lord.

12. Maintain

Watchmen maintain things for the Lord. They are maintenance people. They may not set vision, build or plant in the way that some do, but they maintain. They keep things working well and prevent breakdowns. They maintain the anointing, integrity, health and many other necessary blessings of the kingdom.

In summary, God is raising up prophetic intercessors—watchmen—*to keep the serpent out!* Men and women who will "lean forward, peering into the distance," watching for the enemy's attacks. Sentries, bodyguards, gatekeepers, boundary setters and preservers in His kingdom. It is, indeed, a high calling!

Be Offensive—Lay Siege!

There is another facet to this type of prayer, however, that I now want us to consider. One of the most interesting and surprising things I discovered as I studied these words is that they embody not only protective or defensive meanings, but offensive as well.

The words mean "to besiege or lay siege to a city,"[11] the idea being to watch it to keep people and supplies from coming or going. One definition was "to spy on" or "lie in wait for someone to ambush the person."[12] They are actually translated this way in 2 Samuel 11:16, Isaiah 1:8, Jeremiah 4:16-17, Jeremiah 51:12 and Judges 1:24.

In 1989 when the Lord gave me this teaching, He clearly spoke in my heart that He was releasing the watchman anointing, which would enable individuals to "lay siege to" cities and nations through prayer. Where Satan had taken advantage and held the greater portion, the people of God would be given instruction about how to lay siege to these situations, cutting off his supply lines and removing that which had given him place. They would take back from him people, cities and nations.

This was before there was talk (at least in a broad degree) of reconciliation ceremonies, identificational repentance, spiritual mapping, prayer walks, marches and journeys—all of which are terms associated with systematically removing from Satan his hold on places and people to take them for Christ. These and other strategies are all a part of the watchman anointing God has released to the Church.

The Body of Christ is learning to *systematically* pull down the strongholds of darkness. God is giving us the ability—by His Spirit—to discern the enemy's plans, strengths, weaknesses and points of entry—to cut him off and take nations, cities and individuals through prayer. The strongholds of darkness are being torn down. Those imprisoned in satanic fortresses are being freed. Sieges are being laid in the spirit. God is showing us what to bind and loose, as well as how to do it. There is opposition, of course.

One of the things that keep some from this kind of prayer is the time element. The very concept of laying siege implies a duration of time. It may take days, weeks or years of daily intercession to receive the breakthrough. I certainly believe this can be sped up by more intelligent and informed praying, as well as by the multiplication of power that takes place through agreement.

However, nothing can change the fact that some situations require a degree of time. I laid siege to the cyst in my wife for 30 days. Polly Simchen, whom we spoke of in chapter 10, laid siege to the bondages in her son for 4 years. God gave her and her friends much strategy as they prayed, enlightening them on what to cut off and what to call forth. That is a siege. They discerned Satan's strategies, "spying out" his plans. Was it worth the effort and wait? Absolutely. They gained the greater portion.

This concept of laying siege is well-illustrated in a story about Theresa Mulligan, editor of a newsletter for intercessors called *Breakthrough*, related by Sherrer and Garlock in *How to Pray for Your Family and Friends*. Theresa and a friend had prayer-walked their neighborhood for a season, stopping in front of each house, taking hands and agreeing in prayer for the occupants' salvation.

Soon reports started coming in: A colonel's wife accepted Christ, the teenage daughter of a Jewish family met Jesus, an arthritic woman made a commitment to Christ and a college-age daughter of another family came to the Lord. Even after she moved away, Theresa continued to hear of these former neighbors coming to Christ.[13]

That is laying siege! It is the watchman anointing at its best and anyone can do it.

Taking Cities and Nations for God

I have focused most of my attention in this book to intercession for individuals. I would now like to comment briefly on intercession for cities and nations, especially as it relates to the watchman aspect of laying siege.

Scripture clearly shows that God deals with—relates to—not only individuals, but also groups of people. Because of the principles of authority, responsibility, free will, sowing and reaping, etc., which operate not only on an individual level, but also on the corporate level at which individuals join, God relates to people *groups*. Why?

Many of the decisions we make, the rights and privileges we enjoy, are not individualistic, but are jointly made with the people to whom we relate. For example, I make many decisions privately regarding my personal life. But for our household—our children, finances, home, time, and so on, my wife and I make the decisions together.

The same principle of shared authority can be incrementally expanded all the way up to a national level—from organizations to cities to counties to states to nations. These groupings could be secular or religious. In whatever way a group of people can be said to have rights, decision-making power and freedoms, there is reciprocal responsibility. As the decisions on laws, leaders, morals, interests, tolerances and intolerances are shared, so are the ramifications.

For example, I do not favor abortion, but I cannot escape the effects, though they may be indirect, of God's judgments on this nation due to this tragic holocaust. If God brings drought or inclement weather that affects our crops, I too, will pay higher prices. As He turns us over to our degraded and perverted desires, accidents and illnesses increase, which raise my insurance rates, also. If the judgment happens to be war, I, too, pay for it in higher taxes and share in the grief of lost American lives. Numerous other examples could be given.

Although we may not like it, none can live as an island. Though we as believers can enjoy a certain degree of protection from these judgments—God might increase my prosperity to help me pay higher prices or taxes, for example—there is no way to totally avoid the principle of shared responsibility.

The Corporate Dealings of God

Having given the reason, I want to validate it by listing several ways in which God dealt with cities or regions in Scripture on a corporate level:

1. Cities were addressed or prophesied to: Jonah 1:2; Nahum 3:1; Micah 6:9; Revelation 2 and 3.
2. Cities and nations were judged: Nineveh, Sodom, Gomorrah, Tyre, Sidon, Bethsaida, Capernaum, Jericho, Jerusalem, and others. The nation Israel was judged as a whole on many occasions in Scripture, as were other nations.
3. Cities and nations were forgiven or spared judgment: Nineveh; Sodom could have been, had there been enough righteous people; the nation Israel was forgiven as a whole, as were others.
4. Cities and nations had divine purposes or callings: Israel, Jerusalem, the seven cities of refuge, and many others.
5. Cities were spoken of as being kept or preserved by God: Psalm 127:1.
6. Cities and nations had principalities ruling them: Tyre (see Ezek. 28:12); Persia (see Dan. 10:13); Ephesus (see Acts 19:28); Pergamum (see Rev. 2:12).
7. People groups have a corporate righteousness or sin level: Any nation (see Prov. 14:34); Sodom and Gomorrah (see Gen. 18:20-21); the Amorites (see Gen. 15:16).
8. Cities have a corporate faith or unbelief level: Nazareth (see Mark 6:5-6).
9. Cities have a corporate peace or welfare (see Jer. 29:7).
10. Cities can have revival: Nineveh (see Jon. 3:5-10).
11. Cities can miss revival: Jerusalem (see Luke 19:41-44).

I gave this entire list and the preceding explanation primarily to substantiate one thing: *God deals with people as groups, not just as individuals.* This fact is what also substantiates our intercession for people as groups.

Abraham successfully interceded for a city (see Gen. 18:22-33); Moses interceded for a nation (see Exod. 32:9-14). Exiles from Jerusalem were told to intercede for the cities they now lived in (see Jer. 29:7). We are told in 2 Chronicles 7:14 that our prayers and lifestyles can cause healing for a nation. Ecclesiastes 9:15 and Proverbs 21:22 inform us that wisdom can deliver a city and bring down strongholds.

Without question, God is releasing an anointing to lay siege to cities and nations to take them for Him! He is equipping us to "spy out" the enemy's plans and strongholds, "ambushing" him in the spirit. We are the Melchizedek order of priesthood prophesied in Psalm 110. We're a priestly army, stretching forth the scepter of our conquering hero, ruling in the midst of our enemies. Come on, join us!

For those who are serious about city taking, Peter Wagner's book *Breaking Strongholds in Your City* contains a wealth of information. In it, Victor Lorenzo tells of the three-year plan to evangelize the city of Resistencia, Argentina. One of the key elements of the effort was the spiritual mapping of the city by Lorenzo. Through this mapping he discovered four spiritual powers influencing the city. Lorenzo tells of praying to tear down these powers and the ensuing results:

The next day our team went out to the plaza with the pastors of the Resistencia churches, a group of trained intercessors and Cindy Jacobs. We battled fiercely against the invisible powers over the city for four hours. We attacked them in what we sensed was their hierarchical order, from bottom to top. First came Pombero,

then Curupi, then San La Muerte, then spirit of Free-
masonry, then Queen of Heaven, then the Python spirit whom we suspected functioned as the coordinator of
all the forces of evil in the city. When we finished, an
almost tangible sense of peace and freedom came over
all who had participated. We were confident that this
first battle had been won and that the city could be
claimed for the Lord.

After this, the church in Resistencia was ready for
full-scale evangelization. Unbelievers began to respond
to the gospel as never before. As a result of our three-year
outreach, church attendance increased by 102 percent.
The effect was felt in all social strata of the city. We could
undertake community projects such as providing drinking water for the poor. The public image of the evangelical church improved greatly by gaining respect and
approval from political and social leaders. We were invited to use the media to spread our message. The spiritual
warfare and mapping we were able to do opened new doors
in Resistencia for evangelism, social improvement and
reaping of the spiritual harvest.[14]

That is the watchman anointing! *We can impact our cities and
nations through intercession.* We can lay siege to them, taking them
for God. Strongholds of darkness can become strongholds of light.

Cities Transformed

Canaan, a cursed land (see Gen. 9:25) became the Promised Land
of blessing.

Jerusalem, once a stronghold of evil giants, became the city
of peace.

Seven cities, once ruled by idolaters and wicked giants,
became cities of refuge where people who had accidentally taken

a life fled for safety and protection. Hebron, the most famous of the seven, was formerly called Kiriath-Arba, which means the city of Arba. Arba was the greatest of the Anakim, or giants (see Josh. 14:15). Hebron, its new name, means "association, friendship, fellowship, communion."[15] Fittingly, Abraham, the friend of God, is buried there. Caleb, a man of faith and courage, was used to transform the stronghold of the greatest giant to a place where people ran to find safety and sweet fellowship or communion with God. This can happen to our cities!

Also, as a city of refuge, Hebron was a picture or type of Christ. One who killed accidentally could find safety in one of two places: in a city of refuge (for long-term protection) or holding on to the horns of the altar in the Holy Place (for short-term protection).

In Hebrews 6:18, the Lord draws from both of these pictures in one phrase: "In order that by two unchangeable things, in which it is impossible for God to lie, we may have strong encouragement, we who have fled for *refuge* in *laying hold* of the hope set before us" (emphasis added). Interestingly, individuals who were there for safety had to remain in a city of refuge until the death of the current high priest (see Num. 35:28), after which they were free to go safely. What a picture of our great High Priest who died so that we could go free from judgment and penalty.

My point for this story, other than just to enjoy a beautiful picture of Jesus, is to demonstrate that a former stronghold of giants was transformed into such a place of protection, refuge and fellowship with God that it became a picture of Christ Himself.

Can God do this again today? Can our cities and nations be so thoroughly transformed? Yes, unless God has changed in the last 3,000 years! That is, if He can find some Calebs. . . . If He can find some giant killers. . . . If He can find some "We're well able" attitudes.

He is asking us, as He did Ezekiel, to look on the dry bones of our nation—the men and women, the young and old, the rich and poor, the hurting and those who think they're healthy—and answer the same question he asked the prophet: "Can these bones live?" I say they can. What do you say?

Are You Ready?

We need to be like Sam and Jed. Hearing that a $5,000 bounty had been offered for the capture or killing of wolves, they became bounty hunters. Waking up one night, Sam saw that they were surrounded by 50 pairs of gleaming eyes—ravenous wolves licking hungry chops. "Jed, wake up," he whispered to his sleeping partner. "We're rich!"[16]

We need to see the multitude of unbelievers around us, not as threats, but as opportunities. Our task would be overwhelming were it not for the fact that we are relying on God's strength and ability, not ours. Though a host should encamp against us, we can still be confident (see Ps. 27:3). Gideon's 300 were more than enough to defeat 135,000 with God on their side. If He is for us, who can successfully be against us (see Rom. 8:31)?

Let's do it! Let's let God arise and His enemies be scattered. Let's fill our bag with the stones of victory and run to meet Goliath. Let's take Kiriath-Arba. Let's run through some troops and leap over some walls.

Let's demonstrate the awesomeness of our God. Let's growl! Let's roar! Let's let Jesus live through us.

He is ready—are you?

Are you ready to walk in your calling as an intercessor? . . . To re-present Jesus as the reconciler and the warrior? . . . To distribute His benefits and victory? . . . To meet, to carry away, to set boundaries?

Are you ready to birth, to liberate, to strike the mark? . . .
To fill some bowls, to make some declarations, to watch and pray?
Are you ready?
Remember: "Life is fragile, handle with *PAGA*!"

Questions for Reflection

1. Can you summarize the four conclusions drawn from
   Ephesians 6:18, 1 Peter 5:8 and 2 Corinthians 2:11?
   Using the verses themselves, give reasons for these
   conclusions.

2. Describe the functions and responsibilities of Old
   Testament watchmen. How do they symbolize watching intercession?

3. Where is the first usage of the Hebrew word for
   "watchman" in the Scriptures? What significant
   insight can be drawn from this?

4. Based on the definitions and usages of the three
   words for "watchman," can you give some summary
   statements about the defensive aspect of the watchman anointing? How can you apply this to your
   family? . . . Pastor? . . . Church?

5. Describe the offensive aspect of the watchman
   anointing. Can you relate it to intercession for an
   individual? . . . How about a city?

6. Can you give the reason God deals with groups of
   people, not just with individuals? List three or four
   biblical examples.

7. Think of ways you and your prayer group can lay
   siege to your city. Do it!

DISCUSSION LEADER'S GUIDE

The purpose of this book is to ignite and empower the prayer lives of those who read it. As the group grows in faith and unity, you may want to implement some of the prayer tactics mentioned in the book, such as using prayer cloths, prayer-walking and engaging in spiritual warfare for each other.

As a leader, it is important to be sensitive to the maturity level of the group. It is also important that you do not impose your beliefs on those who differ in the way they worship the Lord.

The optimum-sized discussion group is 10 to 15 people. A smaller group can make continuity a problem when too few members attend. A larger group will require strong leadership skills to create a sense of belonging and meaningful participation for each person.

If you are leading a group that already meets regularly, such as a Sunday School class or weekly home group, decide how many weeks to spend on the series. Be sure to plan for any holidays that may occur during your scheduled meetings.

Use creativity. This book's 14 chapters will fit a regular 13-week quarter if a couple of chapters are paired to provide time for personal sharing.

The first session would provide a perfect time for an open forum to create a sense of unity as you begin the series. A time for introduction followed by nonthreatening questions is often helpful for building close ties within the group. Chapter 1 can be used as the introduction. Consider one or more of the following questions:

1. Are you satisfied with your prayer life? If not, where are you struggling?

2. Why do you think prayer is such a lacking discipline
   in the Body of Christ?
3. What do you hope to gain from studying this book?
4. After reading chapter 1, do you think we should
   pray only once or do you think we need to be persistent? Why?
5. If you could ask God one question about prayer,
   what would it be?

Such questions will create a sense of identity among the
class members and help them to discover their similarities.

Many individual questions may arise that will significantly
contribute to the group's understanding of the subject. Group
members should be encouraged to maintain lists of their questions. Suggest that they be submitted anonymously and combine
them together to eliminate repetition. Many questions may be
answered by the time the series reaches its conclusion. It is, therefore, a good idea to wait until your last session to discuss them.

Enlist a co-leader to assist with calling class members to
remind them of meeting dates, times and places. Your co-leader
can also make arrangements for refreshments and child care.

People will have a greater appreciation for their books if they
are responsible for paying for them. They will also be more apt to
finish the course if they have invested in their own materials.

Be sure to have several extra Bibles available. *The Living Bible*
is often helpful for people who have little or no Bible background; however, it is important to explain that the *NASB* dif-
fers considerably and will be the main version used in this book.

Be aware of the basic principles for group dynamics, such as:

1. Arrange seating in a semicircle with the leader included rather than standing in front. This setting invites
   participation.

2. Create a discussion-friendly atmosphere. The following tips are helpful for guiding discussions:

    a. Receive statements from group members without judgmentalism, even if you disagree with them. If they are clearly unbiblical or unfair, you can ask questions that clarify the issue; but outright rejection of comments will stifle open participation.

    b. If a question or comment deviates from the subject, either suggest that it be dealt with at another time or ask the group if they want to pursue the new issue now.

    c. If one person monopolizes the discussion, direct a few questions specifically to someone else. Or, tactfully interrupt the dominator by saying, "Excuse me, that's a good thought, and I wonder what the rest of us think about that." Talk with the person privately and enlist that person's help in drawing others into the discussion.

    d. Make it easy and comfortable for everyone to share or ask questions, but don't insist that anyone do so. Reluctant participants can warm to the idea of sharing by being asked to read a passage from the book. Pair a shy person with someone else for a discussion apart from the main group, and ask reluctant participants to write down a comment to be shared with the larger group.

    e. If someone asks you a question and you don't know the answer, admit it and move on. If the question calls for insight from personal experience, invite others to comment on it; however, be careful that this sharing is limited. If it requires special knowledge, offer to look for an answer in the library or from a theologian or minister, and report your findings later.

3. Guard against rescuing. The purpose of this group is to learn to pray for others, not fix them. This doesn't mean that poignant moments won't come up or unhappy problems won't be shared, but the group is for sharing and prayer—not fixing others. The leader should be open and honest about wanting to grow with the group instead of coming across as an authority about the subject.

4. Start and stop on time, according to the schedule agreed upon before the series begins. This is especially important for those who have to hire a baby-sitter or arise early for work the next morning.

5. During each session, lead group members in discussing the questions and exercises at the end of each chapter. If you have more than 8 or 10 class members, consider dividing into small groups, then invite each group to share one or two insights with the larger group.

6. Be sensitive. Some people may feel comfortable praying for others, but don't force those who don't. It is necessary to set aside a time either at the beginning or end of the meeting to pray for those in need.

7. Encourage members of the group to pray daily for each other. This will perpetuate a sense of unity and love.

8. As a leader, pray regularly for the sessions and the participants, asking the Holy Spirit to hover over each person throughout the week. The Lord will honor your willingness to guide His people toward a more intimate relationship with Him.

ENDNOTES

Chapter One: The Question Is . . .
1. John L. Mason, *An Enemy Called Average* (Tulsa, OK: Harrison House, 1990), p. 20.
2. Craig Brian Larson, *Illustrations for Preaching and Teaching* (Grand Rapids, MI: Baker Books, 1993), p. 128.
3. Ibid., p. 75.

Chapter Two: The Necessity of Prayer
1. Paul E. Billheimer, *Destined for the Throne* (Fort Washington, PA: Christian Literature Crusade, 1975), p. 51.
2. Ibid.
3. James Strong, *The New Strong's Exhaustive Concordance of the Bible* (Nashville, TN: Thomas Nelson Publishers, 1990), ref. no. 120.
4. William Wilson, *Old Testament Word Studies* (Grand Rapids, MI: Kregel Publications, 1978), p. 236.
5. *The Consolidated Webster Encyclopedic Dictionary* (Chicago: Consolidated Book Publishers, 1954), p. 615.
6. Ibid.
7. Spiros Zodhiates, *Hebrew-Greek Key Study Bible—New American Standard* (Chattanooga, TN: AMG Publishers, 1984; revised edition, 1990), p. 1768.
8. Strong, *The New Strong's Exhaustive Concordance*, ref. no. 1819.
9. R. Laird Harris, Gleason L. Archer Jr., and Bruce K. Waltke, *Theological Wordbook of the Old Testament* (Chicago: Moody Press, 1980; Grand Rapids: William B. Eerdmans Publishing Co., revised edition, 1991), p. 426.
10. Zodhiates, *Hebrew-Greek Key Study Bible*, p. 1826.
11. Andrew Murray, *The Ministry of Intercessory Prayer* (Minneapolis, MN: Bethany House Publishers, 1981), pp. 22-23.
12. Billheimer, *Destined for the Throne*, p. 107.
13. C. Peter Wagner, *Confronting the Powers* (Ventura, CA: Regal Books, 1996), p. 242.
14. Jack W. Hayford, *Prayer Is Invading the Impossible* (South Plainfield, NJ: Logos International, 1977; revised edition, Bridge Publishing, 1995), p. 92, 1977 edition.

Chapter Three: Re-Presenting Jesus
1. *The Consolidated Webster Encyclopedic Dictionary* (Chicago: Consolidated Book Publishers, 1954), p. 384.
2. Ibid., p. 450.
3. James Strong, *The New Strong's Exhaustive Concordance of the Bible* (Nashville, TN: Thomas Nelson Publishers, 1990), ref. no. 1834.
4. Jack Canfield and Mark Victor Hansen, *Chicken Soup for the Soul* (Deerfield Beach, FL: Health Communications, Inc., 1993), p. 74.
5. R. Arthur Mathews, *Born for Battle* (Robesonia, PA: OMF Books, 1978), p. 106.
6. I have used the phrase "enforcing the victory of Calvary" throughout this book. Though not a direct quote, the seed thought was planted in my mind by Paul Billheimer, *Destined for the Throne* (Fort Washington, PA: Christian Literature Crusade, 1975), p. 17.
7. Mathews, *Born for Battle,* p. 160.

Chapter Four: Meetings: The Good, the Bad and the Ugly

1. Francis Brown, S. R. Driver, and Charles A. Briggs, *The New Brown-Driver, Briggs-Gesenius Hebrew and English Lexicon* (Peabody, MA: Hendrickson Publishers, 1979), p. 803.
2. Spiros Zodhiates, *The Complete Word Study Dictionary* (Iowa Falls, IA: Word Bible Publishers, 1992), p. 1375.
3. Ibid.
4. William Wilson, *Old Testament Word Studies* (Grand Rapids, MI: Kregel Publications, 1978), p. 263.
5. Spiros Zodhiates, *Hebrew-Greek Key Study Bible—New American Standard* (Chattanooga, TN: AMG Publishers, 1984; revised edition, 1990), p. 1583.
6. Ibid.
7. Jack Canfield and Mark Victor Hansen, *Chicken Soup for the Soul* (Deerfield Beach, FL: Health Communications, Inc., 1993), p. 74.

Chapter Five: Cheek to Cheek

1. Joseph Henry Thayer, *A Greek-English Lexicon of the New Testament* (Grand Rapids, MI: Baker Book House, 1977), p. 45.
2. Craig Brian Larson, *Illustrations for Preaching and Teaching* (Grand Rapids, MI: Baker Book House, 1993), p. 144.
3. Ibid., p. 99.
4. Francis Brown, S. R. Driver, and Charles A. Briggs, *The New Brown-Driver, Briggs-Gesenius Hebrew and English Lexicon* (Peabody, MA: Hendrickson Publishers, 1979), p. 671.
5. F. F. Bosworth, *Christ the Healer* (Grand Rapids, MI: Baker Book House/Revell, 1973), p. 26.
6. S. D. Gordon, *What It Will Take to Change the World* (Grand Rapids, MI: Baker Book House, 1979), pp. 17-21, adapted.
7. *New American Standard Exhaustive Concordance of the Bible* (Nashville, TN: Holman Bible Publishers, 1981), ref. no. 2428.
8. R. Laird Harris, Gleason L. Archer Jr., and Bruce K. Waltke, *Theological Wordbook of the Old Testament* (Chicago: Moody Press, 1980; Grand Rapids: William B. Eerdmans Publishing Co., revised edition, 1991), p. 453.
9. Spiros Zodhiates, *The Complete Word Study Dictionary* (Iowa Falls, IA: Word Bible Publishers, 1992), p. 1128.
10. Harris, Archer, Waltke, *Theological Wordbook*, p. 453.
11. Words by Julia Ward Howe, America melody attributed to William Steffe.
12. Larson, *Illustrations for Preaching*, p. 26.

Chapter Six: No Trespassing

1. *The Spirit-Filled Bible* (Nashville, TN: Thomas Nelson Publishers, 1991), p. 1097.
2. I first heard the phrase "prayer that sets boundaries" in a live message by Jack Hayford in Dallas, Texas, in 1976. He has since written about this in one of his books.
3. James Strong, *The New Strong's Exhaustive Concordance of the Bible* (Nashville, TN: Thomas Nelson Publishers, 1990), ref. no. 3427.
4. Francis Brown, S. R. Driver, and Charles A. Briggs, *The New Brown-Driver, Briggs-Gesenius Hebrew and English Lexicon* (Peabody, MA: Hendrickson Publishers, 1979), p. 533.
5. Ethelbert W. Bullinger, *A Critical Lexicon and Concordance to the English and Greek New Testament* (Grand Rapids, MI: Zondervan Publishing House, 1975), p. 804.
6. Ibid.

Chapter Seven: Butterflies, Mice, Elephants and Bull's-Eyes

1. Francis Brown, S. R. Driver, and Charles A. Briggs, *The New Brown-Driver, Briggs-Gesenius Hebrew and English Lexicon* (Peabody, MA: Hendrickson Publishers, 1979), p. 803.
2. W. E. Vine, *The Expanded Vine's Expository Dictionary of New Testament Words* (Minneapolis, MN: Bethany House Publishers, 1984), p. 200.
3. Spiros Zodhiates, *Hebrew-Greek Key Study Bible—New American Standard* (Chattanooga, TN: AMG Publishers, 1984; revised edition, 1990), p. 1812.
4. Spiros Zodhiates, *The Complete Word Study Dictionary* (Iowa Falls, IA: Word Bible Publishers, 1992), p. 400.
5. The connection between Genesis 28:11-22 and Romans 8:26-28 along with several of the related thoughts, including the butterfly illustration, I first heard in a live message by Jack Hayford in Dallas, Texas, in 1976. He has since written about this in one of his books.
6. Communicated to me by Israeli student Avi Mizrachi at Christ for the Nations Institute in Dallas, Texas.
7. James Strong, *The New Strong's Exhaustive Concordance of the Bible* (Nashville, TN: Thomas Nelson Publishers, 1990), ref. no. 4878.

Chapter Eight: Supernatural Childbirth

1. *The Consolidated Webster Encyclopedic Dictionary* (Chicago: Consolidated Book Publishers, 1954), p. 749.
2. W. E. Vine, *The Expanded Vine's Expository Dictionary of New Testament Words* (Minneapolis, MN: Bethany House Publishers, 1984), p. 110.
3. James Strong, *The New Strong's Exhaustive Concordance of the Bible* (Nashville, TN: Thomas Nelson Publishers, 1990), ref. no. 8414.
4. Spiros Zodhiates, *Hebrew-Greek Key Study Bible—New American Standard* (Chattanooga, TN: AMG Publishers, 1984; revised edition, 1990), p. 1790.
5. C. F. Keil and F. Delitzsch, *Commentary on the Old Testament*, Volume 1 (Grand Rapids, MI: William B. Eerdmans Publishing Co., reprinted 1991), p. 48.
6. William Wilson, *Old Testament Word Studies* (Grand Rapids, MI: Kregel Publications, 1978), p. 175.
7. *The Consolidated Webster Encyclopedic Dictionary* (Chicago: Consolidated Book Publishers, 1954), p. 89.
8. Francis Brown, S. R. Driver, and Charles A. Briggs, *The New Brown-Driver, Briggs-Gesenius Hebrew and English Lexicon* (Peabody, MA: Hendrickson Publishers, 1979), p. 934.
9. Strong, *The New Strong's Exhaustive Concordance*, ref. no. 3205.
10. Ibid., ref. no. 2342.
11. Ibid., ref. no. 1411.
12. Ibid., ref. no. 1982.
13. Joseph Henry Thayer, *A Greek-English Lexicon of the New Testament* (Grand Rapids, MI: Baker Book House, 1977), p. 242.
14. Spiros Zodhiates, *The Complete Word Study Dictionary* (Iowa Falls, IA: Word Bible Publishers, 1992), p. 1366.
15. Vine, *The Expanded Vine's Expository Dictionary*, p. 268.
16. Craig Brian Larson, *Illustrations for Preaching and Teaching* (Grand Rapids, MI: Baker Books, 1993), p. 165, adapted.

Chapter Nine: Pro Wrestlers

1. R. Arthur Mathews, *Born for Battle* (Robesonia, PA: OMF Books, 1978), p. 113.
2. Jack W. Hayford, *Prayer Is Invading the Impossible* (South Plainfield, NJ: Logos International, 1977; revised edition, Bridge Publishing, 1995), p. 45, 1977 edition.
3. R. Laird Harris, Gleason L. Archer Jr. and Bruce K. Waltke, *Theological Wordbook of the Old Testament* (Chicago: Moody Press, 1980; Grand Rapids: William B. Eerdmans Publishing Co., revised edition, 1991), p. 715.
4. Hayford, *Prayer Is Invading the Impossible*, p. 5.
5. Ethelbert W. Bullinger, *A Critical Lexicon and Concordance to the English and Greek New Testament* (Grand Rapids, MI: Zondervan Publishing House, 1975), p. 400.
6. Spiros Zodhiates, *Hebrew-Greek Key Study Bible—New American Standard* (Chattanooga, TN: AMG Publishers, 1984; revised edition, 1990), p. 1797.
7. Spiros Zodhiates, *The Complete Word Study Dictionary* (Iowa Falls, IA: Word Bible Publishers, 1992), p. 1173.
8. James Strong, *The New Strong's Exhaustive Concordance of the Bible* (Nashville, TN: Thomas Nelson Publishers, 1990), ref. no. 4122.
9. Bullinger, *A Critical Lexicon and Concordance*, p. 28.
10. Geoffrey W. Bromiley, *Theological Dictionary of the New Testament Abridged* (Grand Rapids, MI: William B. Eerdmans Publishing Co., 1985), p. 935.
11. Strong, *The New Strong's Exhaustive Concordance*, ref. no. 4314.
12. Ibid., ref. no. 1747.
13. Ibid., ref. no. 2442.
14. Harris, Archer, Waltke, *Theological Wordbook*, p. 791.
15. Strong, *The New Strong's Exhaustive Concordance*, ref. no. 6960.
16. Zodhiates, *Hebrew-Greek Key Study Bible*, p. 1733.
17. Strong, *The New Strong's Exhaustive Concordance*, ref. no. 4049.
18. Zodhiates, *Hebrew-Greek Key Study Bible*, p. 1796.
19. Ibid.
20. Gordon Lindsay, *The New John G. Lake Sermons* (Dallas: Christ for the Nations, Inc., 1979), pp. 29-30.
21. Strong, *The New Strong's Exhaustive Concordance*, ref. no. 7218.
22. Joseph Henry Thayer, *A Greek-English Lexicon of the New Testament* (Grand Rapids, MI: Baker Book House, 1977), p. 240.
23. Hayford, *Prayer Is Invading the Impossible*, p. 140.
24. Bullinger, *A Critical Lexicon and Concordance*, p. 731.

Chapter Ten: Most High Man

1. Spiros Zodhiates, *The Complete Word Study Dictionary* (Iowa Falls, IA: Word Bible Publishers, 1992), p. 816.
2. James Strong, *The New Strong's Exhaustive Concordance of the Bible* (Nashville, TN: Thomas Nelson Publishers, 1990), ref. no. 575.
3. Craig Brian Larson, *Illustrations for Preaching and Teaching* (Grand Rapids, MI: Baker Books, 1993), p. 98.
4. Zodhiates, *The Complete Word Study Dictionary*, p. 1464.
5. Ibid., p. 1463.
6. Strong, *The New Strong's Exhaustive Concordance*, ref. no. 1994.
7. Ibid., ref. no. 1124.
8. Ibid., ref. no. 3056.
9. Spiros Zodhiates, *Hebrew-Greek Key Study Bible—New American Standard* (Chattanooga, TN: AMG Publishers, 1984; revised edition, 1990), p. 1718.

10. W. E. Vine, *The Expanded Vine's Expository Dictionary of New Testament Words* (Minneapolis, MN: Bethany House Publishers, 1984), p. 125.
11. Strong, *The New Strong's Exhaustive Concordance*, ref. no. 5188.
12. Ibid., ref. no. 5187.
13. Larson, *Illustrations for Preaching*, p. 134.
14. Strong, *The New Strong's Exhaustive Concordance*, ref. no. 1415.
15. Ibid., ref. no. 2507.
16. Walter Bauer, *A Greek-English Lexicon of the New Testament* (Chicago: The University of Chicago Press, 1979), p. 386.
17. Strong, *The New Strong's Exhaustive Concordance*, ref. no. 2192.
18. Zodhiates, *The Complete Word Study Dictionary*, p. 923.
19. Strong, *The New Strong's Exhaustive Concordance*, ref. no. 5313.
20. Bauer, *A Greek-English Lexicon*, p. 851.

Chapter Eleven: The Lightning of God

1. Spiros Zodhiates, *Hebrew-Greek Key Study Bible—New American Standard* (Chattanooga, TN: AMG Publishers, 1984; revised edition, 1990), p. 1846.
2. Craig Brian Larson, *Illustrations for Preaching and Teaching* (Grand Rapids, MI: Baker Books, 1993), p. 133.
3. Ibid., p. 72, adapted.
4. Joseph Henry Thayer, *A Greek-English Lexicon of the New Testament* (Grand Rapids, MI: Baker Book House, 1977), p. 422.
5. James Strong, *The New Strong's Exhaustive Concordance of the Bible* (Nashville, TN: Thomas Nelson Publishers, 1990), ref. no. 7931.

Chapter Twelve: The Substance of Prayer

1. James Strong, *The New Strong's Exhaustive Concordance of the Bible* (Nashville, TN: Thomas Nelson Publishers, 1990), ref. no. 3115.
2. Dick Eastman, *No Easy Road* (Grand Rapids, MI: Baker Book House, 1971), pp. 96-97.
3. Craig Brian Larson, *Illustrations for Preaching and Teaching* (Grand Rapids, MI: Baker Books, 1993), p. 245, adapted.
4. Eastman, *No Easy Road*, pp. 97-98.
5. Larson, *Illustrations for Preaching*, p. 114.
6. Joseph Henry Thayer, *A Greek-English Lexicon of the New Testament* (Grand Rapids, MI: Baker Book House, 1977), p. 38.
7. Jack W. Hayford, *Prayer Is Invading the Impossible* (South Plainfield, NJ: Logos International, 1977; revised edition, Bridge Publishing, 1995), p. 55, 1977 edition.
8. Thayer, *A Greek-English Lexicon*, p. 14.
9. Gordon Lindsay, *Prayer That Moves Mountains* (Dallas: Christ for the Nations, Inc., revised 1994), p. 43.
10. Thayer, *A Greek-English Lexicon*, p. 422.
11. Paul E. Billheimer, *Destined for the Throne* (Fort Washington, PA: Christian Literature Crusade, 1975), p. 107.
12. Strong, *The New Strong's Exhaustive Concordance*, ref. no. 4057.
13. Ibid., ref. no. 5228.
14. Ibid., ref. no. 2596.
15. Larson, *Illustrations for Preaching*, p. 177, adapted.

Chapter Thirteen: Actions That Speak and Words That Perform

1. Cindy Jacobs, *The Voice of God* (Ventura, CA: Regal Books, 1995), pp. 251-253.
2. Sue Curran, *The Praying Church* (Blountville, TN: Shekinah Publishing Company, 1987), p. 140.

3. Elizabeth Alves, *Becoming a Prayer Warrior* (Ventura, CA: Renew Books, 1998), pp. 167-210.

4. Spiros Zodhiates, *Hebrew-Greek Key Study Bible—New American Standard* (Chattanooga, TN: AMG Publishers, 1984; revised edition, 1990), p. 1861.

5. R. Laird Harris, Gleason L. Archer Jr., and Bruce K. Waltke, *Theological Wordbook of the Old Testament* (Chicago: Moody Press, 1980; Grand Rapids: William B. Eerdmans Publishing Co., revised edition, 1991), p. 158.

6. Ibid., p. 118.

7. Ibid., p. 793.

8. James Strong, *The New Strong's Exhaustive Concordance of the Bible* (Nashville, TN: Thomas Nelson Publishers, 1990), ref. no. 4834.

9. Adapted from a message by Pastor Tim Sheets, Middletown, Ohio.

10. Ibid.

11. Dick Eastman, *The Jericho Hour* (Orlando, FL: Creation House, 1994), pp. 10-11, adapted.

Chapter Fourteen: The Watchman Anointing

1. Craig Brian Larson, *Illustrations for Preaching and Teaching* (Grand Rapids, MI: Baker Books, 1993), p. 59, adapted.

2. Cindy Jacobs, *Possessing the Gates of the Enemy* (Grand Rapids, MI: Chosen Books, 1991), pp. 21-22, adapted.

3. Quin Sherrer with Ruthanne Garlock, *How to Pray for Your Family and Friends* (Ann Arbor, MI: Servant Publications, 1990), p. 127.

4. James Strong, *The New Strong's Exhaustive Concordance of the Bible* (Nashville, TN: Thomas Nelson Publishers, 1990), ref. no. 8104.

5. Ibid., ref. no. 5341.

6. Ibid., ref. no. 6822.

7. C. Peter Wagner, *Prayer Shield* (Ventura, CA: Regal Books, 1992), pp. 66-73.

8. Ibid., p. 180.

9. Ibid., p. 177.

10. Sherrer with Garlock, *How to Pray for Your Family*, pp. 152-153, adapted.

11. Spiros Zodhiates, *Hebrew-Greek Key Study Bible—New American Standard* (Chattanooga, TN: AMG Publishers, 1984; revised edition, 1990), p. 1752.

12. Ibid., p. 1787.

13. Sherrer with Garlock, *How to Pray for Your Family*, p. 95, adapted.

14. C. Peter Wagner, *Breaking Strongholds in Your City* (Ventura, CA: Regal Books, 1993), pp. 176-177.

15. Strong, *The New Strong's Exhaustive Concordance*, ref. no. 2275.

16. Larson, *Illustrations for Preaching*, p. 12, adapted.

BIBLIOGRAPHY

Alves, Elizabeth. *Becoming a Prayer Warrior*. Ventura, CA: Renew Books, 1998.

Bauer, Walter. *A Greek-English Lexicon of the New Testament*. Chicago, IL: The University of Chicago Press, 1979.

Billheimer, Paul. *Destined for the Throne*. Fort Washington, PA: Christian Literature Crusade, 1975.

Bosworth, F. F. *Christ the Healer*. Grand Rapids, MI: Baker Book House/Revell, 1973.

Bromiley, Geoffrey W. *Theological Dictionary of the New Testament, Abridged*. Grand Rapids, MI: William B. Eerdmans Publishing Co., 1985.

Brown, Francis, S. R. Driver, and Charles A. Briggs. *The New Brown-Driver, Briggs-Gesenius Hebrew and English Lexicon*. Peabody, MA: Hendrickson Publishers, 1979.

Bullinger, Ethelbert. *A Critical Lexicon and Concordance to the English and Greek New Testament*. Grand Rapids, MI: Zondervan Publishing House, 1975.

Canfield, Jack, and Mark Victor Hansen. *Chicken Soup for the Soul*. Deerfield Beach, FL: Health Communications, Inc., 1993.

The Consolidated Webster Encyclopedic Dictionary. Chicago, IL: Consolidated Book Publishers, 1954.

Curran, Sue. *The Praying Church*. Blountville, TN: Shekinah Publishing Company, 1987.

Eastman, Dick. *The Jericho Hour*. Orlando, FL: Creation House, 1994.

———. *No Easy Road*. Grand Rapids, MI: Baker Book House, 1971.

Gordon, S. D. *What It Will Take to Change the World*. Grand Rapids, MI: Baker Book House, 1979.

Harris, R. Laird, Gleason L. Archer Jr., and Bruce K. Waltke. *Theological Wordbook of the Old Testament*. Chicago, IL: Moody Press, 1980; Grand Rapids: William B. Eerdmans Publishing Co., revised edition, 1991.

Hayford, Jack. *Prayer Is Invading the Impossible*. South Plainfield, NJ: Logos International, 1977; revised edition, Bridge Pub-lishing, 1995.

Jacobs, Cindy. *Possessing the Gates of the Enemy*. Grand Rapids, MI: Chosen Books, 1991.

——. *The Voice of God*. Ventura, CA: Regal Books, 1995.

Keil, C. F., and F. Delitzsch. *Commentary on the Old Testament, Volume 1*. Grand Rapids, MI: William B. Eerdmans Publishing Co., reprinted 1991.

Larson, Craig Brian. *Illustrations for Preaching and Teaching*. Grand Rapids, MI: Baker Books, 1993.

Lindsay, Gordon. *The New John G. Lake Sermons*. Dallas, TX: Christ for the Nations, Inc., 1979.

——. *Prayer That Moves Mountains*. Dallas, TX: Christ for the Nations, Inc., revised 1994.

Mason, John L. *An Enemy Called Average*. Tulsa, OK: 1990.

Mathews, R. Arthur. *Born for Battle*. Robesonia, PA: OMF Books, 1978.

Murray, Andrew. *The Ministry of Intercessory Prayer*. Minneapolis, MN: Bethany House Publishers, 1981.

New American Standard Exhaustive Concordance of the Bible. Nashville, TN: Holman Bible Publishers, 1981.

Sherrer, Quin, and Ruthanne Garlock. *How to Pray for Your Family and Friends*. Ann Arbor, MI: Servant Publications, 1990.

The Spirit-Filled Bible. Nashville, TN: Thomas Nelson Publishers, 1991.

Strong, James. *The New Strong's Exhaustive Concordance of the Bible*. Nashville, TN: Thomas Nelson Publishers, 1990.

Thayer, Joseph Henry. *A Greek-English Lexicon of the New Testament*. Grand Rapids, MI: Baker Book House, 1977.

Vine, W. E. *The Expanded Vine's Expository Dictionary of New Testament Words*. Minneapolis, MN: Bethany House Publishers, 1984.

Wagner, C. Peter. *Breaking Strongholds in Your City*. Ventura, CA: Regal Books, 1993.

——. *Prayer Shield*. Ventura, CA: Regal Books, 1992.

Wilson, William. *Old Testament Word Studies*. Grand Rapids, MI: Kregel Publications, 1978.

Zodhiates, Spiros. *The Complete Word Study Dictionary*. Iowa Falls, IA: Word Bible Publishers, 1992.

——. *Hebrew-Greek Key Study Bible—New American Standard*. Chattanooga, TN: AMG Publishers, 1984; revised edition, 1990.

BOOK TWO

HOW TO PRAY
FOR LOST
LOVED ONES

Praying for the Salvation of Your Friends and Family

DUTCH
SHEETS

THE PERSISTENT KNOCKING

Author and lecturer Leo Buscaglia once talked about a contest he was asked to judge. The purpose of the contest was to find the most caring child. The winner was a four-year-old boy whose next-door neighbor was an elderly gentleman who had recently lost his wife. Upon seeing the man cry, the little boy went into the old gentleman's yard, climbed onto his lap and just sat there. When his mother asked him what he had said to the neighbor, the little boy said, "Nothing. I just helped him cry."

Letting God Cry Through Us

On Wednesday, October 4, 2000, God somehow powerfully touched my heart with His, and for three and a half hours God allowed me to help Him cry over our nation.

Though I have often asked God for His heart toward America, I was in no way ready for the intensity with which it came that night. As I felt God's aching heart for America,

I thought my own heart would break in two. I didn't know it was possible to weep from so deep within. It was not from my head or my emotions; it was from deep in my heart.

That day the Lord placed upon me an incredible burden to call the nation to prayer for the then-upcoming presidential election. I was led by the Lord to issue a prayer alert that ultimately went to millions of people, resulting in a great mobilization of prayer asking God for His man to be placed in office.

I believe God answered the prayers of those many people and gave us the president He wanted America to have. I believe He gave us a man who, like King David, is a man after His heart—a sincere, humble man who loves God and through whom He can work. Not that God is a Republican or a Democrat. It's not about a political party but about finding a person God can use to accomplish His purposes. In ancient Israel, He could not do what He wanted through King Saul, so He looked for a man after His own heart. That person, of course, was David. I believe that, in this election, God heard our prayers and graciously gave us a man after His heart to lead our nation.

My wife and I, along with a few others from our church in Colorado Springs, attended the inauguration of George W. Bush. It was worth every minute of standing in the extremely cold rain—as well as the many hours of prayer and fasting leading up to this day—as I watched and heard Bush, with great conviction, complete his oath of office by saying, "So help me God." Upon the uttering of those words, one well-known minister in attendance was heard to say, "The curse is broken off of America." I, too, believe that it marked a new beginning. We are, indeed, seeing God's grace upon us to heal and save our nation.

Another important result of my experience on October 4 was a fresh awareness of the incredible passion of the Lord to save. I already knew God desired to save America. He had been challenging me for the past few years to believe Him for the saving of this nation, for genuine revival and a great harvest of souls. But on this particular evening, it was different. I literally *felt* God's breaking heart aching to save and heal America.

In my prayers for our nation, the Lord has often led me to Ezekiel 37. In this passage He uses a graveyard of dry bones to reveal Israel's spiritually dead condition to the prophet Ezekiel. As the prophet gazed upon these dry bones, the Lord asked him an interesting question: "Can these bones live?" Ezekiel, not knowing how to respond, simply said, "Oh, Lord God, You know" (see Ezek. 37:3). God's response was to have Ezekiel prophesy to the bones and later to have the wind of the Holy Spirit breathe life into the bones. In the vision the bones came together, and the wind—or breath—of God's Spirit came to them, causing them to live again.

As I said, God has often led me to this passage. It seems I am prompted with the same question about America that God asked Ezekiel about Israel: Can these bones live? I have always tried to summon faith and believe that America will indeed receive a revival that results in Resurrection life. But I must admit there have been times of wavering in which I found it difficult to believe.

However, on that aforementioned evening something changed. I actually *felt* God's passion to save our nation. I identified with His aching heart so strongly that my faith was lifted to a new level. I knew beyond any doubt that the dry bones of America *could* live, because *God desperately wants to save this nation.*

I am fully persuaded that hundreds of thousands of people will be saved in America over the next several years. As God comes to bring salvation to our nation, however, that salvation will come *an individual at a time.* Those born again will be our fathers, mothers, sons, daughters, husbands, wives, friends and neighbors. They will have names and faces, known personally by God.

My purpose for this chapter is to encourage your faith that *God really does want to save those dear to you.* I want your faith to be lifted to a new level. I have found that where faith for the salvation of the lost is concerned, unbelief controls much of the Church. We ask God to send revival and save people, but deep in our hearts we can't believe it is really going to happen. Perhaps it's because we've prayed and waited so long that we are no longer convinced God really will do it.

Persevering in Prayer

Chrissy sleepily answered the phone late one night and heard her older brother's voice on the line. "Sis, I just invited Jesus into my life!" he shouted. "I'm saved! The preacher said to tell someone immediately, so I knew I had to call you because you've prayed for me for so long."

The praying sister sat speechless with the phone in her hand. This brother of hers—the one who had mocked and screamed at her at their mother's funeral when she tried to share Jesus with him—the one who had broken up a pastor's home to marry his third and current wife—this rebel was calling to say he'd accepted Jesus. She could hardly believe it!

Why is it when our loved ones are saved in answer to prayers we've prayed for years, we are always surprised? Could it be that we secretly doubt whether our prayers will really change anything? Or that we've written off the person as hopeless?[1]

I want you to be so convinced that God will save the person you love, the one for whom you pray, that you would be shocked if they *didn't* get saved. I want you to believe God is so passionately in love with people that when you cry for those you love, you realize you're really helping *Him* cry.

Why is this kind of faith so important? First, if we don't really believe God will answer our prayers, we will not pray with any kind of consistency and diligence. We may sporadically ask Him, but we certainly will not persevere. We must have a motivational faith that truly believes He is hearing us and He will answer.

When Raymond's brother was dying, he stood by the hospital bed and said boldly, "Henry, I've prayed for you for years. I'm tired of you cursing the Lord I serve. It's time you accepted Him and all He has done for you! You could very well die tonight! Where would you spend eternity?"

Henry acknowledged his need for God and asked Jesus into his heart right then. Finally, after 15 years, Raymond saw his prayers for his brother dramatically answered just a few days before Henry died. [2]

Like Raymond, we must have faith that doesn't quit!

Faith Releases God's Power

The second reason this issue is so important is that our faith really does release God's power. There is a striking story in Mark 6:1-6 about Christ not working any miracles in His hometown of Nazareth. A careful reading and study of the verses in the original Greek text reveals that Jesus didn't simply choose not to work miracles, but He actually *could not* work miracles in Nazareth because of the unbelief of the people.

I certainly am not implying that Christ did not have enough power or that something was wrong with His spiritual condition. It is clear, however, that somehow his neighbors' unbelief blocked God's power from flowing from Christ to them. The Scriptures don't say He *didn't want to* work miracles or that He chose not to work miracles. Mark 6:5 says, "He *could do no miracle* there except that He laid His hands upon a few sick people and healed them" (emphasis added).

There really is a dynamic of faith wherein unbelief can hinder God's power from flowing to us. In James 1:6,7, we are instructed:

> Ask in faith without any doubting, for the one who doubts is like the surf of the sea driven and tossed by the wind. For let not that man expect that he will receive anything from the Lord.

Again, from this passage it is clear that unbelief can cause us to not receive what we have asked for, even though it may be within the scope of God's will.

Galatians 6:9 (*KJV*) states: "And let us not be weary in well doing: for in due season we shall reap, if we faint not." Again, if we are not able to persevere, which certainly has to do with our faith, then there will be times when we will not reap what we have asked. Jesus said, "If thou canst believe, all things are possible to him that believeth" (Mark 9:23, *KJV*).

It is imperative that we ask in faith when we pray for the salvation of the people we love. We must be convinced that God will answer our prayers, or we will not be sufficiently motivated to ask or to do so with persevering faith. And it is also true that unbelief will block the power of God from being released to answer the prayer.

I can well imagine that some of you are already feeling intimidated, questioning whether you have, or could ever have, enough faith to pray your loved one or friend into the family of God. The answer to your question is an emphatic yes!

Don't allow Satan, that accuser of the brethren, to defeat you before you ever get started. You are of the family of faith. The Holy Spirit, the author of faith, is in you, and you can and will be able to believe. Deep within your spirit it is your nature to walk in faith.

God Turns Our Weakness into Strength

One of my favorite stories in the Bible is that of Abraham and Sarah believing God's promise for a son. What most people don't realize, however, is that they didn't always walk in great faith during the 25 years they waited for Isaac. They wavered in their faith for receiving a son through Sarah—so much so that they conceived a plan to try to fulfill the promise through Hagar, Sarah's maid. Ishmael was the result.

The aged couple were still in doubt when God came again and said to Abraham that Sarah would conceive and bear him a son "at this season next year" (Gen. 17:21). Abraham was 99 years old and Sarah was 90. Abraham laughed at God, and so did Sarah. I probably would have laughed, too. Abraham's "faith-filled" response was, "Oh that Ishmael might live before Thee!" (Gen. 17:18). I have asked God to accept a few of my Ishmaels, too!

Interestingly, in a seeming contradiction, the New Testament states very clearly that it was because of Abraham and Sarah's *great faith* that God was able to fulfill the promise (see Rom. 4:17-22; Heb. 11:11,12). Does the New Testament contradict the Old Testament? Absolutely not.

Romans 4:20 tells us they "*grew* strong in faith" (emphasis added). And here's the good news: They grew into this incredibly strong faith in three short months, at which time Isaac was conceived. Twenty-four years of unbelief was overcome in just three months! From the point of unbelief until Isaac's conception three months later, something transpired to transform them from unbelief to the great faith spoken of in the New Testament.

If God could do this for them, He can do it for you! Abraham and Sarah were not even born again as you are. They didn't have the Holy Spirit abiding within them. Surely we who live on this side of the Cross, with a "better covenant" and "better promises" (Heb. 8:6), can rise to a level of faith as quickly, or even more so. Don't underestimate the Christ in you (see Col. 1:27)!

Sam and Jed refused to walk in anything but faith. Hearing that a $5,000 bounty had been offered for the capture or killing of wolves, they became bounty hunters. Waking up one night, Sam saw that they were surrounded by 50 pairs of gleaming eyes—ravenous wolves licking hungry chops. "Jed, wake up," he whispered to his sleeping partner. "We're rich!"

When the wolves of unbelief and opposition endeavor to erode your faith, and when the circumstances around you scream that you will never receive the Lord's promise, follow the admonition of the prophet Joel:

Let the weak say, I am strong (Joel 3:10, *KJV*).

And see the unbelievers around you not as threats but as opportunities. They really can live, and you can really believe it.

Questions for Wisdom and Faith

1. Why do we fail to be persistent in our prayers?

2. Can a person pray in faith for someone's salvation and not seemingly see this prayer fulfilled? If so, why would this happen?

3. Why does God allow us to experience a small measure of His long-suffering heart over the salvation of other people?

FAITH PAVES THE WAY

There is an old story that recalls how Satan once summoned his top demonic aides to plan strategy against the Church of Jesus Christ. Satan stood at the blackboard lecturing and illustrating the latest tactics in demonic warfare. At the end of this session Satan said, "Now get out there and give your best possible effort to keep believers from winning the lost!" As the demonic hierarchy headed for the door, Satan hollered out, "By the way, be careful! If those Christians ever begin to really believe and act on what they have in the Word of God, then hell help us, all heaven's going to break loose!"

Well, we ARE going to believe. And we ARE going to break heaven loose over people!

God's Assurance

As stated in the first chapter, faith is necessary in order for us to receive our provisions in Christ. The generation of Israel that came out of bondage in Egypt did not receive their inheritance because of their inability to believe. Hebrews 4:1,2 tells us:

Therefore, let us fear lest, while a promise remains of entering His rest, any one of you should seem to have come short of it. For indeed we have had good news preached to us, just as they also; but the word they heard did not profit them, because it was not united by faith in those who heard.

In this chapter we are going to see how our faith can grow to a point where we become assured of seeing God's salvation come to those for whom we pray. First, here are some principles of faith that are essential for us to understand.

Though it may seem obvious, I need to state that faith is not of the mind—it is not positive thinking. It is possible to convince ourselves of something mentally and allow no thoughts of doubt to enter our minds without that being true biblical faith. Biblical faith is of the heart, not the mind (see Mark 11:23; Rom. 10:10).

Hebrews 11:1 says faith is an assurance of what we ask for—things hoped for. The word "assurance" comes from the Greek word *hupostasis*.[1] This was also the Greek word for a title deed. Biblical faith is knowing with certainty deep in our hearts that we have what we ask God for, just as surely as a title deed proves that we own a piece of property.

The same verse in the *King James Version* tells us that faith is our evidence of things we cannot see. "Evidence" is from the Greek word *elegchos*,[2] which literally means the proof of the charges in a legal court case that results in a conviction. The word was used in a court of law for evidence significant enough to prove a case and result in a conviction. In other words, our faith in God's Word or His promises is all the evidence we need to validate our conviction.

If there is not a deep, settled faith in you for the salvation of the one for whom you are praying—or for anything else for that matter—please don't be intimidated. Your faith simply needs to grow. The Bible teaches that faith is like a mustard seed. The point of Jesus' mustard seed parable is not that we need faith the size of a mustard seed. Though some translations word it that way, it is not entirely accurate. Jesus does not tell us we need faith *the size of* a mustard seed. He says we need faith that is *like* a mustard seed. The point is that the seed starts out tiny but grows into a tree.

Romans 12:3 teaches that each of us is given "a measure of faith." The Greek word *metron*, which is translated "measure," means "a limited portion."[3] Romans 1:17, however, states that we go from faith to faith. In other words, our faith must grow.

Paul commended the Thessalonian church, saying, "Your faith is greatly enlarged" (2 Thess. 1:3). *Huperauxano*, the Greek word translated "greatly enlarged," means "to increase above ordinary degree."[4] Our faith can do this also.

Earlier I referred to Romans 4, where it says that Abraham grew strong in faith. The phrase being "fully assured" in Romans 4:21 is very significant. It comes from the Greek word *plerophoreo*, which is a combination of the words *pleros*, meaning "full," and *phero*, meaning "to carry."[5] Together they give us the literal definition "to bring in full measure." In other words, Abraham started with a measure of faith that grew to full measure.

How does this happen?

Nurturing the Seeds of Faith

Our faith grows by a revelation of the Word of God as we feed and meditate on it (see Josh. 1:8; Ps. 1:2; Rom. 10:17). Doing this transforms God's Word from a seed (see Mark 4:1-9,13-20; 1 Pet. 1:23) to full fruition.

We start with a promise from God's Word. As we meditate on that promise, the Holy Spirit infuses it with His life, causing it to grow and multiply in us. Our part is to feed on and meditate in the Word of God. The Holy Spirit's part is to cause it to grow.

George Müller, a great man of faith, had this to say about the maturing of our faith:

> You ask how may I, a true believer, have my faith strengthened? Here is the answer: "Every good gift and every perfect gift is from above, and comes down from the Father of lights, with whom there is no variation or shadow of turning" (Jas. 1:17, *NKJV*). As the increase of faith is a good gift, it must come from God; therefore, He ought to be asked for this blessing. The following means, however, ought to be used.
>
> First, carefully read the Word of God and meditate on it. Through reading the Word of God, and especially through meditation on the Word of God, the believer becomes more acquainted with the nature and character of God. Thus he sees more and more, besides His holiness and justice, what a kind,

loving, gracious, merciful, mighty, wise and faithful God He is.

He will rely upon the willingness of God to help him because he has not only learned from the Scriptures what a kind, good, merciful, gracious and faithful being God is; but he has also seen in the Word of God how, in a great variety of instances, God has proved Himself to be so. And the consideration of this, if God has become known to us through prayer and meditation on His own Word, will lead us with a measure of confidence, in general at least, to rely upon Him. Thus the reading of the Word of God, together with meditation on it, will be one special means to strengthen our faith.[6]

As we approach God's Word with the intention of planting seeds that can grow into great faith, we should meditate specifically on scriptures that pertain to our need. In other words, if you need faith for someone's salvation, feed on promises relating to that subject. If you need to increase your faith in God as your provider, meditate on Scriptures that address this particular area of truth.

Perhaps a short explanation of biblical meditation is appropriate. Scriptural meditation does not mean attempting to clear the mind, as in Transcendental Meditation. I am not talking about having a blank mind in order to receive any and every thought communication that might be sent our way. This unbiblical form of meditation gives way to demonic thoughts.

Biblical meditation, however, means to ponder, muse on, think about and even mutter to one's self. In other words, it is repetitious thinking on and speaking of God's Word. This allows the Holy Spirit to transform the Word from information in the mind to revelation of the heart.

Ten Signposts Toward God's Saving Grace

I would like to give you 10 proofs from the Scriptures that God wants to save your loved ones. As you think and meditate on these truths, they will cause your faith to grow and you, too, will have great faith—a full measure! The Holy Spirit may give you other Scriptures, too. In no way do I consider this list to be complete.

God Wants All to Be Saved

The Scriptures tell us that God is "not willing that any should perish, but that all should come to repentance" (2 Pet. 3:9, *KJV*). He could not make His will any clearer. It is His desire for every person to believe upon Christ and be born again. We don't have to wonder what God wants for the person for whom we are praying.

God Is Able to Save

"Behold, the LORD'S hand is not so short that it cannot save" (Isa. 59:1). We must believe not only that God wants to but that He *can* save. He is not weak; He *can* do this. His hand is very powerful and somehow He can bend, shape and change the perspective of unbelievers and bring them to a realization and understanding of the truth. He can break off of them every satanic stronghold and bring them to a knowledge of the truth.

While hitchhiking home, Roger Simms was picked up by an older gentleman in an expensive car. They talked about many things, including Mr. Hanover's business in Chicago. Roger felt a strong compulsion to witness, but was apprehensive about witnessing to a wealthy businessman. Finally, nearing his destination, Roger spoke up.

"Mr. Hanover," began Roger, "I want to share something very important with you." He explained the way of salvation and asked if Mr. Hanover would like to receive Christ as his Savior. To Roger's astonishment, the businessman pulled over to the side of the road, bowed his head, wept and prayed the prayer of salvation. He thanked Roger, saying, "This is the greatest thing that has ever happened to me."

Five years later, while in Chicago on a business trip, Roger went to Hanover Enterprises. The receptionist told him it would be impossible to see Mr. Hanover, but Mrs. Hanover was available. A little disappointed, he followed her into an office.

After exchanging greetings, Roger explained how Mr. Hanover had kindly given him a ride years ago. Suddenly interested, Mrs. Hanover asked when this had happened. When Roger told her it was on May 7, five years earlier, she asked if anything unusual had happened during his ride.

Roger hesitated, wondering if giving his witness had been a source of contention. But, feeling the prompting of the Lord, he told her that he had shared the gospel message and that her husband had accepted the Lord into his heart.

She began to sob uncontrollably. After a few minutes, she explained that she had thought her prayers for her husband's salvation had not been answered. After leaving Roger at his destination, Mr. Hanover had died that day in a horrible head-on collision.[7]

God is faithful, and He is definitely capable!

Salvation Is His to Give

"Salvation belongs to the LORD" (Ps. 3:8). God is a God of salvation; He owns it. Since it belongs to Him, He can give it away! It is His nature, a part of who He is, to confer His gift of salvation to people. He will do this for the person for whom you pray.

His Very Name Is Savior

"And you shall call His name Jesus, for it is He who will save His people from their sins" (Matt. 1:21). The Hebrew name *Yeshua* comes from the word *yasha*, which means "save."[8] He is called *Yeshua* because He is the Savior. Think about it: He chose to call Himself "the One who saves." He loves to save. He wants to save! Salvation is who He is. He will save

your loved one, your friend, your neighbor! He wants to—
it's His name.

The angel said to the shepherds, "Do not be afraid; for
behold, I bring you good news of a *great joy which shall be for
all the people*; for today in the city of David there has been
born for you a Savior, who is Christ the Lord" (Luke 2:10,11,
emphasis added).

"For it is for this we labor and strive, because we have
fixed our hope on the living God, *who is the Savior of all men,*
especially of believers" (1 Tim. 4:10, emphasis added).

Charles Finney shared the following testimony of a father
who realized the Lord's intense desire to save his family:

> I knew a father who was a good man, but who had
> misconceptions about the prayer of faith. His whole
> family of children had grown up, without one of
> them being converted. One day his son grew ill and
> seemed ready to die. The father prayed, but the son
> grew worse and was sinking into the grave without
> hope. The father prayed until his anguish was un-
> utterable. He finally prayed (there seemed no prospect
> of his son surviving), pouring out his soul as if he
> would not be denied.
>
> Later, he got an assurance that his son would
> not only live, but be converted. God also assured
> him that not only this one, but his whole family
> would be converted to God. He came into the house
> and told his family his son would not die. They were
> astonished at him. "I tell you," he said, "he will not

die. And no child of mine will ever die in his sins."
That man's children were all converted years ago.

What do you think of that? Was that fanaticism? If you believe it was, it is because you know nothing about the prayer of faith. Do you pray like this man prayed? Do you live in such a manner that you can offer such prayers for your children?[9]

You can. Believe in the Savior! What He did for this father, He will do for you.

God's Passion to Save
While on earth as a human, the Lord would rather reach out to save a sinner than eat (see John 4). Christ, even as a flesh-and-blood human being with very real human appetites, cared much more about saving an immoral, hurting, lonely woman than about meeting His own needs. He found much more excitement and satisfaction in saving the lost than in feeding His body. Immediately afterward, when encouraged by His disciples to eat, He simply said, "I have food to eat that you do not know about" (John 4:32). He was so excited about what happened with this lady that He had lost His appetite!

He Was Willing to Become Human to Save Us
While in heaven as God, He chose to become human in order to save us rather than to remain God only. In other words, He went to the unfathomable extent of becoming a human in order to save humanity. It meant that much to

Him. He loves us so much that He would rather pay the price of becoming one of us than for us to remain outside His family. "For there is one God, and one mediator also between God and men, the man Christ Jesus" (1 Tim. 2:5).

He Was Willing to Die to Save Us

When faced with the agony of the cross, which was for our salvation, Jesus chose torture, humiliation and death instead of angelic deliverance. He could have called upon legions of angels to deliver Him (see Matt. 26:53). His desire to save us was and is so intense that no price or sacrifice was too great. He did it for your loved one. Go ahead, put a face to the price He paid!

In his book *Written in Blood*, Robert Coleman tells the story of a little boy whose sister needed a blood transfusion. The doctor had explained that she had the same disease the boy had recovered from two years earlier. Her only chance for recovery was a transfusion from someone who had previously conquered the disease. Since the two children had the same rare blood type, the boy was the ideal donor.

"Would you give your blood to Mary?" the doctor asked.

Johnny hesitated. His lower lip started to tremble. Then he smiled and said, "Sure, for my sister."

Soon the two children were wheeled into the hospital room—Mary, pale and thin; Johnny, robust and healthy. Neither spoke, but when their eyes met, Johnny grinned.

As the nurse inserted the needle into his arm, Johnny's smile faded. He watched the blood flow through the tube. With the ordeal almost over, his voice, slightly shaky, broke the silence, "Doctor, when do I die?"

Only then did the doctor realize why Johnny had hesitated, why his lip had trembled when he'd agreed to donate his blood. He'd thought giving his blood to his sister meant giving up his life. In that brief moment, he'd made his great decision.

Johnny, fortunately, didn't have to die to save his sister. Each of us, however, has a condition more serious than Mary's, and it required Jesus to give not just His blood but His life.[10]

He did it gladly.

God Desires to Show Mercy

God was willing to spare an entire wicked city, Sodom, even though it was so profoundly wicked. He told Abraham He would spare the city if even 10 righteous people could be found (see Gen. 18:32). He desires to show mercy rather than judgment toward sinners. If He was willing to spare Sodom, He is willing to spare your friend or family member—yes, even if they are bound by great perversion.

Jesus Came to Seek and Save the Lost

Jesus said He came to seek—what a great word—and to save the lost (see Luke 19:10). He is still seeking them today.

He is on a quest. Let Him use you to satisfy His seeking heart! Speak this truth to your heart every day. Go to sleep at night thinking about it. Faith will come.

Salvation Is the Theme of the Bible

The Bible is the story of God's desire to save a fallen human race. The book of Genesis brings us very quickly to the Fall. The rest of the Bible is God's story of His heart toward the human race and His plan to save us from our sins.

After much worry and stress, author Quin Sherrer came to a point of faith for her three children to be touched by God's transforming power. Let her testimony encourage you as you allow your faith to grow:

> Though the Scriptures boldly declare God's almighty power and Christ's victory over Satan, we often struggle to believe that His Word is really true *for us.* Or that His power and victory will be applied to our situation.
>
> Paul Billheimer states, "Unbelief in the integrity of the Word is the first great cause for prayerlessness." We must put our confidence in the reliability of God's Word and choose to believe God is who He says He is, and that He will do what He said He will do.
>
> When I began diligently praying for my children, the Lord led me to meditate on this verse: "All your children shall be taught by the LORD, and great shall be the peace of your children" (Isa. 54:13, *NKJV*).

Some weeks later, after putting one child on a plane following a Labor Day visit, my heart was heavy. There was no indication of a turning toward the Lord. In church later that day, as I closed my eyes in prayer, I suddenly had an inner vision of all three of our children with arms raised, praising the Lord.

I went home and recorded it in my prayer diary. I began to declare with my mouth, "The Lord *is* my children's teacher . . . their peace shall be great. Thank you, Lord, that You will fulfill Your promise, and someday I *will* see them praising You."

Eight months later, each child came from a different city to meet me in Orlando for Mother's Day. During worship in church that morning, I looked up to see all three of them, hands raised, praising the Lord! What a Mother's Day gift!

I learned what I say with my mouth is important. It is all too easy to talk about the negatives in a situation, when instead I should open my mouth to wield the Sword of the Spirit by quoting the Word of God and declaring what God says in the matter (see Heb. 4:12).[11]

God's heart is to save. Meditate on and feed your heart with these truths, as well as any He may reveal to you. You will soon become fully convinced that the God who saves, will. Then, according to Psalm 126:5,6, after you help Him cry, you can help Him rejoice!

Dutch Sheets

Bedrock for Your Faith

Here are several additional Scriptures you can meditate on to build your faith:

Crying Out to God
The LORD hears when I call to Him (Ps. 4:3).

I have called upon Thee, for Thou wilt answer me, O God (Ps. 17:6).

But as for me, I will watch expectantly for the LORD; I will wait for the God of my salvation. My God will hear me (Mic. 7:7).

And it will come about that whoever calls on the name of the LORD will be delivered (Joel 2:32).

Hunger for His Blessing
Wilt Thou not Thyself revive us again, that Thy people may rejoice in Thee? Show us Thy lovingkindness, O LORD, and grant us Thy salvation (Ps. 85:6,7).

For I will pour out water on the thirsty land and streams on the dry ground; I will pour out My Spirit on your offspring, and My blessing on your descendants (Isa. 44:3).

Wooing People to His Kingdom
He that winneth souls is wise (Prov. 11:30, *KJV*).

Now all these things are from God, who reconciled us to Himself through Christ, and gave us the ministry of reconciliation, namely, that God was in Christ reconciling the world to Himself, not counting their trespasses against them, and He has committed to us the word of reconciliation (2 Cor. 5:18,19).

Praying in Faith

If you abide in Me, and My words abide in you, ask whatever you wish, and it shall be done for you (John 15:7).

Truly, truly, I say to you, if you shall ask the Father for anything, He will give it to you in My name. Until now you have asked for nothing in My name; ask, and you will receive, that your joy may be made full (John 16:23,24).

Believe in the Lord Jesus, and you shall be saved, you and your household (Acts 16:31).

The effective prayer of a righteous man can accomplish much (James 5:16).

God's Touch of Salvation

The LORD has bared His holy arm in the sight of all the nations, that all the ends of the earth may see the salvation of our God (Isa. 52:10).

Thus says the LORD, "Preserve justice, and do righteousness, for My salvation is about to come and My righteousness to be revealed" (Isa. 56:1).

And all flesh shall see the salvation of God (Luke 3:6).

For the grace of God has appeared, bringing salvation to all men (Titus 2:11,12).

Hence, also, He is able to save forever those who draw near to God through Him, since He always lives to make intercession for them (Heb. 7:25).

God's Amazing Love

"For I have no pleasure in the death of anyone who dies," declares the LORD God. "Therefore, repent and live" (Ezek. 18:32).

For the Son of Man has come to save that which was lost (Matt. 18:11).

Thus it is not the will of your Father who is in heaven that one of these little ones perish (Matt. 18:14).

I tell you that in the same way, there will be more joy in heaven over one sinner who repents, than over ninety-nine righteous persons who need no repentance (Luke 15:7).

For God so loved the world, that He gave His only begotten Son, that whoever believes in Him should not perish, but have eternal life (John 3:16).

But we should always give thanks to God for you, brethren beloved by the Lord, because God has chosen you from the beginning for salvation through sanctification by the Spirit and faith in the truth (2 Thess. 2:13,14).

It is a trustworthy statement, deserving full acceptance, that Christ Jesus came into the world to save sinners (1 Tim. 1:15).

Questions for Wisdom and Faith

1. How do you express your faith on a daily basis?

2. When is your faith the weakest? When is it the strongest?

3. Is there a difference between faith that is nurtured over time and the gift of faith the apostle Paul describes in 1 Corinthians 12:9?

4. What is the most powerful or inspiring passage of Scripture that builds your faith? Why?

3

BEING STRATEGIC
IN SALVATION

An executive hirer, a "head-hunter" who goes out and hires corporate executives for other firms, once told Josh Mc-Dowell, "When I get an executive that I'm trying to hire for someone else, I like to disarm him. I offer him a drink, take my coat off, then my vest, undo my tie, throw up my feet and talk about baseball, football, family, whatever, until he's all relaxed. Then, when I think I've got him relaxed, I lean over, look him square in the eye and say, 'What's your purpose in life?' It's amazing how top executives fall apart at that question.

"Well, I was interviewing this fellow the other day, had him all disarmed, with my feet up on his desk, talking about football. Then I leaned up and said, 'What's your purpose in life, Bob?' And he said, without blinking an eye, 'To go to heaven and take as many people with me as I can.' For the first time in my career I was speechless."[1]

As Christians, that's our purpose, too. And we're going to fulfill it.

Removing the Veil

Acts 13:36 says that King David "served the purpose of God in his own generation." Our purpose as a generation is to bring in the greatest harvest of souls the world has ever seen. What an honor! But to accomplish that purpose, we have some important and fulfilling work to do. And much of it involves strategic prayer to loose our loved ones from Satan's grasp.

The Bible tells us there is a veil that keeps unbelievers from clearly seeing the gospel:

> And even if our gospel is veiled, it is veiled to those who are perishing, in whose case the god of this world has blinded the minds of the unbelieving, that they might not see the light of the gospel of the glory of Christ, who is the image of God (2 Cor. 4:3,4).

The word "veiled" is translated from the Greek word *kalupsis*, which means "to hide, cover up, wrap around."[2] It is important to realize that unbelievers don't see the gospel because they *can't* see it. There is a veil, or covering, over their minds that prevents them from clearly seeing the light and truth of the gospel. We have been given a part to play in lifting this veil off their minds.

Related to this concept of the veil is the Greek word for "revelation," *apokalupsis*. This word is simply the prefix *apo*, which means "off or away,"[3] added to the word *kalupsis*. Literally, then, a revelation is an unveiling, or uncovering. Until unbelievers have an unveiling—a revelation—they won't, indeed they can't, understand the gospel because the veil prevents them from comprehending it. Satan's goal is to hide the truth of the gospel in order to keep unbelievers in his grasp.

Before Tom was saved, he had this to say about his inability to comprehend the gospel: "As clear and simple as the gospel is to me now, it was just as confusing to me before. Oh, I thought I understood it, but I now know it was going right over my head. Then one day it was as though someone peeled back a covering and, for the first time, I truly understood what was being said."

What gives place to this veil? How does Satan, as 2 Corinthians 4:4 says, blind the minds of the unbelieving? The word "blinded" in this verse comes from the Greek word *tuphloo*, which means "to dull the intellect; to make blind."[4] Satan has an ability to dull the unbeliever's thinking where the gospel is concerned. The root word of *tuphloo*, *tupho*, has the meaning of making smoke.[5] Therefore, the blindness in this passage can be compared to a smoke screen that clouds or darkens the air to the point that a person cannot see clearly.

From this same root comes the word *tuphoo* that is used for being high-minded, proud or inflated with self-conceit.[6] The picture is of one who is "puffed up," much like smoke puffs up or billows. The blindness of the unbeliever to the gospel is directly linked to the root of pride that Satan passed on to humankind in the Garden.

The root of pride that came at the Fall causes unbelievers to think humanity's knowledge is greater than God's. This leads not to a knowledge dependent on God but to an independent knowledge that looks to one's own mind and intellect as the judge of truth. This inward quest for knowledge glorifies one's own reasoning ability and causes a rejection of God's knowledge. Because everything is filtered through this inward knowledge, all of which is inundated with pride, it usually translates into the exalting and serving of self and its desires.

Simply stated, *self* loves *self* and anything that satisfies and exalts *self*. Any message that preaches *self-denial*, or even that *self* needs to be saved (which certainly includes the gospel), is offensive to *self*.

The only answer to this self-god is death—the Cross—where we die with Christ. The only problem is self wants so desperately to live. The very nature of pride is to be self-serving and preserving. Thus, the very thing that needs to die is bent on living and must remain the enemy of God in order to do so. No wonder Paul said, "O wretched man that I am!" (Rom. 7:24, *KJV*).

Dealing Pride a Death Blow

Understanding this blinding ability of pride provides a tremendous clue in how to pray effectively for the lost. We must attack the root of pride! Most rejection of Christ, whether from the works motivation of most false religions or the simple fact that most people don't want to give lordship of their lives to another, is due to the veil of pride. This satanically initiated stronghold is the ultimate enemy of Christ and will be dealt with in finality when every knee bows and every tongue confesses that Christ is Lord. Pride will be dealt its final blow!

Ern Grover tells the following story of visiting a woman who had recently become blind:

Mrs. Avery, a woman who had recently lost her sight, invited me to join her outside in the dusk for a cup of tea. On the way outside, she scooped up a handful of cat food. She capably navigated her way to her usual seat at the table in her tiny yard. I sat down beside her and in complete darkness we listened to the sounds of her world. She identified crickets, bullfrogs, a passing motorist, the neighbor's barking dog and the meow of Mrs. Blackwell's cat. She asked me to take her hand and to point it at the north star. I started to get misty-eyed, witnessing this woman, a friend to many, coping with her new challenge of blindness. We sat sipping our tea in silent companionship for a few minutes.

Reaching into her pocket, she fingered a few of the dry nuggets of cat food. Making a "kissing" noise, she held her hand close to the ground. I could barely see the image of a cat sauntering toward her chair and nuzzling its nose in the palm of her hand. A second and then a third cat emerged from the darkness. As I watched her feed and pet her little friends, I smiled at her kindness.

As my eyes adjusted to the dark and my vision became clearer, I almost leaped out of my chair when I realized she was feeding a family of skunks!

Holding my seat, gritting my teeth and hoping I wouldn't startle her little friends, I nervously took another sip of tea. Her conversation never wavered as she continued to feed and pat the skunks circling her ankles. Then, as quickly and stealthily as they had emerged from the dark shadows, they left.[7]

Though not caused by pride, Mrs. Avery's blindness is nonetheless a fitting picture of the reality-distorting ability of pride. Though convincing ourselves of the rightness of our self-serving lifestyles and desires, it is really a terribly odorous fallen creature we humans feed when we serve the exalted god of self.

How do we deal with the vision-altering force of pride inflicted upon us by the deceived, yet deceptive, serpent himself, Satan? The Bible offers a fascinating and enlightening passage that identifies a solution for the pride problem, as well as giving other key strategies, which we will look at in the next chapter, for effectively praying for unbelievers.

For though we walk in the flesh, we do not war according to the flesh, for the weapons of our warfare are not of the flesh, but divinely powerful for the destruction of fortresses. We are destroying speculations and every lofty thing raised up against the knowledge of God, and we are taking every thought captive to the obedience of Christ (2 Cor. 10:3-5).

Although most Christians have interpreted these verses as something we are to do for ourselves, which is also appropriate, the context is certainly that of spiritual warfare for others, as clarified by *The Living Bible*. While reading this paraphrase, please especially notice the references and inferences to the root of pride and its cousin, rebellion. You will be encouraged by the absoluteness of the promises.

It is true that I am an ordinary, weak human being, but I don't use human plans and methods to win my battles. I use God's mighty weapons, not those made by men, to knock down the devil's strongholds. These weapons can break down every proud argument against God and every wall that can be built to keep men from finding Him. With these weapons I can capture rebels and bring them back to God, and change them into men whose hearts' desire is obedience to Christ (2 Cor. 10:3-5, *TLB*).

Let's take a deeper look at what God says here about how to deal with this skunk. Knowing that we often overlook the obvious, God first of all clearly states that our weapons of warfare are not human. We will never win people to Christ on an intellectual basis, nor will we do it through innovative techniques or methods alone. Certainly, a continual barrage of nagging and harassing questions won't bring them to the Lord.

Christian author Quin Sherrer sees the problem clearly when she states:

I've talked with many women who believed it was their responsibility to do everything in their power to "make" their husbands become Christians, but by their manipulative scheming, they only succeeded in turning their husbands away from any interest in spiritual matters. As many wives have learned the hard way, only the Holy Spirit can reveal to an individual the truth of who Jesus is (see John 16:8-13).[8]

Though continued pleading and nagging doesn't often work, sometimes we talk people into a salvation prayer without a true revelation (unveiling), but there is usually no real change because there is no true biblical repentance, which only comes from biblical revelation. When we approach people on a human basis, especially if they feel we are pressuring them, we generally make things worse. The root of pride in them rises up and defends itself, saying essentially, *I don't want anyone else controlling me or telling me what to do.* The irony is that if we attack this pride on a human level, we will only strengthen it.

God's Armory for Breaking Human Pride
However, if we would only realize it, we do have weapons that are "divinely powerful." God says, "Instead of using yours, I'll let you use Mine. Yours won't work; Mine will." *Dunatos*, one of the New Testament Greek words for miracle, is the word translated "powerful."[9] These weapons empowered by God will work miracles. The word is also translated

"possible." Do you know anyone who seems impossible to reach? Will it take a miracle? With this power, their salvation is possible.

Paul Billheimer, a twentieth-century authority on prayer and author of *Destined for the Throne,* said his own salvation resulted from spiritual warfare waged on his behalf. He explains:

> My mother used these weapons on me. I was as hostile to God as any sinner. I was fighting with all my might. But the time came when it was easier to lay down my arms of rebellion than to continue my resistance. The pressure exerted upon me by the Holy Spirit became so powerful that I voluntarily sought relief by yielding my rebellious will. The wooing of divine love was so strong that of my own free will I fell into the arms of redeeming grace. I became a willing "captive."[10]

What are these weapons we use in our warfare?

- *All forms of prayer.* Ephesians 6:18 mentions prayer in the context of the warfare we're in: "With all prayer and petition pray at all times in the Spirit, and with this in view, be on the alert with all perseverance and petition for all the saints." This would include supplication, agreement with other Christians, travail, praying in the Spirit, binding and loosing—any biblical form of prayer.

- *Praise.* Psalm 149:5-9 is a powerful reference to how God uses our praise of Him as a weapon. "Let the godly ones exult in glory; let them sing for joy on their beds. Let the high praises of God be in their mouth, and a two-edged sword in their hand" (vv. 5,6). Always praise God for the salvation of the one(s) for whom you are praying.

- *The Word of God.* Ephesians 6:17: "And take the helmet of salvation, and the sword of the Spirit, which is the word of God." Speaking Scriptures that apply to your situation releases great power against the enemy. Jesus demonstrated this when He was confronted by Satan in the wilderness (see Matt. 4; Luke 4).

- *The name of Jesus.* Mark 16:17 states, "And these signs will accompany those who have believed: in My name they will cast out demons, they will speak with new tongues." Though praying in the name of Jesus is our access to the Father, it is also a powerful weapon against demonic powers and strongholds. Luke 10:17 tells us demons were subject to the disciples in Christ's name.

One of the things these weapons will help produce is enlightenment in the unbeliever. The word "light" in 2 Corinthians 4:4 is translated from the Greek word *photismos*, which means "illumination."[11] It is related to another word in Ephesians 1:18, "enlightened," which is translated from the word *photizo*—"to let in light,"[12] and is similar in meaning to revelation, or "lifting the veil." It is easy to see the English words "photo" or "photograph" in these words, and, indeed, they are derived from them.

What happens when one takes a photo? The shutter on the camera opens, letting in light, which brings an image. If the shutter on the camera does not open, there will be no image or picture regardless of how beautiful the scenery or elaborate the setting.

The same is true in the souls of human beings. And this is exactly what is being communicated—in photography language, as it were—in 2 Corinthians 4. It makes no difference how glorious our Jesus or how wonderful our message. If the veil (shutter) is not removed, there will be no true image (picture) of Christ.

In *The Trivialization of God*, Donald McCullough quotes Freeman Patterson, noted Canadian photographer, describing barriers that prevented him from seeing the best photo possibilities:

Letting go of the self is an essential precondition to real seeing. When you let go of yourself, you abandon any preconceptions about the subject matter which might cramp you into photographing in a certain predetermined way.

When you let go, new conceptions arise from your direct experience of the subject matter, and new ideas and feelings will guide you as you make pictures.[13]

What an appropriate phrase, "letting go of the self." In the same way that a photographer must remove barriers and see things differently, so must the sinner. If not, the picture of Christ is inferior at best.

We must ask God to lift the veil from unbelievers' spiritual eyes. Ask Him for enlightenment to come to the one for whom you are praying. Paul prayed for the Ephesians:

> That the God of our Lord Jesus Christ, the Father of glory, may give to you a spirit of wisdom and of revelation in the knowledge of Him. I pray that the eyes of your heart may be enlightened, so that you may know what is the hope of His calling, what are the riches of the glory of His inheritance in the saints (Eph. 1:17,18).

If these Ephesians, already born again, needed revelation and enlightenment to grow in Christ, how much more must it happen for the unbeliever! Ask for it.

Information Versus Revelation

This brings us to a very important point. We need to understand the difference between *information* and *revelation*. Information is of the mind. However, biblical revelation, which involves and affects the mind, originates from the heart. Spiritual power is only released through revelation knowledge. The written word (*graphe*)[14] must become the living word (*logos*).[15] Even as believers, we must not just read, but abide or meditate in the Word, praying as the psalmist: "Open my eyes, that I may behold wonderful things from Thy law" (Ps. 119:18). The word "open," *galah*, also means "unveil or uncover"[16]—revelation.

Information can come immediately, but revelation is normally a process. As the parable of the sower demonstrates, all biblical truth comes in seed form. Early in my walk with the Lord, I was frustrated because the wonderful truths I had heard from some outstanding teachers were not working for me. When I heard the teachings, they had seemed powerful to me. I left the meetings saying, "I will never be the same!" But a few weeks and months later, I was the same.

As I complained to God and questioned the truth of what I had heard, the Lord spoke words to me that have radically changed my life: "Son, all truth comes to you in seed form. It may be fruit in the person sharing it, but it is seed to you. Whether or not it bears fruit depends on what you do with it. Spiritual information seeds must grow into fruit-producing revelation."

Knowledge or information alone, which is what humans have glorified and where they have begun their quest for meaning ever since the Fall, does not produce salvation. It does not necessarily lead to a true knowledge of God. Jesus said to the Pharisees, "You search the Scriptures, because you think that in them you have eternal life; and it is these that bear witness of Me" (John 5:39). He said to them on another occasion, "You plan to kill me, because My word has no entrance (makes no progress, does not find any place) in you" (John 8:37, *AMP*).

The Pharisees knew the Scriptures (*graphe*) probably better than you or I, but they did not know God. Information from the Word had not progressed to revelation. Many theologians today know the Scriptures thoroughly but don't know God well. Some, perhaps, do not know Him at all. They couldn't sit quietly in His presence for two hours without being bored silly. They have much information but little or no revelation. Revelation makes the Scriptures "spirit" and "life" (John 6:63). It makes them live.

Why is this so important? Because we are forever short-circuiting God's process and, in so doing, short-circuiting the results. It is only revelation that leads to biblical faith and true change. Without it we are simply appealing to a fallen, selfish, humanistic mind created at the Fall that is always asking, "What's in it for me?" When we appeal to this mentality through human wisdom and intellect alone, we often preach a humanistic "What's in it for them?" gospel, and we produce—at best—humanistic, self-centered converts.

If, on the other hand, we preach a pure gospel, including repentance and the laying down of a person's own life (lordship of Christ), unbelievers are sure to reject it *unless* they receive a biblical revelation. In fact, our gospel often sounds ridiculous or moronic to them: "But a natural man does not accept the things of the Spirit of God; for they are foolishness to him, and he cannot understand them, because they are spiritually appraised" (1 Cor. 2:14). The word "foolishness" is *moria*, from which we get the word "moron."[17] What is the solution? *We must allow the Holy*

Spirit time to birth true repentance in unbelievers through God-given revelation.

Revelation Backed with the Fire Power of Prayer

As we have stated, we must ask God to bring this revelation to the unbeliever. The hearing of the gospel isn't enough; prayer must accompany it.

- Pray that the person's heart be prepared, so that it will be "good soil" for the seed (Mark 4:8).

- Pray that Satan not be able to steal the seeds of truth (see Mark 4:15), and that nothing else will be able to destroy the seeds (see Mark 4:16-19).

- Pray that the Word becomes revelation through the lifting of the veil (see 2 Cor. 4:3,4). An excellent verse to use in prayer is Ephesians 1:17: "That the God of our Lord Jesus Christ, the Father of glory, may give to you a spirit of wisdom and of revelation in the knowledge of Him."

- Pray that the root of pride in them be broken (see 2 Cor. 10:3-5).

- Pray that the person comes to true repentance (see 2 Pet. 3:9). Second Timothy 2:25,26 is a wonderful passage to pray over individuals in this regard: "God may grant them repentance leading to the knowledge of the truth, and they may come to their senses and escape from the snare of the devil, having been held captive by him to do his will."

Repentance does not mean to "turn and go another way." That change of direction is the *result* of repentance, not repentance itself, and is taken from the Greek word *epistrepho*, which is often translated "converted" or "turn."[18] Repentance—*metanoia*—means to have "a new knowledge or understanding"[19]—a change of mind. In biblical contexts, repentance is a new understanding that comes from God through an unveiling (revelation) and results in a new direction or lifestyle. It is necessary because of the turning to our own knowledge or understanding at the Fall.

J. Edwin Orr, the revivalist and historian, was with Billy Graham when the evangelist addressed a meeting in Beverly Hills attended by the notorious gangster Mickey Cohen.

"He expressed some interest in the message," Orr later wrote, "so several of us talked with him, including Dr. Graham, but he made no commitment until some time later when another friend urged him—with Revelation 3:20 as a warrant—to invite Jesus Christ into his life.

"This he professed to do, but his life subsequently gave no evidence of repentance, 'the mighty change of mind, heart and life.' He rebuked our friend, telling him, 'You did not tell me that I would have to give up my work!' He meant his rackets. 'You did not tell me that I would have to give up my friends!' He meant his gangster associates.

"He had heard that so-and-so was a Christian cowboy, so-and-so was a Christian actress, so-and-so was a Christian senator, and he really thought he could be a Christian gangster.

"The fact is," said Orr, drawing the lesson, "repentance is the missing note in much modern evangelism."[20]

This "missing note in much modern evangelism"—biblical repentance—would produce God-centered Christians, not self-centered ones. It is the reversing of the effects of the Fall through Adam. Humanity chose their own wisdom, their own knowledge of good and evil, right and wrong. Humanity now needs "a new knowledge from God." Paul said in Acts 26:18 he was called "to open their eyes"—enlightenment, unveiling, revelation, repentance—"*so that* they may turn (*epistrepho*) from darkness to light" (emphasis added).

We help to create this "new knowledge" (repentance) through intercession. Our prayers play a part in the lifting of the veil (revelation) and the opening of the shutter (enlightenment).

Some dear friends of mine, Mell and Paula Winger, have seen many family members come to Christ as they have faithfully interceded for them through the years. The testimony regarding Paula's younger brother is especially powerful:

Doug Giles had an extremely ungodly lifestyle and was living in total rebellion. He hated the gospel message and was so repelled by our faith in Christ that he would leave the house when we came for dinner. We began devoting one night each week to pray and fast for Doug's salvation. We did this weekly for a year and a half, praying that he would be able to see the truth of the gospel, binding the spirit of rebellion that was controlling him and asking God to soften his heart so that he might be drawn to Him. Then, although we were no longer setting aside every Monday night to intercede for him, we continued to pray these and other principles for Doug during the next six years. Finally, one night while attending a Christian concert, he received Christ as his Savior. That was 17 years ago, and today Doug has a powerful evangelistic ministry based out of Miami, Florida.

I have heard Doug minister, and I can attest to the ministry he has. God is no respecter of persons—what He did through the prayer of Mell and Paula, He will do through yours.

Questions for Wisdom and Faith

1. If God is the one who draws people to Him, why is it important to be strategic in how we share the gospel?

2. What are the various kinds of veils (filters) that hinder people from accepting Christ as Lord? In your opinion, what is the most difficult veil that clouds the heart and mind?

3. Does sharing Scripture make people hard of heart, or does it break through their defenses and reservations?

4. Can believers (even acting in a sincere manner) hinder someone from entering the Kingdom by what they say and do?

SPIRITUAL WARFARE
FOR THE LOST

When Eileen from Baton Rouge heard me teach on "Spiritual Warfare for the Lost," she knew it was for her. She had been saved for 21 years and had been praying for her father for 26 years with no results. He had been raised in an occult atmosphere and was a hardened military man who never responded in any way to her many and varied attempts to reach him with the gospel.

She went home from the conference where she had heard me teach, pulled out her notes and began to diligently follow them in praying for her father. She also called her mother, gave her a condensed version of my teaching and told her there was a window of opportunity where he would be able to hear and respond. Four days before he died, her father prayed and accepted the Lord as his Savior.

Eileen went on to say,

I couldn't really celebrate Thanksgiving this year until I called and thanked you for sharing this teaching that showed me how to effectively pray for my dad with eternal results. I also shared this with our church, and several people came to me afterwards saying they now have hope to pray again. I wanted you to know that your teaching is having domino effects and impacting the lives of many. Thank you!

Assaulting Strongholds of Mind and Heart

There is an absolute connection between spiritual warfare and intercession, especially in regards to praying for the lost. As we stated in the previous chapter, we have a role in removing the veil that blinds their minds. Part of the veil that blinds unbelievers is the strongholds referred to in 2 Corinthians 10:4: "For the weapons of our warfare are not carnal, but mighty through God to the pulling down of strongholds" (*KJV*). The *New American Standard Bible* states it this way: "For the weapons of our warfare are not of the flesh, but divinely powerful for the destruction of fortresses." The word "stronghold" is translated from the Greek word *ochuroma*, coming from the root word *echo*, which means "to have or hold."[1] This word for "stronghold" (*KJV*) or "fortress" (*NASB*) is literally a place from which to *hold* something *strongly*. It is also the word for a fort, a castle or a prison. Strongholds are not demons; they are places from which demons rule.

In essence, Satan has a place of strength *within* unbelievers from which he can imprison or hold on to them strongly. They are prisoners, captives, slaves. Christ was sent "to proclaim release to the *captives*" (Luke 4:18, emphasis added). We participate in the destruction of these "prisons" through spiritual warfare. What happened for Eileen and her father can happen for you.

I love the concept embodied in the word "destruction," or as the *KJV* says, "pulling down." These words are translated from the Greek word, *kathairesis*. This important and powerful word has a couple of pertinent meanings. One of them is "to bring down with violence or demolish" something.[2] God's plan is for us to become demolition agents, violently tearing down Satan's strongholds.

I remember as a small child watching the destruction of an old brick school. I was fascinated as the huge cement ball, attached to a gigantic crane, was swung time after time into the building, crashing through walls and ceilings and bringing incredible destruction. I suppose this would be, in one sense, a viable picture of our warfare as we systematically—one divine blow at a time—work destruction on the strongholds of darkness. It truly does usually happen this way—a systematic, ongoing, one-blow-at-a-time war against Satan's strongholds.

Yet I saw another huge building in Dallas, Texas, demolished several years ago. This edifice was much larger than the school I had seen destroyed as a child. This one covered nearly an entire city block, or at least it seemed that way to me. The demolition crew didn't use a wrecking ball for this one. And it didn't take days—it took seconds. They used dynamite strategically placed by experts to demolish this major structure in less than 10 seconds.

Since the phrase "divinely powerful" is the word
dunatos,[3] from which we get the English word "dynamite," I
like to think that this, in some ways, can also be a picture
of our intercession. Unlike a detonated physical building,
we don't usually see the answer to our intercession within
seconds—we may be strategically placing the dynamite of
the Spirit for days, weeks or months. But every time we take
up our spiritual weapons and use them against the strongholds of the enemy, we are placing our explosive charges in
strategic places. And sooner or later the Holy Detonator of
heaven is going to say "Enough!" There will be a mighty explosion in the spirit, a stronghold will crumble to the
ground and people will fall to their knees. Consider this
beautiful story:

> Ellen was a mother and widow who persistently
> prayed for her five children after she was left to rear
> them alone. When gathering them around their fa-
> ther's casket, she had prayed, "Lord, I don't have
> anything to give You except myself and these chil-
> dren, but we commit ourselves to You and trust You
> to take care of us."
>
> Hardships hit, but with her faith in God stead-
> fast, she continually declared, "We're going to make
> it!" When the state welfare agent wanted to place
> one boy, Charles, in an orphanage to lighten her
> load, she refused. "We may not look like much, but
> we're going to make it," she announced stubbornly
> to the agent who came to the farm to get Charles.

Years passed. The children stayed true to the Lord, and most of them entered the ministry—all except one. When the middle boy, Melvin, joined the army, he fell into the ways of the world, married an unbeliever, and forsook the faith of his childhood. Ellen never stopped praying for her wayward son. Every time friends or family members lamented over Melvin's spiritual condition, she had a standard response: "God doesn't lie—I'll never stop believing. My boy's going to make it."

One day, Charles received word that his unsaved brother Melvin had died suddenly of a heart attack. He immediately flew to Boston and went directly to the funeral home. As he stood before his brother's casket, wondering how his mother would respond to the shocking news, Melvin's wife came into the room.

"Charles, I want to tell you something that happened last night that I think will make you feel better," she said. "I had gone to bed ahead of Melvin. A little later he went from room to room to tell all the children goodnight, then came to our bedroom. But instead of getting into bed, he did something I've never seen him do in all the years we've been married. He knelt beside the bed and began praying. Then I noticed he was praying in a strange language—a language I've never heard him speak before. After a little while he got into bed and went to sleep. Early this morning he had the heart attack and died."

His fears relieved, Charles phoned his mother's home and recounted the story. "Well, Mom, what do you think?" he asked.

Strong and confident, her voice came back so real he could almost see her Irish eyes sparkling. "I think my boy made it!" Ellen said triumphantly.[4]

The one you are praying for is going to make it, as well. God is going to show you just how to pray so that you can demolish every part of Satan's fortress.

"We are destroying speculations and every lofty thing raised up against the knowledge of God, and we are taking every thought captive to the obedience of Christ" (2 Cor. 10:5). Verse 4 says our divinely empowered weapons are for the destruction or demolition of strongholds, and verse 5 elaborates more fully on just what comprises the strongholds we're going to demolish. In other words, the Holy Spirit breaks down for us exactly what the stronghold or prison is made of. This is critical information as we begin to war for the lost.

Breaking the Foundations of Resistance

Specifically, He shares with us three major components of the fortress or prison. These are the things we will begin to call out in prayer and demolish as we war over individuals with our divinely empowered weapons.

The first aspect of the stronghold He mentions is "speculations"—*logismos* (plural *logismoi*). This word speaks not of the scattered individual thoughts of humans but of their calculative reasoning, their wisdom or logic.[5] Our word "logic" is actually derived from this Greek root. *Logismos* is the sum total of the accumulated wisdom and information learned over time. It becomes what one really believes—the person's mind-set. The Moffatt translation calls them "theories." Humanity, before the Fall, got their wisdom and logic—their beliefs—from God. Now James 3:15 tells us they come from the earth, the soul or intellect and demons.

The word *logismos* includes philosophies (conscious or unconscious), religions, humanism, atheism, Hinduism, Buddhism, Islam, racism, intellectualism, Judaism, materialism, roots of rejection, perversions, alcoholism, other addictions—anything that causes a person to think a certain way.

> One mom travailed in prayer for some time about her drug-addicted daughter. One evening while lying on her face in prayer, she heard the Lord's quiet voice promising that [her daughter would] soon be set free. Wiping her tears, that mom got up and began praising God. She continued praising God for victory, though there was no outward change in her daughter. Five long months passed. Then, when the daughter overdosed, she was ready for help. After some Christian counseling, she was set free.[6]

Though there were no doubt other *logismoi* in this daughter, one was drug addiction, which controlled her thinking.

How does a *logismos* blind an individual? How do they veil truth? The way the human mind functions dictates that when people hear the gospel, before they even have time to think or reason about what they are hearing, it is filtered through the subconscious or memory where all other information—including these *logismoi*—is stored. This means that unbelievers don't hear only what we are saying, they hear what we are saying *plus* what they already believe.

In the past, before realizing the distorted perception of the unbeliever, I often wondered why people could hear and reject powerful gospel presentations. Now I understand that what the unbelievers heard was filtered through a belief system—a veil—that caused them to hear something totally different. When "hearing" the gospel message, they didn't hear what I heard, see what I saw or understand what I understood. The fourth verse of 2 Corinthians 4 clearly states this: "that they might not *see* the light of the gospel of the glory of Christ, who is the *image* of God" (emphasis added). They simply do not see the same image of Christ that we do. To clearly see Him is to love and want Him.

In his novel *My Lovely Enemy*, Canadian Mennonite author Rudy Wiebe aptly pictures how different the same thing looks to different people:

It could be like standing on your head in order to see the world clearer. . . . If one morning you began walking on your hands, the whole world would be hanging. The trees, these ugly brick and tile buildings wouldn't be fixed here so solid and reassuring; they'd be pendant. The more safe and reliable they seem now, the more helpless they'd be then.[7]

The same world would look very different, depending on the way it was seen. The same is true with the message of Jesus Christ. People's *logismoi* distort, color or turn upside down their perceptions of the gospel message.

For example, I was sharing the gospel with a girl who had been horribly abused. "God is love," I said. "He loves you so much He sent His Son to die for you." She heard more than what I said. I know because she said to me, "Oh? If He is love, why would He have allowed me to be so abused? Doesn't sound like a loving God to me." That is a *logismos*—a belief, a philosophy, her wisdom, her logic. Someone will need to intercede for her and help tear down the *logismos* with "divinely powerful" weapons. The Holy Spirit will need to remove that veil, allowing her to see clearly.

On another occasion, I was sharing the gospel with a fellow who had a *logismos* I call "good-ol'-boy-ism." He was just too nice a guy to think he needed saving. "I'm a pretty good guy," he said. "I don't cheat on my wife, beat my kids, lie, curse or steal. I don't think God would send me to hell." His *logismos*, or belief system, was that a person can be good enough to get to heaven.

How does the gospel break through these arguments? Certainly the gospel of truth itself has power to break down some of this when anointed by the Holy Spirit. But it usually takes a long period of time—if you can get them to listen. It is much wiser to plow the ground ahead of time, preparing for the reception of the seed by pulling down these strongholds, as George Müller and his team did for orphans in their care.

The spiritual condition of the orphans generally brought great sorrow to our hearts, because there were so few among them who were in earnest about their souls and resting on the atoning death of the Lord Jesus for salvation. Our sorrow led us to lay it on the whole staff of assistants, matrons and teachers to seek earnestly for the Lord's blessing on the souls of the children. This was done in our united prayer meetings and, I have reason to believe, in secret sessions of prayer as well.

In the year 1872, in answer to and as a result of our private and united prayers, there were more believers by far among the orphans than ever. On January 8, 1872, the Lord began to work among them, and this work continued more or less afterward.

At the end of July 1872, I received the statements of all the matrons and teachers in the five houses, who reported to me that, after careful observation and conversation, they had good reason to believe that 729 of the orphans then under our care were believers in the Lord Jesus. This number of believing orphans was by far greater than we had ever had before, for which we adore and praise the Lord![8]

Perhaps you already know what these *logismoi* are in the person for whom you are praying. If not, ask the Holy Spirit to reveal them to you. He will. And when He does, call them by name, quoting 2 Corinthians 10:3-5. Say, "In the name of the Lord Jesus Christ I am destroying you, stronghold of . . ." Do it daily until the person comes to Christ.

> During Operation Desert Storm, the Iraqi war machine was overwhelmed by the Coalition Forces' ability to strike strategic targets with never-seen-before accuracy. Unknown to the Iraqis, the Allied Supreme Command had dropped Special Operations Forces (SOF) deep behind enemy lines. These men provided bombing coordinates for military targets and firsthand reports on the effectiveness of subsequent bombing missions.
>
> To avoid unintended targets, pinpoint bombing was often required. A soldier from a SOF unit standing on the ground would request an aircraft high overhead to drop a laser-guided missile. Using a handheld laser, the soldier would point at the target. The missile would hone in on the soldier's target for the hit.[9]

In much the same way, our prayers focus the attention of God's powerful weapons on the *logismos* fortresses of Satan in the minds of unbelievers.

The second part of the stronghold we must demolish is "every lofty thing raised up against the knowledge of God." I like using the *KJV* for this verse because it uses "high thing" to translate the Greek word *hupsoma*, which is actually the same root word for "Most High" God. It actually means "any elevated place or thing."[10] This is referring to the same root of pride we discovered hidden in the word "blinded" in 2 Corinthians 4:3,4. It is the "most highness" that came to humanity at the Fall when Adam and Eve bought the lie, "You will be like God" (Gen. 3:5).

By disobeying God, humankind, like Satan, exalted themselves to a place of equality with the Most High. We became, however, not the Most High but our own most high, filled with pride. One leading lexicon even defined *hupsoma* as "all pride that rises up."[11] The word would then encompass all mind-sets that exalt themselves against the knowledge of God. It involves a desire to rule our own lives, decide for ourselves right and wrong and basically be our own god.

The good news is that we can also tear down this stronghold in people through spiritual warfare so they can humble themselves and bow their knees to Christ. An example of this power is seen below:

Darlene's husband died of a heart attack and her older son was killed by a highway sniper—both within one year. Sean, her only remaining child, moved back home to help her with their struggling family business.

Darlene soon realized with dismay that Sean had strayed far from the Lord he had once served. He never read his Bible or went to church, and he was very cold in his attitude toward her.

"Stay out of my room," he barked at her one day when she had gone into his room for something. "I'll take care of my things in there."

To keep peace, Darlene tried to leave Sean to himself. But many nights she walked the floor praying for her son, pleading with God to intervene in his life. One day she went into his room to get dirty laundry and found a marijuana plant growing under a special light he'd rigged in the closet.

Standing there, getting more and more angry at the devil, she screamed at the plant. "Die, in the name of Jesus! I curse you and forbid you to live in this house."

The next day the plant was dead.

That night as she again walked the floor praying for Sean, she felt the Holy Spirit leading her to pray, *Lord, I give You my son. Give me back a brother in the Lord.*

From then on her prayers changed. She began to praise the Lord that Sean was going to become a brother in the Lord to her. She stopped begging God but continued to thank Him for the work He would do in Sean's life.

Two weeks later, her son came in early on a Saturday night. He knew Darlene always had a prayer meeting and Bible study going on then. Finding the Bible teacher and his wife still there, Sean began querying them. Before the night was over, Sean asked for God's forgiveness and promised to follow Jesus for the rest of his life.

"God did give me a brother in the Lord," Darlene said, rejoicing. "Almost ten years have passed, and Sean is still walking with the Lord."[12]

The pride in this young man's life—his desire to rebel against authority and rule his own life—was torn down, demolished through intercession.

Read 2 Corinthians 10:5 again, this time from *The Living Bible*:

> These weapons can break down every proud argument against God and every wall that can be built to keep men from finding Him. With these weapons I can capture rebels and bring them back to God, and change them into men whose hearts' desire is obedience to Christ.

I like the "cans" and "everys" in this verse. The Lord doesn't wish us luck or tell us that we will win a few once in awhile. He lets us know we can break down every proud argument and every wall; we can capture rebels! And we must!

With this in mind, consider the third aspect of strongholds. The Lord tells us we can take "every thought captive to the obedience of Christ." The word "thought" is *noema*, which also means plans, schemes, devices or plots.[13] It refers to the spontaneous thoughts and temptations Satan uses to assault the unbelievers, as well as the schemes and plans he uses to keep them in darkness. In intercession we must declare boldly that *no weapon* of Satan's will prosper. We must bind his plans and stand against them through prayer. We can and should pray that the unbeliever be shielded from Satan's thoughts and temptations.

Never stop praying for "hopeless" cases, for no one is beyond the Lord's ability to convict and convert. Consider the example of E. Howard Cadle. His mother was a Christian, but his father was an alcoholic. Cadle began emulating his father, drinking and out of control, and soon was in the clutches of the crime syndicate.

Every night at eight o'clock, his mother knelt by his bed praying. One evening, Cadle pulled a gun on a man and squeezed the trigger, but the weapon never fired and was quickly knocked away. Cadle noticed that it was exactly eight o'clock, and somehow he'd been spared from committing murder.

He continued headlong in vice, however, and his health deteriorated to where the doctor told him he had only six months to live. Dragging himself home, penniless and pitiful, he collapsed in his mother's arms, saying, "Mother, I've broken your heart. I'd like to be saved, but I've sinned too much."

The elderly woman opened her Bible and read Isaiah 1:18: *"Though your sins are like scarlet, they shall be as white as snow."* That morning, March 14, 1914, Cadle started life anew. The change in him was dramatic and permanent.

With Christ now in his heart, he turned his con skills into honest pursuits and started making money, giving 75 percent of it to the Lord's work. He helped finance crusades in which thousands were converted and became one of America's earliest and most popular radio evangelists.

He once said: "Until He calls me, I shall preach the same gospel that caused my mother to pray for me. And when I have preached my last sermon, I want to sit at His feet and say, 'Thank You, Jesus, for saving me.'"[14]

Like Mrs. Cadle, we can turn unbelievers "from darkness to light and from the dominion of Satan to God" (Acts 26:18). We are called to enforce and make effectual the freedom Christ procured.

The unbeliever cannot war for himself. He cannot and will not overcome the strongholds of darkness, and he will not understand the gospel until the veil lifts. We must take our divinely dynamic weapons and fight. The powers of darkness will resist, but "do not be afraid of them, remember the Lord who is great and awesome, and fight for your brothers, your sons, your daughters, your wives, and your houses" (Neh. 4:14).

Questions for Wisdom and Faith

1. What philosophy *(logismoi)* is the most subtle in affecting nonbelievers today? Can such a philosophy affect a Christian, too?

2. What aspect of pride *(hupsoma)* hindered you from becoming a follower of Christ? Why?

3. What does it mean to capture a thought *(noema)* to the obedience of Christ? Is that self-discipline?

What thoughts in your life need to be taken captive?

4. What kinds of spiritual fruit (see Gal. 5) come from our laboring and wrestling for the salvation of others through prayer?

BEARING GOD'S
HEARTBREAKING BURDENS

The Lord does and will give His people a taste of His own long-suffering heart and His desire that all should come to know Him. Consider this story:

John "Praying" Hyde grew up hearing his father, a minister, often mention the needs of overseas mission fields and praying for laborers to be sent forth. At McCormick Theological Seminary, John committed himself to foreign evangelism and, following graduation, he sailed for Bombay.

Initially overcome by the difficulties of climate and language, John preached from village to village but grew discouraged as there were few converts. Then he discovered Isaiah 62:6,7, which became his personal motto. He began praying with remarkable intensity—missing meals, meetings and preaching appointments. As he spent days and nights in prayer, revival began to come down upon his labors in India.

At the beginning of 1908, he prayed earnestly to win at least one soul to Christ every day. By December 31, he had recorded over four hundred converts. The following year, the Lord laid two souls per day on his heart, and his prayer was again answered. The next year he prayed for four souls daily with similar results.

Once, stopping at a cottage for water, Praying Hyde pleaded with God for ten souls. He presented the gospel to the family, and, by the end of his visit, all nine members of the family had been saved. But what of number ten? Suddenly a nephew who had been outside ran into the room and was promptly converted.

Hyde's great missionary work flowed from his prayer life like water from a faucet, and he finally wore himself out in prayer, staying on his knees, night after night, year after year, reminding God of his promises and giving the Lord no rest. The great prayer warrior died on February 17, 1912, his last words being: *Bol, Visu Masih, Ki Jah*—"Shout the victory of Jesus Christ!"[1]

I don't necessarily want you to "wear yourself out in prayer" to the point of death, as some say Praying Hyde did, but I do want to talk to you about passion . . . tears . . . allowing God's heart to be born in and released from you.

The Passion to Pray

At the risk of sounding self-serving, or perhaps even prideful, I want to share a little more with you about my experience of October 4, 2000, when God moved upon me for America. I do so cautiously and somewhat hesitantly because the time was very personal and precious. But perhaps it will help us understand some things I consider very important.

God had moved upon me very powerfully during the worship that evening, but not with tears or intercession. It was a wonderful intimacy that, paradoxically, became mixed with a sense of foreboding or heaviness. Not until one of my associates articulated a burden for the elections, warning of the intense warfare surrounding it and its outcome so precariously hanging in the balance, did I realize what God was placing on me.

Intending to go ahead and deliver my message, I walked to the podium. As I opened my Bible, what I can only describe as a wave of God's presence overwhelmed me in a matter of seconds. I explained to our congregation that I didn't know exactly what was happening, but that I knew I couldn't speak. The wave continued and within seconds I was weeping uncontrollably. Thus began three and a half hours of deep intercession for America, specifically for the upcoming presidential election.

By the time the evening was over, I knew several things:

1. This was to be the most important election in decades. God had brought the nation to a point

where the spiritual decline of the last 30 to 40 years could begin to turn. If the opportunity wasn't seized now, however, it would take decades before it would be available again.

2. This would only take place if God's person was elected. (Not that our faith should ever be in a person or political party, but God can work through some people and not others. For example, he had to remove King Saul and appoint David, a man after God's heart, to lead Israel).

3. If the election were held at that moment, God's person would not win.

4. God was NOT going to change this and give us His choice without the prayers and repentance from the Body of Christ. He wouldn't do it in spite of us; He would only do it *through* us—if there were enough prayers and a true repentance in the Church of America.

5. I didn't know what "enough" was. I only knew I had to issue the call to pray.

God graciously anointed the prayer alert we issued and within days a massive prayer movement was underway. Of course, as the election unfolded, the degree of the warfare became obvious. Not only an election but the future of a nation hung in the balance.

I, and many others, carried this burden of the Lord from early October until the day Vice President Gore conceded. For me, it was overwhelming at times. I wept often. Though it may sound strange, occasionally I would drape the American flag around me and pray for hours again, often with many tears. I sometimes felt—though I knew I was one of many—that I was carrying the weight of a nation on my shoulders.

At one point I asked God to remove the burden. It was becoming too unbearable; emotionally I was becoming overwhelmed. I knew the future of America was being determined: a harvest of millions, a generation of youth, millions of unborn babies, even millions of unsaved people from around the world would be affected by what happened.

God did not remove the burden, but He did give me grace and understanding to carry it. He showed me how to do it from my heart by the power of the Holy Spirit, and not from my mind and emotions. It was still heavy and at times emotional, but I was walking in the Spirit, not my own strength, and could therefore endure it. I am fully convinced that our prayers—those of the Body of Christ—determined the outcome of the election.

Bearing a Measure of God's Burden

Why have I shared this? To help explain the power of tears, of passion, of allowing God to touch us with His heart so He can pray through us. When Nehemiah heard the spiritual condition of his nation, Israel, he "sat down and wept and mourned for days" (Neh. 1:4). Ezra did as well, "weeping and prostrating himself before the house of God" and others "wept bitterly" with Ezra (Ezra 10:1). Both situations resulted in breakthroughs. *There are times when only God's passionate heart, released through us, will produce the needed results.* Charles Finney relates the following story:

> A minister once related a story to me about a town that had not had a revival in many years. The Church was nearly extinct, the youth were all unconverted and desolation reigned unbroken. There lived, in a retired part of the town, an aged blacksmith who stammered so badly that it was painful to hear him speak. One Friday, as he worked in his shop, alone, he became very upset about the state of the Church and of the impenitent. His agony became so great that he had to put away his work, lock the shop door, and spend the afternoon in prayer.
>
> He continued to pray all day. Then he asked his minister to arrange a conference meeting. After some hesitation, the minister consented, even though he feared few people would attend. He called the meeting the same evening at a large private house. When evening came, more people assembled than could be accommodated in the house. All were silent for a time, until one sinner broke out in tears and said, "If anyone could pray, would he pray for me?" Another followed, and another, and still another, until people from every part of town were under deep conviction. It was also remarkable that they

all dated their conviction to the hour the old man prayed in his shop. A powerful revival followed. Thus this stammering old man's prayer prevailed, and as a prince, he had power with God.[2]

By sharing this story, as well as what transpired with me, I run the risk of making you feel that if you're not weeping for someone's salvation, your prayers won't be effective. Please don't interpret what I'm saying in this way. My spiritual passion isn't always released through tears, nor will yours be; there are many biblical ways to pray and to release our faith. In fact, most of the time, my intercession does not involve tears.

What I am saying is that we must allow ourselves to receive the burden of the Lord. We must let His heart for people become ours, so much so that when we pray, it is really Him praying through us.

The apostle Paul wrote to the Corinthian believers and said that God "gave us the ministry of reconciliation, namely, that God was in Christ reconciling the world to Himself, not counting their trespasses against them, and He has committed to us the word of reconciliation. Therefore, we are ambassadors for Christ, *as though God were entreating through us; we beg you on behalf of Christ,* be reconciled to God" (2 Cor. 5:18-20, emphasis added). Paul used strong words: "entreating" and "beg." Yet he said, in essence, that he was actually doing it for God.

Just a couple of verses later in 2 Corinthians 6:1, he uses the phrase "working together with Him." Romans 8:26 says

God "helps" us in our intercession. The word is *sunantilam-banomai*, which means "to take hold of together with against." If we let Him, the Holy Spirit will help us in prayer by allowing us to partake of His compassion for the lost. Certainly this is one of the ways He takes hold with us in intercession.

The great Charles Finney said it this way:

> His prayers seem to flow from the intercessor's heart like water: "O LORD, revive Thy work" (Hab. 3:2). Sometimes this feeling is very deep. This is by no means enthusiasm. It is just what Paul felt when he said, "My little children, of whom I travail in birth" (Gal. 4:19). I do not mean to say that it is essential to have this great distress in order to have the spirit of prayer. But this deep, continual, earnest desire for the salvation of sinners is what constitutes the spirit of prayer for a revival.[3]

Passionate Caring

The following two passages on tears describe the passion of which Finney speaks. Interpret the tears, however, as passionate caring, not necessarily as literal tears, which is certainly the spirit of what God is saying. Psalm 126:5,6 states: "Those who sow in tears shall reap with joyful shouting. He who goes to and fro weeping, carrying his bag of seed, shall indeed come again with a shout of joy, bringing his sheaves with him."

Our tears are called seeds in these verses. In others words, God uses them to produce a harvest. The word for seed, *zera*, means not only "seed" or "crop" but also "offspring, progeny or family."⁴ It's not that difficult to see the symbolism. God uses our "tear seeds" to bring forth His family!

Or perhaps we want to apply it to our family. Remember *zera*, the word for seed, also means family. When we weep in intercession (or remember, pray passionately) for our family, the prayer seeds (*zera*) we are sowing will grow into a family (*zera*) harvest! In other words, the seeds of intercession you sow will grow into saved children, spouses, parents, etc. That will be our harvest. Hallelujah!

Another great verse on tears is Psalm 56:8: "Thou hast taken account of my wanderings; put my tears in Thy bottle. Are they not in Thy book?" The bottle referred to here isn't just a storage container. It is the word *nodah*, meaning a skin used to transform juice to wine or cream to butter.⁵ Again, God is trying to tell us our tears (or passionate prayers) will be transformed into something else. God will store them and *use* them, not *waste* them. And when He is finished, they will be changed into wine—fruitfulness. Where intercession for the lost is concerned, this fruit will be saved people.

Go ahead and become a person of passion. You cannot do so on your own, but the passionate God—the very passion that sent Him to the Cross—is in you. "Zeal for [His] house" (Ps. 69:9; John 2:17) is yours for the asking. This kind of passion is exemplified well in the following story:

Police don't know where Deborah Kemp found the strength, but she knows. Her six-year-old daughter,

Ashleye, was in the back seat. Deborah had just finished putting gas in her car when a man attempted to steal her car. The thirty-four-year-old mother was dragged on her knees for several blocks as she clung to the door and steering wheel of the moving car. "I wasn't trying to be a hero," she said. "I was concerned about my baby . . . that was part of me in that car." Kemp eventually pulled the suspect from the car and beat him with an anti-theft club device while he apologized and begged her to stop. The driverless car went out of control and smashed into a restaurant, breaking a gas line. That's when the child woke up. Kemp suffered only ripped pants and bloody knees. The child was not injured. The suspect couldn't walk due to leg injuries he incurred.[6]

Passionless people change nothing. But people like Deborah Kemp, motivated by passionate love, refuse to allow Satan, the thief, to steal, kill and destroy God's "babies." Refuse to be lukewarm in your approach to lost souls. Be hot. Let His love constrain you (see 2 Cor. 5:14, *KJV*). He really does want to love through you.

He is waiting for you to ask.

Questions for Wisdom and Faith

1. Can we choose to accept God's heartache over certain people and events or does the Lord lay it upon us regardless?

2. Does bearing God's burdens entail feelings alone? Are we moved to reason, understand, and articulate more clearly what the burden is to ourselves and to others?

3. In some of our pleadings to God in prayer, does the Lord say "no" to our knocking?

4. How do we distinguish between what is God's burden for us to pray versus something that is our own personal burden? Or are they one and the same?

LABOR-INTENSIVE REALITIES

It's wonderful to see the overflow, or domino effect, that sometimes happens when we pray for family members. Lorraine's family is an example of this principle. For years she prayed for her brother Stuart and his family to come to Christ. His typical response was, "Don't bother me with talk about religion."

Then one day Stuart called to tell Lorraine that his son, Bart, was getting out of jail. "Can you and your husband help him find a place to stay?" Stuart asked. "The jail is not that far from where you live." Lorraine and her husband agreed to invite Bart to stay with them. After he moved into their upstairs bedroom, they learned that, while in jail, he had had an encounter with God. As a spiritually hungry new Christian, Bart became involved in a local church and began to work in a Christian ministry. As he grew in faith, he became eager for his father to also know Christ in an intimate way.

Lorraine knew that God was answering her prayers for Stuart when he agreed to attend a Christian men's rally with Bart and her husband. While there, Bart asked his dad if he would like to accept Christ as his Savior and Lord, and Stuart responded affirmatively. Lorraine's prayers of more than 40 years were answered when Bart led his own father in a salvation prayer.[1]

During her years of intercession for her brother, Lorraine probably never envisioned that Stuart would come to the Lord through this sequence of events. But as a result of her prayers, this father and son were both brought to salvation in Christ.

God's Birthers

Prayer releases power from the Holy Spirit, which brings about the new birth or salvation. We are "birthers" for God. The Holy Spirit wants to bring forth spiritual sons and daughters through our intercession. Jesus said in John 7:38: "From his *innermost being* shall flow rivers of living water" (emphasis added). "Innermost being" is translated from the Greek word *koilia*, which means "womb."[2] We are the womb of God upon the earth. We are not the source of life, but we are carriers of the source of life. We do not generate life; but we release, through prayer, Him who does. All of us can and should regularly involve ourselves in intercession for the lost, realizing it will cause people to be born again.

Please understand that we don't birth anything spiritually; the Holy Spirit does. He is the birthing agent of the Godhead (see Luke 1:34,35; John 3:3-8). He is the power source of the Godhead (see Luke 4:14,18; Acts 1:8; 10:38).

He is the power behind Creation which, as we will see, is likened to a birthing (see Gen. 1). He is the one who supplies power to God's will, giving it life and substance. He gives birth to the will of God. He is the one who breathes God's life into people, bringing physical and spiritual life (see Gen. 2:7; Ezek. 37:9,10,14; Acts 2:1-4). Concerning salvation, we call this the new birth or the new creation. Anything we might accomplish in intercession that results in someone being born again would have to be because our prayers caused or released the Holy Spirit to do something.

For example, Elijah as a human being couldn't birth or produce rain. Yet, James 5:17,18 tells us that his prayers did. Paul couldn't birth through travailing prayer the new birth or maturity in the Galatians, yet Galatians 4:19 implies that his intercession did. We cannot produce spiritual sons and daughters through our human abilities, yet Isaiah 66:7,8 tells us that our travail can. If we cannot create or birth these things through our own power or ability, then it seems fairly obvious that our prayers must in some way cause or release the Holy Spirit to do so.

Ephesians 3:20,21 states:

Now to Him who is able to do exceeding abundantly beyond all that we ask or think, according to the power that works within us, to Him be the glory in the church and in Christ Jesus to all generations forever and ever. Amen.

The word for "exceeding abundantly beyond" is the same word for the abundant grace of God in Romans 5:20.

The word is *huperperissos*. *Perissos* means "superabundant,"[3] *huper* means "beyond" or "more than."[4] Together, they would mean superabundantly with more added to that. That's like saying "more than more than." Ephesians 3:20 says He has enough power to do more than we can ask or think with more added to that—more than more than.

God's Womb—the Church

So, why are we often deficient? The power source is obviously not the problem. The rest of Ephesians 3:20 gives us a clue. It tells us He is going to do this more than more than enough "according to the power that works within us." Wuest translates the phrase "in the measure of the power which is operative in us." The word "measure" is *kata*, which not only contains the implication of that which is measured in us, but Strong says it is also used at times with the connotation of "distribution."[5] He is going to do this superabundantly more than we can ask or think in the measure of the power that is distributed from us.

There is literal power from the Holy Spirit that can be released from us. The power of God that brings life, healing and wholeness to the earth flows out from us—the Church. Please don't picture some throne in heaven and feel like that's the only place from which His power flows. He has now made His throne in our hearts and we are the temple of the Holy Spirit. We are the *naos* of God. In 1 Corinthians 3:16 and 6:19 this word is used and literally means "holy of holies."[6] We are now the holy of holies, the dwelling place of God upon the earth. When He moves to release power upon the earth, it doesn't have to shoot out of the sky somewhere—it comes from His people where His Spirit dwells upon the earth. We, the Body of Christ, are God's womb from which His life is birthed or released upon the earth. The life that Christ produces flows from the womb of the Church.

Inducing Spiritual Labor

You must release through prayer the power of God inside of you on a consistent basis. James 5:16 (*KJV*) says, "The *effectual fervent* prayer of a righteous man availeth much" (emphasis added). Wuest translates it this way: "A prayer of a righteous person is able to do much as it operates." Notice the verse doesn't say, "A prayer of a righteous person is able to do much because it causes God to operate."

It certainly does this, but that's not what this verse is telling us. It says, "A prayer of a righteous person is able to do much as it—*the prayer*—operates" (emphasis added). The *Amplified* translation reads, "The earnest (heartfelt, continued) prayer of a righteous man makes tremendous power available [dynamic in its working]." The point is that our prayers release the power of the Holy Spirit to work. Notice the word "continued." The *Amplified* captures the present tense meaning of the verb. We do this continuously until we see results. We have the power inside of us that created the world—the same power that went into the depths of the earth and took the keys from the kingdom of darkness. We must release it, and we do so by prayer.

Rosy was the first person in her devout Buddhist family in China to receive Christ. The tradition in her family was for the parents to take her and her siblings to the temple every week. They paid the Buddhist priests to write prayers and predictions of good luck for each of the children. The papers containing these writings were burned at an altar; then the ashes were stirred up in water and the children had to drink the mixture. The parents did this thinking it would assure the safety and well-being of their children. "The truth is, we actually were ingesting demons every week," Rosy said.

Rosy first heard the gospel message at a youth camp when she was 18. She accepted the Lord as her Savior and began to eagerly study the Bible. She memorized Scripture and began praying for her immediate family to receive Christ. At first they completely rejected Rosy and her newfound faith, but as Rosy continued to release the power of the Holy Spirit through prayer, one by one they began responding to the gospel. During a period of several years, she led every family member to the Lord. For many years she and her husband have been in full-time ministry, mostly in Asia, and now their son is preparing to do missions work among Muslims.[7]

Rosy's continued intercession for her family is a wonderful example of how people can be loosed from the kingdom of darkness as the power of the Holy Spirit is released through prayer.

Understanding, then, that it is the Holy Spirit's power actually doing the work, I want to say unequivocally that *prayer releases the power of the Holy Spirit to bring about the new birth.* To demonstrate this, various Scriptures use the same words that describe what the Holy Spirit does in birthing or bringing forth life as are used to describe what our prayers accomplish.

Genesis 1:1,2 (*KJV*) says, "In the beginning . . . the earth was without form and void." The words "without form" are translated from the Hebrew word *tohuw,* which means "a desolation; to lie waste; a desert;"[8] "confusion;"[9] "empty (barren)."[10] Sounds like lost people to me (we'll make the connection shortly).

Verse 2 goes on to say, "The Spirit of God moved upon the face of the waters." The Hebrew word *rachaph,* which is translated "moved" in this verse, literally means "to brood over."[11] "Brood" comes from the root word "breed," which means to bring forth offspring. In fact, this phrase in the *Amplified* translation reads, "The Spirit of God was moving, hovering, *brooding* over the face of the waters" (emphasis added). In using this term to describe Creation, the Holy Spirit is using the analogy of birthing something. When the Holy Spirit brooded, or hovered, over the earth, He was releasing His creative power at the words of Jesus, giving birth to what Christ spoke.

Psalm 90:2 confirms this, actually calling what the Holy Spirit did at Creation a birthing when it uses two important

Hebrew words: "Before the mountains were born (*yalad*), or Thou didst give birth to (*chuwl*) the earth and the world, even from everlasting to everlasting, Thou art God."

Although the words are not translated "travail" in this verse, *yalad* and *chuwl* are also the primary Hebrew words for travail. Each one is translated variously in the Old Testament: "bring forth," "born," "give birth to," "travail," among others (for examples see Deut. 32:18; Job 15:7; 39:1). Regardless of how they are translated, the concept is that of giving birth to something. It is not always referring to a literal, physical birth but is often used for the idea of creating. We do the same thing in our vocabulary. We might say an idea, vision or nation was born or conceived. We're obviously not speaking of a physical birth but of something new coming into being. In much the same way, Psalm 90:2 likens the Genesis account of Creation to a birthing.

Now, let's make the prayer connection. These are the very same words used in Isaiah 66:8: "As soon as Zion *travailed [chuwl]* she also *brought forth [yalad]* her sons." This is extremely important! What the Holy Spirit was doing in Genesis when He "brought forth" or "gave birth to" the earth and the world is exactly what He wants to do through our prayers in bringing forth spiritual sons and daughters. He wants to hover around (*tohuw*) lost, lifeless, confused, spiritually barren individuals, releasing His awesome power to convict, break bondages, bring revelation and draw them to Himself in order to cause the new birth or new creation in them. *Yes, the Holy Spirit wants to birth through our prayers!* And if He can do so to create all we see around us, He can certainly do it in the one for whom you are praying. Consider this story:

When Pam gave her life back to the Lord, she felt compelled to take up the prayer mantle of her deceased mother and grandmother and intercede for her siblings. The five children had been raised by a godly mother who, as Pam says, "stood on the Word that promised if she taught them the way of the Lord, when they were old they would not depart from it. Mother and Grandmother prayed for years for this household."

After their deaths, the children strayed far from the Lord, and Satan made his bid to trap them in the world. Of special concern was O'Brien, a brother who became drawn into relationships with unbelieving women. Then, while stationed in Asia, he married a Buddhist. Pam was heartbroken that he had rejected the Lord and embraced a false god instead.

But Pam continued to pray, asking the Holy Spirit to hover around her brother and his wife—to break bondages, release revelation and draw them to Himself. She asked God to also remember the many prayers of their grandmother and mother. Finally, after two years, she was overjoyed to receive O'Brien's phone call: "Sis, I want you to know I found the Lord. I love Jesus, and I'm going to stay with the Lord. All the prayers for me were not in vain."

Shortly afterwards, he came to visit Pam, bringing his Buddhist wife with him. Pam immediately took them to visit her spiritual mom, JoAnne. Before they left her house, JoAnne had led O'Brien's wife to Jesus.[12]

Tohuw people—lost, confused, deceived, spiritually barren—can be brought to salvation if the Holy Spirit is released to hover. Buddhists and rebellious brothers are not a problem for Him; that is, if we pray. Don't call them unsaved, call them pre-saved and get on with it.

The second example of the Holy Spirit hovering, bringing forth life out of lifelessness, is in Deuteronomy 32:10-18. All four of the previously mentioned Hebrew words are used in this passage: *tohuw, rachaph, yalad* and *chuwl*. In this passage Moses is recounting to the Israelites their history and speaks of Israel as an individual, obviously referring back to Abraham, the father of the nation. In verse 10, Moses says God found him in a *tohuw* situation—in other words, lifeless or barren.

Abraham was in the same barren condition the earth was in prior to the Creation. Neither he nor Sarah had the ability at this point to produce life. They were sterile, lifeless. We are then told in verse 11 that like an eagle hovers (*rachaphs*) over its young, the Lord hovered over them. The Holy Spirit brooded over Abraham and Sarah, releasing His life and power, giving them the ability to conceive!

We read in Hebrews 11:11 that by faith Sarah received *dunamis* (the miraculous power of the Holy Spirit)[13] to conceive. As He hovered, God was actually birthing a nation in them. Later in the passage (Deut. 32:18) *yalad* and *chuwl*, the primary Hebrew words for travail or giving birth, are used: "You neglected the Rock who begot you, and forgot the God who gave you birth." The identical words are chosen in this passage to describe the Holy Spirit's hovering over Abraham and Sarah to bring forth life as were used in the Genesis Creation and in Isaiah 66:8. The hovering that brought forth natural Israel will also bring forth spiritual Israel as He *rachaphs* through our intercession.

Our third example of the Holy Spirit bringing forth life as He hovered, or brooded over, is found in Luke 1:35, the conception of Christ in Mary. The angel of the Lord came to Mary telling her that she would bear a child. She responded by asking, "How can this be, since I am a virgin?" (v. 34).

The answer was, "The Holy Spirit will come upon you, and the power of the Most High will overshadow you" (v. 35). Overshadow is the Greek word *episkiazo,* which means "to cast a shade upon; to envelope in a haze of brilliancy; to invest with supernatural influence."[14] It is in some ways a counterpart for the Hebrew word *rachaph.* Thayer says it is used "of the Holy Spirit exerting creative energy upon the womb of the Virgin Mary and impregnating it."[15]

The word is only used three times in the New Testament. At the transfiguration of Jesus in Matthew 17:5, the passage says the cloud of the Lord "overshadowed" them. It is also used in Acts 5:15 when people were trying to get close to Peter—in his "shadow"—that they might be healed. Have you ever wondered how Peter's shadow could heal anyone?

It didn't. What was actually happening was that the Holy Spirit was moving out from Peter—hovering and *rachaphing*—and when individuals stepped into the cloud, or overshadowing, they were healed.

Intercession releases the Holy Spirit to hover around an individual, enveloping that person with His power and life, bringing conviction of sin and breaking strongholds. We are His birthing vessels, His incubation chambers. He desperately wants to release His creative birthing power through us, bringing forth the fruit of Calvary. He wants to use us in *tohuw* (lifeless, fruitless, desolate, barren) situations, releasing His life into them. As He did at Creation, He wants to bring forth new creations in Christ Jesus. As with Israel when He hovered over the barren bodies of Abraham and Sarah, bringing forth a nation, He wants to bring forth spiritual Israel from us. As with Mary when He hovered, bringing forth, or conceiving, the Christ in her, He desires to bring forth Christ in people through our intercession. Here's an excellent example:

One morning a phone call from her son interrupted Quin Sherrer's busy schedule. "Mom, my roommate's mother is dying of throat cancer in a military hospital near you," he said. "He has recently accepted Jesus, but he's concerned because his mother doesn't know the Lord. Would you go see her and pray for her?"

When Quin and her prayer partner, Fran, walked into the hospital room, Beatrice was in such pain she could barely talk. "Did you know your son Mickey has become a Christian?" Quin asked, getting right to the point of the visit. "My son rooms with him and has seen such a happy change in him. In fact, Mickey is concerned about your spiritual condition."

"Yes, he told me. I'm glad for him, but it's just too late for me," Beatrice said. Assuring her that it was not too late and that Jesus would accept her right where she was, Fran read several Scripture verses while Quin silently prayed that the Holy Spirit would come and hover around Beatrice, bringing forth new life.

Finally, Beatrice said that she was ready to ask Him to forgive her and be her Savior and Lord. She quietly prayed, "Lord Jesus, please forgive me for my rebellion and for running from You. Come live in my heart. I want to be Yours."

Quin visited her a few more times in the hospital, taking her a Bible and praying with her, before Beatrice died a few weeks later. While at the funeral home, Quin shared with Mickey regarding his mother's salvation experience. An elderly woman standing nearby spoke up, "Forgive me for listening in, but I'm Beatrice's mother. I can't remember a day when I didn't pray for my only daughter to come to the Lord."

"Well, dear, your prayers were answered," Quin said.

"She made it to heaven!" the woman exclaimed, wiping tears from her eyes. "She actually accepted Jesus just days before she died! Thank You, Jesus! Thank You, Lord, for Your faithfulness."[16]

The prayers of Beatrice's mother and son, as well as those of Quin and Fran, had released the creative, birthing power of the Holy Spirit to hover around Beatrice, bringing her to salvation.

Birthing Midwives—God's Word and Declarations of Faith

Decreeing God's Word and speaking forth Spirit-led declarations are two of the ways we release the birthing power of the Holy Spirit. They do not release Him in the sense that He is bound—God obviously is not bound. But, His creative power, energy and ability that come forth through His Word are released upon the earth as we speak them for Him. We are His partners, His representatives.

There is incredible power and creative ability in God's spoken Word. The Hebrew word *asah* is often used in association with the declared Word of God. *Asah* means "to work, do, make, create, construct, build and accomplish."[17] Nations, seas, the heavens and all creation are spoken of as being created (*asah*) by the word of God (see Pss. 33:6; 86:9; 95:5; 96:5; 148:1-6).

Listen to these other well-known verses that speak of God's Word accomplishing or creating:

> God is not a man, that He should lie, nor a son of man, that He should repent. Has He said, and will He not do (*asah*) it? Or has He spoken, and will He not make it good? (Num. 23:19).

> So shall My word be which goes forth from My mouth; it shall not return to Me empty, without accomplishing (*asah*) what I desire, and without succeeding in the matter for which I sent it (Isa. 55:11).

Then the LORD said to me, 'You have seen well, for
I am watching over My word to perform (*asah*) it'
(Jer. 1:12).

Please realize that when God said these things, He was
not talking about speaking from the clouds. He was referring to what He had been saying and was still saying to people through His servants. In essence He was declaring.
"These men's words are My words. They are My voice. Their
words won't return to Me void, but will do exactly what I
send them to do through these vessels. They will do, accomplish and perform—they will *asah*!"

We must understand that it is not an issue of what
our words would normally do. It is rather speaking *for God*
that releases His power to accomplish something. Isn't
this what happens as we preach or declare the gospel,
which "is the power of God for salvation" (Rom. 1:16)?
Our mouths, speaking God's Word, release the power inherent in the gospel. This is also what happens when we
speak His Word as a sword in spiritual warfare (see Eph.
6:17). He infuses our words with divine power. Holy
Spirit-inspired declarations are powerful because they release the power of God into situations. We become the
voice of God upon the earth.

Evelyn's Bible was marked with pen and tears as,
for years, she prayed God's Word for her family.
"I remember calling out Isaiah 49:25 and 54:13,"
she said, "reminding God that He would save our

sons and daughter and that they would be taught of the Lord."

After visiting her son Ken on the East Coast, her heart was deeply grieved for him. On her return flight home, she prayed, "God, I know all the Scriptures that are there to stand on for my family, but I need something new and fresh so I can fight the good fight for my son." She opened a small book of Proverbs she had with her, and suddenly a verse seemed to leap off the page, birthing faith in her for Ken: "You can also be very sure that God will rescue the children of the godly" (Prov. 11:21, *TLB*). Wondering why she had never noticed this verse before, she realized this was a Bible version she usually didn't use. It was as though the Lord was saying to her, "You may know all the Scriptures, but you don't know all the versions!"

Little did Evelyn realize that ahead lay many years of prayer and warfare for Ken, as he became increasingly hard, bitter and angry. But Evelyn and her husband persevered in declaring the Word of God over their son, continuing to pray that God would indeed rescue him. Finally, the day came when Ken called to tell them he had repented and turned to the Lord.

"I'll never forget the moment he came home. There he stood, so visibly changed! Ken's countenance, dark for so many years, now was lit up with that inward glow that only Jesus can give."[18]

As this mother released the power of God over her son's life, the spoken Word of God accomplished what it was sent forth to do.

The word in the New Testament for "confession" is *homologia*, which means "say the same thing."[19] Biblical confession is saying what God says—no more, no less. If it isn't what God is saying about a situation, it does nothing. But if it is what He says, it accomplishes much.

The Word of God is called a "seed" in the Scriptures. The root word in Greek is *speiro*. *Spora* and *sperma* are variations of the word, both of which are translated "seed" in the New Testament. It is easy to see the English words "spore" and "sperm" in them.

God's method of reproducing or bringing forth life is His Word, by which we are born again (see 1 Pet. 1:23), cleansed (see John 15:3), matured (see Matt. 13:23), freed (see John 8:31,32), healed (see Ps. 107:20)—as well as many other results. When God speaks His Word, He is sprinkling seeds that will bring forth. The Word of God is never ineffective; it will always produce. When we speak God's Word into situations, as the Holy Spirit directs, we are sprinkling the seeds of God, which then gives Him the ability to cause life to come forth!

Job 22:28 declares, "You will also decree a thing, and it will be established for you." The word "decree" means literally "decide and decree"[20]—determines something and then decrees it. The actual meaning of *omer*, the word translated "thing" is "a word, a command, a promise."[21]

A more precise wording would be, "You shall decree or declare a word." Then He says it will be established for you. "Establish" is the word *qum*, meaning not only to establish but also to "arise or stand up."[22] Here's what I believe God is saying: "You shall decree a word and it will rise up. You shall sprinkle My seed. It will arise (grow) and establish something in the earth." Some would contend that we cannot command God to do something. I would agree. But there is a great difference between dictating and simply being a spokesperson. We are not telling God what to do. We are decreeing *for* Him, releasing His Word to perform its work.

Job 6:25 (*KJV*) reads: "How forcible are right words!" "Forcible" is the word *marats*, which also means "to press."[23] As the signet ring of a king presses a document with his seal, our words also seal things. They seal our salvation, the promises of God, our destinies and many other things (see Prov. 18:20-21; Matt. 12:37; Mark 11:23; Rom. 10:8-10).

Ecclesiastes 12:11 (*KJV*) tells us "The words of the wise are as goads, and as nails fastened by the masters of assemblies." Our words act as nails, constructing things in the spirit. Just as a nail is used to keep a board in place, words are used to keep God's promises in place, allowing them to build or construct (one of the meanings of *asah*) things in the spirit.

Ezekiel and the valley of dry bones is an example of declaration. "[Speak] to these bones!" (Ezek. 37:4, *AMP*), God said to the prophet.

Can you imagine what Ezekiel thought? *Speak to them? God, if You want something said to skeletons, why don't You just do it?* But Ezekiel obeyed and said, "O dry bones, hear the word of the Lord." And they did! Bone came to bone and flesh came on them.

There was no life in them, however, and Ezekiel's next assignment amazes me more than prophesying to the bones. The Lord told him *"Prophesy to the breath"* (v. 9). Later in the passage we're told that the breath he was prophesying to was the Holy Spirit. God didn't say, "Prophesy *by* the Holy Spirit," nor did He say, "Prophesy *for* the Holy Spirit." God said, "I want you to prophesy *to* the Holy Spirit." Ezekiel did and the Spirit of God did what a man told Him to. Incredible! Did the prophet actually command the Holy Spirit? Not really. He wasn't commanding God; He was commanding *for* God.

Apply these principles to intercession for the lost. As you declare God's Word over those for whom you pray, you are releasing the hovering of the Holy Spirit to birth the new creation (*asah*). Speak life and deliverance over them. Speak conviction, revelation and repentance. God will perform His Word.

Questions for Wisdom and Faith

1. What do you feel is the role of a Christian in God's birthing process?

2. Is it possible for us to negatively affect a spiritual birth in progress?

3. What is the critical element in spiritual birthing? Is it prayer, the Scriptures, declarations of faith . . . ?

4. When a new life in Christ is born, what are the critical nutrients for maturity and strength in Christ?

5. Should believers be experiencing numerous spiritual births in and around their lives each day?

ENDNOTES

Chapter One: The Persistent Knocking

1. Quin Sherrer and Ruthanne Garlock, *How to Pray for Your Family and Friends* (Ann Arbor, MI: Servant Publications, 1990), p. 80.
2. Ibid., p. 81.

Chapter Two: Faith Paves the Way

1. James Strong, *The New Strong's Exhaustive Concordance of the Bible* (Nashville, TN: Thomas Nelson Publishers, 1990), Greek Dictionary, ref. no. 5287.
2. Ibid., ref. no. 1650.
3. Ibid., ref. no. 3358.
4. Ibid., ref. no. 5232.
5. Ibid., ref. no. 4135.
6. George Müller, *Release the Power of Prayer* (New Kensington, PA: Whitaker House, 1999), pp. 46, 47.
7. Alice Gray, *Stories for the Heart* (Sisters, OR: Multnomah Publishers, 1996), pp. 255-257.
8. Strong, *The New Strong's Exhaustive Concordance of the Bible, Hebrew and Chaldee Dictionary*, ref. no. 3467.
9. Charles G. Finney, *How to Experience Revival* (New Kensington, PA: Whitaker House, 1984), p. 58.
10. Craig Brian Larson, *Illustrations for Preaching and Teaching* (Grand Rapids, MI: Baker Books, 1993), p. 25.
11. Quin Sherrer and Ruthanne Garlock, *How to Pray for Your Family and Friends* (Ann Arbor, MI: Servant Publications, 1990), pp. 134, 135.

Chapter Three: Being Strategic in Salvation

1. Alice Gray, *Stories for the Heart* (Sisters, OR: Multnomah Publishers, 1996), p. 109.
2. Spiros Zodhiates, *The Complete Word Study Dictionary* (Iowa Falls, IA: Word Bible Publishers, 1992), p. 816.
3. James Strong, *The New Strong's Exhaustive Concordance of the Bible* (Nashville, TN: Thomas Nelson Publishers, 1990), Greek Dictionary, ref. no. 575.
4. W. E. Vine, *The Expanded Vine's Expository Dictionary of New Testament Words* (Minneapolis, MN: Bethany House Publishers, 1984), p. 125.
5. Strong, *The New Strong's Exhaustive Concordance of the Bible, Greek Dictionary*, ref. no. 5188.
6. Ibid., Greek Dictionary, ref. no. 5187.
7. Azriela Jaffe, *Heart Warmers* (Holbrook, MA: Adams Media Corporation, 2000), pp. 10-12.

8. Quin Sherrer and Ruthanne Garlock, *How to Pray for Your Family and Friends* (Ann Arbor, MI: Servant Publications, 1990), p. 44.

9. Strong, *The New Strong's Exhaustive Concordance of the Bible, Greek Dictionary,* ref. no. 1415.

10. Paul Billheimer, *Destined for the Throne* (Christian Literature Crusade: Fort Washington, PA, 1975), p. 67.

11. Zodhiates, *The Complete Word Study Dictionary,* p. 1464.

12. Ibid., p. 1463.

13. Edward K. Rowell, *Fresh Illustrations for Preaching and Teaching* (Grand Rapids, MI: Baker Books, 1997), p. 182.

14. Strong, *The New Strong's Exhaustive Concordance of the Bible, Greek Dictionary,* ref. no. 1124.

15. Ibid., *Greek Dictionary,* ref. no. 3056.

16. Spiros Zodhiates, *Hebrew-Greek Key Study Bible—New American Standard, rev. ed.* (Chattanooga, TN: AMG Publishers, 1990), p. 1718.

17. Ibid., p. 1858.

18. Ibid., p. 1834.

19. Ibid., p. 1856.

20. Robert J. Morgan, *Real Stories for the Soul* (Nashville, TN: Thomas Nelson Publishers, 2000), pp. 226, 227.

Chapter Four: Spiritual Warfare for the Lost

1. James Strong, *The New Strong's Exhaustive Concordance of the Bible* (Nashville, TN: Thomas Nelson Publishers, 1990), Greek Dictionary, ref. no. 2192.

2. Ibid., ref. no. 2507.

3. Ibid., ref. no. 1415.

4. Quin Sherrer and Ruthanne Garlock, *How to Pray for Your Family and Friends* (Ann Arbor, MI: Servant Publications, 1990), pp. 158, 159.

5. Spiros Zodhiates, *The Complete Word Study Dictionary* (Iowa Falls, IA: Word Bible Publishers, 1992), p. 923.

6. Sherrer and Garlock, *How to Pray for Your Family and Friends,* pp. 163, 164.

7. Craig Brian Larson, *Illustrations for Preaching and Teaching* (Grand Rapids, MI: Baker Books, 1993), p. 239.

8. George Müller, *Release the Power of Prayer* (New Kensington, PA: Whitaker House, 1999), pp. 86, 87.

9. Edward K. Rowell, *Fresh Illustrations for Preaching and Teaching* (Grand Rapids, MI: Baker Books, 1997), p. 196.

10. Strong, *The New Strong's Exhaustive Concordance, Greek Dictionary,* ref. no. 5313.

11. Walter Bauer, *A Greek-English Lexicon of the New Testament* (Chicago: The University of Chicago Press, 1979), p. 386.

12. Sherrer and Garlock, *How to Pray for Your Family and Friends,* pp. 36, 37.

13. Zodhiates, *Hebrew-Greek Key Study Bible—New American Standard,* p. 1797.

14. Robert J. Morgan, *Real Stories for the Soul* (Nashville, TN: Thomas Nelson Publishers, 2000), pp. 141-143.

Chapter Five: Bearing God's Heartbreaking Burdens

1. Robert J. Morgan, *Real Stories for the Soul* (Nashville, TN: Thomas Nelson Publishers, 2000), pp. 199-201.
2. Charles G. Finney, *How to Experience Revival* (New Kensington, PA: Whitaker House, 1984), pp. 49, 50.
3. Ibid., p. 12.
4. Spiros Zodhiates, *Hebrew-Greek Key Study Bible—New American Standard* (Chattanooga, TN: AMG Publishers, 1990), p. 1723.
5. James Strong, *The New Strong's Exhaustive Concordance* (Nashville, TN: Thomas Nelson Publishers, 1990), Hebrew and Chaldee Dictionary, ref. no. 4997.
6. "More Than Her Car," *Parables, Etc.*, July 1995, http://www.autoillustrator.com (accessed February 1, 2000).

Chapter Six: Labor-Intensive Realities

1. Quin Sherrer and Ruthanne Garlock, *Praying Prodigals Home* (Ventura, CA: Regal Books, 2000), adapted from pp. 89, 90.
2. W. E. Vine, *The Expanded Vine's Expository Dictionary of New Testament Words* (Minneapolis, MN: Bethany House Publishers, 1984), p. 110.
3. James Strong, *The New Strong's Exhaustive Concordance of the Bible* (Nashville, TN: Thomas Nelson Publishers, 1990), Greek Dictionary, ref. no. 4057.
4. Ibid., ref. no. 5228.
5. Ibid., ref. no. 2596.
6. Joseph Henry Thayer, *A Greek-English Lexicon of the New Testament* (Grand Rapids, MI: Baker Book House, 1977), p. 422.
7. Sherrer and Garlock, *Praying Prodigals Home*, adapted from pp. 124, 125.
8. Strong, *The New Strong's Exhaustive Concordance of the Bible, Hebrew and Chaldee Dictionary*, ref. no. 8414.
9. Spiros Zodhiates, *Hebrew-Greek Key Study Bible—New American Standard*, rev. ed. (Chattanooga, TN: AMG Publishers, 1990), p. 1790.
10. C. F. Keil and F. Delitzsch, *Commentary on the Old Testament*, vol. 1 (Grand Rapids, MI: Williams B. Eerdmans, 1991), p. 48.
11. William Wilson, *Old Testament Word Studies* (Grand Rapids, MI: Kregel Publications, 1978), p. 175.
12. Sherrer and Garlock, *Praying Prodigals Home*, adapted from pp. 131-133.
13. Strong, *The New Strong's Exhaustive Concordance of the Bible, Greek Dictionary*, ref. no. 1411.
14. Ibid., ref. no. 1982.
15. Thayer, *A Greek-English Lexicon of the New Testament*, p. 242.
16. Quin Sherrer, *Good Night, Lord* (Ventura, CA: Regal Books, 2000), pp. 197, 198.
17. Zodhiates, *Hebrew-Greek Key Study Bible—New American Standard*, p. 1763.
18. Sherrer and Garlock, *Praying Prodigals Home*, adapted from pp. 47-49.
19. Zodhiates, *Hebrew-Greek Key Study Bible—New American Standard*, p. 1861.

20. R. Laird Harris, Gleason L. Archer Jr. and Bruce K. Waltke, *Theological Wordbook of the Old Testament* (Grand Rapids, MI: Williams B. Eerdmans, 1991), p, 158.

21. Ibid., p. 118.

22. Ibid., p. 793.

23. Strong, *The New Strong's Exhaustive Concordance of the Bible, Hebrew and Chaldee Dictionary,* ref. no. 4834.

BOOK THREE

WATCHMAN
PRAYER

Keeping the Enemy Out While Protecting Your
Family, Home and Community

DUTCH
SHEETS

1

LOOKING FOR A FEW GOOD WATCHMEN

━━━━━━━━━━━━◈━━━━━━━━━━━━

Be Careful What You Watch For

The only thing worse than shopping is watching someone shop. Except for my wife, of course. I don't mind at all following her around a mall for two or three hours. I show my interest periodically with pleasant little grunts—"Umph"; "Uh-huh"; "Ahh-hum." Sometimes I get downright wordy—"Yes"; "No"; "Sure"; "HOW MUCH?!" I've gotten pretty quick at correcting that one: "Wow, what a deal!" I hastily add. About the closest thing I can compare "shopper watching" to would be watching a sewing match.

Which is why I'm sitting in the food court writing while my wife and youngest daughter, Hannah, shop. It's one of those outlet malls where they sell you the flawed stuff "on sale." My oldest daughter, Sarah, who is 10 years old, is with me, reading. She doesn't like shopping, either—yet. I informed her on the way to our "food court refuge" of the gene in her—which God gave all women—that simply hasn't kicked in yet. Told her not to worry, it'll happen. (I first shared this story several years ago in my book *Intercessory Prayer*. Sarah's shopping gene has since fully kicked in. She has matured nicely in this essential aspect of womanhood. I'm still eating in food courts—by myself now—and "umph"ing once in a while.)

In my studies of this genetic plague—most of them done through conversing with other men in food courts—I have discovered that no one knows for sure when the gene kicks in or what triggers it. It can hit anytime between the ages of 6 and 13. Sometimes it happens in the middle of the night; they just wake up with the shakes—flu-like symptoms. When it happened with Hannah, I was ready to anoint her with oil, until my wife, Ceci, informed me it wouldn't help.

"What do you mean it won't help?" I asked in surprise. "Of course it will."

"No," she said, "it's her shopping gene kicking in. We've got to get her to a mall—fast."

Mom was right, of course. She usually is. Hannah came home proudly holding her shopping bag, looking like she'd just caught her first fish. Women! Who can figure?

To prove my point, I just counted the men and women in the food court and surrounding stores—26 females and 9 males. Half the males were kids that had been dragged there against their wills. Another was writing—yours truly—and the rest were grunting, "Uh-huh." I felt sorry for one guy; he actually looked like a zombie. I think he finally cracked under the stress. Either that or he was suffering from food-court food poisoning.

Ceci and Hannah are back now, getting something to drink and showing us their "deals." I'm grunting. Ceci is merely dropping Hannah off so she can run back for one more thing. Seven-year-olds—apprentice shoppers—can't always keep up with the pros. They haven't had enough aerobics classes, for which the real motivation is shopping conditioning. (Hannah's stamina has increased remarkably since then. Ceci assured me regularly during my daughters' growing-up years that they were both right on schedule in this all-important phase of development—she urged me "not to worry." The thought never crossed my mind!)

Why couldn't God have made women to like normal things, such as sitting in a woods for days in sub-zero weather, waiting for a deer or elk to walk by? Now that's my idea of exciting watching! . . . Or watching a football game! I'm not into TV too much—unless it's a good sporting event. Ceci doesn't always understand me in this area, but she is kind about it. "Who are you rooting for?" she sometimes asks.

"I don't care who wins," I often reply.

"Are these any of your favorite teams?"

"No, not really."

"A favorite player or two, perhaps?"

"Naw, I don't know much about these guys at all."

"Then why are you watching the game?" she asks with a quizzical expression.

"Because it's football," I reply as patiently as I possibly can. Sometimes people can't figure out the obvious. I'll tell you what puzzles me—why she and my two daughters like to watch stuff that makes them cry. Go figure!

Many kinds of watching take place: TV watching, parade watching, watching the clock, stock market watching, bird watching (ranks right up there with sewing matches to me) and a thousand other things. I like to watch kids laugh. I hate to watch people cry. I've watched individuals born; I've watched others die.

I once watched a lady in San Pedro, Guatemala, look for a watch. It was her husband's—he died in the earthquake of 1976. So did three of her kids. All she and her surviving infant had left were the clothes on their backs. Their small adobe home was a mound of dirt.

When our interpreter asked her what she was digging for, she replied. "A bag of beans we had and my husband's watch. He was sleeping about here when he was killed," she said, pointing at an area of approximately 10 square feet. "It would mean so much to me if I could find his watch."

We started digging.

Although it was like looking for a needle in a haystack, we asked God to help us and waded into the three-feet-deep dirt. Right then I'd have charged hell for that watch. We found it an hour or so later.

"Muchas gracias," she repeated through tears as she clutched the inexpensive watch to her breast.

"Treasure" is such a relative term, I thought as I wiped my eyes. *I wish the world could see this. Maybe some priorities would change.*

I watched another quake victim, holding her three-year-old daughter, walk away from a food line in which I was serving. She was the last in line for the soup. As she held out the jar she had found, we looked at her and said, "No más" (which means "No more"). Then I watched her walk away, holding her hungry child.

Things got all messed up at that point in my life. Neat little lists of needs disappeared. Certain important goals became strangely irrelevant. Things that mattered suddenly didn't. Bank accounts were looked at differently; success was redefined. Funny how one glance into four eyes can bring such chaos. In many ways, order has never been restored.

Be careful what you watch.[1]

Watchmen Need God's 20/20 Vision

This introduction was taken from the final chapter of my first book, *Intercessory Prayer*. The chapter dealt with what I called the "watchman anointing." I want to pick up where I ended that book and develop fully the concept of the watchman. It is a facet of prayer being greatly emphasized by the Holy Spirit in this hour, and it must be understood.

God is certainly not finished with the prayer movement around the world. In fact, He wants to transform it from a "movement" to a lifestyle. Movements come and movements go; sometimes that's good and sometimes that's bad. Wouldn't it be sad if 20 years from now the prayer movement of the 1990s was only a "was," spoken of as the good old days!

Will our chapter of history be titled:

- Opportunities Left Unseized
- They Began Well, but . . .
- What Could Have Been?

I trust not. I hope our legacy is similar to King David's: He served God's purpose for his generation (see Acts 13:36). Or maybe like that of the Early Church: They turned their world upside down (see Acts 17:6, *AMP*).

If you're like me, I know you want to finish well. My hope is that prayer becomes the *lifestyle* of the Church and that the movement keeps moving until it takes root. By the grace and power of the Holy Spirit, we can make it so!

Yes, our history is yet to be written. Much is waiting for us: Testimonies are waiting to be created; a generation of youth is waiting to be born again; dry bones are waiting for breath (see Ezek. 37); homes are waiting to be healed; addictions are waiting to be broken; untold millions are waiting to hear the gospel for the first time. Note some alarming statistics:

- In 2002, 2.3 million juveniles were arrested in the United States. Forty-three percent of those arrests were for violent crimes.[2]

- Five thousand young Americans kill themselves each year, making suicide the third highest cause of death among 10- to 24-year-olds.[3]

- Two-thirds of students in grades 6 to 12 say they could obtain a firearm in 24 hours. Six percent of high school students have carried a gun in the last 30 days.[4]

- In 2005, there were nearly 900,000 reports of child abuse and neglect in the U.S. Between 1997 and 2003, more than 4,000 children died as a result of abuse or neglect.[5]

- Forty-seven percent of U.S. teens in grades 9 to 12 had sexual intercourse in 2003. Sixty-two percent of students in grade 12 report having had sex.[6]

- The ratio of abortions per live births remains at roughly 25 percent.[7]

- The number of born-again Christians in America has not significantly changed in the last 10 years.[8]

- Between 1991 and 2004, U.S. church attendance declined more than 6 percent.[9] (This means that we have lost ground.)

- The majority of Americans believe "that the Holy Spirit is a symbol of God's power and presence but not a living entity, that Satan does not exist, and that there are many paths by which we may experience eternal salvation."[10]

- In 2007, 46 percent of Christians who call themselves born again denied the existence of Satan.[11]

We need a wake-up call. There simply is no hope for America apart from revival.

If watchmen had been on duty, these and other shocking events could have been averted. Satan takes advantage of us when the watchman concept of prayer is not operating, as is made clear in the following verse: "In order that no advantage be taken of us by Satan; for we are not ignorant of his schemes" (2 Cor. 2:11). The context is forgiveness, but a general principle is also revealed, which is very applicable to our subject. Let's analyze the verse more closely.

The word "ignorant" is from the Greek verb *agnoeo*, which means to be "without knowledge or understanding of."[12] Our English word "agnostic" is derived from it. Technically, an agnostic is not a person who is unsure if he or she believes in God, although we now use the word this way. In actuality, however, an agnostic is a person who does not know or understand, regardless of the subject. We also get the word "ignore" from the same root. In this verse we're urged not to ignore or be an agnostic—without understanding—where the devil is concerned.

"Schemes" is from the word *noema*, which literally means "thought." The verse is essentially saying, "Don't be without understanding of the way Satan thinks." *Noema* came to also mean "plans, schemes, plots, devices"[13] because these things are born in the thoughts of the mind. For greater insight, let's insert all these concepts into the verse: "Don't be without understanding of the way your enemy thinks and operates—of his plans, plots, schemes and devices." Is there not also a subtle promise here? If God suggests we are not to be ignorant of Satan's schemes, He must be willing to reveal them to us.

What if we are unaware of his schemes? He'll take advantage of us. The word "advantage" is derived from *pleonekteo*, which is a compound word meaning literally "to have or hold the greater portion" (*pleon*—"the greater part"; *echo*—"to have or hold").[14] It is easy to see why this is a word for "covet." It also means "overreach."[15]

In boxing, the person who has the longer reach has the advantage and usually gets in more blows. The word *pleonekteo* is also translated "make a gain"; Satan makes a lot of gains on those who are unaware of his ways. Bullinger says *pleonekteo* means "to make a prey of, to defraud."[16] Let's put all of these definitions together: "To the degree we are ignorant of the way our adversary thinks and operates—of his plans, plots, schemes and devices—to that degree he will gain on us, prey on us, defraud us of what is ours and have or hold the greater portion."

The greater portion of what? Whatever! Our homes, marriages, families, communities, money, government, nation and more. In the 1970s and 1980s, the Church in America was without understanding of what Satan was planning, and he got the greater portion of our schools. The same could be said of our government and many of our churches!

Have you ever been taken advantage of? Have you ever received the smaller portion? In my Bible-college days we had a way of enlightening the superspiritual who thought it necessary to intercede for the world while giving thanks for a meal. They were *ignorant* of our *scheme* when we asked them to pray over the food. While they traversed the globe, we enjoyed *the greater portion* of their meals! It was a real test of their true spirituality. (I am deeply embarrassed by this abominable practice in my past and would never do it today. But for those of you who feel you must intercede over your food, save it for your prayer closet!)

Paul was taken advantage of in 1 Thessalonians 2:18. Satan gained on him (*pleonekteo*) in the ongoing war over spreading the gospel: "For we wanted to come to you—I, Paul, more than once—and yet Satan thwarted us." We know Paul won more battles than he lost. But he was human and at times Satan succeeded in thwarting his plans. Please notice it doesn't say God changed His mind about where Paul was to go. It clearly says that Satan hindered him. Those people who would have us think that Satan can do nothing except what God allows and that we are to ignore him, should reread these two verses. God doesn't ignore the devil and neither should we. And he certainly does a lot of things God doesn't *allow* him to do.

The only sense in which it can be said that God allows everything that happens on Earth is that He created the laws and principles—sowing and reaping, cause and effect and the free will of humans—that govern the earth. We, however, implement these principles and determine much of what we reap and experience. It is truly God and humans working together. Satan, too, understands these laws and uses them to his advantage whenever possible.[17]

Consider the following comments that reflect how easy it is for humans to blame God for failures, mishaps and consequences that are the result of human effort and Satan's role in human affairs:

- In *Christianity Today,* Philip Yancey writes: "When Princess Diana died, I got a phone call from a television producer. 'Can you appear on our show?' he asked. 'We want you to explain how God could possibly allow such a terrible accident.'"

- At the 1994 Winter Olympics, when speed skater Dan Jansen's hand scraped the ice, causing him to lose the 500-meter race, his wife, Robin, cried out, "Why, God, again? God can't be that cruel!"

- A young woman wrote James Dobson this letter: "Four years ago, I was dating a man and became pregnant. I was so devastated! I asked God, 'Why have You allowed this to happen to me?'"

- In a professional bout, boxer Ray "Boom-Boom" Mancini slammed his Korean opponent with a hard right, causing a massive cerebral hemorrhage. At a press conference after the Korean's death, Mancini said, "Sometimes I wonder why God does the things he does."

- Susan Smith, who pushed her car with her two sons in it, into a lake to drown and then blamed a black carjacker for the deed, wrote in her official confession:

"I dropped to the lowest point when I allowed my children to go down that ramp into the water without me. I took off running and screaming, 'Oh God! Oh God, no! What have I done? Why did you let this happen?'"

- I once watched a television interview with a famous Hollywood actress whose lover had rolled off a yacht in a drunken stupor and drowned. The actress, who probably had not thought about God in months, looked at the camera, her lovely face contorted by grief, and asked, bizarrely, "How could a loving God let this happen?"[18]

Let's understand the ways of God and not credit Him for the results of our actions and Satan's. Let the responsibility fall where it should fall.

Two more verses give additional insight. The first is Ephesians 6:18: "With all prayer and petition pray at all times in the Spirit, and with this in view, *be on the alert* with all perseverance and petition for all the saints" (italics mine). The *King James Version* uses the word "watching" for the phrase "be on the alert."

The second verse is 1 Peter 5:8: "Be of sober spirit, *be on the alert*. Your adversary, the devil, prowls about like a roaring lion, seeking someone to devour" (italics mine). Again, other translations use the word "watchful." The context of both verses is spiritual warfare. Each mentions our adversary and challenges us to alertness or watchfulness, both for ourselves and for our brothers and sisters in Christ.

I want to draw four conclusions from these three verses—Ephesians 6:18, 1 Peter 5:8 and 2 Corinthians 2:11—as an introduction for our study of the watchman anointing:

1. *Protection from the attacks of our enemy—even for believers—is not automatic.* There is a part for us to play.

Though God is sovereign, this does not mean He is literally in control of everything that happens. He has left much to the decisions and actions of humankind. If God were going to protect or safeguard us from Satan's attacks regardless of what we did, these verses would be totally irrelevant to Christians. Somewhere in our theology, we must find a place for human responsibility. At some point we must begin to believe that we matter, that we're relevant, for ourselves and for others.

2. *God's plan is to warn or alert us to Satan's tactics.* This is deduced from the simple fact that, since God says not to be *unaware* of Satan's tactics, He must be willing to make us *aware* of them. If He says to be on the alert, this must mean that if we are, He will alert us. God wouldn't ask of us something He wasn't also going to enable us to accomplish.

3. *We must be alert—remain watchful—or we won't be aware of God's attempts to warn us of Satan's attacks and plans.* If these attacks were always going to be obvious, alertness wouldn't be necessary. Isaiah 56:10 speaks of blind watchmen. What a picture! I'm afraid it has been a fairly good description of many of us in our watching roles. We're often like the disciples of old: we have eyes, but we do not see (see Mark 8:18). It's time we do more than gaze; we must alertly watch!

4. *If we are not alert and watchful, and if we are ignorant of Satan's schemes, he will take the bigger portion.* He will gain on us, taking advantage of our ignorance. Contrary to popular belief, we really can be destroyed

due to ignorance (see Hosea 4:6). We may not like to admit it, but Satan really has gained a lot of territory in America.

We cannot deny the reality of spiritual conflict. If we do, we act in denial, and the results can be disastrous.

Don't be like the desert nomad who awakened hungrily one night and decided he'd have a midnight snack. Lighting a candle, he grabbed a date and took a bite. Holding the date to the candle, he saw a worm, whereupon he threw the date out of the tent. Biting into the second date, he found another worm and threw it away, also. Deciding he might not get anything to eat if this continued, he blew out the candle and ate the dates.[19]

Sometimes we, too, prefer the darkness of denial to the light of truth. Though the truth really does hurt at times, it is still truth. Denial doesn't change it. Where Satan has made gains, let's admit it and determine to take them back![20]

Watchmen Wanted

The first example of a failed watchman is recorded in the Bible and affects each one of us every day. The watchman's name was Adam. God told him in Genesis 2:15 to "keep" the garden. The word "keep" is the Hebrew word *shamar*, which is one of the three Old Testament words used for a watchman. I will define these three words in great depth over the next few chapters, but for now, suffice it to say, one of the main concepts of the word involves protection and preservation.

Adam was told to *protect* the garden, *watching* for attacks from the evil one, the serpent. Why do I assert this? Because first of all, it is much in keeping with the nature of God to have warned him. To have done otherwise would not have been consistent with God's character. Second, neither Adam nor Eve seemed shocked when a snake talked to them. It evidently didn't come as a total surprise. Third, what else could there have been before the Fall to guard, keep or protect themselves from in the garden? Only the serpent.[21] The first responsibility of watchmen is to keep the serpent out of their God-given gardens.

The serpent has been interloping ever since, seeking to grab the greater portion. He has sunk his venomous fangs into many portions of America and the world. The fruit of the poisonous venom is terrifying. Consider these reports concerning a young, identity-less generation of Americans:

- In 2005, more than 721,000 10- to 24-year-olds were treated in emergency rooms for injuries related to violence. In the same year, nearly 8 percent of students in grades 9 to 12 reported being injured by or threatened with a weapon at school, while more than 6 percent reported staying home from school because they felt unsafe.[22]

- On April 20, 1999, two young men wearing long, black trench coats opened fire in a suburban high school in Littleton, Colorado, injuring as many as 23 students and killing 12 students and 1 teacher, and then they killed themselves.

- On February 9, 2000, a six-year-old in Mount Morris Township, Michigan, took his uncle's gun to school and fatally shot a six-year-old classmate.

- On April 23, 2003, a 14-year-old boy at Red Lion Area Junior High School in Pennsylvania shot the school's principal in the chest and then turned the gun on himself.

· On March 21, 2005, a 16-year-old student in Red Lake, Minnesota, killed 10 people, including himself and his grandfather, and wounded 15 others.

· On April 16, 2007, in the deadliest school shooting in U.S. history, a young English major at Virginia Tech in Blacksburg, Virginia, fatally shot 33 people, including himself, and injured 23 others.[23]

Our precious gardens are full of demons—we need some watchmen!

Tragedies such as these can and must be eliminated. I challenge you to make a difference. Learn the power of prayer and apply the principles of the watchman. We must take back the portions Satan has seized in our nation and around the world. Let's become spiritually militant and aggressive as we deal with the serpent and his stealing, killing and destroying. Let there be no more agnostics where Satan is concerned. Let's expose and STOP HIM! Let's get him out of our gardens!

All across America thousands of youth are meeting in Torch Grab rallies where they are encouraged to pick up the torch of Columbine High School martyrs Cassie Bernall and Rachel Scott. Many are responding with total commitment and abandonment to God, picking up the torch and accepting the call to reach their generation for Christ.

The blood of these martyrs cries from the ground, "Revival to this generation!" The same ears that heard the blood-cry of righteous Abel hear those of righteous Cassie and Rachel. The fire of the torches they carried is spreading to other torches across this land. Once again, the blood of the martyrs will be the seeds of revival.

What of us? What of we watchmen who are exhorted by God to guard this generation and birth a revival? Must not our commitment match that of our fallen young comrades and their successors? Is this not a cause worth abandoning ourselves to? My good friend Solveig Henderson states it well for each of us. I pray you'll agree.

I'm abandoned to You, Jesus,
I surrender to the call.
I don't want to have my own way,
'Cause I know through that I'll fall.
So I come and fall on You, Lord.
I will answer when You knock.
When I'm weak You are my stronghold,
*   my security, my Rock.*

I'm abandoned to You, Jesus,
You're the treasure that I seek.
Anything that I've held sacred,
By comparison is bleak.
In my travels You're my journey,
You're my road, my map, my guide.
You're my final destination.
I say yes.[24]

The call goes out for watchmen. Can you hear it? Surrender to the call!

2

GOD'S ALARM SYSTEM

~❦~

The Big Picture on God's Watchmen

We recently built a new, custom home—and I'm still saved. This is due much more to the grace of God and a detailed wife than anything else. From overruns to misunderstood instructions to contractor delays, there were plenty of opportunities to lose it when we were building our home. Thank God for a detail-oriented wife who did most of our work, a good Christian builder who walks in integrity and the grace of God.

When beginning the project, we started with the big picture and then worked our way down to the details. I was more involved in the big picture, thank goodness. I'm a big-picture, bottom-line, "don't bore me with the details" kind of guy. "What's it gonna look like?" and "How much will it cost?" were about as deep as my questions got.

When I share my bright ideas and lofty visions, Ceci always wants to talk details: "What about this?" "Have you thought of that?" "Who is going to do this and such?"

"That's for someone else to worry about," I quickly and impatiently respond. "I have a dream. Don't bother me with all that stuff."

It really doesn't matter to me that "all that stuff" will no doubt make or break the project. Thinking about all that stuff would break *me*—raise my blood pressure and give me stress.

So I don't administrate. I leave that for the weird people God made with abnormal desires.

I have a friend, Randall Gant, who told me the other day he actually loves to solve problems. I'm afraid this dear brother has a problem someone needs to help *him* solve. He told me he woke up the other day thinking about a flow chart. He was serious! I was ready to pray for him; he, on the other hand, was excited. He thinks God made him this way. My theology won't let me believe God is that cruel. People like him weren't born this way—they probably did something really bad as children and this is their punishment.

What does all that have to do with this book? Not much—I just needed to get it off my chest! But there is some relevance. In this chapter we're going to look at the big picture where watchmen are concerned: the broad concepts and definitions as opposed to specific principles and how-tos. In subsequent chapters we'll get to some details—God have mercy on my soon-to-be-troubled soul!

So, for you detail people . . . chill! We'll make you happy later.

For you big-picture people . . . enjoy! Relax! Indulge yourself! Dream a little.

The Role of Watchmen

Those of you who have read my book *Intercessory Prayer* (in other words, the most spiritual of you!) will recall that I sometimes refer to spiritual abilities and activities as anointings. This is simply because anything we accomplish of eternal value is brought about by the ability and empowerment of the Holy Spirit. Through anointings of the Holy Spirit, Jesus preached, liberated spiritual captives, healed people and did other good works (see Luke 4:18-19; Acts 10:38). In the Old Testament, kings were anointed to rule and priests were anointed to serve and to minister. For us as well, it is the anointing of the Holy Spirit that enables us to adequately perform spiritual activities.

In this book I use the phrase "watchman anointing." This is not done to imply that only a select few with unique callings can operate in this type of prayer activity. Nor is it insinuating that we wait on some heavenly visitation before moving into this type of prayer. It is simply a way of stating and reminding us that the Holy Spirit will empower us and give us the ability to function in this wonderful ministry.

The three primary Hebrew words in the Old Testament for watchman are *natsar*, *shamar* and *tsaphah*. These words have both a defensive or protective connotation and an offensive or aggressive application, with the defensive aspect being the most prominent in the Scriptures. We will discuss the defensive meanings in these next chapters, then later examine the offensive aspect.

Combining the definitions of these three words, which are used almost synonymously, their defensive concept essentially means *to guard or protect through watching over or concealing*. While applied to many subjects—crops, people, cities, etc.—the concept is usually *preservation*.

The two New Testament Greek words for "watching," *gregoreuo* and *agrupneo*, also refer to protection but they have the literal meanings of "being awake" or "sleepless." The picture is that of a sentry, lookout or night watchman who is supposed to remain awake and alert, watching for signs of trouble. Hence the translation at times "be on the alert" (see Luke 21:36, 1 Cor. 16:13, Eph. 6:18, 1 Pet. 5:8).

As He does so often in Scripture, the Holy Spirit uses these practical, physical activities of watchmen to symbolize spiritual functions, usually in reference to prophetic warnings and intercessory prayer.

Watching for Wolves, Thieves and Enemy Assaults

Let's broaden our understanding of biblical watchmen by look-ing at the two most prominent contextual usages of the word in the Old Testament:

- Watching over and protecting crops
- Watchmen on the walls of cities

First, those who watched crops were stationed on rocks, buildings or towers to provide a better range of vision. Towers or outposts in the fields usually had sleeping quarters because it was necessary to keep watch day and night during harvest. The watchmen would take shifts—one working, one sleeping—and thereby "watch" 24 hours a day.

This has great symbolism for us. Seasons of harvest neces-sitate a more urgent need for watchmen, as the "thief" (see John 10:10) is going to do all he can to steal the harvest and keep the greater portion. It is little wonder that God has pre-ceded the greatest harvest of souls the world has ever known—which is now happening—with the greatest prayer awakening in history. The Lord of the harvest is wise. I can assure you He has 24-hour sentries watching the harvest. May we be able to say with our Lord, "Of those You have given me, not one of them perished" (see John 17:12).

Paul and Silas were in danger of losing a very significant harvest in Acts 16. They had been supernaturally led westward into Europe with the message of Christ and had witnessed the first European convert, Lydia (see Acts 16:6-15). At this time a girl with a spirit of divination (Greek: *puthon*—python)[1] began to follow Paul and Silas, saying, "These men are bond-servants of the Most High God, who are proclaiming to you the way of salvation" (v. 17).

Paul, discerning by the Holy Spirit her demonization, turned and commanded the spirit to leave her; and she was instantly delivered. Had Paul not discerned by the Spirit this girl's true condition, but accepted her endorsement, it could have seriously damaged his credibility. At the very least it may have allowed a mixture into this newborn Church, creating the delusion that Christianity and divination were compatible.

This point is also made by Gordon Lindsay in his commentary on Acts:

Satan is clever in his relentless war against God and His people. The evil spirit, of course, immediately recognized Paul and his party as bearers of the true message of God, and it might have denounced them vehemently. But a different strategy was adopted by Satan, who no doubt was following the party's fortunes with malevolent interest. Why not identify the religion of the oracles with that of Christianity? This would confuse and mislead the people so they would not understand that Christianity had no relation whatever with the heathen gods of Greece.[2]

Peter Wagner points out that Satan's strategy failed and instead worked toward the prospering of the gospel:

This episode of strategic-level spiritual warfare would affect the whole city of Philippi. Therefore, the more public the battle the better. If Paul had cast out the Python spirit the first day, few would have known about it. But when it finally happened, it turned out to be a major public display of the power of God over the power of Satan, and the territorial spirit over Philippi was thoroughly embarrassed. The strongman had been bound in the name of Jesus. The way had been opened for the gospel to spread and for a powerful church to be planted.[3]

Because of Paul's ability to discern and deal with the serpent's subtle attempt to steal the early harvest in Europe, a great church was planted at Philippi. Remember the first responsibility of watchmen, as seen from Adam's assignment to keep or protect the garden, is to keep the serpent out. Paul did this in Philippi. (Isn't it interesting that the spirit's name was that of a serpent?)

Second, watchmen were also posted on the city walls usually near the gates, where they functioned as sentries. This is described in the following Old Testament references:

For thus the Lord says to me, "Go, station the lookout, let him report what he sees. When he sees riders, horsemen in pairs, a train of donkeys, a train of camels, let him pay close attention, very close attention." Then the lookout called, "O Lord, I stand continually by day on the watchtower, and I am stationed every night at my guard post" (Isa. 21:6-8).

Lift up a signal against the walls of Babylon; post a strong guard, station sentries, place men in ambush! For the Lord has both purposed and performed what He spoke concerning the inhabitants of Babylon (Jer. 51:12).

On your walls, O Jerusalem, I have appointed watchmen; all day and all night they will never keep silent. You who remind the Lord, take no rest for yourselves (Isa. 62:6).

From the walls of the cities, they watched for two things: messengers and enemies. Their purpose in watching for messengers was to inform the gatekeepers when to open the gates and when to keep them closed. In those days runners were used to carry messages from city to city, and the watchmen would cry out when a messenger was coming. Skilled watchmen could sometimes even recognize the runners "by their stride" before ever seeing their faces. In 2 Samuel 18:27 the watchman said, "The running . . . is like the running of Ahimaaz." Do you see any important symbolism here?

Seasoned watchmen are often alerted by the Holy Spirit, before ever having any concrete evidence, that certain messengers are not to be trusted. They recognize wolves sent to devour the flock, or hirelings with improper motives, and bring warnings to those in leadership. Being alerted by their stride—something just doesn't seem right—watchmen sense and discern. To be sure, we must guard against human suspicion and judging after the flesh. But I have learned to listen to my trusted watchmen (one of whom is my wife) when uneasiness prevails about so and so. They are usually right. At times, these watchmen are unable to give me specific reasons, which is difficult for my analytical mind, but I have learned to trust them.

In *The New Yorker*, Sara Mosle recounts:

On March 18, 1937, a spark ignited a cloud of natural gas that had accumulated in the basement of the London, Texas, school. The blast killed 293 people, most of them children. The explosion happened because the local school board wanted to cut heating costs. Natural gas, the by-product of petroleum extraction, was siphoned from a neighboring oil company's pipeline to fuel the building's furnace free of charge. London never recovered from the blast that turned the phrase "boom town" into a bitter joke. The one positive effect of this disastrous event was government regulation requiring companies to add an odorant to natural gas. The distinctive aroma is now so familiar that we often forget natural gas is naturally odorless.[4]

Many of Satan's activities are "odorless"—hidden from our natural senses. God has added odorants to the evil one's works, however, that can be discerned by spiritual senses. Hebrews 5:14 tells us, "But solid food is for the mature, who because of practice have their senses trained to discern good and evil." Most false doctrine, division and general destruction in the Body of Christ could be averted if the watchmen would exercise these senses and the leaders would listen! Peter speaks of this need in 2 Peter 2:1-2:

> But false prophets also arose among the people, just as there will also be false teachers among you, who will secretly introduce destructive heresies, even denying the Master who bought them, bringing swift destruction upon themselves. And many will follow their sensuality, and because of them the way of the truth will be maligned.

Paul warned the Ephesians of it in Acts 20:28-31:

> Be on guard for yourselves and for all the flock, among which the Holy Spirit has made you overseers, to shepherd the church of God which He purchased with His own blood. I know that after my departure savage wolves will come in among you, not sparing the flock; and from among your own selves men will arise, speaking perverse things, to draw away the disciples after them. Therefore be on the alert, remembering that night and day for a period of three years I did not cease to admonish each one with tears.

Evidently these Ephesians heeded Paul's advice for the Lord commended them in Revelation 2:2 (italics mine):

> I know your deeds and your toil and perseverance, and that you cannot endure evil men, and *you put to the test those who call themselves apostles, and they are not, and you found them to be false.*

The watchmen on the wall also looked for enemies. When they saw potential danger approaching, they sounded an alarm, either by a shout or with a trumpet blast. Soldiers could then prepare themselves for battle and defend the city. Watchmen do this today, in a spiritual sense. They alert the Body of Christ to attacks of the enemy, sounding the alarm. When the watchmen are functioning properly, we need never be caught *off guard* by Satan and his forces. This may seem somewhat idealistic, but I'm convinced of its truth. I don't believe God ever intends for Satan to "take advantage" or get the bigger portion (see 2 Cor. 2:11). The famed "Dutch evangelist Corrie ten Boom was right to observe: 'It's a poor soldier indeed who does not recognize the enemy.' The key to victory in both natural and spiritual warfare is to clearly identify the enemy, and to understand his character and methods."[5]

As watchmen we do not live in fear of our adversary, nor do we live in ignorance of him. Contrary to what some would teach, alertness and vigilance are not synonymous with preoccupation. I must warn you, it is a common tactic of the enemy to dissuade Christians from watching for him by accusing them of a wrong emphasis.

Sadly enough, this message is often purported by well-meaning Christians. They teach that Satan is to be ignored or that little attention is to be paid him. No passage in the Bible supports this. Certainly we are not to become infatuated with

Satan, but a good soldier is a well-informed soldier concerning his enemy. Be infatuated with and in awe of Jesus—be aware of the enemy. Love worship, not warfare; but when necessary, go to war. And post the sentries!

A classic story that stresses the importance of being vigilant was seen in the conflict between the Arabs and Turks in the early part of this century:

> Aqaba in 1917 seemed impregnable. Any enemy vessel approaching the port would have to face the battery of huge naval guns above the town. Behind Aqaba in every direction lay barren, waterless, inhospitable desert. To the east lay the deadly "anvil of the sun." The Turks believed Aqaba to be safe from any attack. But they were wrong.
>
> Lawrence of Arabia led a force of irregular Arab cavalry across the "anvil of the sun." Together, they rallied support among the local people. On July 6, 1917, the Arab forces swept into Aqaba from the north, from the blind side. A climactic moment of the magnificent film *Lawrence of Arabia* is the long, panning shot of the Arabs on their camels and horses, with Lawrence at their head, galloping past the gigantic naval guns that are completely powerless to stop them. The guns were facing in the wrong direction. Aqaba fell, and the Turkish hold on Palestine was broken, to be replaced by the British mandate and eventually by the State of Israel.
>
> The Turks failed to defend Aqaba because they made two mistakes. They did not know their enemy, and they did not have the right weapons.
>
> We must be careful not to make the same mistakes, Ephesians 6:12 makes it very clear who our enemy is: "Our struggle is not against flesh and blood, but against

the rulers, against the authorities, against the powers of this dark world."[6]

We, too, must be aware of our enemy. Do we major on Satan or his demons? No, but we must discern their activities and, unlike these Turks, never walk in ignorance.

We are watchmen warriors who neither emphasize nor ignore the devil. We follow our loving Savior while remembering that He is also a mighty warrior. Through Him we are more than conquerors!

The Many Kinds of Watchmen Today

Before we move on to the next chapter and look at more specific definitions and applications of the watchman anointing, this is a good place to comment on the various realms of calling as watchmen. The anointing and responsibility to function in this needed activity can range from doing it for an individual person or home to watching for a nation or nations.

Cindy Jacobs of Generals of Intercession and Dr. C. Peter Wagner of Global Harvest Ministries are certainly watchmen for nations. While ministering abroad, it is not uncommon for them to receive insight and direction that, when acted on and prayed over properly, has significant impact on the particular nation involved.

Cindy Jacobs tells of how the Lord powerfully impacted the nation of Argentina as she and other intercessors sought His strategy for that nation. As they prayed for wisdom and insight, the Lord revealed various strongholds that needed to be dealt with and directed them to pray at the Plaza Mayo in Buenos Aires. The significance of this location was emphasized as they realized this plaza was surrounded by several buildings representing each of the strongholds that needed prayer. As Cindy led the prayer team from one building to the next, the Lord directed them specifically how to pray regarding each stronghold. They asked God to come heal and restore this nation.

The remarkable changes in Argentina since that time of prayer have been amazing! The run-down plaza has been restored from the ground up. The Argentine Agriculture Department issued a report that the land suddenly began to produce for no known reason; the fertility of the land increased without receiving any improvements. The Congress gave hectares of land to the native peoples as restitution. The inflation rate dropped from 3,000 percent to 1.5 percent. The *Wall Street Journal* reported, "There is a revival in the economy of Argentina, but nobody knows why." History indeed belongs to the watchman intercessor![7]

Peter Wagner, though in a totally different manifestation of the watchman anointing, seems to have incredible insight as to trends and themes the Holy Spirit is emphasizing to the Church around the world. As would a watchman on the wall of a city waiting for messengers, he alerts the Body of Christ to the message of the Spirit. The recent prayer movement is a prime example, and Peter has been one of its leading voices. Though particularly impacting America, it has also had a profound impact on other nations.

In 1997, the Lord instructed Peter and his wife, Doris, to take a prayer journey to Turkey. While debriefing at home later about Turkey, "Operation Queen's Palace" was born—a strategy to have teams of intercessors from the nations of the world participate in a massive prayer initiative. As Turkey and Ephesus are included in both the 10/40 Window and the 40/70 Window, Turkey appears to be the principal hinge nation for this area of the world. It is also the recognized spawning grounds for worldwide goddess worship. The Queen of Heaven (Operation "Queen's Palace") is considered a chief principality commissioned by Satan to keep unbelievers in spiritual darkness. She is at the spiritual roots of Islam, with ancient Ephesus as one of her principal power centers.

Operation Queen's Palace was undoubtedly one of the most significant actions ever taken to push back the forces of darkness so that the light of the gospel can penetrate the hearts of unbelievers blinded to the love of Jesus Christ. Multiple prophetic prayer initiatives were held throughout the world, specifically targeted against every known manifestation of the power of the Queen of Heaven. Operation Queen's Palace culminated at Celebration Ephesus on October 1, 1999, where over 5,000 people gathered in the ancient Ephesian amphitheater to worship the Lord Jesus Christ and declare the Word of God for over four hours. Undoubtedly, the impact of these events will continue to reverberate throughout the nations of the world, as the strongholds of Satan are broken and multitudes come into the kingdom of God.[8]

Other individuals seem to have more of a calling as watchmen to a particular nation. Although he also ministers internationally, Chuck Pierce of Glory of Zion is a watchman I believe fits this description. He frequently has prophetic insight for all or part of America, which helps to thwart the powers of darkness and release the kingdom of God. I would not presume to define his calling for him—perhaps he is an international watchman as well—but my observations of his ministry have been limited to the United States.

The Holy Spirit frequently gives Chuck Pierce specific insight as to what needs to be done and how to pray concerning certain regions of the United States. When obeyed, breakthroughs always follow. Barbara Wentroble shares one of these experiences in her book *Prophetic Intercession*:

I remember a prophecy told to me in 1994 by Chuck Pierce. He had just returned from speaking at a meeting in Houston. While ministering, the Lord gave him a vision and spoke a prophetic word through him. The word from the Lord said that the next 24 days would be critical. God was looking at Houston and would break structures that were holding back revelation. He said the revelation would be released like rain. The prophecy continued to say that as the people looked, a river would begin to rise in the east. A literal fire would be on the river and come to the city. There was instruction for intercessors to gather together and pray during the night. The prayers would limit the destruction that would come to the area.

God was calling intercessors to pray for 24 days. Deborah DeGar, an intercessor from the Houston area, alerted local churches. She also led a prayer meeting from 3:00 A.M. to 6:00 A.M. during those 24 days. Exactly 24 days later, Houston experienced one of the worst floods recorded in the history of the city. The San Jacinto River, east of the city, flooded throughout Houston. A gas line broke and caused a literal fire on the river. As a result of the prophetic warning followed by the fulfillment of the prophetic word, the city experienced a new move of the Holy Spirit.[9]

This is a clear example of a watchman issuing a warning to a city, and watchmen intercessors responding properly.

A friend of mine, whom we'll call Margie, is another example of a watchman for a nation. At the age of 12, the Lord called her to pray for America and told her she would one day live in Washington, DC. She moved there in 1974, and her call to intercession increased in 1976. Still serving today in our nation's capital, she continues to be devoted to daily intercession for America. Margie has helped coordinate dozens of prayer excursions on and around Capitol Hill. God has given her great favor with church and government leaders alike. She has personally met with many members of Congress to pray for them and to offer biblical counsel.

Because of her long tenure of prayer in DC, Margie has a tremendous authority there in the Spirit, as well as very keen discernment. Our church, Springs Harvest Fellowship, has relied on her expertise on several occasions, allowing her to set the prayer agenda for prayer teams we send to Washington, DC.

Before they left, the Lord gave her five specific reasons why the prayer team we were sending at that time should focus on the financial arena of our nation. She and the team sought the Lord for spiritual insight, specific words, proclamations and prophetic acts, and also received briefings from knowledgeable people regarding several strategic places. As God uncovered hidden information, the Holy Spirit alerted them to the seriousness of the situation. They followed the Lord's directives and spent several days praying specifically in various locations. Almost immediately, significant events began to take place. We believe God will continue to move in this area as a result of these watching prayers over this realm of our nation.

Watchmen are also assigned to other geographical areas, such as specific regions, states, cities and even neighborhoods. The United States Spiritual Warfare Network now has individuals coordinating intercession for all 50 states. They're watchmen for their individual states and coordinate other intercessors who watch smaller regions. God is literally blanketing America with prayer. The results will be increased harvest and ultimately revival. For example:

When intercessors in Texas became aware of an upcoming vote in Willow Park, they took their places as watchmen for that area. The county had been a dry county

for years, meaning that liquor-by-the-drink was not allowed. No beer was sold at the grocery stores and there
weren't any bars. In Willow Park's upcoming election
some groups were trying to pass a liquor-by-the-drink
law. Not wanting the atmosphere that would come with
the bars and liquor sales to infiltrate their community,
these watchmen prayed and fasted for three days. They
prayed against the bondage of addiction and that people would come out to vote against the proposal. It came
as no surprise that this law was defeated by a landslide.
When God establishes His watchmen to pray His will,
He will hear their prayers.[10]

There are also watchmen assigned to churches, individuals
and, of course, families. These roles will be discussed in detail
later in the book. Each of us should be involved in those realms
of watching intercession. As we do so more faithfully and effectively, much will change.

Let's find our place on the wall, watchmen. *San Francisco
Chronicle* columnist Herb Caen writes, "Every morning in Africa,
a gazelle wakes up. It knows it must run faster than the fastest
lion or it will be killed. Every morning a lion wakes up. It knows
it must outrun the slowest gazelle or it will starve to death. It
doesn't matter whether you are a lion or a gazelle; when the sun
comes up, you'd better be running."[11]

Let's run the race on our knees!

LISTEN SLOWLY

―――――― ⁘ ――――――

God Is All Ears

I love hanging out in the woods. I like the solitude, but I also enjoy watching the animals. I've observed birds, squirrels, rabbits, coyotes, deer, elk, antelope and probably a dozen or so other creatures in the wild. Once in a while I love to sit still enough for them to get close, and then I make them aware of my presence by moving slightly or making some sort of noise.

When wild animals hear something or someone, they suddenly come to *attention* and are "all ears." Their ears prick up, listening intently for the slightest sound, as they know their very lives may depend on how well they listen. They have learned to *pay attention*.

The Hebrew word *qashab* describes this sort of alertness. Zodhiates defines it as "to prick up the ears, i.e., sharpening them like an alert animal; *to pay attention*"[1] (italics mine). Whether observing a domesticated animal or one in the wild, I'm sure most of you have witnessed this twitching or pricking of the ears when an animal comes to *attention*.

God does this. I'm not implying His ears twitch or prick up, but this pictorial word, *qashab*, is used to describe His attention's being captured by His children talking to Him. Psalm 66:19 refers to this: "But certainly God has heard; He has *given heed* to the voice of my prayer" (italics mine). Several other verses in the psalms and elsewhere also use *qashab* to describe the Father's *attentive* listening to our prayers (see Pss. 17:1; 55:2; 61:1; 86:6; 130:2; and 142:6).

In the same way that His eyes roam to and fro throughout the earth, seeking those whose hearts are truly His (see 2 Chron. 16:9), His ears are always listening for the voices of His children. When He hears us, our words capture His *attention* like an animal's coming to alertness—He is all ears. He loves us so much!

In his book *Stress Fractures*, Charles Swindoll writes:

I vividly remember some time back being caught in the undertow of too many commitments in too few days. It wasn't long before I was snapping at my wife and our children, choking down my food at mealtimes, and feeling irritated at those unexpected interruptions through the day. Before long, things around our home started reflecting the pattern of my hurry-up style. It was becoming unbearable.

I distinctly recall after supper one evening the words of our younger daughter, Colleen. She wanted to tell me about something important that had happened to her at school that day. She hurriedly began, "Daddy-I-wanna-tell-you-somethin'-and-I'll-tell-you-really-fast."

Suddenly realizing her frustration, I answered, "Honey, you can tell me . . . and you don't have to tell me really fast. Say it slowly."

I'll never forget her answer: "Then listen slowly."[2]

You'll never find yourself having to say to your heavenly Father, "Then listen slowly." He has all the time in the world where you are concerned.

My secretary, Joy Anderson, tells of a similar, humorous family story:

While my sister-in-law was busy in the kitchen preparing dinner and planning for various family and church activities, her young daughter continued to talk to her about many different important things in her life, to which her mother would periodically respond, "Uh-huh." Finally, wanting to do something to make this more of a two-sided conversation, the little girl tugged on her mother's arm to get her full *attention*. Once she knew her mother was really listening to her, she said, "Mom, why don't you talk for a while now, and I'll say 'Uh-huh.'"

I want to say this to you—God is never so preoccupied that He isn't really listening to you. You'll never find Him so involved with someone else, or so intent on running the universe, that He feigns *attentiveness* to you, mumbling "Uh-huhs," while actually thinking about something else. He can't wait to visit with you!

Pay Close Attention

Psalm 34:15 combines both the *attentive* eyes and the *attentive* ears into one verse: "The eyes of the Lord are toward the righteous, and His ears are open to their cry." The psalmist goes on to say in verse 17, "The righteous cry, and the Lord hears and delivers them out of all their troubles." "Hears" in verse 17, though translated from a different Hebrew word, *shama*, is just as meaningful: "to hear intelligently with *attention*; to eavesdrop. The main idea is perceiving a message or sensing a sound."[3] Zodhiates goes on to say that *shama* is a synonym of *qashab*.

God is eavesdropping on us, waiting for us to speak a few words to Him. I love that! He just can't wait to visit with His kids. And when we do talk to Him, He gives great *attention* to what we're saying. His eavesdropping certainly isn't from the legalistic perspective some seem to believe of Him. God isn't sitting in heaven with His rod of discipline or scorebook, just waiting for us to make a mistake or say something wrong. He is listening because He so loves to communicate with us.

A picture of God's heart toward us and our inability to comprehend can be seen in the story of the boy who thought he was going to be shot. "Belden C. Lane writes in the *Christian Century* about English raconteur T. H. White, who recalls in *The Book of Merlyn* a boyhood experience. 'My father made me a wooden castle big enough to get into, and he fixed real pistol barrels beneath its battlements to fire a salute on my birthday, but made me sit in front the first night . . . to receive the salute, and I, believing I was to be shot, cried.'"[4]

So many people do not understand God's heart toward His kids. He is waiting, longing for a visit; they are waiting to be "shot." Controlled by our own fears and distorted perceptions of who God really is, we rob ourselves and Him of the pleasure He intended for the relationship.

Malachi 3:16 is another verse that uses the word *qashab* to describe the Father's careful *attention* toward us: "Then those who feared the Lord spoke to one another, and the Lord gave *attention* and heard it, and a book of remembrance was written before Him for those who fear the Lord and who esteem His name" (italics mine).

The context of this verse is God's pronouncing judgment due to rebellion and apostasy. Does a serious and important activity such as this keep Him from hearing His own and listening to them? No way! His compassion and relational desires toward us are never outweighed by wrath and the judgment of His enemies.

As absolutely thrilling as this is, it is only half of the needed understanding for watchmen. Our *attentiveness* to the Father is equally as important as the Father's *attentiveness* to us. The same word, *qashab*, is also used to describe our intense listening to God (see Prov. 4:20-22; 5:1; 7:24). The pricking of an animal's ears should also be descriptive of our intense desire to listen for the voice of our Father.

This kind of attentiveness is crucial for a proper functioning as a watchman. In this and the next two chapters, we will mention no less than 18 different ways the three Hebrew and two Greek words for "watchman" or "watching" are translated in the Scriptures. Each concept will give us different insights into what it means to be a watchman. Can you guess what the first translation is? It is: "PAY ATTENTION!"

Listen for Him—He's listening for you. It is important to recognize that there are different degrees of listening. In Matthew 11:15, Jesus said, "He who has ears to hear, let him hear." In other words, some were listening to Him without really hearing.

Do You Hear What I Hear?

Several years ago, my daughter Hannah was on my lap while I was engrossed in something very important on TV—I think it was a football game. She, only three or four years old at the time, of course wasn't interested in the game. (For some weird reason, she, like most girls her age, still isn't very interested in football.)

As children do, *especially girls*, she was jabbering incessantly. Between first downs and touchdowns I was uh-huhing and nodding. Finally, she took her two small index fingers, placed them on my cheeks, turned my face toward hers and teasingly said, "Dad, look me in the eyes and listen to me."

Women are taught these things at a young age!

For those of you now burdened for me and planning to send me articles from Dr. Dobson on child rearing, please don't! This was a humorous occasion—Hannah and I enjoyed a good laugh. Please be assured that we do have serious and uninterrupted conversations, giving full *attention* to each other.

Tim Hansel, in *When I Relax I Feel Guilty*, points out the different levels of listening with the following story:

> An American Indian was in downtown New York, walking with his friend who lived in New York City. Suddenly he said, "I hear a cricket."
>
> "Oh, you're crazy," his friend replied.
>
> "No, I hear a cricket. I do! I'm sure of it."
>
> "It's the noon hour. There are people bustling around, cars honking, taxis squealing, noises from the city. I'm sure you can't hear it."
>
> "I'm sure I do." He listened *attentively* and then walked to the corner, across the street, and looked all around. Finally on the corner he found a shrub in a large cement planter. He dug beneath the leaves and found a cricket. His friend was astounded. But the Cherokee said, "No. My ears are no different from yours. It simply depends on what you are listening to. Here, let me show you." He reached into his pocket and pulled out a handful of change—a few quarters, some dimes, nickels and pennies. And he dropped it on the concrete. Every head within a block turned. "You see what I mean?" he said as he began picking up his coins. "It all depends on what you are listening for."[5]

It isn't that God so rarely speaks. I believe we're not hearing Him because we listen so infrequently and have not trained ourselves to hear His voice.

When Ceci asks me, "What did I just say?" I immediately start squirming. She knows I wasn't really hearing her. I usually apologize with a "Sorry, God was telling me something" or some similar lie. (Not really—lighten up!)

In her book *Becoming a Prayer Warrior*, Beth Alves shares the following important wisdom on being *attentive* to the Lord:

> Many times you and I don't hear God's directive because we have not inclined our ear to Him. The prerequisite to hearing is listening! Often we are so busy talking ourselves that we can't possibly hear Him. And yet, He wants us to be so attuned to His voice that we can even hear Him in the midst of a crowd. Someone has said that we have one mouth and two ears because we need to listen twice as much as we speak.
>
> And as we listen, we find that God's tone of voice changes just like ours does. Sometimes the Lord speaks with a loud thunder; other times He speaks in a still small voice. The Word commands us to keep on the alert; keep watching and waiting. When He calls us to intercede for someone, the Holy Spirit will reveal strongholds, special burdens, battle plans of the enemy, actions to take and prayer strategies. We must learn to identify His voice and to be sensitive to responding quickly. Remember, listening gets better as intimacy deepens.[6]

Our need for *attentiveness* to the Father is also described by a word used in 1 Corinthians 7:35: "This I say for your own benefit; not to put a restraint upon you, but to promote what is seemly, and to secure *undistracted devotion* to the Lord" (italics mine). "Undistracted devotion" is translated from the Greek word *euprosedros*, which literally means "sitting well towards."[7] *Prosedreuo* by itself means "to sit near."[8] The prefix *eu-* means "well" and strengthens the emphasis from sitting near to sitting very near or "well towards."

You've probably observed individuals so engrossed in what another is saying that they sit very near and also lean toward the person, hanging on every word. That is *euprosedros*. It's probably what Mary was doing at the feet of Jesus in Luke 10:39. No doubt this is what the two unnamed disciples were doing as they listened to the resurrected Christ open the Scriptures concerning Himself to them (see Luke 24:13-35). "Were not our hearts burning within us while He was speaking to us?" was their testimony (v. 32).

In his sermon "The Disciple's Prayer," Haddon Robinson recalls:

> When our children were small, we played a game. I'd take some coins in my fist. They'd sit on my lap and work to get my fingers open. According to the international rules of finger opening, once the finger was open, it couldn't be closed again. They would work at it, until they got the pennies in my hand. They would jump down and run away, filled with glee and delight. Just kids. Just a game.
>
> Sometimes when we come to God, we come for the pennies in his hand. "Lord, I need a passing grade. Help me to study"; "Lord, I need a job"; "Lord, my mother is ill."
>
> We reach for the pennies.[9]

When God grants the request, we walk away. More important than the pennies in God's hand is God Himself.

Prayer Is a Two-Way Conversation

I used to play a similar game with my grandpa, Bill Henkel. When we visited him as young children, he would often hide a quarter or 50-cent piece in his hand. (For you youngsters, yes, they used to have half-dollars.) After teasing us for a while, he would give us the coin, which we knew all along would be ours. Off we would dash to the ice cream store or candy shop. (And yes, back then you could do that with a quarter!)

Years later, however, my interest in Grandpa changed. I didn't care as much about his hand as I did his face, eyes and voice. I loved to sit very close to him and ask questions about his childhood, my mother's upbringing, his conversion to Christ or just life in general. I would *euprosedros*—sit as close as possible—and listen intently.

It wasn't that Grandpa was such a great storyteller, but simply that *he* was telling the stories. I wanted to know as much as I possibly could from him and about him before he moved to heaven, which is where he now lives.

Have you graduated from the Father's hand to His heart, His face and His voice? Or do you settle for pennies?

"Great," you might say. "Inspirational. Motivating. But how does all of this relate to watchmen?" Because, the watchman aspect of intercession must entail a two-way conversation, not a one-way prayer or petition.

We can glean many excellent strategies in how to function as watchmen from Quin Sherrer and Ruthanne Garlock. The following quote is from their book *How to Pray for Your Family and Friends*:

> Waiting is a very important part of prayer. Very often we must *wait* to hear God's still, small voice within our hearts, or *wait* for Him to speak to us through His Word. We would think it terribly rude if a friend came for a visit, sat down and related all his concerns, then got up and left without giving us an opportunity to speak. Sadly, many people behave that way toward God during their prayer time. Answered prayer, I've discovered, results not from some formula, but from maintaining

an intimate relationship with our Lord Jesus and Father God.[10]

The watchman anointing has everything to do with relationship, as should every area of ministry. As watchmen, while fellowshipping with Him, we wait on promptings, warnings and directives from the precious Holy Spirit. We *pay attention*, "giving ear" to Him. We listen—all ears.

In her book *Possessing the Gates of the Enemy*, Cindy Jacobs alerts watchman intercessors to the necessity of being *attentive* to what the Lord is saying to us:

> Prophetic intercessors . . . get up early every morning and "check in" with the Lord to find out what their prayer assignment is for the day. . . . Although I have things for which I pray daily, God sometimes preempts these requests for those on His heart. I have found that God's daily prayer alerts may or may not be the same as those on my prayer list. Being an intercessor [watchman] requires quite a bit of discipline in the emotional realm because often I would rather pray my own concerns than the ones that God will give me. This is when I "seek first the Kingdom of God" instead of my personal burdens.

Cindy goes on to share several ways the Lord alerts her to pray for a specific person:

- She sees someone who reminds her of another individual and realizes she is to pray for that person.
- She sees the name of someone, or a similar name, and then seeks the Lord's direction as to how to pray for that person.

• Her thoughts turn to a person she has not seen for years and knows they need prayer.

Cindy is convinced that God alerts many people to pray in this manner, but they simply do not recognize the signals.[11]

As we listen and *pay attention*, He will alert us to a person or situation that needs to be covered in prayer. We respond by praying, and He responds by answering the prayer. That is divine/human partnership.

• We speak. He listens.
• He speaks. We listen.
• We pray. He answers.

This is God and family synergistically working together for good in the earth. Second Corinthians 6:1 says, "And *working together* with Him" (italics mine). Working together is the word *sunergeo*, from which we get the English word "synergism" or "synergy." Synergism is "the combined action of two or more which have a greater total effect than the sum of their individual effects."[12] I've been told that a rope made of three strands woven together is 100 times stronger than one strand. That's synergism. Can you imagine God saying there is a synergistic effect when we work together with Him? All of the multiplication of power must come from His strand! Rusty Stevens, a Navigators director in Virginia Beach, Virginia, tells this story:

As I feverishly pushed the lawn mower around our yard, I wondered if I'd finish before dinner. Mikey, our six-year-old, walked up and, without even asking, stepped in front of me and placed his hands on the mower handle. Knowing that he wanted to help me, I quit pushing.

The mower quickly slowed to a stop. Chuckling inwardly at his struggles, I resisted the urge to say, "Get out of here, kid. You're in my way," and said instead, "Here, Son. I'll help you." As I resumed pushing, I bowed my back and leaned forward, and walked spread-legged to avoid colliding with Mikey. The grass cutting continued, but more slowly, and less efficiently than before, because Mikey was "helping" me.

Suddenly, tears came to my eyes as it hit me: *This is the way my heavenly Father allows me to "help" him build his kingdom!* I pictured my heavenly Father at work seeking, saving and transforming the lost, and there I was, with my weak hands "helping." He chooses to stoop grace-fully to allow me to co-labor with Him.[13]

Grab a handle and push! Don't disappoint Dad. He desper-ately wants to partner with us. Where do you think our parental instincts and love for our kids come from? They originate from the heavenly Father in whose image we're made.

In the book *Intercessory Prayer*, I write a great deal about in-tercession being a partnering with God. As a form of interces-sion, the watchman anointing certainly is this as well. It is all about the divine-human partnership in which God provides the wisdom, direction and power, and we supply the body and voice. His is the kingdom, power and glory. Ours is the asking. We can't do it without Him. He won't do it without us.

It all starts with relationship—actively listening to Him and believing He is actively listening to us. Don't allow your prayers to be a one-way conversation. If they are, you will never be an ef-fective watchman intercessor.

Listen slowly. He is.

WATCHMEN ARE GARDENERS

The Wee Watchman in My Car

"I'm gonna blow your doors off!"

My frustration could no longer be contained on this particular morning's commute to teach at Christ For The Nations Institute in Dallas, Texas. I was running late that day, and as was often the case, my two-year-old daughter, Sarah, was with me so she could attend the children's classes.

When we pulled out of our subdivision, we ended up behind an elderly man driving an old pickup truck at about 20 miles per hour. After following him for about five minutes on a country road, we finally turned onto a four-lane highway. By this time I had totally lost my patience, and as I zoomed by his vehicle I mumbled, "Man, I'm gonna blow your doors off!"

My little girl was quiet for the next two or three miles, which I thought was rather unusual. Then, with great concern in her voice, she asked, "Daddy, why are you going to blow that man's doors off?" While watching *Sesame Street*, she had recently heard the story of the three little pigs and the big bad wolf who blew their houses down. Now she was picturing me literally blowing the doors off this man's truck! She had obviously been thinking about this since hearing my exclamation and was rather alarmed and puzzled.

Try explaining to a two-year-old why passing a car is described by some as "blowing their doors off." Then, of course, she needed to know that I really didn't dislike this elderly gentleman, just his driving.

About another mile down the road, I passed another car and said, "Would you get out of my way?!"

"Daddy, who are you talking to?"

"The man in the car we just went around."

"Can he hear you?" she asked very sincerely.

"No, of course not," I replied.

"Then why are you talking to him?" was her next logical question.

I thought about explaining to her that it's a very sensible thing to do because it relieves stress and causes one's driving experience to be much more satisfying and peaceful, but I didn't think a two-year-old would understand such profound logic.

After this enlightening experience, I realized I would need to be more careful about what I said. My children were listening to me!

What Watchmen Do Best

In the previous chapter we discussed the need for watchmen to listen to the Lord. In this chapter we are going to look at several other uses of the Hebrew and Greek words for "watchman" to help paint a clearer picture of what they do. We will discuss these individually in great detail, but first notice how the definitions—those we've already reviewed and those we will cover in this chapter—are related and even have a certain progression:

- pay attention, listen (discussed in the last chapter);
- beware, be aware, don't be unaware;
- be on the alert, stay awake, remain sober; and
- observe, be observant, be an observer; see or behold.

Let's explore these concepts one at a time, studying the various strategies they communicate.

Beware! Be Aware!

Watchmen must *beware . . . be aware*. If we are not aware, we are obviously *unaware*, or ignorant, as we discussed in chapter 1; and this can give our adversary a distinct advantage.

"Wary" is also a word related to "beware." We must be wary regarding our enemy. Webster defines wary as "on one's guard, on the lookout for danger or trickery."[1] We are not to fear our enemy, Satan, but we are to be aware of him and his subtleties.

Theologians have what is known as the law of first mention. This refers to the general rule that the first time a major subject is mentioned in the Bible, significant facts are given concerning it that will remain consistent and relevant throughout the Scriptures.

For example, the first mention of the serpent—Satan—is in Genesis 3:1: "Now the serpent was more *crafty* than any beast of the field which the Lord God had made. And he said to the woman, 'Indeed, has God said, "You shall not eat from any tree of the garden"?' " (italics mine). It is easy to see this law at work here, as the verse speaks of Satan's subtlety or craftiness. God is informing us of one of the most important things we must remember about Satan: He is far more dangerous to us as the crafty serpent than as a roaring lion.[2]

"Crafty" is the Hebrew word *aruwm*, taken from *aram*, which means "to be bare or smooth."[3] We use the same concept in our English language. Someone who is crafty or wily is often referred to as slick or as a smooth operator. Such is the case with Satan. He is very cunning, and we must be wary of his attacks and deceptions. He is always seeking to steal, kill, destroy (see John 10:10) and grab the bigger portions—and he does it with great skill.

Adam wasn't wary enough of the serpent in the garden. He heard and saw him but wasn't aware of his plans. He wasn't paying attention. Therefore, he allowed Satan to invade and violate his garden.

The devil is after our "gardens," too—our families, homes, marriages, churches, cities, etc. Our responsibility as watchmen is to keep the devil out, and this is best illustrated in Edward K. Rowell's book *Fresh Illustrations for Preaching and Teaching*.

> In *First Things First*, A. Roger Merrill tells of a business consultant who decided to landscape his grounds. He hired a woman with a doctorate in horticulture who was extremely knowledgeable. Because the business consultant was very busy and traveled a lot, he kept emphasizing to her the need to create his garden in a way that would require little or no maintenance on his part. He insisted on automatic sprinklers and other labor-saving devices. Finally she stopped and said, "There's one thing you need to deal with before we go any further. If there's no gardener, there's no garden!"[4]

Watchmen are gardeners. When there's no gardener, there's no garden! Let's determine to be gardeners and keep our gardens.

This same word "crafty" is used in Joshua 9:4, describing a plan the Gibeonites used to deceive Israel: "They also acted *craftily* and set out as envoys, and took worn-out sacks on their donkeys, and wineskins, worn-out and torn and mended" (italics mine). The *King James Version* says they acted "wilily." The *KJV* also says in Ephesians 6:11: "Put on the whole armour of God, that ye may be able to stand against the *wiles* of the devil" (italics mine).

Remember Wile E. Coyote on the old cartoon show *The Road Runner*? In his devious cunning, he continually endeavored to think of new ways to capture Road Runner. Road Runner always seemed to escape, however, and Wile E. Coyote's evil plans most often boomeranged.

God has similar plans for Wily Serpent. His desire is always for us to escape and for Satan's schemes to backfire on him. Picture this same relationship between Israel and the Wily Gibeonites.

The Wily Gibeonites

The Gibeonites were one of the Canaanite tribes that Joshua and Israel were supposed to destroy. They deceived the Israelites, however, into believing they had come from a far country in order to enter a covenant with them. Joshua and the people neglected to pray about this—always a part of Satan's subtlety—and were therefore deceived into entering a binding, covenantal agreement with them. The serpent's entry into their garden was progressing wonderfully . . . the watchmen were asleep.

The Israelites were not without warning. In Exodus 34:12, Israel was told, "*Watch* yourself that you make no covenant with the inhabitants of the land into which you are going [or it will] become a snare in your midst" (italics mine). The Israelites failed in their responsibility to watch, and just as the verse warned, the snare was laid.

We can conclude from the Israelites' suspicion of the Gibeonites that God was obviously trying to alert Israel. Joshua 9:7 says, "The men of Israel said to the Hivites (Gibeonites), 'Perhaps you are living within our land; how then shall we make a covenant with you?'" Rather than heeding this caution, however, they acted on what they saw. The Israelites weren't *wary* . . . weren't *paying attention* . . . weren't *watching*. We must remember things are not always as they appear.

There is a memorable story that teaches a humorous lesson about how we perceive events:

A traveler, between flights at an airport, went to a lounge and bought a small package of cookies. Then she sat down and began reading a newspaper. Gradually, she became aware of a rustling noise. From behind her paper, she was flabbergasted to see a neatly dressed man helping himself to her cookies. Not wanting to make a scene, she leaned over and took a cookie herself.

A minute or two passed, and then came more rustling. He was helping himself to another cookie! By this time, they had come to the end of the package, but she was so angry she didn't dare allow herself to say anything. Then, as if to add insult to injury, the man broke the remaining cookie in two, pushed half across to her, and ate the other half and left.

Still fuming some time later when her flight was announced, the woman opened her handbag to get her ticket. To her shock and embarrassment, there she found her pack of unopened cookies![5]

How amazing it is to discover how wrong our assumptions can be!

Though Israel "ate the wrong cookies" and was subsequently taken advantage of, there is a positive ending to this story. Upon seeking God's solution to this problem—better late than never—Joshua received instruction that painted an amazing picture of Christ's victory over the serpent at Calvary and demonstrated His ability to reverse our failures.

The craftiness of the Gibeonites was used to typify Satan's craftiness. Joshua was told to make these Gibeonites "hewers of wood and drawers of water for the congregation *and for the altar of the LORD*" (Josh. 9:27, italics mine). The altar of the Lord, where the blood of atonement was shed, symbolized the cross. Just as the *crafty* Gibeonites were used to prepare the sacrifices, God used Satan, *the crafty one*, to make preparations for the ultimate sacrifice—Christ's crucifixion.

The outcome of this story is an incredible assurance that God can reverse the subtleties of our adversary, the devil, and use them to bring about good. Through God's amazing wisdom, which always supersedes Satan's subtlety, our mistakes can actually become the instruments of His redemptive purposes. This, of course, can only happen if we, like Joshua, cooperate with Him.

Have you been deceived by Satan? Have you fallen prey to his subtleties? Is the serpent in your garden? The cross is God's ultimate proof that He can turn the circumstances around and even bring good through them.

Wily False Brethren Today

God helps watchmen by pointing out what needs to be seen and heard to aid the growth and health of a church. An excellent example of the importance of focusing on the right thing at the right time is seen in this baseball story:

> One of the classic baseball television shots comes from the 1975 World Series, in which NBC captured Carlton Fisk, jumping up and down, waving his arms, trying to coax his hit to stay fair. It did—for a home run.
>
> That colorful close-up would have been missed had the cameraman followed the ball with his camera, as was his responsibility. But the cameraman inside the Fenway Park scoreboard had one eye on a rat that was circling him. So instead of focusing the camera on the ball, he left it on Fisk.[6]

Rats and serpents, they seem somehow to go together, don't they? If you smell a rat in your situation, don't panic. God has plenty of rat traps. Through the watchman anointing you can discern the enemy's trap and set one of your own.

The New Testament has its own brand of Gibeonites of which we are to be wary. Galatians 2:4 speaks of "false brethren who had sneaked in" and Jude 4 says "certain persons have crept in unnoticed." There are people who come into churches or ministries with impure motives. If not discovered soon enough, they can do great damage. The anointing of the watchman will detect them, and they can either be exposed or neutralized in prayer so that they are unable to create problems.

A balancing word of caution should be given, however, concerning this wariness we must have. We are to be watchmen, not watchdogs. Some individuals become so suspicious of others they act more like guard dogs, not trusting anyone, than watchmen who guard only against evil.

Others are led into a deception of preoccupation when they become overly demon or devil conscious. This, too, is a part of Satan's craftiness. We must be aware and wary of him, but not so preoccupied with him that we conjure up demonic attacks and plans.

The two Greek words for "watching" in prayer mean to be on the alert, stay awake and remain sober. How descriptive! In order to pay attention, listen and beware, watchmen must stay awake and sober. Alertness is imperative. The failure of the United States at Pearl Harbor is a tragic picture of failed watchmen.

United States officials and commanders failed to pay attention in the critical weeks, days and hours prior to 7:55 A.M., December 7, 1941. If those in strategic leadership had realized the necessity to listen and beware, the results of the attack on Pearl Harbor could have been drastically different.

In meetings with both the Secretary of the Navy and the President, Admiral Richardson of the Pacific Fleet alerted them to the danger of the United States fleet remaining at Pearl Harbor. He was wary that the Japanese would realize the United States military's vulnerability and would act quickly to take advantage of the situation. His warnings, however, were ignored and he was dismissed shortly thereafter.

The commanders at Pearl Harbor, Admiral Kimmel and Lieutenant General Short, were alerted to the impending danger of war on October 16, November 24 and November 27. Not believing an attack was possible, they only took precautions against Japanese sabotage. In fact, instead of strategically moving to the logical point of attack in the northwest, the entire fleet was moored in the harbor. Some personnel were even allowed to go on shore leave. Would it have made a difference had they stayed awake and remained sober at their posts?

Four hours before the attack, a United States destroyer in the Pacific sighted a Japanese submarine. Evidently not being alert to the imminent danger, no one on the destroyer reported the attack. Also, an army private (practicing on the radar set after its normal closing time) notified his superior officer of an approaching large squadron of planes. The lieutenant, however, neglected to listen and beware, but instead passed it off as being the group of B-17s that was expected from the United States.

The enemy gained the greater portion in this attack. More than 2,300 American servicemen were killed and over 1,100 were wounded; two battleships were destroyed and six others were heavily damaged; several lesser vessels were put out of action and more than 150 United States planes were wrecked. The Japanese lost less than 100 men and sacrificed only 29 planes and five midget submarines. Their task force escaped without being attacked.

The lack of alertness and false estimation of the enemy's capabilities and intentions were primary reasons this attack resulted in such devastation. Military and civilian officials in Washington, as well as the commanders at Pearl Harbor, had failed to observe and pay attention to the many warnings of impending attack. Their neglect to listen and to beware of the

approaching danger allowed the enemy's plans to be successful.[7] Frequently, we believers ignore warnings from Scripture
and the Holy Spirit. The cost is often great.

Sentry Duty

The three Hebrew words for "watchman" are also translated
"observe," "see" and "behold." Jesus told His disciples to "keep
watching and praying" (Matt. 26:41, italics mine). Colossians 4:2
says to "Continue in prayer, and *watch* in the same with thanksgiving" (*KJV*, italics mine). If we do *watch* and pray, the Holy
Spirit will cause us to *see* or *observe* things that need prayer. Just
recently an intercessor approached me with great concern about
an aspect of our fellowship. She *pays attention—observes, watching*
in prayer. And she *saw* something that needed to be prayed
through immediately. I agreed. The following day we prayed
with other intercessors in the church about the situation. Because she was paying attention, Satan didn't get the bigger portion. (We prayed and God intervened.)

Proverbs 29:18 is a very familiar verse that describes our
need as watchmen to see: "Where there is no vision, the people
perish: but he that keepeth the law, happy is he" (*KJV*). Most of
our interpretations of this verse are pretty shallow.

The word "vision" does not refer only to plans or dreams
concerning the future. It is translated from the Hebrew word
chazown, which means "a mental sight, a dream, a vision, a revelation, an oracle, a prophecy." *Chazown* comes from *chazah*
meaning "to see."[8] In this verse it refers to any form of communication from God to us. A good translation would be, "Where
there is no communication from God, the people perish."

The Hebrew word *para*, translated "perish," is also revelatory. It means, among other things, "to make bare or naked."
Moses came off the mountain and found the Israelites *para*,

or "naked" (see Exod. 32:25, *KJV*), worshiping the golden calf. They were "uncovered."[9]

We often speak of "prayer coverings," or "covering" a person, event or organization in prayer. To be without this covering can create a vulnerability—people are exposed to attacks of the enemy. In order to provide this covering with the utmost effectiveness, we must have warnings and promptings (*chazown*) from the Holy Spirit. In other words, "without communication from the Holy Spirit, the people are uncovered."

On the other hand, if we are walking in the anointing of the watchman, if we are paying attention, the Holy Spirit will make us aware of Satan's schemes and attacks. We will see them and can take action.

I recall ministering in Oregon several years ago. My first night of speaking, I became disoriented, confused and slightly dizzy. I wondered at first if it was a physical illness and then I began to think it was simply fatigue. I pushed through it, relying more heavily on my notes, and made it through the message.

After the service, I began to sense the Holy Spirit's alerting me that it was witchcraft. The pastor of the church strongly agreed. Upon calling home to alert my intercessors, it was a great comfort to hear they had already discerned the attack and were covering me in prayer. Some had actually sensed it and *prayed while it was happening*. They smelled a rat! It never affected me again during the conference.

That is the watchman anointing!

Pay attention, intercessors. Watch! Listen! The crafty one is always seeking to destroy lives and hinder the work of God. He is no match, however, for the Holy Spirit who is waiting to partner with you, enabling you to smell the rat and keep your garden.

5

COVER ME! I'M GOING IN!

―――※◆※―――

My "Little Joe" Dream

I must have watched too many Westerns as a child. I was having a very detailed dream, one so realistic my body and mouth were into it. My vigorous kicking and unintelligible mumblings awakened my wife, Ceci, who then awakened me.

"Are you okay? Are you dreaming?" she asked.

"Little Joe," I mumbled, still half asleep.

"What? Did you say 'Little Joe'?"

"Yeah. Little Joe Cartwright." For those of you deprived of the experience, or too young to have been around, Little Joe (played by the late Michael Landon) was one of the characters on the hit Western television series *Bonanza*.

"I dreamed I was Little Joe," I repeated. "And I was fighting a big dude in a boxing match. I was terrified of him and my strategy was to keep moving so fast he couldn't hit me." Thus the kicking.

Ceci, insensitive as she was, thought it was hilarious. That's because she wasn't in the boxing ring with a man whose main goal was to beat her senseless. She still brings it up once in a while, especially when I'm having a graphic dream. "Who are you this time?" she chuckles. "Muhammad Ali?"

An often-used expression in Westerns was "cover me." This, of course, was said by those who were running into the open during gun battles. They wanted enough gunfire aimed toward the enemy to prevent the enemy from successfully firing upon them. Little Joe said it several times. As we shall soon see, we also cover each other, not with guns but with prayer.

Prayer Coverage

In this chapter we will consider five more definitions of "watchman" that will enable us to provide effective prayer coverage.

Protector

"Protect" or "protector" are translations of the Hebrew words for "watchman." Psalm 121:5,7-8 tells us, "The Lord is your keeper [*shamar*] . . . The Lord will protect [*shamar*] you from all evil; He will keep [*shamar*] your soul. The Lord will guard [*shamar*] your going out and your coming in from this time forth and forever." Four times the Holy Spirit uses this watchman word *shamar* to assure us of His protection. The English word "protect" comes from two Latin words: *pro*, meaning "before," and *tego*, meaning "to cover; to cover or shield from danger or injury."[1] One of the ways this protection comes is through the watchman anointing. Quin Sherrer and Ruthanne Garlock share the following two testimonies of prayer coverage in their book *A Woman's Guide to Spiritual Warfare*:

> Janet's six-year-old son, Kevin, came in from school one day with a defiant, sassy attitude.
>
> "What did you do in school today, son?" Janet asked, puzzled by his mood.
>
> "Played with a crystal ball the teacher brought. We asked it all kinds of questions," he answered.
>
> "Lord, what shall I do about this?" Janet, a new Christian, prayed silently. From deep within she heard,

Break the witchcraft and curses that come with it.

"Kevin, come sit on my lap for a minute," she said, still asking the Lord *how* to follow the directions she'd just received. She gave Kevin a big hug as he climbed on her lap. Surprised, she heard herself saying, "Father, in the name of Jesus I break the power of witchcraft and curses, and I take back from the enemy the ground he has stolen from my son. We give that ground back to You, Lord. Thank you for your protection and your blessing upon Kevin."

After prayer, Kevin immediately changed back to her happy, sweet-natured kid. "That was my introduction to dealing with invisible evil forces," Janet said. "In a nutshell, I quickly learned about spiritual warfare, and I'm still using it for both of my children."

Kevin is grown now, and drives a huge cattle transport trailer-truck across the country. One night Janet woke up four times, and each time she "saw" a truck going off the road. The truck was the eighteen-wheeler Kevin was driving.

"I began binding the spirits of death and calamity, then I asked the Lord to send angels to keep my son's truck on the road. I did it four times that night," she remembers.

"At dawn Kevin called to say, 'Mom, I'm back in town, but I'm too tired to drive home. Four times last night my truck almost went off the road. Were you praying?' "[2]

Janet fulfilled the role of a watchman as she covered her son from the evils of witchcraft and from physical harm. She was a *protector*—a role that is possible for each of us if we allow the Holy Spirit to help us walk in this anointing.

Keeper

"Keep" and "keeper" are also ways the words are used. Adam, as mentioned in chapter 1, was instructed to keep (*shamar*) the garden (see Gen. 2:15). He was the watchman, assigned by God to *protect* what was given him, *keeping* it from the serpent. *Keeping* the serpent out of our gardens is the primary assignment of watchmen.

"Assignment" is a very appropriate and revealing term. God's gifts are also His assignments. He frequently spoke of "giving" Canaan to Abraham and his descendants. Psalm 115:16 states that He has "given" the earth to the sons of men. This word "give" (*nathan*) means to give a charge, assignment or possession. God was assigning stewardship of the earth to humans. He was assigning the land to Abraham and his seed. This is why Israel had to *take* what God was *giving*.

The Lord has given gifts to us as well, which, like Israel's of old, are also assignments: children, ministries, churches, cities, nations, and many other things. Adam failed in the assignment to protect his gift. He lost his garden. Israel, too, failed in many ways and had crop failure. We must determine, with tenacious persistence, that we will not tolerate the serpent in our gardens.

Freda Lindsay, cofounder with her late husband, Gordon Lindsay, of Christ For The Nations missions organization and Christ For The Nations Institute in Dallas, Texas, has for several decades walked in the watchman anointing. Decades ago, they were doing and teaching what is thought today by many in the Body of Christ to be new. In her book *My Diary Secrets*, Dr. Lindsay tells of her and her husband's prayer efforts to keep the serpent out of their family garden:

> I recall when Carole began drifting away from the Lord in her high school years. And when she chose a liberal, secular college that neither her father nor I approved

of, she borrowed money on her own and attended. . . .
My heart was broken, and I recall one Christmas when
she failed to come home I was sick in my soul. How
could we be spiritual leaders when our daughter was
behaving as she did? Refusing to come to church. Refusing to read the Bible. Wanting no part of anything
spiritual. Wanting no part of her family.

I recall one Saturday night in particular I walked
the floor all night long praying, not knowing where
Carole had gone. I couldn't even think of sleeping. . . .
Then Gordon decided to set aside a time of fasting and
praying for Carole. The days stretched into weeks, and
finally I became greatly concerned about him—so much
so that I was afraid he would lose his health. When I
said to him that I felt he might die from too much fasting, his answer was, "Either Carole will have to die or I
will. If she continues in life as she is, she will kill herself
and my ministry. So I really don't have a choice."

After 30 days of fasting Gordon felt that God had
answered prayer and that she would come to the Lord,
though we did not see any immediate change. But each
day after that I began to claim what God's Word said
about Carole's soul being saved. Through a remarkable
series of events the Lord did bring Carole to Himself.
She received a call to Israel and has served the Lord
there faithfully for many years. I have always felt that
Gordon's prolonged fasting projected Carole into the
ministry which the Lord finally gave her.[3]

What God asks us to do, He equips us to do. Adam could
have kept the serpent out of the garden had he relied on the
Lord to aid him. We, like Gordon Lindsay, must pursue with
tenacity the goal of keeping and protecting that which is ours.

Guard

"Guard" and "bodyguard" are also usages of the watchman words. We must *guard* carefully that which is entrusted to us, whether it be human beings or spiritual treasures. We are called to *guard* and *protect* one another both spiritually and physically. We are *bodyguards*—shields—who cover one another. Paul told Timothy to "*guard* . . . the treasure which has been entrusted to you" (2 Tim. 1:14, emphasis mine), referring to spiritual gifts and callings.

In her book *Prophetic Intercession*, Barbara Wentroble shares a testimony about the vital importance of spiritually *guarding* one another:

> I remember a time when my mother-in-law experienced a flow of the river of intercession during a very strategic moment. She was sitting in her living room at 9:30 A.M. Suddenly, she felt a sensation of fear and danger, accompanied by an urgency to pray for her son (my husband) Dale. At first she did not understand where this was coming from. Recognizing she had nothing to fear and was not in danger, she asked the Lord to reveal what this was. This was a wise and necessary move, because gaining understanding is an important first step in effective prayer. An inner prompting will alert you to something your mind does not quite comprehend. At these times just ask the Lord to help you know how He wants you to pray.
>
> After asking the Lord to reveal to her how to pray, Dale's mom then felt a deep impression that it was Dale who was in danger. She prayed for several minutes and then felt the "burden" lift. Later that night she called our home to ask Dale what he had been doing at 9:30 in the morning. "Oh, that's easy," he replied. "I remember

because I looked at my watch. Another man was talking to me while we were standing out in the plant at work. There had been some remodeling in the plant over the past several weeks, and we were discussing the progress. All of a sudden I felt an urgency to move from the place where we were standing. We quickly moved to another spot about 20 feet away. Just as quickly as we moved, a large steel beam fell from the ceiling and landed in the very spot where I had been standing."

A strategic moment! Often I have wondered what would have happened if Dale's mom had not sought the Lord and received her instructions for prayer. Would Dale and the other man be alive? Could they have been paralyzed or deformed from the injury? How many tragedies occur each day because we do not know how to hear the Lord speak so that we can respond in prayer?[4]

Beth Alves adds additional insight in how we can respond effectively when God alerts us to *guard* and *protect* at strategic times:

Daniel 10 records an instance when Daniel received a message from God concerning a great conflict between the angelic hosts. The Hebrew word translated "message" is sometimes translated "burden." Often when God gives you a message or a word, there is a heaviness or a burden placed upon you to pray that word into action. Sometimes the directive will be to pray the Word of God. At other times you may be led to do warfare against the enemy forces. Sometimes intercession may cause an anguish of heart, or a wrestling within your spirit.

You must be available to receive a prayer message or prayer burden from God. And when the Lord reveals His secrets to you in this way, it is a holy trust; do not take the matter lightly. If you feel the power of the Holy Spirit moving within your heart, be obedient to cry out to God on behalf of a spiritual leader, a nation or an individual as the Spirit brings names and places to your mind. Effective prayer requires availability, sensitivity and obedience.[5]

Knowing Beth as I do, I know she practices these things. Having been a watchman in the Body of Christ for many years, she speaks with great authority and wisdom on this subject. Heed her counsel. Be available, sensitive and obedient; and you will be an effective *bodyguard* in the Spirit.

Doorkeeper and Gatekeeper

Two more protective usages of the watchman words are "doorkeeper" and "gatekeeper." As watchmen of old guarded gates and doors of cities or vineyards, we, too, guard entrances. We are responsible and able to determine who or what is allowed into homes, churches, cities and other places.

Barbara Wentroble tells of another experience when she functioned in the role of a gatekeeper at the Lord's prompting:

Several years ago Dale and I were part of a citywide pastors' prayer meeting. After praying for about 15 minutes, my attention was drawn to another pastor in the room. I had never seen him before and didn't know anything about him. As my eyes fastened on him, the Lord began to speak to me about him. I did not expect this. I had come with my husband to pray. The group was not used to women speaking up, and I wanted to be a quiet pastor's wife. *Lord, please tell this to one of the men pastors. I want to be obedient, but I don't want to tell this pastor what You are saying.* My begging God didn't make any difference. He just kept speaking and gently nudging me to be obedient.

At the end of the prayer session, time was given for sharing anything the pastors felt God was saying. One after another shared. I kept waiting. Surely, someone had heard the Lord concerning the pastor the Lord had spoken to me about. However, no one even addressed the matter. "Is there anyone else who has heard something from the Lord?" the leader asked. After much hesitation, I indicated I needed to give a "word" to the new pastor. Permission was granted, and I began.

"You are in the midst of a great conflict in your church," I said. "God has granted you an incredible gift of mercy, and the mercy is overriding the wisdom He has for you in this situation. There is a man in your church who is involved in the finances of the church, and he is causing problems." At that moment the pastor pulled a big handkerchief from his pocket, put his face in it and sobbed so loudly it was hard to hear what I was saying.

"The Lord says you need to deal with the situation," I went on, "because it is affecting your whole church. You already know what to do, but you have been hesitant because of your mercy. If you will be obedient to the Lord, healing and restoration will come to your church. The finances will change, and you will have more than enough to meet the needs."

Quickly, I sat down in my chair as the pastor continued to sob for several minutes. Months later I met the pastor while shopping in a local grocery store. "Barbara, I have to tell you what happened. When you spoke the word to me at the prayer meeting, I knew who you were talking about. God had already been dealing with me about the situation, but I did not want to confront it. I did what the Lord said, and now our church has experienced a breakthrough. There is peace for the first time, and our offerings have increased greatly." As I thanked him for sharing the story with me, I also prayed, *Lord teach me how to hear You more and more in times of intercession.*[6]

This pastor was called by God, as are all pastors, to cover and protect his fellowship. He was a watchman. Through the prophetic anointing of another watchman to listen, he was able to guard his church and be the gatekeeper he was intended to be. Pastors, we have the right and the ability to do this.

In the same way pastors guard their churches, parents are called by God to be doorkeepers or gatekeepers of their homes. As watchmen, we have responsibility and authority from the Lord to determine what enters. We do not have to allow the serpent in! If he is already there, we should run him out.

Sometimes we must be very aggressive in our dealings with the enemy. Gordon Lindsay used to say every Christian should pray at least one violent prayer every day. He was, of course, speaking of spiritual warfare. Dr. Lindsay tells of their fervent prayer for their son Dennis when he was on a path of rebellion:

> Our youngest son, Dennis, began having his problems as a result of selecting companions at school whose lives were anything but exemplary. Gordon counseled with him, and when that didn't work he would discipline him. But finally the day came when he said to me, "We will have to choose another method." We gave ourselves to more fervent prayer.
>
> While Gordon was away, I could not get Dennis to go to school. He would stay out late at night and would want to sleep all day. When his father returned home,

there was a real confrontation. Dennis ran from his own bedroom into ours and locked the door. When he didn't open to his father, his dad knelt in front of the locked door and prayed for most of an hour, calling on God to stop him in his tracks at any cost. To save his soul. To rain judgment upon him if necessary, but to use love if possible.

Dennis had not even a radio in the room, so there was no way of escaping hearing his father's praying. I am sure that prayer made a lasting impression upon his life, for shortly after this Dennis decided to go to a Christian college where he found himself and where he also met his future wife.[7]

Dennis is now a respected author and teacher and is the president of Christ For The Nations. The Lindsays knew how to deal with the serpent—with faith, aggressive prayer and persistence. They understood their role as doorkeepers.

Intercessors and pastors, we are gatekeepers, not only of our homes and churches, but also of our cities. We must guard what comes into them, and God will certainly hold us responsible for stewarding our assignment. It is both sobering and encouraging for me to read Exodus 32:25: "Now . . . Moses saw that the people were out of control—*for Aaron had let them* get out of control to be a derision among their enemies" (italics mine).

The sobering reality is that God held one man, Aaron, responsible for allowing this rebellion and idolatry. On the other hand, the fact that he was held responsible is encouraging as it communicates that Aaron could have stopped this tragedy. Had he functioned in his God-given assignment as the gatekeeper, he could have kept the serpent out. God would have supported him, squelching the rebellion, just as He supported Moses a few verses later.

Preserver

"Preserving" or "preserver" and "maintain" are also watchman words. Watchmen are maintenance people. They maintain things, keeping them in good operating condition.

According to the Associated Press, on December 14, 1996, a 763-foot grain freighter, the *Bright Field*, was heading down the Mississippi at New Orleans, Louisiana, when it lost control, veered toward the shore, and crashed into a riverside shopping mall. At the time the Riverwalk Mall was crowded with some 1,000 shoppers, and 116 people were injured. The impact of the freighter demolished parts of the wharf, which is the site of two hundred shops and restaurants as well as the adjoining Hilton Hotel.

The ship had lost control at the stretch in the Mississippi that is considered the most dangerous to navigate. After investigating the accident for a year, the Coast Guard reported that the freighter had lost control because the engine had shut down. The engine had shut down because of low oil pressure. The oil pressure was low because of a clogged oil filter. And the oil filter was clogged because the ship's crew had failed to maintain the engine properly.[8]

Many spiritual ships run aground because maintenance prayer is ignored. First Kings 8:44-45 tells us, "When Thy people go out to battle against their enemy, by whatever way Thou shalt send them, and they pray to the Lord toward the city which Thou hast chosen and the house which I have built for Thy name, then hear in heaven their prayer and their supplication, and *maintain* their cause" (italics mine). Righteous causes are maintained by prayer.

Joshua's ship ran aground and Israel's cause suffered a breakdown at Ai because Joshua forgot to pray (see Josh. 7). After their previous victory at Jericho, Joshua and Israel grew overconfident. Instead of seeking the Lord, as they had before defeating Jericho, they assumed the battle with Ai would not be difficult. "Only about two or three thousand men need go up to Ai . . . for they are few" (Josh. 7:3). Had Joshua, or perhaps one of the other leaders, sought the Lord in prayer *before* the battle, God would have told them then—before the defeat—about Achan's sin of taking forbidden spoils of Jericho. Had this been the case, Israel would not have had to suffer such a humiliating defeat. Watching prayer maintains the cause!

Watchmen *preserve*, which is "to keep in the same state; keep from decay or spoilage."[9] We keep the serpent from spoiling homes, relationships, individuals and other precious things. In 1 Thessalonians 5:23 Paul prayed for the Thessalonian believers that the "God of peace Himself sanctify you entirely; and may your spirit and soul and body be *preserved* complete, without blame at the coming of our Lord Jesus Christ" (italics mine). The prayers of watchmen *preserve* the lives of other individuals—spirit, soul and body.

Watchmen are also to *preserve* moves of the Holy Spirit. It is a sad fact that revivals usually wane after two to three years. They could be prolonged if those involved operated more in the watchman anointing. Paul addressed the Galatians, "You foolish Galatians, who has bewitched you . . . ?" (Gal. 3:1). They had allowed false doctrine to creep into their midst, compromising the gospel. The doorkeepers—watchmen—weren't on duty. The sentries had fallen asleep on the job and spoilage occurred.

The Corinthian church had allowed division, immorality and other carnal ways to invade their midst (see 1 Cor. 1:10-12; 5:1). Perhaps the *maintenance crew* was asleep. The church at Thyatira had allowed infiltration by the spirit Jezebel (see Rev. 2:20).

There are, no doubt, many reasons why improper doctrines and compromise enter churches and why moves of the Holy Spirit are hindered or stopped. One of them, however, is a lack of prayer—watching prayer. The serpent is allowed in with his poisonous venom. Spoilage occurs. Harvests are stolen.

God is awakening us, the Church, at this hour to our powerful arsenal of weapons. We are realizing that God's plan is always for His people to win and Satan to lose. The serpent's authority has been stripped from him, his headship crushed (see Gen. 3:15).

The volunteer army of Psalm 110 is being positioned. Training is intense, but the fruit is and will be worth it. Now is the time to enlist. Enter the declared war on the serpent. You are a part of the overcoming Church against which the gates of hell won't prevail.

Run the evil one out of your house!

Drive him out of your city!

Keep him out of your garden!

Take up the challenge I once saw on the T-shirt of a young Christian warrior: "Get on your knees and fight like a man!"

WATCHMAN—LAY SIEGE!

When Jericho Falls

"See, I have given Jericho into your hand, with its king and the valiant warriors. Shout! For the Lord has given you the city" (Josh. 6:2,16).

Jericho. What a great story! Also a source of tremendous encouragement, it has for centuries spawned many wonderful faith-inspiring sermons and songs. It seemed so easy: march, shout, gather the spoils.

Your Town, U.S.A.—what a different story. March, shout, no spoils . . . march, shout, no spoils . . . march, shout, no spoils.

Frustration. Disillusionment. Unbelief. Despair.

May I remind you that in both of the above verses God said He *had* given Jericho to Israel before there was any change whatsoever. Has He done that with you? Has He given you your city, and yet it still looks the same?

I have good news for you. When God states He has done something, from then on, as far as He is concerned, it is a done deal—He *has* given. This is a chapter about taking, possessing, and laying hold of. "Fight the good fight of the faith; *lay hold* of the eternal life to which you were summoned and [for which] you confessed the good confession [of faith] before many witnesses" (1 Tim. 6:12, *AMP*, italics mine). I am referring primarily to taking cities, though the watchman connection is applicable to any place or person needing to be captured for Christ.

Obviously, I'm not foolish enough to attempt to do in one chapter what others have required entire books to accomplish, i.e., fully explain key strategies of city taking. My goals are quite simple really: first, to encourage and to spark faith in you that our cities can be taken for Christ; second, to connect the strategies involved in city taking with the watchman anointing.

It is well worth considering that events in Scripture didn't always happen as quickly as it appears they did. Though the book of Joshua can be read in a couple of hours, the conquest of Canaan under Joshua's leadership probably took about seven years. The entire book covers a period of approximately 25 years. And at the end of the book, all the tribes of Israel still had not fully conquered all of their territories (see Judg. 1:27-36).

Later in Israel's history, after a grand and glorious beginning, they experienced a 16-year delay in the rebuilding of the Temple (see Ezra 3-4). Through the ministry of the prophet Haggai, courage and faith to continue came. Delays, setbacks and long-term campaigns are not uncommon in the kingdom of God. Though God has facilitated an acceleration in the pace of world evangelization, endurance and patience are still very key factors.

What am I saying? You may not be as far behind as you think! Hang in there! We play until we win. God has given us our cities, even though it may not yet look like it.

Is this comparison with Joshua and Israel valid? Can we really take our cities, or is that a lofty but unattainable goal? Consider these reports of city taking shared by George Otis, Jr., in his book *Informed Intercession.*

Cali, Columbia

The Cali drug cartel was considered the largest, richest and most well-organized criminal organization in history, exporting 500 million dollars worth of cocaine a month. The cartel owned as many as 12,000 properties in the city. Drug money controlled everything, including the banks, politicians and law enforcement. Crime and murder were rampant with as many as 15 people a day killed by thugs. In the spiritual arena, the church was anemic and divided.

Then God initiated a work of prayer and unity. In May 1995, over 25,000 people filled the civic auditorium and prayed all night for breakthrough in their city. Within 48 hours, Cali experienced its first 24-hour period with no homicides in as long as anyone could remember. The police force was purged of 900 cartel-linked officers. The Columbian government began to crack down on the drug lords and, with a force of 6,500 commandos, captured most of the leaders.

Through unity and much prayer, the believers in Cali finally experienced their breakthrough. For years after, they held all-night prayer rallies every 90 days with thousands of people in attendance. Great openness to the gospel existed at every level of society. Across the board, church growth exploded due to new converts; one church grew to 35,000 members—and is still growing! Denominational affiliation and location had little to do with it. By the year 2000, this marvelous revival had gone on for 36 consecutive months.

Almolonga, Guatemala

In the 1970s Almolonga was idolatrous and economically depressed. Alcoholism was rampant, poverty and violence the norm. Families suffered terribly due to the depravity that ruled. The gospel did not prosper; persecution of Christian leaders was common.

In 1974, a series of five-hour prayer vigils began, and shortly thereafter God began to move. Deliverance and healings began to break forth, even resurrections from the dead.

Conversions began to take place at such a rate that 90 percent of the 19,000 people in Almolonga became evangelical Christians.

The revival impacted every area of life: families, businesses, even the produce of the land. Nicknamed "America's Vegetable Garden," the fields produced three harvests per year, with five-pound beets, carrots bigger than a man's arm and cabbages the size of basketballs.

Crime disappeared so much that, in 1994, the last of the four jails closed. Aftershocks of the revival in Almolonga continue to this day.

Hemet, California

Once called a pastor's graveyard, Hemet was filled with occult activity and had in fact become, as Pastor Bob Beckett described it, "a cult haven." The Moonies, Mormons, Sheep People (a drug-dealing cult that professed Christianity), the Church of Scientology and the Maharishi Yogi all had made Hemet a headquarters of sorts.

Gangs had plagued the city for a century, with some gangs boasting third-generation members. Drugs were rampant, and Hemet Valley became the methamphetamine capital of the West Coast. Some law enforcement officials were so corrupt they transported dope in their police cruisers.

By 2000, all that had changed. Cult membership all but disappeared, with most of the groups gone altogether. The drug trade dropped nearly 75 percent and corruption in law enforcement was drastically reduced. Gang involvement seriously declined—one entire gang came to Christ. Church attendance doubled, and where there was once division and apathy, unity among churches prevailed. Pulpit swapping became common and quarterly concerts of prayer and citywide prayer revivals continue to bring change.[1]

God in Your City

"Great!" you may be saying. "But what do those places have to do with my city, and what do they have to do with the watchman anointing?" Everything.

First of all, the Bible states, "What God has done for one city, He'll do for another." You didn't know this was in the Bible? Sure you did. You just didn't recognize the Sheets paraphrase. Most translations read something like, "God is no respecter of persons" (Acts 10:34, *KJV*).

Another verse says, "God wants to save people in your city just as much as those in Hemet, Cali and Almolonga." I'm sure you've caught on by now. This is an interpretation of 2 Peter 3:9: "The Lord is . . . not willing that any should perish, but that all should come to repentance" (*KJV*).

Yes, there is hope for your city and mine. There is hope for America. We are not at the mercy of sin, sinners, politicians, Satan or demons. Refuse to place control of your destiny in any of these! Choose to believe God is wiser than the devil.

If God wants to bring revival to America, and He does, then we can have revival. We, the Church, hold the keys. We are His body—His hands, feet, voice—and what He does, He'll do through us. We're Plan A and there is no Plan B.

No one said that it would be easy. To the contrary, words such as "persecution," "tribulation," "fight," "warfare," "wrestle," "endurance" and others like them are all applied to us in Scripture. But so are words such as "victory," "faith," "overcomer," "conqueror," "power," "authority," "harvest" and "miracle."

I want to state with boldness: If you are willing to obey God fully, walk in faith and never give up, you can have anything God wants you to have. And that absolutely includes revival in your local community.

The Offensive Power of a Watchman

What of the watchman? What does all this have to do with watching intercession? The answer to that lies in a revelation the Holy Spirit gave me in 1988. "Study the watchman concept" were the words I heard from Him.

"I already know about watchmen" was my *humble* response.

"I know more than you do" was the Holy Spirit's quick and confident answer. "Study the concept of the watchman!"

He was right, as usual. It was then I discovered that there is more to the watchman anointing than defensive or protective connotations. There is also an offensive or aggressive aspect of watching. The Hebrew words are translated "to besiege,"[2] "spy"[3] and "ambush"[4] (see Judg. 1:24; 2 Sam. 11:16; Isa. 1:8; Jer. 4:17; Pss. 56:6; 71:10), because all of these things involve watching.

"I am about to release a fresh anointing to the Church," the Holy Spirit continued, "that will enable My people to take individuals, cities, regions and nations for Me. New strategies will emerge, fresh concepts of discerning Satan's strongholds will be released (i.e., *spying*) and *sieges* will be put in place that will eventually break Satan's hold over people and places.

"It will be a broad work, with strategies coming from many different sources. I will give one part of a plan to one person, another to others. This will take place simultaneously, and often one ministry or person won't even realize they are a part of a larger scheme. But I will be cutting off Satan's strength from every direction, as through the watchman anointing My people discern from Me."

This was several years ago, before terms such as "prayer walking," "prayer journeys," "spiritual mapping," "identificational repentance," "reconciliation ceremonies," "territorial spirits" and others were being used. I'm sure they may have existed in some people's thinking, but most of the Body of Christ had never heard of them. And I'm relatively certain that some didn't exist at all.

Since that time literally *millions* of believers around the world have not only understood and embraced these concepts, but have *put them into practice!* The learning curve in the recent prayer movement is off the charts. In the words of Peter Wagner, certainly one of the well-known fathers of the movement, "The prayer movement around the world is out of control."

Of course, we haven't "arrived" in our understandings and activations, but we are progressing toward the mark at an amazing pace. Not too long ago, you would have had to look long and hard to find a ministry that existed solely for the purpose of training intercessors and establishing prayer. Now there are dozens, including several major denominations, that have entire departments committed to the facilitating of prayer. It is no wonder we are making such progress in world evangelism.

Much of the praying falls under the category of the watchman anointing. *Spying* has taken place as the enemy's strongholds and plans have been discerned. *Sieges* are under way all over the world. The watchman anointing is in place. I am so confident heaven's strategies will not fail that I have a bold prediction: *During the next several decades, testimonies like those of Cali, Almolonga and Hemet will become common.*

Otis, after relating the stories of Cali, Almolonga, Hemet and several others, asks the all-important question: "Are these revivals reproducible?" His answer is encouraging:

Bump into this same story 10 or 12 times, however, and your confidence will rise. You now have an established pattern, and patterns are compelling. Laden with reproducible principles, patterns transform inspirational stories into potent models.

My own investigation into the factors responsible for transformed communities has yielded several major "hits." These include, but are not limited to, the following five stimuli:

1. Persevering leadership (see Neh. 6:1-16)
2. Fervent, united prayer (see Jon. 3:5-10)
3. Social reconciliation (see Matt. 5:23-24; 18:15-20)
4. Public power encounters (see Acts 9:32-35)
5. Diagnostic research/spiritual mapping (see Josh. 18:8-10)

Although each of these factors recurs often enough to be considered common, two of them—persevering leadership and fervent united prayer—are present in all of our transformation case studies.[5]

Strategies for a Watchman Taking a City

As we make diligent efforts to study and implement principles shared in resources such as the above-mentioned books—and doing so is absolutely essential—God will release to us this anointing of the Holy Spirit. This will enable us to transform our communities with precision and excellence. Don't try to copy these principles as formulas. The key to success is listening to the Holy Spirit give insight on how to accurately implement them in our regions.

Start immediately. It may take several years, as it did with the three cities mentioned and with Joshua and Israel, but God *has* given us our cities.

In his book *Warfare Prayer*, Dr. C. Peter Wagner shares six strategies he feels are essential to making a permanent spiritual impact on your city. Watchmen for cities should take heed to these important points:

1. Select a manageable geographical area with discernible spiritual boundaries.

2. Secure the unity of the pastors and other Christian leaders in the area and begin to pray together on a regular basis.

3. Project a clear image that the effort is not an activity simply of Pentecostals and charismatics, but of the whole Body of Christ.

4. Assure the spiritual preparation of participating leaders and other Christians through repentance, humility and holiness.

5. Research the historical background of the city in order to reveal spiritual forces shaping the city.

6. Work with intercessors especially gifted and called to strategic-level warfare, seeking God's revelation of: (a) the redemptive gift or gifts of the city; (b) Satan's strongholds in the city; (c) territorial spirits assigned to the city; (d) corporate sin past and present that needs to be dealt with; and (e) God's plan of attack and timing.[6]

Bob Beckett, in the book *Commitment to Conquer* (which is his personal version of the transformation of Hemet), would agree with Otis and Wagner, while also emphasizing a long-term commitment to the community to which God has called a person. His arguments and corresponding personal testimony concerning regional commitment make an overwhelming case for its importance.

I could not agree more with Bob's contention. I have personally gone through a time of recommitment to my city, Colorado Springs. In January 1999, I received a significant visitation from the Lord, during which He put a new mantle and some specific assignments on me for America. There is no need for details, but it was the most significant encounter I have ever had with the Lord.

One of the results of this impartation was an overwhelming burden for this nation. It was difficult for me to mention America, Washington, DC, or even our president without weeping. The burden for America was so heavy that it became difficult to focus on my own city. This, added to the incredible pace I have kept up the past three to four years and the resulting weariness, caused my vision and passion for Colorado Springs to diminish significantly. After some well-timed *kairos* (the Greek word for an opportune time, a distinct moment)[7] attacks of Satan, I simply had no strength of will to continue in what amounted to two full-time jobs.

By midsummer I had pretty well convinced myself that God wanted me to lay down my pastorate and call to this city in order to focus on the nation. It came as a surprise to me when the Lord was able to finally make clear that He was not releasing me from my calling to this church and community.

I then found myself in the challenging position of needing vision and passion restored for my own city, which I'm glad to say has happened. I can assure you, however, that *as passion and love for my city waned, my anointing and ability to minister to it did as well.* If you do not have a love and commitment for your city, this is where your revival must begin.

Recognizing Weaknesses

A few of our experiences in trying to take Colorado Springs for Christ could perhaps be beneficial for some of you. We have had our share of victories and setbacks. It is not uncommon for reputations to exceed reality—sometimes negatively, other times positively. Colorado Springs would fall into the latter category.

We in our city are not where we are reputed to be in prayer, unity, salvations and city transformation. In some ways I actually saw regression throughout the 1990s. The good news is that several pastors and leaders are determined to walk in unity and prayer and carry a genuine passion to see revival in our city. In spite of our weaknesses, we have great hope that this will occur.

One of the difficult paradoxes of the Kingdom is to acknowledge negative realities while still walking in faith. Some in our city have been accused of pessimism and a negative spirit when trying to point out weaknesses. They have neither, however. It is possible to acknowledge weaknesses while walking in genuine faith.

The first step in fixing a problem is recognizing and understanding it. Romans 4:19, using Abraham as an example of faith, tells us *"without becoming weak in faith* he *contemplated* his own body" (italics mine). Though the *King James Version* says, "he *considered* not his own body" (italics mine), making it seem as though we shouldn't even acknowledge difficult circumstances, the Greek word used (*kataneo*) doesn't corroborate this. It actually means "to contemplate or attentively consider; to observe fully."[8]

Abraham didn't grow strong in faith because he *refused* to acknowledge the natural circumstances. He grew strong in faith *while* acknowledging—even contemplating—his and Sarah's conditions but respecting the promise of God so much that it carried more weight than the earthly reality.

One of the errors in some faith teaching springs from a misunderstanding of this verse. People are taught to deny or to ignore realities, such as sickness or financial lack. Acknowledging them is taught to be unbelief or a faith destroyer. This is not biblical.

Applying this acknowledgment of existing realities to taking our cities, we must honestly admit our lacks and weaknesses:

disunity, apathy, prayerlessness, past sins and others. We can then go to God, confess our needs and find His answers. Beckett acknowledges this is one of the things that caused change for his congregation and city.

"For five solid years, five days a week, our church prayed every morning for one hour. . . . We had anywhere from ten to one hundred people at those meetings." Though he acknowledges fruit in individuals' lives, Beckett says, "The only problem was, at the end of those five years of faithful intercession, totaling about 1,300 hours of corporate prayer, Hemet had not changed one bit."[9]

He began to ask hard questions and was honest with himself about the lack of change. When he did this, God was gracious to give answers. He will for the rest of us, as well.

In spite of our weaknesses in Colorado Springs, there are many reasons for encouragement. Our faith, like Abraham's of old, is growing. So is momentum in the Spirit. Here are some watchman activities in which we have been involved during the last several years and which have and will continue to bear fruit. (I am not implying that our efforts are unique; they simply are ones I am aware of. Others, I am certain, could add to the list.)

On three different occasions, our congregation moved our Sunday morning service to a strategic downtown park so we could publicly worship the Lord and intercede for our city while in this key location.

Our church and several other congregations combined our Sunday morning services on two occasions and met together in a nonchurch location for the purpose of breakthrough for Colorado Springs. Others have done this as well.

For almost two years we had joint weekly Wednesday evening services, with as many as 20 churches represented.

During the same two-year period, we led and hosted hundreds of hours of multichurch prayer meetings for our city.

This was in addition to other pastoral prayer meetings in our city—of which there were several. Many other regular prayer meetings also focused on interceding for this city.

In the spring of 1999, after having been warned by two nationally known and respected prophets that the walls of our city were down due to pride and other issues, many churches participated in 40 days of around-the-clock praise. During the same period, solemn assemblies were held for repentance of pride and other sins, along with several prayer meetings also held to intercede for the city. This resulted in tremendous breakthrough. We have credible evidence that a mass school shooting, like the one in Littleton, Colorado, was planned for Colorado Springs. Instead of following through with the act, however, the young man involved turned himself in to authorities. We believe this tragedy was prevented because of the praise, repentance and prayer—both ours and that of others.

The week after the Littleton massacre, New Life Church prepared a wonderful prayer guide that lists all of our city's high schools and their superintendents. This booklet was distributed in churches throughout the city and enabled believers in Colorado Springs to pray with what Otis calls "informed intercession."[10] We believe this, too, helped ward off violence in our city.

Cindy Jacobs oversaw a very extensive spiritual mapping of our area, with individuals from several churches working together on the project.

As a result of this effort, we have implemented offensive prayer strategies and have conducted periodic citywide prayer and praise services at key locations. Other such meetings are forthcoming, as we are determined to take back what Satan has stolen.

These and other efforts are encouraging signs that God is, indeed, giving us insight and strategy to impact our city. We will not be satisfied until we see thousands come to Christ and our city transformed. These efforts, along with those being conducted by others, are aspects of the watchman anointing. They are spirit-led assignments of discerning (spying) and laying siege to our city.

The very concept of a siege implies time and process. Delays can be expected but also overcome. Though most revivals seem sudden, they are really a culmination of much that has happened to prepare the way. Galatians 6:9 tells us, "Let us not lose heart in doing good, for in due time we will reap if we do not grow weary." "Due time" in this verse is the word *kairos*. The point is simple: our "doing good" will create an opportune season of "reaping," if we don't "grow weary" and give up.

The Divine Shift

Since the visitation from the Lord that I mentioned earlier in the chapter, I have been to the Washington, DC, area many times to pray and to minister. Believing God gave me a strategic assignment to do this, I have added these journeys to an already crowded schedule. My purpose has been (and still is) to generate more prayer for that city and for our nation and also to impart faith for revival in the Body of Christ there. While ministering recently in DC, the Holy Spirit kept bringing to me the phrase "the divine shift."

While meditating on this phrase, the Holy Spirit began to teach me that a *kairos* season is simply a *phase* of the *process*. In other words, through the working of the Holy Spirit in and through the Church, as well as His masterful aligning even in the unsaved world, *chronos* (the general passage of time)[11] BECOMES *kairos*. They are separate but linked. They are different but parts of the same process. We cannot have one without the other, for in fact, *it is the chronos time that produces the kairos time.*

Daniel 2:20-21 speaks of the divine shift: "Blessed be the name of God forever and ever! For wisdom and might are His! He changes the times and the seasons, He removes kings and sets up kings. He gives wisdom to the wise and knowledge to those who have understanding!" (*AMP*). This changing of the times and seasons also takes place, for example, in our individual lives again and again as we move from one phase to another. The Scriptures tell us we go from

- brighter to brighter paths (see Prov. 4:18),
- faith to faith (see Rom. 1:17),
- strength to strength (see Ps. 84:7), and
- glory to glory (see 2 Cor. 3:18).

The passage in Psalm 84 that speaks of going "from strength to strength" begins by saying in verse 6, "passing through the valley of Baca [weeping] they make it a spring." Then in verse 7 is the phrase "from strength to strength." It is in the *chronos* time of weeping, where all seems difficult and fruitless, that the work is done to allow God to transform *chronos* to *kairos*.

After God made promises to Abraham concerning the nation that would come from him through Sarah, there was a 24-year *chronos* season requiring faithfulness, commitment and patience. Though not perfectly, Abraham and Sarah made it through this time until the divine shift occurred, transforming *chronos* to *kairos* in Genesis 18:10: "I will surely return to you at this time next year; and behold, Sarah your wife shall have a son."

The word for "time" in this verse is the Hebrew word *eth*, which is an equivalent for the Greek word *kairos*.[12] *Chronos* became *kairos*!

After refusing to believe and respond to God properly, Israel was forced to wander for 40 years in the wilderness. In Joshua 1, the divine shift occurred as God changed the season to *kairos*. "Within three days," He said, "you are to cross this Jordan" (Josh. 1:11).

After his dramatic conversion in Acts 9, Saul—later named Paul—went into a lengthy season of *chronos*. It was those 12 years of faithful study, equipping and transformation on the Potter's wheel that allowed the Holy Spirit to cause the divine shift in Acts 13, changing *chronos* to *kairos*. "While they were ministering to the Lord and fasting, the Holy Spirit said, 'Set apart for Me Barnabas and Saul for the work to which I have called them'" (v. 2).

In the 1940s through the 1980s, much of Europe was under a shroud of Communist oppression and bondage. The Iron Curtain held millions of hopeless souls in captivity, while a seemingly helpless world looked on. During this *chronos* time of seeming inactivity, much was happening in the Spirit. Untold thousands of prayers went up for the liberation of this sector of the world and the fall of Communism.

In what seemed like a day, God created the divine shift. *Chronos* was transformed into *kairos*, and the Iron Curtain came down. This didn't happen in spite of the *chronos* season; it happened *because of* what was taking place in and through the *chronos* season.

Hang in there! You may be only days from your *kairos*. The divine shift may be imminent. Your faithfulness now will help create it.

Your city may seem far from revival. Don't grow weary in your doing of good. He is faithful who promised, and He *has* given you your city. The watchman anointing is in place in the Body of Christ. Walk in it!

Let the sieges continue!

The shift is coming!

ARMED AND LOADED
WITH PRAYER

Prayer Changes Everything

When George McCluskey married and started a family, he decided to invest one hour a day in prayer, because he wanted his kids to follow Christ. After a time, he expanded his prayers to include his grandchildren and great-grandchildren. Every day between 11:00 A.M. and noon, he prayed for the next three generations.

As the years went by, his two daughters committed their lives to Christ and married men who went into full-time ministry. The two couples produced four girls and one boy. Each of the girls married a minister, and the boy became a pastor.

The first two children born to this generation were both boys. Upon graduation from high school, the two cousins chose the same college and became roommates. During their sophomore year, one boy decided to go into the ministry. The other didn't. He undoubtedly felt some pressure to continue the family legacy, but he chose instead to pursue his interest in psychology.

He earned his doctorate and eventually wrote books for parents that became bestsellers. He started a radio program heard on more than a thousand stations each day. The man's name—James Dobson.[1]

Talk about the power of prayer! The next time you're blessed by *Focus on the Family* or one of Dr. Dobson's books, thank God for a generational watchman, George McCluskey. Many kids aren't as blessed with praying fathers.

At a 1994 Promise Keepers conference in Denton, Texas, Pastor James Ryle told his story:

> When he was two years old, his father was sent to prison. When he was seven, authorities placed him in an orphanage. At 19, he had a car wreck that killed a friend. He sold drugs to raise money for his legal fee, and the law caught up to him. He was arrested, charged with a felony and sent to prison.
>
> While in prison James accepted Christ, and after he served his time, he eventually went into the ministry. Years later he sought out his father to reconcile with him. When they got together, the conversation turned to prison life.
>
> James's father asked, "Which prison were you in?"
>
> James told him, and his father was taken aback. "I helped build that prison," he said. He had been a welder who went from place to place building penitentiaries.
>
> Pastor Ryle concluded, "I was in the prison my father built."[2]

Indeed! In more ways than one.

These are amazing stories, powerfully contrasting two possibilities. We can either build prisons for our children or through prayer build fruitful lives that bless others.

All We Can Do Is Pray

The same stories could be told by millions around the world. Change the names, a detail here and there, but the bottom lines

are the same: success or failure, life or death, fruitfulness or bar-
renness, bondage or freedom—results that are largely determined by the influence of righteous or unrighteous parents.
Never underestimate the power of a praying parent!

In this book, we have often mentioned the concept of watchmen keeping the serpent out of our gardens. In the following
quote, Jamie Buckingham comments on the importance of doing this through watching prayer:

> You may not think your little field is very important. But
> God has set you in your field as a watchman. Most of us
> don't realize it, but our sphere of influence is much
> larger than we can ever imagine—and will continue on
> for generations to come, be it good or evil. It's a wonder-
> ful responsibility—frightening at times—but wonderful.
> Always remember, though, you're never in your watch-
> tower alone. Jesus is ever with you and His Spirit will
> whisper just the things you need to say and do.[3]

And it's never too late to start!

At a family Christmas gathering, an 81-year-old grandmother was complaining that her life was useless.
"But Granny," her 31-year-old grandson protested,
"you can go out of this world in a blaze of glory as an
intercessor!"

It got her attention. "I don't know how to intercede
for others," she said to her daughter-in-law. "Would you
teach me?" That night she had her first prayer lesson as
they spread out a world map on the table, got out the
Bible and began to pray over various countries and for
missionaries they knew. They also made a list of relatives for whom she could pray.

This "useless granny" is launched on a whole new adventure that can change her perspective on life.[4]

Unforgettable Bombs

I've often heard the phrase "All we can do is pray." That misguided statement reminds me of the amazing role played by some Czechs in World War II:

> In Elmer Bendiner's book, *The Fall of Fortresses*, he describes one bombing run over the German city of Kassel: "Our B-17 (*The Tondelayo*) was barraged by flack from Nazi anti-aircraft guns. That was not unusual, but on this particular occasion our gas tanks were hit. Later, as I reflected on the miracle of a twenty-millimeter shell piercing the fuel tank without touching off an explosion, our pilot, Bohn Fawkes, told me it was not quite that simple.
>
> "On the morning following the raid, Bohn had gone down to ask our crew chief for that shell as a souvenir of unbelievable luck. The crew chief told Bohn that not just one shell but eleven had been found in the gas tanks—eleven unexploded shells where only one was sufficient to blast us out of the sky. It was as if the sea had been parted for us. Even after thirty-five years, so awesome an event leaves me shaken, especially after I heard the rest of the story from Bohn.
>
> "He was told that the shells had been sent to the armorers to be defused. The armorers told him that Intelligence had picked them up. They could not say why at the time, but Bohn eventually sought out the answer. Apparently when the armorers opened each of those shells, they found no explosive charge. They were as

clean as a whistle and just as harmless. Empty? Not all of them.

"One contained a carefully rolled piece of paper. On it was a scrawl in Czech. The Intelligence people scoured our base for a man who could read Czech. Eventually, they found one to decipher the note. It set us marveling. Translated, the note read: 'This is all we can do for you now.' "[5]

All we can do?! The pilots on that B-17 certainly didn't have a small opinion of what these Czechs had done. Nor did the wives, children or grandchildren of those soldiers. Not to mention the lives they saved in the future as they helped deliver the world from Adolf Hitler. "All we can do . . . !"

This is often what I think when I hear people bemoan their helplessness or lack of contribution as they announce, "All we can do is pray." What better activity could a person possibly do? We can impact the world, secure destinies and affect eternity through prayer.

Prayers and Prodigals

As we think about the importance of watching intercession for individuals, most of us probably think immediately of our families, as well we should. Our personal gardens, as our opening stories reveal, are where we must begin. Quin Sherrer has taught much on the subject of praying for family members. In her book *Good Night, Lord*, she relates an occasion of interceding for her son:

I clearly remember a day when the Lord spoke to me about my teenage son, Keith, as I walked the beach. Deeply concerned about his spiritual condition, I felt he was drifting further and further from the Lord. My only recourse was prayer. I realized that as a parent, I had made so many mistakes. So I asked the Lord to forgive me.

That afternoon, as I walked alone, I proclaimed aloud Scriptures tucked away in my heart. "The seed of the righteous shall be delivered," I shouted into the wind. "Because of Jesus' blood I am righteous and my children are my seed and they shall be delivered," I paraphrased. "All my children shall be taught of the Lord, and great will be their peace," I paraphrased again. (See Prov. 11:21; Isa. 54:13, *KJV.*)

Over and over I repeated scriptural promises God had given me for my children. I desperately needed an answer for my son. After more than an hour of this, I reached down and picked up a small brown shell being tossed about by the waves. "Trust me to polish and perfect your son," the Lord seemed to whisper to my spirit as I turned the shell over in my hand.

I took my shell home, cleaned it and set it where I could see it whenever I cooked. "Lord, You promised," I would say some days as I cradled it in my palm. Even after Keith left for college and I saw little change, I thanked God for His word that He and He alone would perfect my son whom I loved so very much.

Our prayer battle ended one night when Keith called to ask his father and me to forgive him; we asked him to forgive us, too. He had started his pilgrimage back to the Lord. After college and a short career in graphic arts, he enrolled in Bible school.

Not long ago Keith finished seven years of service with the Youth With A Mission organization (YWAM). . . . Today he's a godly husband to a wonderful wife and the father of two young daughters. My "promise shell" still sits in my kitchen, testimony to a prayer answer God gave me so many years ago.[6]

That promise shell is also a watchman shell, for that is the watchman anointing! Quin also shares prayer steps she uses in being a watchman for her children:

- be specific;
- pray Scripture passages aloud;
- write down your prayers;
- pray in accordance with God's will;
- pray for your children's future.[7]

In another of her books, *The Spiritual Warrior's Prayer Guide*, she and Ruthanne Garlock give biblical examples of how to do this by offering the following scriptural prayers:

- that Jesus Christ be formed in our children (see Gal. 4:19);

- that our children—the seed of the righteous—will be delivered from the evil one (see Prov. 11:21, *KJV*; Matt. 6:13);

- that our children will be taught of the Lord and their peace will be great (see Isa. 54:13);

- that they will train themselves to discern good from evil and have a good conscience toward God (see Heb. 5:14; 1 Pet. 3:21);

- that God's laws will be in their minds and on their hearts (see Heb. 8:10);

- that they will choose companions who are wise—not fools, nor sexually immoral, nor drunkards, nor idolaters, nor slanderers, nor swindlers (see Prov. 13:20; 1 Cor. 5:11);

- that they will remain sexually pure and keep themselves only for their spouse, asking God for His grace to keep such a commitment (see Eph. 5:3,31-33);

- that they will honor their parents (see Eph. 6:1-3).[8]

In chapter 6 we taught that the concept of the watchman involves aggressively laying siege, not just protecting. Ruthanne Garlock shares a powerful testimony of someone who implemented this aspect of the watchman anointing for an unsaved family member:

Sue, a former student, called one day and asked Ruthanne to pray for her unsaved father who had terminal cancer. Sue and her mother had prayed for years for him to accept Jesus. Now near death, he was very bitter, blaming God for his illness.

"How can we lead him to Christ when he is so angry?" Sue asked me.

"The problem is, he's believing Satan's lie that God is his enemy," I responded. "He needs to see that God is his only source of help. I suggest you bind the lying spirit that has deceived him. Then just shower your father with unconditional love; don't preach to him anymore."

Sue's mother and brother picked up extension phones, and I prayed while they agreed: "Thank you, Father, that it is your desire to bring Sue's dad into your kingdom. We take authority in the name of Jesus and bind the deceiving spirits that are lying to him. We ask the Holy Spirit to reveal the truth that you love him. Lord, cause him to come to his senses and escape from the trap of the devil. We ask this in Jesus' name, Amen."

I suggested they continue this strategy. "Use the authority Jesus gave you to forbid the enemy to speak to your father." About six weeks later Sue called to tell me her father had died. But just before he died, he received Jesus as his Lord.

"One day as I walked through the living room where he was lying on the sofa, I went over and hugged him and said, 'I love you, Dad,'" Sue related. "Tears came to his eyes—it was the first time I had ever seen him cry. As I began to share with him about the Lord, I could tell the Holy Spirit had already prepared his heart. He willingly accepted Jesus right then!"[9]

That is the watchman anointing bearing fruit. Siege walls were built by prayer, prohibiting Satan from continuing to lie to this father. As a result, this man is in heaven today. A similar story is told of prayer for a husband, with a few other strategies also implemented:

While visiting my friend Barbara in Germany last spring, I listened fascinated one evening as her husband, Russell, an Air Force officer, explained to a group packed into their dining room about the meaning of the Passover meal we were about to eat. As a Bible study teacher, he had spent hours preparing the lesson, the food and the table.

After we'd eaten, I helped Barbara in the kitchen. "Russ is really turned on to the Lord!" I exclaimed. "I still remember the Sunday years ago when you asked me to pray for him. He was so wrapped up in his career he had no time for God, and he was so reserved—almost stiff in those days. But now, he is not only a mighty man of God, he's a terrific Bible teacher. What did you do besides pray a lot during the time he wasn't following the Lord?"

As Barbara shared, I jotted down her answers:

- I had many intercessors join me in praying for him.

- I was single-minded in my goal—determined that my words and my behavior would make him thirsty for the Lord. I asked the Lord to keep His joy bubbling out of me.

- Russ liked to show off our home and my cooking by having company over, so I often invited Christians to share meals with us. He enjoyed that—especially meeting Christian men, whom he found fun to be around.

- The children and I kept going to church.

- Russ began to go with me to a Bible study— probably out of curiosity, but also because I had such joy. Then he started going to church with the family.

Russ finally decided to make Jesus his personal Lord. He immediately had a hunger to know the Word of God, and began spending hours each week studying the Bible.[10]

These stories point out that when we lay siege through intercession, it is essential for us to allow the Holy Spirit to give us the strategy needed at each specific moment. I always try to find the principles of God's Word that apply to my situation and then ask the Holy Spirit how to apply them in that particular instance. He is always faithful in doing this because He desires to see God's will accomplished even more than I do.

The Watchman's Prayer of Protection

As we have stressed in previous chapters, protection is an important aspect of the watchman anointing. Watchmen are guards, bodyguards, doorkeepers and, generally speaking, those who protect by covering in prayer. The following story tells of a mother's prayer for her children, which also resulted in protection for others:

> Irene, a young praying mother in Texas, has formed the habit of praying for the schools her children attend every morning when she drives them there. On Mondays she gives extra time and attention to praying for the schools, the teachers and the pupils.
>
> Last year, a few weeks into the fall semester, she felt the Holy Spirit urging her to pray over the parking lot at the middle school her seventh-grader attends. She did this for three days in a row. The first two days she drove around the perimeter of the parking lot, binding the enemy from doing any evil work there, asking God to protect everyone coming and going, and praying in tongues.
>
> On the third day Irene got out of the car and walked around the parking lot, praying and claiming the Scripture the Lord gave her: "I will give you every place where you set your foot" (Josh. 1:3).
>
> A few weeks later, a disturbed student from an abusive home shot the assistant principal in that same parking lot. The bullet missed his spine by two inches and lodged in his stomach. After surgery he recovered with no

complications and returned to his job in six weeks. The student received much-needed professional counseling.

"I'm convinced the incident would have been much worse had it not been for the prayer," Irene declared. "We just never know what lies ahead when the Holy Spirit gives specific directions for prayer. We must be obedient."[11]

I like Irene's attitude. Some people would have immediately questioned why this incident still happened when she had prayed so faithfully. She chose to believe—and I certainly agree—that her prayers allowed the Lord to change the enemy's plans and prevent greater tragedy.

In the nineteenth chapter of Joshua, the word *paga* (intercession) is used several times. The passage describes the dimensions or boundaries of each of the tribes of Israel. It has been translated in several ways in different Bible translations, including "reached to," "touched," "bordered," "boundary." The *Spirit-Filled Bible* says that *paga*, when used in this context, is the extent to which a boundary reaches.[12]

Does it surprise you that the word used for intercession, *paga*, is also translated "boundary"? It really shouldn't. It only seems logical to me that perimeters of protection be linked to prayer. I want to state emphatically: We CAN build boundaries of protection around ourselves and others through intercession. What a comfort to know that this truth is inherent in the very meaning of the word. And it is certainly consistent with the watchman anointing.

Strategic Boundaries

This facet of intercession is not only to be something we do on a *general*, regular basis for our family and loved ones. There are also *specific* times when the Holy Spirit will alert us to particular situations that need protective prayer. These are what the Scriptures call *kairos* times. As previously mentioned, there are two Greek words for "time." One is *chronos*, which is time in general, the general "time in which anything *is* done" (italics mine).[13] The other word, *kairos*, is the strategic or "right time; the opportune point of time at which something *should* be done" (italics mine).[14]

- A window of opportunity would be *kairos* time.
- A well-timed attack in war would be *kairos* time.
- When someone is in danger or about to be attacked by Satan, that is a *kairos* time.
- What time it is would be *chronos* time.
- The Bible speaks of well-timed (*kairos*) temptations (see Luke 4:13; 8:13).
- The Scriptures also inform us of strategically timed persecution (see Acts 12:1; 19:23).

Ephesians 6:18, the context of which is spiritual warfare, says we are to "be on the alert . . . for all the saints" and "pray at all (*kairos*) times in the Spirit." He is not telling us to pray all the time, which would be *chronos*, but to pray at all strategic times (*kairos*). In other words, we are in a war and if we are alert, He will warn us of the well-timed attacks (*kairos*) of the enemy so we can create a boundary (*paga*) of protection by praying.

Beth Alves shares the following testimony, which illustrates this:

An example from my own life involves a favorite cousin I hadn't seen in about 10 years. I crawled out of bed in the middle of the night for a glass of water when a picture of my cousin canvassed my mind. Suddenly I dropped to my knees and began to cry out, "God, don't let Mike move! Keep him still, Lord! Keep him still! Oh God, please don't let him move! Hold him, Lord! Hold him!"

Even though I was pleading on Mike's behalf with my words, I remember thinking, *This is really ridiculous. Why am I praying this?* Then the words ceased, and when they did, I could not muster another word. So I got up, drank a glass of water and started back toward the bedroom. Again I fell to the floor and began to cry out with a grave sense of urgency. "Don't let him move, God! Don't let Mike move! Stay still! Stay still!" The words came to an abrupt end. This time I thought, *Oh, no! This must be a nightmare!*

I had no feeling inside of me other than the feeling to pray. I got up and began to pace the floor, wondering what in the world that was all about. One more time I took a few steps toward the bedroom when again I dropped to the floor. Only this time I was yelling, "Get him up, Lord! Get him to run! Run, Mike! Lord, help him to run ... run ... run! Let him run, God! Run, run, run!" After several minutes, a calm came over me and I returned to bed for the night.

The following day, I called my aunt to see if she could help me put the pieces together about my puzzling outcries the night before. She informed me that Mike was in Vietnam. The experience still made very little sense.

Finally, a month later my aunt called to read a letter she had received. The letter told how Mike, who was a pilot, had been shot down and landed in a tree. He had been warned to get out of the area as quickly as possible, but explained that just a few hundred yards from the crash site, he fell into a bush. "Mom," he

wrote, "it was like I was pinned down. I felt like somebody was sitting on me. The Vietcong came and were
unknowingly standing on my pant leg while looking
up at my parachute in the tree. They turned around
and began to slash the bushes with their bayonets. It
looked safe, so I started to get up and was about to run
when once again I fell into the bush as though someone were pushing me. I laid there for a couple of minutes when suddenly I had an impulse to get up and run.
I heard a helicopter so I sprinted through the wooded
area, following the direction of the noise, to an open
space where I was whisked off to safety. The helicopter
crew said they came in response to my beeper. And yet,
it had not been working when I was shot down." That,
dear ones, is intercession![15]

Shirley Dobson shared the following story of praying for
her daughter, Danae, which illustrates the combined watchman concepts we've been speaking of, as well as *kairos* and *paga*:

I was at home one rainy weekend and looking forward
to working on several projects I had set aside for just
such a time. Both Jim and Ryan [their son] were in
Northern California on a hunting trip, and Danae had
plans for the evening with one of her friends. She had
previously asked for permission to use the family car
for her outing.

Secretly happy to have some time to myself, I turned
on some music and was busy at work when suddenly a
heaviness descended upon me. Feelings of unexplainable
anxiety and fear for Danae washed over me. I thought,
*This is silly. She's out with her friend, having a good time. I'm
sure she is all right.* Instead of lessening, the apprehension

I felt grew more intense. Finally, I slipped into the bedroom, closed the door and got down on my knees.

"Lord," I prayed, "I don't know why I am experiencing such fear about Danae, but if she is in any danger, I ask You to send guardian angels to watch over, protect and bring her home safely." I continued praying for a time and then got up and went back to work. The burden lifted to some degree, but I still sensed an uneasiness.

Forty-five minutes later I heard a knock on the door. Opening it, I found a policeman standing on my porch. He asked me if I owned a red car and I replied in the affirmative. "I found it upside down on a mountain road, Mrs. Dobson. Who was driving? Was it your husband?" he questioned. Danae had been driving the red car. I now realized why the Lord had impressed me to pray. Later I was to realize just how powerful that time of intercession had been on her behalf.

While he [the policeman] was there, the hospital emergency room called. They wouldn't tell me details. I found Danae very shaken with her left hand badly injured, swollen and bleeding. She had used her left arm and hand to brace herself as the car rolled over, and the car had actually rolled on her hand. We were told she could have lost her hand had her palm been facing down. Fortunately, a noted hand surgeon was in the hospital that night and was able to operate immediately. Another answer to prayer.

Later, we were to learn the whole story. Even though she had been driving very slowly, the rain had washed gravel over the oil-slick road, causing her to skid as she rounded the curve. She became very scared and lost control as most young drivers would. The car landed upside down in the middle of the road. If she had gone another 30 feet, the car would have plunged off the road and down a 500-foot embankment. There was no guardrail. With much gratitude in my heart, I thought about my prayer in light of the accident and saw legions of angels lined up against the road, keeping her car from sliding over the edge. Another answer to prayer! Danae quickly recovered, regaining full use of her left hand and we gave much praise to the Lord.[16]

Boundaries of protection! *Kairos*-timed prayer! The watchman!

Boundaries of Protection over National and Spiritual Leaders

The Scriptures also teach that we are to watch over governmental and spiritual leaders. "First of all, then, I urge that entreaties and prayers, petitions and thanksgivings, be made on behalf of all men, for kings and all who are in authority, in order that we may lead a tranquil and quiet life in all godliness and dignity" (1 Tim. 2:1-2). Dr. Freda Lindsay tells a remarkable story of a watchman's intervention in the life of her late husband, Gordon:

Many years ago, Gordon left for a round-the-world trip. Before he went, Mrs. Anna Schrader had said by the Spirit that this would be a dangerous trip. The prophecy mentioned that when Gordon got to Hong Kong as he would look to his right there would be danger. After Gordon left, Mrs. Schrader called me and urged that we get several people to pray for Gordon, as Satan was going to try to take his life. We did pray, and I committed the matter to the Lord.

Gordon went to Tokyo, and after he finished his business there he planned to go to Hiroshima. But in

Tokyo the man who was to take him there suddenly found it was impossible for him to go. Gordon was greatly disappointed. He then was confronted with the decision of whether to take a train by himself to Hiroshima or to go on to his next destination.

He said he struggled all evening in prayer, not knowing what to do—wanting to go to Hiroshima but yet somewhat hesitant about going alone. Finally, after several hours of indecision and vacillating back and forth, he felt a strong urge to go on to his next destination. He caught the first plane out, and when he stepped off the plane in Hong Kong, remembering what Mrs. Schrader had said, he looked to the right. All he saw was a big Canadian plane sitting there with a long line of people climbing the ramp. His Hong Kong host appeared shortly, and Gordon dismissed the matter from his mind.

The next morning when he awoke he found a newspaper that had been placed under his door. Pictured there were the ruins of the large Canadian plane which he had seen loading! It crashed and 64 people were dead! [This was the danger to the right, confirming the accuracy of the word.]

The following day he picked up another paper, and to his amazement read that the BOAC plane he was scheduled to fly on had he gone to Hiroshima had crashed, killing 124 people! It had exploded over Mt. Fuji, killing everyone on board, including 89 Americans. It was one of the world's worst commercial disasters. The papers listed that day, March 4, as the "darkest single day in commercial aviation" with both planes going down—yet our great God was able to protect Gordon![17]

Peter Wagner relates the story of a pastor who walked in the watchman ministry and the resulting fruit. As you will see from this testimony, we often aren't aware how far-reaching our prayers can be:

A young Brazilian man named Jesuel was sent out by his local church as a church-planting missionary to neighboring Peru. Soon after he arrived, he was discussing with some friends the strategy to plant their first church. During this discussion, Jesuel reported, a demon calling himself "Prince of Peru" appeared to him. The demon said, "Go back to your own land or you will die in Peru!"

Within a week of this confrontation, Jesuel became critically ill. He sought medical care, but the doctors could give him no hope of recovery. They informed him that, although he was young, he needed to face the fact that he was on his deathbed.

As he fought for his life, a nearby pastor, who believed in two-way prayer, was suddenly impressed by God to go to the hospital and pray for a certain young man who was there. He had never heard of Jesuel, nor did he know why this Brazilian might have come to Peru. He obeyed God, though, prayed for Jesuel, and Jesuel was miraculously healed and released from the hospital.

Jesuel then went to a town in northern Peru where, after four weeks of fruitless evangelistic efforts, he discovered that the Catholic church had not been used for six months. He befriended the church's caretaker and led him to Christ. The two of them decided they would ring the church bells and call the townspeople together for a Mass. When the bell rang, people came to the church from all directions and 100 gave their lives to Christ that day.

Many more were saved and nurtured until nearby Catholic priests heard what was going on and put a stop to it. Jesuel, however, simply moved to another place and planted five more churches in Peru before returning to Brazil to be married.[18]

Jesuel saw a lot of fruit, but an unnamed watchman also has much fruit stored up in heaven. Thank God for faithful intercessors!

Peter Wagner also summarizes a suggested daily praying guide put together by Beth Alves. The guide is focused on spiritual leaders and covers various aspects of their ministry in a community:

- *Sunday*: Favor with God (spiritual revelation, anointing, holiness).

- *Monday*: Favor with others (congregations, ministry staff, unsaved).

- *Tuesday*: Increased vision (wisdom and enlightenment, motives, guidance).

- *Wednesday*: Spirit, Soul, Body (health, appearance, attitudes, spiritual and physical wholeness).

- *Thursday*: Protection (temptation, deception, enemies).

- *Friday*: Finances (priorities, blessings).

- *Saturday*: Family (general, spouse, children).[19]

As important as this is, our prayers for others shouldn't be limited to family members and authority figures. Friends, neighbors and anyone else the Holy Spirit impresses upon our hearts should be watched over. Jesus prayed for Peter that his faith not fail him during a critical time of temptation. "Simon, Simon, behold, Satan has demanded permission to sift you like wheat; but I have prayed for you, that your faith may not fail; and you, when once you have turned again, strengthen your brothers" (Luke 22:31-32).

It seems only right that, as our example, Christ would have walked in the watchman anointing. I am sure it was His intercession that kept Peter from falling away. Our intercession can do the same for our brothers and sisters in Christ.

Neighborhood Guidelines

For those who want to begin praying for your neighbors, here are some guidelines to use as you ask the Lord to show you your own neighborhood from His perspective:

- Ask God to show you what strategy He wants you to use in reaching out to your neighbors—get-acquainted meals, coffee klatschs or similar social gatherings.

- Ask God to open up opportunities for building friendships and for performing services for your neighbors. Think creatively!

- Ask God to show you any areas where perhaps you need to be reconciled with one or more of your neighbors. Confess any sins the Holy Spirit reveals in this area.

- Search Scripture for a special word for each neighbor and expect God to speak to your heart specifically.

- After any neighbors commit their lives to Jesus, be willing to continue to walk with them as they are nurtured and grow in the Word and in the Body of Christ.[20]

Praying and caring for our neighborhoods cultivates peace and kindness. Writer Quin Sherrer provides enormous insight in this area:

> Could our communities be truly transformed by Christ if every neighbor and neighborhood were prayed for daily? God's heart desire is for all people to be saved and for all to "live peaceful and quiet lives in all godliness and holiness" (1 Tim. 2:2, *NIV*).
>
> Christians from numerous churches in our city came together this spring to pray for our neighborhoods. The goal was for each person or couple to pray blessings over five neighbors, then to be available to them when needed. We agreed to pray: Five blessings for five neighbors for five minutes a day five days a week for five weeks.
>
> Each member of our congregation willing to participate took a sheet of paper with this suggestion on it: Who is your neighbor? Jesus described a neighbor as someone you meet along life's road who needs your help. Think of the word BLESS to remember five important ways to pray for your neighbors:
>
> B— Body—health, protection, strength
> L— Labor—work, income, security
> E— Emotions—joy, peace, hope
> S— Social—love, marriage, family, friends
> S— Spiritual—salvation, faith, grace
>
> Always pray with a clean heart. The prayers of the righteous are "powerful and effective" (Jas. 5:16). Pray with compassion. Be like Christ, who was moved with compassion toward the needy (Matt. 9:36). Pray with persistence (Acts 12:5; Jas. 5:17).[21]

Miracles occur in all kinds of neighborhoods. For instance, in Charlotte, North Carolina, scores of women have conducted prayer walks. Mary Lance Sisk has witnessed many miracles in the community and notes that a great portion of the results stem from small neighborhood prayer triplets (three people praying together) that are being formed as the movement grows:

> "I believe the key to the healing of the United States is going to be neighborhood by neighborhood, with women doing it!" she said. "Evangelism is a lifestyle of love which results from having Jesus' heart for the lost." Mary Lance encourages women to intercede daily for their neighbors and to pray for God to raise up a prayer movement in each neighborhood. She takes literally Jesus' command to "Love your neighbor as yourself," and Peter's admonition to "proclaim the praises of Him who called you out of darkness into His marvelous light" (1 Pet. 2:9, *NKJV*).
>
> Walking on her street, she makes it a habit to proclaim Scripture. "Lord, we invite the King of Glory to come in. Come forth and bring Your glory into this neighborhood. Release Your blessing to the families here." One of her neighborhood's most successful events is called "Meet You At The Corner." The neighbors gather on the Saturday morning before Easter for a short service declaring "He is Alive." They share refreshments and fellowship. Flyers are distributed door to door—even the children come along with their parents.
>
> "We're able to share about the resurrected Lord in a contextual way," Mary Lance said. "It's one of the best ways in the world to meet your neighbors."[22]

Walking in the Compassion of the Greatest Watchman

Whether praying for family members, leaders, friends or neighbors, one of the greatest keys to walking in the watchman calling is to allow oneself to walk in the compassion of the greatest Watchman. As we partake of Christ's High Priest anointing, we too will be touched with the feelings of others' infirmities.

Joseph Damien was a nineteenth-century missionary who ministered to people with leprosy on the island of Molokai, Hawaii. Those suffering grew to love him and revered the sacrificial life he lived out before them. One morning before Damien was to lead daily worship, he was pouring some hot water into a cup when the water swirled out and fell onto his bare foot. It took him a moment to realize that he had not felt any sensation. Gripped by the sudden fear of what this could mean, he poured more hot water on the same spot. No feeling whatsoever.

Damien immediately knew what had happened. As he walked tearfully to deliver his sermon, no one at first noticed the difference in his opening line. He normally began every sermon with "My fellow believers." But this morning he began with, "My fellow lepers."[23]

My fellow watchmen, most of us will never be called to be a leper to save others. Our lives will probably not be laid down in a literal sense, but every believer is called to a life of prayer. We are also called to be our brother's *keeper*—yes, the word is "watchman." Let the love of God constrain you to pick up the serpent-killing mantle God is offering.

Use it daily!

8

KEEPING WATCH OVER YOURSELF

─────◆◇◆─────

My Father-in-Law's Test

My father-in-law, James Merchant, is a watchman for his family. I've now assumed the primary role of watching over his daughter, Ceci, but for years he did an admirable job. Actually, her real name is Celia—that's what he calls her (pronounced by him and others in Mississippi "Say-ya").

I'll never forget my first meeting with him. Ceci and I met in Bible school, and I had already decided I wanted to marry her before her mom and dad met me. Mr. James Watchman-for-Say-ya Merchant decided on his own unique way of checking my work ethic and submission to elders on my first visit to their farm.

After a wonderful Mississippi breakfast of bacon, eggs and the absolutely best biscuits in the world made by my mother-in-law, Melba, James said to me, "I need some help with the cows today."

"Sure," I said, looking for ways to prove I was worthy of his daughter.

We then proceeded to vaccinate and tag 40 calves. My job was to catch them, push them down the chute and hold them, while James did the smart work of tagging and vaccinating. Scared baby calves do the same thing scared puppies do—mess all over themselves. Correction, they mess all over themselves and who-ever happens to be scaring, catching, pushing and holding them *from behind.*

By the time we finished, I was an amazing mixture of mud, perspiration, calf manure and urine—pretty much from head to toe. Mr. James Watchman-for-Say-ya Merchant was as clean as a whistle and smiling from ear to ear.

On our return from the barn, Say-ya met us outside with a big smile of her own. Being as absolutely crazy about me as she was, her whole world revolved around my passing this test. Seeing her daddy's smile, she knew all was well. Still grinning herself, she began—from a distance, due to my odorous condition—hosing me off. Strangely, for the next two weeks people seemed to avoid me like the plague. I was a little rank for a while—even the dogs didn't come near me—but I was a happy man.

Pity the poor guys who come asking Mr. Dutch Watchman-for-Sarah-and-Hannah Sheets for my daughters' hands in marriage one day. I've had 22 years so far to reflect and to improve on this testing process.

We've spoken about watching for many things throughout this book—nations, cities, neighborhoods, harvests, individuals (daughters—get 'em, James!)—but the watching target of this chapter may surprise you: It's ourselves. While not primarily related to prayer, this certainly has to do with the watchman anointing.

Guard Your Heart

"*Watch* over your heart with all diligence for from it flows the springs of life" (Prov. 4:23, italics mine). "Watch" is translated from *natsar*, one of our words for watchman. Yes, as important as it is to watch for others, we are also to be watchmen for our own hearts, guarding what we allow to enter. The word "heart" in this verse is the Hebrew word *leb*. Although this could mean the physical heart, it is used "figuratively for the feelings, the will and even the intellect."[1] This would include the soul—the mind, will and emotions. Again, we are told to be watchmen over them with all diligence.

Deuteronomy 4:15,23 instructs us to watch and guard against idolatry. Deuteronomy 6:12 tells us to watch ourselves, making certain blessing and prosperity don't cause us to forget the Lord. There are many areas we must watch, and as door-keepers of our own souls we determine what is allowed in, which then determines who we are in word and in deed.

Proverbs 23:7 gives tremendous insight to this, "For as he thinks within himself, so he is." "Thinks" (*shaar*) is a very inter-esting word. In fact, it's a watchman word. It doesn't literally mean to think; that was a derived, figurative meaning. It actu-ally means "to split or open; to act as a gatekeeper."[2] In other words, we are who we are because of what is allowed into our minds, *causing* a particular way of thinking. The verse is actually saying, "Whatever a person lets into his soul, so he will be." Each of us is the product of what we allow to access our minds and hearts. The context of the verse, in keeping with this reasoning, tells us to be careful with whom we associate. We are, indeed, watchmen for our own souls—our minds and emotions. It is critical that we act as gatekeepers or doorkeepers of our hearts.

Further explanation of the way the mind works will help us as watchmen. We, as human beings, are not controlled by that which is true. We are controlled by *what we believe to be true*, whether it is or not. Deceptions, lies and distorted perceptions all can control us, even though untrue. This is the biblical con-cept of a stronghold—a prison in the mind (see 2 Cor. 10:4) built by the distortions and deceptions of the enemy.

Even latent beliefs, buried deep in our subconscious, con-trol us whether true or not. An article in *Readers Digest* stated that "when people who fear snakes are shown a picture of a snake, sensors on their skin will detect sweat, a sign of anxiety, even though the people say they do not feel fear. The sweat shows up even when a picture is presented so rapidly that the subject has no conscious awareness of seeing it."[3]

Once a concept or philosophy has embedded itself into the deepest recesses of one's mind and memory, the belief center, the mind considers it to be truth and functions accordingly. And what is believed to be true *will* control the person, whether it is true or not. Thus Proverbs says, "So he [or she] is" (Prov. 23:7).

I once knew a lady who, for the first three years of her marriage, was unable to enter a physical union with her husband. She had been molested as a child, and though she tried to convince herself that her todays didn't need to be controlled by her yesterdays, she was unsuccessful. The stronghold in her belief center was too strong. A siege was necessary. As is often the case, her key to freedom was forgiving, which released the Holy Spirit to do the necessary work in her soul—her mind and emotions.

Comparing the human soul to the rings of a tree is helpful in understanding strongholds. The history of a tree can be read in its annual rings. If there has been drought, it will show in the rings. The same is true for plagues of insects, fires and also healthy years.

In the same way, everything we have experienced is recorded in our souls. If we could slice them open and see their "rings," we could read their histories. We might see great rejection in one year and the death of someone close, molestation or other harmful events in other years. Though some of what happens is beyond our control, these events can still lead to strongholds.

This is why Proverbs 4:23 says we must guard our souls, carefully determining what is allowed to enter. And though we cannot control everything placed there, we can be gatekeepers who strategically watch over what does and doesn't have access. If we do not, Satan will succeed in establishing strongholds.

Strongholds in the Heart and Mind

But what if strongholds already exist in a person's mind or emotions? Many people have allowed in much unbiblical information before becoming Christians. Others have allowed great amounts of perversion and unclean thinking to be engrained into their souls. Still others have experienced great trauma, rejection or other emotional wounds before coming to Christ. All of these things can be used to establish strongholds within them, causing certain patterns of acting and thinking.

A person doesn't have to be born again long before discovering that the new birth did not erase all that had been previously programmed into the mind and emotions. We can certainly guard what comes into our souls in the future, but what of the strongholds, wrong ways of thinking, fears and other destructive soul patterns already there?

We must *lay siege* to them! As mentioned previously, "watch" in Proverbs 4:23 is *natsar* (one of our watchman words) and also means "to lay siege." By the power of the Holy Spirit we can see these strongholds torn down. "The weapons we fight with . . . have divine power to demolish strongholds" (2 Cor. 10:4-5, *NIV*). The New Testament calls this renewing our minds (see Rom. 12:1-2), which is done through the Word of God. I have wonderful news for you—there is hope for a troubled, bound or wounded soul!

The Liberating Power of God's Word

How do we accomplish this renewing of the soul? First of all, we must remember that a siege implies a process over time. One of the misconceptions of trying to renew the soul is assuming it can be changed simply by a quality choice. In reality, however, a person is not able to overcome a stronghold, established mindset or habit just by choosing to be different. That is only the first step of a *process*. What must be chosen is the *process of change*. I realize you probably don't like that—I don't either. When I need fixing, I want to be fixed quickly. But if it were that simple, New Year's resolutions would work. I rest my case.

Several years ago the Holy Spirit spoke a phrase to my heart that tremendously helped me understand this process. I was thinking about John 8:32: "And you shall know the truth, and the truth shall make you free." Knowing this verse was speaking about the truth of His Word, I was wondering why it hadn't become reality in my life.

Most of us, if honest, would have to acknowledge that our experiences don't always line up with the Scriptures. For example, we are more than conquerors, but we are sometimes conquered by bad attitudes, sin, unbelief or other weaknesses. We're told we need never fear, but most Christians do.

Why doesn't the Word work for me? I thought while meditating about this verse in John.

Because all truth comes in seed form, He so clearly spoke to my heart. *What you do with the seed after it is planted will determine whether or not it bears fruit in you.*

Suddenly, many other passages of Scripture made sense: the parables of the sower (see Matt. 13; Mark 4; Luke 8); the renewing of the mind (see Rom. 12:1-2); abiding in the Vine by abiding in His Word (see John 15), and others. All of these involve planting seeds and working the process.

I discovered, that day and during subsequent studies, that this process of applying God's Word is both *constructive* and *destructive*. It is a healing scalpel and a destroying sword. It is a watering nutrient and a pruning knife. Through it God gives life to those who believe and releases judgment to those who don't. And most importantly, I realized that its work in me was a process.

The word "transformed" in Romans 12:2 and 2 Corinthians 3:18 confirms this. It is *metamorphoo*, from which we get the English word "metamorphosis." The concept is a process of change from one form or state to another from the inside out. The Holy Spirit within wants to go to work on us, changing what is contrary to Scripture that produces unwholeness in us. His greatest surgical tool is the Word.

In 1977 I witnessed a horribly gruesome automobile accident. The violence was indescribable. Being one of the first on the scene, I watched a young man die. Through the trauma of this event, a spirit of fear tried to overpower me. Using the indelibly imprinted scene I had witnessed, with relentless tenacity, it warred against my soul.

I felt fear all the time. I felt fear of being alone, fear of the dark, fear of the unknown and fear of just about everything imaginable. I couldn't sleep at night because of the replayed horror I had witnessed and the spirit that was using it. I *knew* this was a spirit of fear, trying to use this trauma to create a stronghold. Somehow I realized if I ever yielded to the fear, it would then own me. By refusing to act on it, I didn't yield to it but always pushed through and did what I needed to do in spite of the feelings of fear.

The Holy Spirit made real to me the incredible power of His Word as a sword. He showed me that I would have to wage all-out war against this spirit and the trauma to my emotions by using "the sword of the Spirit, which is the word of God" (Eph. 6:17). I obeyed. For close to a month, nearly all the time, I meditated on and spoke Scriptures concerning freedom from fear. Every possible moment I kept God's Word on my mind and tongue—I was laying siege, releasing the anointing.

I believe it took so long because of the incredible trauma to my emotions when I witnessed the gruesome accident. But one day, as suddenly as it came, the fear and the spirit left.

The Word had made me free, the seeds had born fruit, the siege was successful.

Hebrews 4:12-13 describes laying siege to the soul with the Word: "For the word of God is living and active and sharper than any two-edged sword, and piercing as far as the division of soul and spirit, of both joints and marrow, and able to judge the thoughts and intentions of the heart. And there is no creature hidden from His sight, but all things are open and laid bare to the eyes of Him with whom we have to do."

These wonderful verses give tremendous insight to the transforming ability of the Scriptures to heal that which needs healing and destroy the strongholds in the soul. The words "laid bare" in verse 13 are from the Greek word *trachelizo*, which literally means "to seize and bend back the neck, exposing the throat, as with an animal being slaughtered or sacrificed."[4] The word was also used to describe battlefield action. Need I say more?

Ugly? Yes. Graphic? Very.

But this strong and violent word is describing what His Word can do—not to us—but to the problem areas of the soul. We are meant to see the power of His Word and the intensity of our great High Priest against those things in our souls that work against our well-being and the life of His Spirit.

Though we are guilty of sin and rebellion toward God, He brings us life through His Word and His Spirit. This story of a war memorial often reminds me of how believers can be counted as dead in sin but be made alive in Christ:

> The Vietnam Veteran's Memorial is striking for its simplicity. Etched in a black granite wall are the names of 58,156 Americans who died in that war. Since its opening in 1982, the stark monument has stirred deep emotions. Some visitors walk its length slowly, reverently, and without pause. Others stop before certain names,

remembering their son or sweetheart or fellow soldier, wiping away tears, tracing the names with their fingers.

For three Vietnam veterans—Robert Bedker, Willard Craig, and Darrall Lausch—a visit to the memorial must be especially poignant, for they can walk up to the long ebony wall and find their own names carved in the stone. Because of data-coding errors, each of them was incorrectly listed as killed in action.

Dead, but alive—a perfect description of the Christian.[5]

God has some wonderful lists in heaven. One list contains "the certificate of debt consisting of decrees against us" (Col. 2:14). It contains all the curses resulting from sin, all of our weaknesses, bruises, wounds and fears. Your name is on one such list, followed by the phrase "crucified with Christ" (Gal. 2:20). There is another list called the Lamb's book of life (see Rev. 13:8). If you're born again, your name is there as well, followed by the phrase "nevertheless [he/she] live[s]" (Gal. 2:20, KJV). We are, indeed, dead but alive.

Hebrews 4:12 speaks of this life and death and is amazingly rich with promise. A short summary will bless, equip and encourage you in your work of laying siege to the soul. Here are some amplifications:

"The Word of God is *living*" (italics mine). "Living" comes from the Greek word *zao* from *zoe*, which means the life of God—"actively alive."[6] The Word of God is also "*active*" (italics mine). In Greek "active" is *energas*—"working, toiling, operative, effectual, energized."[7] An amplification of the verse to this point might be: "The Word of God is alive—actively alive—it is filled with the life of God and is full of His energy. It toils and works in us and is operative and effectual." In addition, the Word of God is "*piercing*" (italics mine). "Piercing" comes from the word *diikneomai*: from *dia*—"the channel of an act"; and from *hikanos*—"to arrive; competent, ample, attain the desired end, sufficient, adequate, enough."[8]

Let's add this to the amplification we already have: "The Word of God is alive—actively alive—it is filled with the life of God and is full of His energy. It toils and works in us and is operative and effectual. It is sharp enough and is fully competent (adequate, sufficient, ample, has enough ability) to channel itself through the various areas of the soul and spirit, reaching its desired end and attaining its desired goal. It is fully adequate! It will arrive! And it will accomplish its goal once it gets there!"

Wow! What a promise!

Moreover, in "as far as the *division* of soul and spirit" (italics mine), the word "division" comes from *merismos*, which means "a separation and distribution; to divide or disunite; to apportion."[9] The Word of God will *divide* or *separate* the soul and spirit, *distributing* to each what it needs, and the phrase "and able to *judge*" comes from *kritikos*—"to judge or critique."[10]

One more time! "The Word of God is alive—actively alive—it is filled with the life of God and is full of His energy. It toils and works in us and is operative and effectual. It is sharp enough and fully competent (adequate, sufficient, ample, has enough ability) to channel itself through the various areas of the soul and spirit, reaching its desired end and attaining its desired goal. It is fully adequate! It will arrive and will accomplish its goal once it gets there! It will divide between the soul and spirit, apportioning to each what is needed as it critiques the thoughts and intentions of the heart." Now let's add an amplification of verse 13 to the mix: "when necessary it lays the knife to the throat of anything found in the soul that is contrary to His Word."

How's that for laying siege! Yes, as watchmen, we guard the entrance to our souls. But we also deal aggressively with anything already working there that wars against the spirit. With the sword of the Spirit, we drive it out!

A soul that has been transformed—successfully laid siege to—by the Word is a weaned soul. Have you ever heard of a weaned soul? I didn't think so. The Bible speaks of one, however. The word is *gamal*, meaning "ripen, mature, wean."[11] It is sometimes translated "deal bountifully" because when a plant has bountiful provision, it *matures* and the fruit *ripens*. When a baby has bountiful provision, it *matures* and is *weaned*. Psalms 116:7; 131:1-2 and 142:7 use this word to speak of the soul.

"Return to your rest, O my soul, for the Lord has *dealt bountifully* with you" (Ps. 116:7, italics mine).

"O Lord, my heart is not proud, nor my eyes haughty; nor do I involve myself in great matters, or in things too difficult for me. Surely I have composed and quieted my soul; like a *weaned* child rests against his mother, my soul is like a *weaned* child within me" (Ps. 131:1-2, italics mine).

"Bring my soul out of prison, so that I may give thanks to Thy name; the righteous will surround me, for Thou wilt *deal bountifully* with me" (Ps. 142:7, italics mine).

God wants our souls to be well fed by His word, growing strong and maturing to the point that we think the way He thinks. He wants them weaned of pride, carnality and bondages. His desire is for us to lay siege to any strongholds of the enemy there, allowing the sword of His Word to slay all that is opposed to Him. Watchmen are warriors and sometimes the war is within themselves!

Once we have our souls weaned from that which oppresses them, they can be at rest, as stated in the above verses from Psalms 116 and 131. God wants us to have restful souls that truly walk in His peace. If there is a part of your soul that is not yet under the peaceful influence of your Shepherd, the Holy Spirit will help you lay siege to it, freeing you from that stronghold.

Take up your watchman sword and go to war. He guarantees your victory.

THE WATCHMAN'S ALLY

Parting in Our Best Interests

"It is better for you that I leave" is what Jesus told His followers (see John 16:7). What a seemingly ridiculous, asinine statement! After watching Him raise the dead, heal lepers, walk on water, calm raging storms with a word, deliver the insane, pay taxes with fish-mouth money—the list seems endless—can you imagine the shock of the disciples at such a statement?

Of course, He was forever shocking them with His words and actions. They must have thought with surprise and astonishment, "There He goes again!" I can almost see them waiting until He turned His head and then rolling their eyes at one another.

A short time before, He had mentioned going to prepare dwelling places for them in the presence of the Father. "Of course, you know where I'm going," He stated rather matter of factly (John 14:4, Sheets's paraphrase).

"We don't have the slightest idea what you're talking about" (Sheets's paraphrase of John 14:5), Thomas finally had the brass to say. Thank God for Thomas! If he could express his frustration at some of God's words and ways, so can I. (And I do once in a while!)

Peter also spoke out his frustration at times. On a different occasion, he finally had enough of Christ's seemingly confusing words and decided Jesus just needed a good rebuke. Unlike Thomas, he *didn't* get away with it. I suppose the lesson learned is this: plead ignorance with God; disagree even, but don't rebuke Him.

Jesus' declaration in John 16:7 that His leaving would be good for them was probably different, however. It was one thing to see and hear things beyond their comprehension. But when Jesus started talking about suffering, dying or, as in this case, leaving, I imagine that started pushing a few panic buttons.

How could His leaving possibly be advantageous for them? He was God in the flesh, for heaven's sake. The answer lies in two understandings. The first has to do with Christ's choice of the word "advantage," or as the *KJV* says, "expedient." The word is *sumphero* and literally means "to bring together."[1] Since the *bringing* of right things or people *together* produces benefit, advantage or profit, the word was used for these concepts of advantage or expediency.

Christ was saying in essence, "My leaving will cause a new connection, a joining together which will be of tremendous benefit to you . . . yes, of even greater benefit than My actually being here with you."

The second necessary contextual understanding is simply with whom that new connection would be. Jesus was, of course, speaking of the Holy Spirit. "I will bring you together with the Holy Spirit." "This," He was stating, "will be even more *advantageous* than having Me here with you in the flesh. The bodily limitation of My being in only one place at a time will not be so with Him. In fact, not only will He be *with* you, He'll be *in* you. *You will become His body—His hands, feet and mouth! He'll touch through you, speak through you and move through you.*"

I don't think any of us have fully grasped the ramifications of this. Our operative "mere men" (see 1 Cor. 3:3) levels of fruit and power confirm this assertion. Suffice it to say Jesus meant it when He said, "It's better for you if I leave."

Craig Larson offers this illustration:

Consider the power and greatness of the One who created the universe and inhabits every square inch.

Begin with our solar system. At the speed of light,
186,000 miles a second, sunlight takes eight minutes
to reach the earth. That same light takes five more
hours to reach the farthest planet in our solar system,
Pluto. After leaving our solar system that same sunlight must travel for four years and four months to
reach the next star in the universe. That is a distance
of 40 trillion kilometers—mere shoutin' distance in
the universe!

The sun resides in the Milky Way Galaxy, which is
shaped like a flying saucer, flat and with a bulge in the
center. Our sun is roughly three-quarters of the way to
the edge of the galaxy. To get a feel for that distance, if
our solar system were one inch across, the distance to
the center of the Milky Way Galaxy would be 379 miles.
Our galaxy contains hundreds of billions of stars.

Yet the Milky Way is but one of roughly one trillion
galaxies in the universe. Says astronomer Allan Sandage,
"Galaxies are to astronomy what atoms are to physics."

There are twenty galaxies in what is called our local
group. The next sort of grouping in the universe is called
a supercluster of galaxies. Within our supercluster, the
nearest cluster of galaxies, called Virgo, is 50 million
light years away. (A light year is the distance light travels
in one year. To get a feel for the distance of one light
year, if you drove your car at 55 miles per hour, it would
take you 12.2 million years to travel one light year.)

Astronomers estimate that the distance across the
universe is roughly 40 billion light years and that there
are roughly 100 billion trillion stars.

And the Lord Almighty is the Creator of it all.[2]

This God dwells in you! What could we be with true revelation of this? Probably true Christians—little Christs!

Listen to two leading Christian voices describe the work of the Holy Spirit in their lives. Jack Hayford says:

- It is the Spirit who keeps the Word alive, and progressively being "incarnated" in me.

- It is the Spirit who infuses prayer and praise with passion and begets vital faith for the supernatural.

- It is the Spirit who teaches and instructs me so that the "mirror" of the Word shines Jesus in and crowds sin out.

- It is the Spirit who brings gifts and giftedness for power-ministry to my life.

- It is the Spirit who will bring love, graciousness, and a spirit of unity to my heart; so that I not only love the lost and want to see people brought to Christ, but I love all other Christians, and refuse to become an instrument of injury to Christ's body—the Church.[3]

Bill Bright states it this way:

- He guides us (John 16:13), empowers us (Mic. 3:8) and makes us holy (Rom. 15:16). He bears witness in our lives (Rom. 8:16), comforts us (John 14:16-26), gives us joy (Rom. 14:17).

- As our teacher of spiritual truths, the Holy Spirit illuminates our minds with insights into the mind of Christ (1 Cor. 2:12,13) and reveals to us the hidden things of God (Isa. 40:13,14).

- As you are filled with the Holy Spirit, the Bible becomes alive, prayer becomes vital, your witness becomes effective and obedience becomes a joy. Then, as a result of your obedience in these areas, your faith grows and you become more mature in your spiritual life.[4]

Great stuff! The Holy Spirit is all of this and more. And having brought us to this point, I want to make an emphatic and very dogmatic statement. *The single greatest key to eternal success in any Christian endeavor is allowing the full work of the Holy Spirit in and through us.* This is true for our personal growth and development, and it is certainly true concerning all ministry. In spite of this, He is largely ignored and taken for granted.

If we are to become skilled watchmen, we must become increasingly led and instructed by the Holy Spirit. Watchmen watch Him! He was Christ's helper, and He must be ours as well. Jesus was filled with, led, empowered and anointed by the Holy Spirit (see Luke 4). Acts 10:38 again says Christ derived His power from the Holy Spirit, and our power flows from the same source—the Holy Spirit (see Acts 1:8).

In a seminary missions class, Herbert Jackson told how, as a new missionary, he was assigned a car that would not start without a push.

After pondering his problem, he devised a plan. He went to the school near his home, got permission to take some children out of class, and had them push his car off. As he made his rounds, he would either park on a hill or leave his car running. He used this ingenious procedure for two years.

Ill health forced the Jackson family to leave, and a new missionary came to that station. When Jackson proudly began to explain his arrangement for getting the car started, the new man began looking under the hood. Before the explanation was complete, the new missionary interrupted, "Why Dr. Jackson, I believe the only trouble is this loose cable." He gave the cable a twist, stepped into the car, pushed the switch, and to Jackson's astonishment, the engine roared to life.

For two years needless trouble had become routine. The power was there all the time. Only a loose connection kept Jackson from putting the power to work.

J. B. Phillips paraphrases Ephesians 1:19-20, "How tremendous is the power available to us who believe in God." When we make firm our connection with the Holy Spirit, His life and power flow through us.[5]

Our Battle Partner

There are two references in Scripture to the Holy Spirit's being our Helper. One is the aforementioned verse, John 16:7: "But I tell you the truth, it is to your advantage that I go away; for if I do not go away, the *Helper* shall not come to you; but if I go, I will send Him to you." Here the word is *parakletos*, which literally means "called to another's side to aid, help or support."[6] While often used to describe a legal advocate or attorney, it is not limited to this, but includes any and every means of helping.

Another interesting use of the term *parakletos* was in ancient warfare. "Greek soldiers went into battle in pairs so when the enemy attacked, they could draw together back-to-back, covering each other's blind side. One's battle partner was the *paraclete*."[7]

Yes, our greatest partner in battle is the Holy Spirit! As Samson of old, we become more than conquerors when He is our strength.

The Amplified Bible uses no less than seven terms to describe or translate the concept of the Holy Spirit as our *paraclete*: "Comforter, Counselor, Helper, Advocate, Intercessor, Strengthener, Standby." The point is simple yet broad. The Holy Spirit has been sent to help us in every aspect of our life and ministry. *He is the key to success!* We must lean heavily on Him, watchmen.

The second passage that refers to the Holy Spirit's helping us is Romans 8:26: "And in the same way the Spirit also *helps* our weakness; for we do not know how to pray as we should, but the Spirit Himself intercedes for us with groanings too deep for words" (italics mine). The Greek word is *sunantilambonomai*. It is a compound word made up of three words. *Sun* means "together with"; *anti*, "against"; and *lambano*, "to take hold of."[8] Putting them together, a very literal meaning of the word would be "take hold of together with against."

How's that for help?!

In situations where we're experiencing difficulty in obtaining results, the Holy Spirit wants to take hold of the situation with us, adding His strength to ours. He also wants to help or take hold with us by directing us how to pray, "for we know not what we should pray for as we ought" (Rom. 8:26, *KJV*).

Although the context of 2 Corinthians 12:9 is not prayer, praying in the Spirit is perhaps the greatest example of when His strength is made complete in our weaknesses. Realizing our weaknesses and our inability to produce results causes us to look to Him for help. If we allow Him to pray through us, He will take hold together with us. We just have to believe that when the Holy Spirit takes hold, something is going to move!

Please notice that both the word "helps" and its literal definition "takes hold *together* with against" imply not that He is doing it *for* us but *with* us. In other words, this isn't something the Holy Spirit is simply doing in us, with or without our participation. No, we involve Him by praying in the Spirit, which is actually allowing Him to pray through us.

As I shared in *Intercessory Prayer*, several years ago my wife, Ceci, developed a pain in her abdomen. An ovarian cyst was discovered, and she was advised to have surgery. However, her doctor was a believer and, being confident this was not life threatening, agreed to give us two months to pursue healing through prayer.

We prayed for Ceci with every biblical method we knew of: laying on of hands, elders anointing her with oil, the prayer of agreement, etc. No change in her condition occurred, and I realized we were going to have to obtain this healing through perseverance and laying hold by faith (see 1 Tim. 6:12). That, by the way, is the way most answers to prayer come—not as instant miracles, but through fighting the fight of faith and patience. This perseverance is part of the watchman concept of laying siege. Most of the time we need this long-term siege mentality. For a fuller treatment of why persistence is needed in prayer, I strongly encourage you to read chapter 12 in my book *Intercessory Prayer*.

I felt I needed to spend an hour a day praying for Ceci. I began my prayer times by stating my reason for approaching the Father. Then I referred to the Scriptures on which I was basing my petition. I would quote them, thanking the Father for His Word and Jesus for providing healing. This usually took no more than five or six minutes. I prayed in the Spirit for the remainder of the hour. This siege went on for a month.

After a couple of weeks of this, one afternoon the Lord showed me a picture as I was praying in the Spirit. I saw myself holding this cyst in my hand, squeezing the life out of it. I did not yet know that the literal meaning of "helps" in Romans 8 was "taking hold of together with against," but the Holy Spirit was teaching me a wonderful truth.

I knew, of course, that I couldn't really get my hands on the cyst; but He was showing me that as I allowed Him to pray through me, He was taking hold with me against the thing. Obviously, it was His power making the difference.

It sort of reminds me of the mouse and the elephant who were best friends. They hung out together all the time, the mouse riding on the elephant's back. One day they crossed a wooden bridge, causing it to bow, creak and sway under their combined weight. After they were across, the mouse, impressed over their ability to make such an impact, said to the elephant, "We sure shook up that bridge, didn't we?"

Kind of reminds me of some of our advertisements and testimonials. You'd think He was the mouse and we were the elephant. (Maybe that's why we don't shake many bridges.)

After seeing the picture of myself squeezing the life out of the cyst, I asked Ceci if there was any change in her condition. "Yes, the pain is decreasing," she informed me.

The doctor's response was "If the pain is decreasing, the cyst must be shrinking. Keep doing whatever it is you're doing." The siege was working.

I tried hard to make sure I wasn't conjuring up any mental images, but twice more the Holy Spirit showed me this same picture. Each time the cyst was smaller. The last of them, which was the third time overall, was about a month into the process. In the picture the cyst was about the size of a quarter, and as I prayed, it vanished in my hand. I knew the Lord was letting me know the work was finished. Even though Ceci said there was still a very small amount of discomfort, I could not bring myself to pray about it any further. I knew it was done.

Three days later she informed me that all the pain and discomfort was gone. The subsequent ultrasound confirmed what we already knew in our hearts—no more cyst! The watchman anointing was a major part of this wonderful healing.

The Many Roles of the Holy Spirit

One further reference and some amplified definitions will give us even more insight into the role of our Helper. Second Corinthians 13:14 says, "The grace of the Lord Jesus Christ, and the love of God, and the *fellowship of the Holy Spirit*, be with you all." The word "fellowship" here is *koinonia* and is rich with meaning, as can be seen in the following definitions:

Fellowship; Communion

The word *koinonia* implies that the Holy Spirit wants intimacy with us. This very word is used in 1 Corinthians 10:16 to describe the Lord's table, the bread and the wine. This is appropriate since it is the Lord's shed blood and broken body that bring us into covenantal, intimate *communion* with Him.

The Holy Spirit wants to commune with us. He has much to say if we learn to listen. He is the means to all revelation from God. He is the Teacher. He is a part of the Godhead we're to be in relationship with. Let Him fellowship and commune with you.

At times His fellowship with you requires no speaking. Some communion is heart to heart.

Rowell provides this illustration:

In his book *Good Morning Merry Sunshine*, Chicago Tribune columnist Bob Greene chronicles his infant daughter's first year of life. When little Amanda began crawling, he records: "This is something I'm having trouble getting used to. I will be in bed reading a book or watching TV. And I will look down at the foot of the bed and there will be Amanda's head staring back at me.

"Apparently I've become one of the objects that fascinates her. . . . It's so strange. After months of having to go to her, now she is choosing to come to me. I don't know quite how to react. All I can figure is that she likes the idea of coming in and looking at me. She doesn't expect anything in return. I'll return her gaze and in a few minutes she'll decide she wants to be back in the living room and off she'll crawl again."

The simple pleasure of looking at the one you love
is what we enjoy each time we worship God and bask in
His presence.[9]

At times I crawl up to God for a look. Just knowing He is
looking back is enough. At other times He shares His heart
while I'm gazing.

There is an amazing picture of this sort of intimacy in the
following Scriptures:

- For the devious are an abomination to the Lord; but He
  is *intimate* with the upright (Prov. 3:32, italics mine).

- The *secret* of the Lord is for those who fear Him, and
  He will make them know His covenant (Ps. 25:14, italics mine).

The words "secret" and "intimacy" are translated from the
same Hebrew word *cowd*, which means "couch, cushion or pillow."[10] The picture is one of two intimate friends seated on a
couch, sharing their most intimate thoughts with one another. Or perhaps of a wife and husband sharing a pillow, conversing intimately.

"Do you really think God wants that kind of relationship,
Sheets?" you may be asking.

Absolutely! Abraham was His friend. David was a man after God's heart (see 1 Sam. 13:14). If that didn't mean so much
to the Lord, why did He share it three times in Scripture? Enoch
walked with Him until God took him on to heaven (see Gen.
5:22,24). The disciples were called His friends (see John 15:15).

We can be His friends, too.

Several years ago, I was ministering in Toronto. My last
morning there, as I was packing my bags and thinking about
my final session, I was also visiting with the Holy Spirit. I wasn't

in intercession, and it wasn't during my quiet time. It was simply communing while working, sharing some of my inner thoughts with Him, much the same way I might have done with my wife had she been there.

Suddenly He spoke to me. It was as natural and matter of fact as if two friends were sharing their hearts. "Japan is really on My heart this morning," the Holy Spirit said.

This surprised me because I've never thought about God's having one place on His heart more than others. I've always figured He had *every place* on His heart all the time. And the phrase "on My heart" surprised me as well. It was more than on His mind; this was something deeper—very important to Him. I felt as though He were letting me into His very heart.

He then said to me, "I must have Japan. It is a gate to Asia and I must have it. There is tremendous warfare over the nation right now. Would you pray for Japan this morning in your session?"

How do you like that?! Not a command, "Pray for Japan," but a question, "Would you?" He was *asking* me!

"Of course we will, Holy Spirit," I said. "We would be honored to do that." And we did! Such an anointing and burden came upon the assembly—tears, travail, intense intercession. It went on for about 45 minutes, at which time I had to leave for the airport. They continued—how long I do not know.

God brought tremendous insight to us in that session of how to pray for Japan. He spoke to us prophetically some promises to lay hold of and to declare over the nation. It was glorious. I'm told that somehow many believers in Japan have heard about it and been very encouraged. Japan will be saved! (I'm not implying this only because of our prayers that day. I simply have strong faith concerning this nation.)

This watching and subsequent intercession were born out of fellowship with the Holy Spirit.

Dutch Sheets

Sharing Together; Participation in or with Something or Someone

The Holy Spirit wants to share His strength, power, wisdom and information with us. He is desirous of participating with us in life's endeavors. He certainly wants to participate with us in our prayer lives.

Paul Grabill interviewed Eric Harrah, who, prior to his conversion to Christ in 1997, had been the second largest abortion provider in the United States. Harrah recalls how the supernatural working of the Holy Spirit through Steve Stupar played a part in his decision:

> "A week before I gave my life back to Christ, we were sitting at a restaurant and Steve said he wanted to confirm three things the Holy Spirit had revealed to him. He asked me if the name John meant anything to me; I replied it was my grandfather's name. He asked if I knew a girl in a plaid outfit and a white shirt; I knew that was my sister because my grandfather had a picture of her in that school outfit. I wasn't too impressed, though, because everyone knew my grandfather and that I had a sister.
>
> "Then he said the Holy Spirit had revealed to him a plate that had blue pills with white bands on it, and wanted to know if that meant anything to me. I denied it at first, but later called him and told him its significance. About a week before, after coming home with joint pains, I decided to take some pain medication. As I went to take one of my blue pills with the white band, I said to myself, *Enough is enough—tonight is a good night to die*. I dumped all the blue pills onto a plate; then got my other medication and dumped all of them on the plate too. As I started to put the first pill in my mouth, my

dog barked and looked at me as if to say, Who's going to take care of me? I knew nobody would, so I put the pills back in their containers.

"It was amazing to me that the Holy Ghost revealed such details to him. I knew it was time to give in."

One reason God gives us the power of the Holy Spirit is to help us win lost people to Christ.[11]

Watchmen learn to *partner* with Him, and partnership with the Holy Spirit causes their prayer success rate to climb significantly!

Distribution; Impart

The Holy Spirit desires to *distribute*, or *impart*, to us all that we need to function well in life and certainly as watchmen. This verse, 2 Corinthians 13:14, is saying, "May the Holy Spirit impart to you," "May He distribute to you," of His vast resources and gifts.

I love it when the Holy Spirit distributes revelation to me as I study His Word. I then take great joy in distributing it to others.

I find it very fulfilling when, through the power of the Holy Spirit, I am used to impart a spiritual gift or perhaps power for healing to another person. Paul spoke of this in Romans 1:11: "For I long to see you in order that I may impart some spiritual gift to you, that you may be established." He also said Timothy received spiritual gifts through impartation (see 1 Tim. 4:14 and 2 Tim. 1:6). Moses imparted to Joshua a spirit of wisdom (see Deut. 34:9).

How would a human being have the ability to impart a spiritual gift if not by the power of the Holy Spirit? Does this still happen today? Of course it does.

The Holy Spirit wants to impart to us, as watchmen, information that will help us in our prayers. Jane Hamon tells of a dream He gave to her, bringing information that helped save their church from great problems:

> I once dreamed that someone poisoned the leader of our ministry with the intent of killing him. He did not die, but became very sick. As pastors of the church, my husband and I stood up to ask for special prayer on behalf of our leader. Before we could pray, however, someone came running up and whispered in my ear that we shouldn't announce what had happened because the person who had done the poisoning was right in our church. No one's name was mentioned.
>
> When I awakened from the dream I felt concerned. I recorded the dream and began to pray about what it meant. I felt that it was indicating a spiritual attack that was coming against not only the leader, but the ministry as well and that its intent was to bring death; not only physical death, but a death of the vision as well. This death would come as a result of a poisoning of minds and would be perpetuated from within. I examined my heart right away to see if the Lord would show me anything in my heart that could be poisoning me.
>
> Before 9:00 A.M. that morning I received two phone calls. One was from one of our church intercessors who had been praying and felt that the Lord had showed him that there was a spiritual infiltration in our church and that it was trying to bring death. He specifically mentioned the name of our leader but felt that the whole church was being affected as well. The second phone call was similar, but this individual had a dream that revealed a spirit of death coming against our church.
>
> My dream, plus the two additional confirmations to what I felt the dream meant caused us to begin to

pray as a church and war against the plans of the enemy. Since we don't wrestle against flesh and blood, but against a spiritual foe, this is where the battle was won (see Eph. 6:12).[12]

Partaking

This is a logical follow-up to the previous definition. The Holy Spirit not only wants to distribute and impart to us, He wants us to partake of Him. If we will not partake, He cannot impart. Much of what He wants to give is missed because of unbelief and ignorance.

Read the verse again with faith: "May you partake of the Holy Spirit!" What a statement! Let's draw from Him daily—strength, ability, compassion, power and an ability to watch.

Quin Sherrer tells of a friend who partook of the Holy Spirit's ability to watch for her possessions:

> I was rooming with Ruthie at a Christian conference when she told me how God had protected her property. One night during the church service she heard a voice: "Your house is being robbed." She tried to dismiss the thought. She'd lived in that house for thirty years and there had been no burglaries in her neighborhood. But the more she thought about it, the more it seemed to her that the inner voice she had heard was the Holy Spirit warning her.
>
> "Lord, if our house is being robbed, please send an angel—no, Lord, send a warring angel—to frighten the burglar off." Then she began to quote Scriptures, praying for protection: "No evil will come near our dwelling place. . . . No weapon formed against us shall prosper. . . ."
>
> Sure enough, when she and her husband arrived home, their back patio door was smashed in and

everything inside was in disarray—drawers open and stuff scattered everywhere. The next day, when the police officer came to get a list of the things they knew were missing, all they had to report was one pillow case. He told them that's what a burglar usually takes to stash the valuables. "As far as we can tell nothing is missing—not even my good gold jewelry," Ruthie told him.

He looked around at her china, silver, gold vases. "With all these beautiful things, I don't understand why you weren't robbed blind. Something obviously frightened away the intruder. He left in a hurry," the policeman said.

Two other houses in her neighborhood were robbed that night. Ruthie is sure God sent a warring angel of protection, as she had prayed and asked Him to do.[13]

Partake of the Holy Spirit's love and communion, yes. But also draw on His supernatural ability to protect that which belongs to you.

Partnership; Companionship

What an amazing thought! The Holy Spirit is saying to us, "I want to be your partner and companion. Allow Me to partner with you in your prayer life. Let me be your companion as you walk through the Word each day. Let me join with you in this calling to be a watchman. We can accomplish much together!" Wow!

Bob Beckett, whom we've already mentioned as one of the Hemet, California, pastors used to impact that city, shares of many situations where the Holy Spirit supernaturally gave the correct strategy for prayer. Until they learned to listen for that strategy, allowing the Holy Spirit to be their watchman partner, the fruit was very limited. Beckett says:

We knew the value of prayer. We knew how to bind demonic forces. We were willing to put in the time and energy. We did not have enough understanding, however, of what our enemy was doing to hold Hemet in bondage. We did not know how to aim our prayers in such a way as to destroy Satan's strongholds—fortresses that exist both in the mind and in particular locations.

The first thing we had to do was find out the Lord's agenda for our community. What was it He wanted us to tackle in our warfare praying? How were we to approach various problems? What was God's highest priority in our town? If we wanted to see His Kingdom come and His will be done in Hemet, we needed to know what His will was.[14]

As they grew in their ability to follow the Holy Spirit's directives, things began to change rapidly. Beckett goes on to say:

An understanding of "smart bomb praying"—prayers armed with warheads of specific information regarding issues of darkness within our community—moved us into strategic-level intercession, delivering smart bomb prayers on behalf of a geographical location (in our case, Hemet). And as The Dwelling Place [our church] moved toward accurate, strategic-level praying, we began to find out what really—and I mean *really*—was going on in our city.

The Lord revealed more and more to us as we prayed. Because we knew where problems had the greatest grip and why those areas were more affected, we learned what we were hitting with our prayers. After a while, when we prayed, we could go back and evaluate our progress. If we did not see significant changes, we knew to go back and pray some more.

Eventually we started seeing breakthroughs in our community. Nothing has fulfilled me more as a pastor than watching this city I love so dearly become more infiltrated with the Kingdom of God. God allowed us to arrive at the place where we could employ smart bomb strategies in our intercession.[15]

Smart bomb strategies in intercession come from the smart Holy Spirit, not smart Christians. We don't know enough to function as watchmen without Him. Let your Prayer Partner help!

Time Never Wasted

Koinonia means not only partnership but companionship as well. Let me say, without fear of error, that God longs for and craves companionship with us. That's why He made us. It's why Jesus came—to redeem us back into relationship with Him. Let it happen.

In *The Effective Father*, Gordon MacDonald shares a story that exemplifies the nature of companionship:

It is said of Boswell, the famous biographer of Samuel Johnson, that he often referred to a special day in his childhood when his father took him fishing. The day was fixed in his mind, and he often reflected upon many things his father had taught him in the course of their fishing experience together.

After having heard of that particular excursion so often, it occurred to someone much later to check the journal that Boswell's father kept and determine what had been said about the fishing trip from the parental perspective. Turning to that date, the reader found only

one sentence entered: "Gone fishing today with my son;
a day wasted."[16]

Do you consider time spent with Him wasted? He doesn't!
And neither do wise watchmen.

10

WATCHMEN AREN'T WATCHDOGS

※⟡※

The Day My Dog TP'd the Yard

Mercedes. I have one. No, not a car or a sports utility van—she's a dog. A big boxer my wife and daughters named Mercedes. I just called her "One More." We already had two small dogs, Cocoa and Missy. We felt "led" to get a big dog because the rural area we recently moved to has coyotes and foxes, and our two small dogs look like coyote and fox food.

So along came Mercedes. The protector! Man's best friend. (Excuse me, ladies, "*People's* best friend.") Cocoa and Missy's bodyguard.

It didn't take long for Mercedes to establish herself as the tormenting, *"I'm still a puppy—let me see what I can get into"* bodyguard. The two small dogs begged us to get rid of her. We could see it in their eyes. By the time she was nine months old and 65 pounds, they pleaded with us to excommunicate her, not fully understanding the eating habits of coyotes and foxes. Well, maybe they did. Perhaps they saw it as a way out.

Mercedes loves to assert her dominance over the smaller dogs. One of the ways that she does this is standing over them—literally. She straddles them, positioning herself over and around them, stating in essence, "I'm in charge here." Of course, she doesn't hurt them. She doesn't have to; they obey her quickly. Once in a while she sits on them lightly, just to emphasize her dominance.

Not long ago, she did it to me. I was lying face down on the floor when she came, straddled me and sat down with her posterior on mine. Fixing a proud, assertive look on her face, she stared from me, to Ceci, to the kids. We all knew what she was saying, "I'm in charge here. Don't think for a minute that you are the head of this household."

Once she was even on the roof with me—yes, the roof. I was hanging Christmas lights and went through Hannah's bedroom window to get to the roof. The next thing I knew, there she was, inspecting my work and giving me one of those "Do you know what you're doing?" looks. You'd think she would have been scared. No way. I had to chase her all over the roof to capture and remove her. I'm now known in the neighborhood as the guy who chases dogs on roofs.

Ceci and the girls finally took her to obedience school. I think it worked—they came home barking (bear with my humor).

One day Mercedes TP'd (toilet papered) the yard of our previous home. No, I'm not kidding. She TP'd my yard! I saw this trail of toilet paper leaving the powder room (for all you guys, that's a half-bathroom kept clean all the time for guests), leading to the patio doors. Because the backyard was fenced, we sometimes left the door open so the dogs (Cocoa, Missy and Mercedes the Tormenting Protector) could wander in and out.

It was beautiful. You wouldn't think a dog could make such designs: figure eights, donuts, stripes and much more—real works of art. My neighbors couldn't believe a dog really did it, that is, until they saw her proudly standing guard over her work. She wouldn't let me clean it up for days.

I've had my church TP'd a few times. Well, not exactly, not with toilet paper. But believe me, I've had some major sheep messes to clean up. I have a sign in my office: "TP Happens." Some of those messy sheep were intercessors. They would probably consider themselves watchmen. Watchdogs would be more accurate. Most of my intercessors are wonderful, and I certainly don't throw out the good with the bad; but nonetheless, I've known some real, as I heard one person state it, "granola" intercessors: fruits, flakes and nuts.

Some so-called watchmen see demons behind every tree, have visions daily and dream "prophetic" dreams every night. They're downright scary and they give true watchman intercessors a bad name. My advice to pastors and leaders is not to reject the prophetic, including watching intercessors, just because of a few strange ones. In spite of the strange ones, I agree with Bob Beckett: "It is a wise pastor who understands and encourages the intercessors of the congregation to use their God-given gifts to help him or her fulfill the position of gatekeeper."[1]

Sensible Watchmen

The purpose of this chapter is to give practical instruction that will help keep us balanced and make our gifts a blessing. As watchmen, we must ask ourselves at least three major questions when processing information that comes to us supernaturally.

- Is the information from God? (In other words, we must discern the source.)

- What does it mean? (We must interpret the information correctly.)

- What do I do with it? (We must determine the course of action.)

Whether it comes in the form of voices, impressions, visions or dreams, all information must be carefully tested. Perhaps you are considering a dream. The first obvious round of questions consists of these: Was it given by the Holy Spirit, or did it originate in the subconscious mind? It may have even come from a demon. How can we be certain a revelation, warning or prompting is from the Holy Spirit and not our own imagination or fears?

Dr. Freda Lindsay tells of an important dream from the Holy Spirit, which was almost overlooked:

> After paying out the property we had purchased behind Christian Center, we were now ready to launch into the construction of the headquarters for Christ For The Nations and the printing building. Actually, we were overcrowded in every department to say the least.
>
> Throughout the Bible there are instances where God spoke to individuals through dreams. One such experience came to me the night of November 13, 1968. I dreamed that the men who were constructing our new headquarters building were placing it at the wrong end of the property. After a bit I woke up, fell asleep again and dreamed virtually the same dream. Again I woke up, fell asleep and dreamed the same dream the third time.
>
> When morning came I couldn't figure out what it was all about, as I was sure the contractor knew exactly which end of the property to put the building on. And so I dismissed it from my mind.
>
> We were leaving in two days to take a tour group to Israel. The day before leaving, Gordon and I drove over to the building site. As I stood there looking at the pegs outlining the location of the building, I was surprised to see that it was at the opposite end of the property from where we had planned it. I mentioned this to Gordon and he calmly remarked, "Oh, these are no doubt just preliminary stakes and have nothing to do with the location of the building."

> Suddenly recalling the three dreams I had had the night before, I said to Gordon, "Let's talk to the foreman."
>
> To our amazement he confirmed what I suspected. He had misunderstood, and was actually putting the building at the opposite end of the property from where we wanted it. This would have caused no end of problems as we needed the print shop loading docks next to the street. The warning dream had come just in time![2]

A mistake that seemed too outlandish to be true was, indeed, being made. Had Dr. Lindsay not given credence to the dream, great problems would have resulted.

While we don't want to say every impression that comes to us is from God, we also don't want to ignore promptings of the Spirit out of naiveté or fear of being wrong. First Thessalonians 5:21 instructs us to "Examine everything carefully; hold fast to that which is good." The word "examine" is *dokimazo*, which means to put something to the test or put it on trial.[3] The context is receiving supernatural information. The preceding verses warn not to quench the Spirit or despise prophecy. The Holy Spirit's balanced instruction to us is, "Don't be afraid of the subjective realm of supernatural revelation. At the same time, don't buy everything that comes along. Test it."

Acid Tests

There are three basic ways we judge revelation: (1) the Scriptures, (2) wise counsel, and (3) confirmation.

The Scriptures

The Word of God is the absolute authority in the life of a Christian. Any alleged revelation that contradicts the Bible is not from the Holy Spirit. For example, if someone told me God led him or her to leave their current spouse in order to marry another—and they have—I would know immediately they were deceived. The Holy Spirit who wrote Matthew 19:6 wouldn't contradict it: "Consequently they are no longer two, but one flesh. What therefore God has joined together, let no man separate."

Beth Alves says in her book *Becoming a Prayer Warrior*, "Satan does not want you to hear God's voice because your partnership with the Lord can wreak havoc on his kingdom."[4] She goes on to share 13 excellent guidelines to hearing the voice of God and eight ways to test what is heard. My purpose in this chapter isn't to thoroughly teach how to hear from God. It would be presumptive of me, if not foolish, to give such a cursory treatment to such an important subject. My intent is simply to share a few guidelines and boundaries for us as watchmen.

I would strongly encourage you to study books such as *Becoming a Prayer Warrior* by Beth Alves, *Listen, God Is Speaking to You* by Quin Sherrer and *The Voice of God* by Cindy Jacobs, as these are wonderfully complete and balanced teachings on how to hear God speak. We often don't want to take the time to do something such as this, but to ignore this responsibility is a sure way to create problems. The following story is all too true:

> In *The Essential Calvin and Hobbes* by Bill Watterson, the cartoon character Calvin says to his tiger friend, Hobbes, "I feel bad that I called Susie names and hurt her feelings. I'm sorry I did it."
>
> "Maybe you should apologize to her," Hobbes suggests.
>
> Calvin ponders this for a moment and replies, "I keep hoping there's a less obvious solution."[5]

Some messes made by irresponsible Christians have obvious solutions. While the Bible is the number one measure by which we judge all information, there are times, however, when

Scripture will not specifically answer the question of whether or not a revelation is of God. Still, the information must harmonize with the general wisdom, ways and character of God in the Word. An example of such a situation is when we receive a caution concerning another person.

In these types of situations, where there is no direct Scripture to validate a word, we should ask ourselves questions such as:

- Does this person bringing the warning seem to have a critical spirit? The Holy Spirit never aligns Himself with the accuser of the brethren.

- Does this person have a proven track record in being able to discern things such as this?

- Is there a legitimate reason why the Holy Spirit would warn me about this person? If there is no potential for involvement with an individual, the Holy Spirit probably wouldn't give information that would affect my trust or acceptance of them.

- Is the warning confirmed by what I perceive in my heart?

- Has anyone else confirmed this caution?

We can see that even where Scripture doesn't give literal answers to our questions, the principles and wisdom it contains are always applicable.

Wise Counsel

The second way of determining the source of information is wise counsel. If we are walking in biblical principles of relationship and accountability, God always has individuals in our lives that can give us sound advice. It is never wise to act on subjective revelation without seeking the wisdom of others, especially if the Scriptures don't address in a literal way what is revealed.

We are all susceptible to prejudices, traditions, past paradigms, misinterpretation of Scripture and, yes, even demonic spirits, all of which can cause us to be misled. True humility is the willingness to allow others to help judge our leanings, leadings and revelations.

I was given a word of warning from a supposed watchman a few years back about another person. I was told, "That individual is a witch. You need to get her out of the church."

I do experience a lot of spiritual warfare, and I know I've had witches in our services, trying to cause problems. Of course, I don't like this and I certainly don't want any to infiltrate our church, becoming "plants" working against us behind the scenes. I did not bear witness with this warning, however, and absolutely didn't want to falsely accuse a sincere person. I have seen people terribly bruised by false accusations of this sort.

What did I do? I sought wise counsel and discreetly asked other discerning people to pray with me. We decided the Lord was telling us this person wasn't a witch, and we disregarded the warning word. As it turns out, she is a wonderful, sincere Christian with a very real, serving heart. Wise counsel is invaluable.

Confirmation

The third way we judge whether or not a revelation or warning is from the Holy Spirit is by asking God for confirmation. I received a strong warning from an intercessor several years ago that a certain individual in ministry was going to die unless steps were taken to help him. The first question I had to answer was, "Is this serious warning from God?"

I asked God for confirmation. Within a week, two more individuals gave me the same warning about the same person, and none of the three people had spoken with the others or heard about their warnings. I had my confirmations.

On another occasion, a prophetic intercessor told me she felt very strongly that I was wrong in rejecting a certain invitation to speak. God confirmed this person's word to me within a week through two other watchmen telling me the same thing. None of them had spoken with each other or had knowledge of the others' warnings. I took the meeting!

This, unlike the death warning, wasn't a life-or-death situation, but it certainly was a word that kept me from missing God's plan for my ministry. Tremendous fruit resulted from that meeting, which would have been missed had I not received and heeded the warning and confirmations.

What Does This Mean?

After we have confirmed that information given to us is indeed from God, we need to ask ourselves, *What does this mean?*

- Is the information symbolic or literal?

- Is this something happening currently or a warning about the future?

- And often in order to determine the proper meaning, we must ask ourselves, *Am I the one who should interpret this information?*

Symbolic or Literal

A few years ago I had a dream, which I knew was from the Holy Spirit. It involved President Clinton, my state of Colorado and myself. It isn't necessary to share the details, but it had symbolic aspects to it and the dream seemed very important. Because I do not feel gifted at interpreting dreams, I asked others to help me and received what I believe was an accurate interpretation. There is wisdom in asking for help in understanding information given to us by the Spirit.

I mentioned previously three warnings concerning the potential death of a fellow minister. One of the warnings came in
the form of a detailed dream. In the dream this individual fell
into what appeared to be a mud puddle but was actually a deep
pit. The only part of his body sticking out of the pit was a foot
with a wool sock on it.

Not feeling competent to fully understand the dream and
its symbolism myself, I asked for help. I knew that three separate
warnings surely indicated the accuracy and seriousness of this
situation. The person interpreting the dream knew from several
details it was a warning about death, but also drew significant
insight from the picture of the wool sock. The man in danger
was a pastor, but the wool sock was a reminder that he was also
a sheep, not just a shepherd, and needed to be carefully pastored
through this time. This was done, the man's life was saved and I
am pleased to say he is well and still in ministry today.

Relating this to the above questions, I first determined that
I was *not* the person to interpret some of the information. Second, we concluded that the warning was definitely for the present. And third, there was symbolic information, which needed
to be interpreted.

Correct Application of Time, Person and Place

Sometimes watchmen receive words from the Holy Spirit and
have difficulty discerning the timing. I have received warnings
from them about situations they thought to be current, which
in reality were concerning the future. Had we not discerned
this, we would have discarded the warnings altogether because
they made no sense at the time they were issued.

One such event several years ago involved an intercessor encouraging me that "the strife among our leadership team was
going to be taken care of by the Lord." She assured me she was
praying about it and had peace that God was intervening.

I wasn't aware of any strife among our team members at the time and was confused. I also grew somewhat alarmed because she was so adamant and is usually accurate. Upon quizzing my staff—even pressing the issue—they all assured me, and finally convinced me, that there were no problems among us.

The Holy Spirit, however, showed us that actually what she was discerning by the Spirit was a future but imminent attack by Satan to divide us. We were then able to pray against it and be alert, watching for it. The attack did come, but it wasn't successful because of the warning of the Holy Spirit and preventive prayer.

I'm certain many warnings from the Holy Spirit are not heeded simply because, like the above story, they didn't make sense at the time or were not properly interpreted. These two things can also result in distrust between the giver and the recipient of the warning.

I experienced another situation in which a lady believed she was alerted that adultery existed in a minister's life. When praying for this minister, she kept hearing the word "adultery." As it turned out, the minister wasn't involved in adultery at all, but Satan had a plan in place to try to snare him in this area. It was exposed and unsuccessful. God was alerting her to what the enemy was *planning*, not what the pastor was *doing*, so she could pray against it.

It is easy to see how words such as these could be misinterpreted and cause great confusion and serious problems. They must be handled very carefully and often with the help of mature leaders.

What to Do with the Information

The last questions that need to be answered when a watchman believes he or she has received information from the Lord are the following:

- What do I do with this information?
- Do I tell anyone else?
- Do I inform leaders?
- Do I alert the person(s) involved?
- Do I simply pray and say nothing?

There have been instances when intercessors came to me with warnings I wish they had never shared. Had they simply prayed for me and not distracted me with the information, it would have been much more beneficial.

For example, there is spiritual warfare happening most of the time in a church or ministry that is making a true impact against the enemy. Satan relentlessly seeks to distract, discourage and destroy what they are doing. So when a watchman comes to me with the warning "Pastor, I feel there is spiritual warfare taking place against us at this time," my first thought is usually *Of course there is.*

I really don't want to be bothered with general statements such as this all the time. The watchmen are probably perceiving correctly, but they do not need to burden me with the information. The Holy Spirit is most likely trying to awaken them to pray against the attacks.

There are other times when leaders definitely need to be informed. On one occasion, I received a warning during a Wednesday evening service that there was spiritual warfare coming against us. I thanked the person that gave the warning and ho-hummed in my mind. Then a second person came with the same warning. I still wasn't too alarmed, but I thought that now it might merit being brought before the congregation for prayer.

When I mentioned it, not with any real gravity, another person in the service raised his hand and asked permission to speak. I knew him well enough to allow him to share and he informed us, "I received a call from a friend in another city today who told me he felt like our church was coming into a major attack of warfare."

My ho-hum turned into an uh-oh. Three warnings in one day, including one from a person in another city, were enough to convince me that this was a major attack. We went into immediate prayer.

I recall the meeting very well. It turned into a very precious time of intercession, but it was also a spiritual bonding among our congregation. Before the night was over, many of them formed a circle around the leadership team and prayed a strong barrier of protection around us.

The attack of the enemy failed and God turned the situation into something positive for our fellowship. What Satan meant for division and disruption became unifying and edifying.

Often watchmen also need to decide whether to alert other intercessors or just to pray themselves. Much damage can come if certain information is shared with immature or indiscreet people. Any information that would damage another's reputation or bring division to a group of people should only be disclosed to those with the God-given responsibility of dealing with it. And information that is unproven or unconfirmed should only be shared with responsible leaders and then only after much prayer.

Cindy Jacobs's book *Possessing the Gates of the Enemy* is an excellent watchman resource. She makes the following point concerning this issue:

> Pray that God will teach you the proper time and place to sound the alarm. God reveals to intercessors the intimate needs of those for whom we intercede. This is a precious trust. The things God shares with us are not to be told to others. Many prayer groups are nothing more than spiritual gossip sessions. If God reveals another

person's weaknesses to you, you need to: Ask for confirmation first to see if you have heard the need accurately. You do not want to pray amiss. If you are sure you are praying accurately, then you need to ask God whether or not to tell the person what you have learned. If you are to tell the person, then pray that God will prepare his or her heart to be receptive.

Many times you will never say anything to the persons for whom you have prayed. God will speak to them in His time and way. This is the most effective means of dealing with weaknesses in those for whom we have prayed. When God tells them they need to change, it does not cause them to feel embarrassed, rejected or wounded.

There are times to sound the alarm to others in your prayer group when you see a danger about to occur in your local church body. If this is the case, go to someone in a spiritual leadership position and share your prayer concern. Leave any further sharing in his or her hands.[6]

A watchman in our church received a word for me a few years back, which wasn't a very pleasant one to give. She struggled over whether or not to share it with me. The Lord ultimately was able to convince her she should. The word spoke of four things in my life God wanted to deal with and remove.

This intercessor didn't like giving the word, and I didn't particularly enjoy receiving it; but it was necessary. The Lord used her to do this because:

- we had an established relationship of trust;
- she could be trusted to tell no one else;
- she did not have a critical, judgmental spirit, but rather came in humility, which helped enable me to receive it;

- she prays for my wife and me regularly;
- she is mature enough not to be disillusioned by weakness in a leader;
- she was bold enough—once she was certain the Holy Spirit was directing her—to bring me the word.

These were not sins of rebellion, immorality, dishonesty or anything else of that nature. They were subtle weaknesses that I couldn't even see at the time, nor could she. "I don't see these things in you," she told me. "But I feel strongly the Lord gave them to me concerning you."

I informed her I didn't see them either, but I believed in her enough to earnestly seek the Lord concerning them. Within a month, God had showed all four of them to me. He and I have been working on them and will continue to do so, if necessary. In this case, the word needed to be shared with me, not just prayed over.

What a blessing this watchman word was to me! Had I not received it, who knows what snares the enemy might have laid for me at some point in time? Thank God for the watchman anointing and a watchman who knew what to do with it.

God has established this precious anointing and high calling in the Church. My prayer is that you will receive it and walk in it daily.

Much is at stake. Our gardens must be protected and preserved from the serpent and his demons. In the words of Nehemiah, "Do not be afraid of them; remember the Lord who is great and awesome, and fight for your brothers, your sons, your daughters, your wives, and your houses" (Neh. 4:14).

Rise up, watchmen, and take your position on the wall. There are cities to be protected, people to be covered and a harvest to be reaped and preserved.

The grandstands of heaven are filled with a great cloud of witnesses, cheering us on as we press toward the mark. Some have paid in blood for the truth we now enjoy and for the incredible spiritual momentum we have had handed to us as a generation.

We must not fail them or the precious Lamb who paid for it all. And we need not fail, if we answer the call. Pick up the sword, watchmen!

11

ESTABLISHING A
PRAYER MINISTRY

Guidelines for Prayer

Many churches have implemented watchman prayer into the various facets of their ministries by organizing and establishing several groups of watchmen so that their church, leadership and ministries are covered in prayer. Specific intercessory teams focus on one particular group or area, such as the leaders, the church's prophetic words, special events, the various departments of the church, each service, outreaches, their cities and the nation.

Dr. Terry Teykl's books *Pray the Price, Blueprint for the House of Prayer, Making Room to Pray, How to Pray After You've Kicked the Dog* and *Mosquito on an Elephant's Rump* give outstanding insight and guidelines into establishing successful prayer in the local church. The remainder of this chapter is taken from these five excellent books. Though the following excerpts will be extremely helpful, I strongly advise that you obtain and use these invaluable books so you can study his entire teachings.

A Prayer Room

Making prayer visible in our churches makes it more likely to happen and encourages more people to participate. We must do everything we can to make prayer appealing, from investing in first-class prayer materials to raising up comfortable, inviting places for people to seek God. Prayer does not have to be mercenary in order to be spiritual.[1]

One of the simplest and yet most profound things that a prayer room offers is a place to be alone and still before God. It promotes humility and a visible dependence on God. Prayer rooms also generate and facilitate other prayer ideas given by the Holy Spirit to affect the whole ministry of the church in the community.[2]

Ten Reasons Your Church Needs a Prayer Room

1. One of the greatest advantages of a prayer room is that it allows us to schedule prayer in a systematic manner, making it more likely to happen. Scheduled prayer is biblical. If you read in the book of Acts, you will see that the disciples had scheduled times of prayer—9:00 A.M. in Acts 2:15; 12:00 noon in Acts 10:9; and 3:00 P.M. in Acts 3 and Acts 10:30. Also, scheduled prayer tends to be perspirational prayer because it is based on a conscious decision to seek God at a given time each week, not on a crisis or feeling.

2. Prayer rooms provide places where information can be gathered and prayed over, promoting agreement in prayer.

3. A prayer room provides an excellent place to keep a record of all the deeds of God in the life of the church—a reminder to thank and praise Him for all He does.

4. Prayer rooms promote ownership of the church vision and serve as tangible, visible reminders of our commitment to pray.

5. The compassion of Jesus is displayed to the community while we make a statement to them about the importance of prayer.

6. A prayer room provides a place where prayer can be practiced and matured—a training center for both corporate and individual prayer.

7. An inclusive impact is made on the church because a prayer room brings everyone to one place to pray.

8. Prayer rooms minister the presence of God to those who come, providing a place where people can be quiet and hear the voice of God. Church staff and prayer counselors can use it when a quiet, private place is needed.

9. Prayer rooms encourage soaking prayer—prolonged periods of prayer—persevering prayer. Sometimes it takes persistent prayer in order to reach a spiritual breakthrough. It's sobering to realize how many prayers fell just short of the mark because we gave up too soon.

10. A prayer room provides a control center for strategic prayer evangelism, for warfare and for other prayer ministries.[3]

A prayer room needs to provide privacy and be closed off from outside distractions. It should be comfortable, with a pleasant atmosphere—an inviting place to enjoy the Lord's presence. It's important that it be safely accessible 24 hours a day, with a telephone and preferably a separate outside entrance that is well-lighted and has a combination lock. It should be inspirational and should have helpful information displayed to guide people as they pray.[4]

Steps for Prayer

Mobilizing your church to pray is a *process*. There are six important steps that can mobilize prayer in your church.[5]

Step One: Pray for Prayer

- Take time to listen to God as you pray for an attitude of prayer to come upon your church.

- Pray with perseverance, knowing that there will be opposition and setbacks.

Step Two: Establish Leadership Support

- It is critical to have the support of the pastor and church leadership.

- Begin praying for God to pour out a spirit of prayer in your congregation.

- Select four or five mature, respected members to serve on a prayer task force that will be responsible for planning and promoting prayer.

Step Three: Lay Groundwork

Assess your church's current prayer status.

- Are there any existing prayer ministries?

- What has been tried in the past?

- Are there any other church ministries into which organized prayer could be incorporated?

- Is there any money in the budget for prayer?

Based on where you are, lay out a master plan that includes:

- Long-term objectives that are measurable
- Short-term goals
- Action steps leading to your short-term goals

Step Four: Teach

Probably the number one stumbling block in mobilizing a church to pray is overlooking or underestimating the importance of education. Teaching the people about God's perspective on prayer is what will give your prayer ministries longevity. For prayer to become the center of church activity, the congregation must have a mindset that makes it so, and that mindset must be nurtured and fed.

Step Five: Implement

Offer a variety of prayer opportunities so that all in the congregation can plug in and feel enthusiastic about their participation. As you plan, consider the seven prayer temperaments and be careful not to zero in on one or two while leaving the others out.

1. Traditional—historical (Matthew)
2. Immediate—spontaneous (Mark)
3. Loving—relational (Luke)
4. Mysterious—contemplative (John)
5. Confrontational—authoritative (Paul)
6. Perceptive—visionary (Peter)
7. Ordered—structured (James)[6]

Recruit and train people to lead and serve. Provide necessary materials and information.

Practice term praying.

- Make sure participants always know when they are to start praying and when they are to stop.

- A definite time frame builds a sense of accomplishment and fulfillment.

- When prayer ministries are implemented, people are more apt to commit to pray again or to pray in a different area.

Step Six: Maintain and Assess

- In a highly visible way, report answers to prayer and give feedback about what is happening through the prayer ministries to the whole congregation.

- Allow two- to three-minute testimonies on a Sunday morning.

- Regularly appreciate those who participate in the prayer ministries.

- Never stop praying for prayer and asking God for new creative ways to pray.

Leadership Support

Leadership is critical to the success of any ministry. Without it, prayer simply will not happen. The support of the pastor is crucial to the success of prayer in the church. Also, there needs to be someone besides the pastor in charge of prayer.[7]

Qualifications of a Prayer Coordinator

1. Has a strong personal prayer life
2. Is spiritually mature
3. Has the gifts of organization, encouragement, leadership and communication
4. Has a good reputation in his or her home congregation and has the confidence of church leaders and other pastors

5. Has enough time to attend key prayer events
6. Is not a pastor[8]

Responsibilities of a Prayer Coordinator

1. Oversee the intercessory prayer ministry
2. Select and enlist prayer leadership
3. Research the church's/city's current prayer ministries
4. Identify key people and enlist their support
5. Gather a wide array of resources on prayer
6. Work closely with pastors and leaders to receive prayer, vision and guidance
7. Help develop and oversee the implementation of the plan
8. Coordinate changes, programs and other activities with the church staff
9. Keep the pastor advised and request the pastor's counsel on significant matters
10. Develop an information network
11. Schedule services offering prayer, as well as orientation and training meetings
12. Schedule and conduct monthly leadership meetings
13. Encourage and promote prayer ministry throughout the church and the community[9]

Lay Groundwork

Develop a long-term prayer plan, one that is realistic and measurable. Give it a time line, assign responsibility, affirm people who pray and celebrate the results. Plans can be well thought out, bold and exciting, but if they do not match up with your church's particular giftings, they will result in unnecessary frustration and disappointment. As you begin to build your prayer ministry, take into account your current status and make sure your plans are realistic. They should challenge you a little, but not so much that failure is inevitable.[10]

Consider the following example of one of Dr. Terry Teykl's experiences:

> After hosting a workshop on the value of having a prayer room, a pastor and his small but dedicated congregation were so excited about the idea, they decided to open up a spare room in their building for twenty-four hour prayer. About six months later the pastor was frustrated and confused. "The people were so excited at first, but after a month or two, interest fell off and it became a struggle. I even feel embarrassed about the fact that we failed. I don't understand what happened."
>
> After visiting with him on the phone, I learned the church had a strong outreach to elderly people and shut-ins in their community, so I suggested that part of the prayer room be designated to reflect the needs and victories of this particular ministry. I also learned they had a core of very active youth who had a vision for their school, so I recommended they hang a special board in the prayer room where kids could leave prayer requests and praise reports, and that the youth be challenged to fill up certain hours in the schedule. Also, because it was a small congregation, they set their total goal as 40 hours of prayer each week, instead of trying to pray around the clock.
>
> Within just a few months, all the time slots were full, testimonies were coming in and the people were excited about the new prayer room. The textbook form of a prayer room had little appeal to keep them motivated. But when it was personalized to reflect and include those things which were important to them, they responded with excitement and a sense of purpose.[11]

Developing a plan of prayer with specific objectives in mind gives intentionality and direction to prayer. Prayer must have organization and accountability to be effective. The greater the order, the more likely the ministry will last. Corporate prayer ministries need structure to keep them on track and focused.[12] The essentials for a praying church are:

- a praying leader who motivates others;

- purpose and direction—prayer plans give scope, limit and direction to intercession in the local church;

- prayer budgets—provide material for training and maintenance of the prayer ministry;

- recruitment—enlist people to pray, orchestrate sign-up methods and build accountability into the prayer ministry; and

- creativity and variety—add interest and enjoyment to prayer ministries.[13]

When organizing a quality prayer room, keep the following tips in mind. A place of prayer should, in appearance and essence, convey the supreme value of prayer in your church. Build into your plan a support base that will sustain the room for at least a year, until it is established.

1. Ask the Father, "What kind of prayer room do You want us to have?"

2. Choose people to lead in the prayer room effort.

3. Develop a statement of purpose for the prayer room. What is the definition of intercessory prayer in your church's prayer room?

4. Choose someone to coordinate the ministry.

5. Select a place in the church for the prayer center.

6. Design a floor plan or format for your prayer room. What pattern will you use? Maps and pictures can be posted on the walls to motivate prayer. A table with a card file can be used for tracking prayer requests. Stations of prayer signifying various needs and subjects can be situated throughout the room so intercessors can move throughout the room praying strategically at each station.[14]

Teach

As you work to initiate prayer in your church, realize that you are asking people to do something that for most Americans is very difficult. We are raised to equate independence, self-reliance and confidence with strength. We believe so strongly in our own capabilities that to ask for help from anyone, even God, is like admitting defeat.[15]

As George Barna stated, "It is not enough for the pastor to pray fervently, nor is it sufficient for a leadership team to pray ardently on behalf of the congregation. Until the church owns prayer as a world-class weapon in the battle against evil and cherishes prayer as a means of intimate and constant communication with God, the turn-around efforts of a Body are severely limited, if not altogether doomed to failure."[16]

An attitude of prayer must be established.

• Build a solid, living theology of prayer (i.e., why pray?).
• Seek a vision for what God wants to do in your specific situation.
• Develop a plan to bring the vision to pass.

- Establish visible leadership for prayer.
- Become familiar with prayer resources.
- Recruit people to pray.
- Train people to pray strategically.
- Turn plans into action.[17]

Churches must be willing to pay the price for a first-class, organized, informed, visible, attractive prayer ministry. Good prayer materials cost money. Having a comprehensive prayer library is a tremendous step toward becoming a house of prayer. We need to be committed to training all of our people to pray, not just some select group who exhibit the gift of intercession. Prayer training must become an integral part of church life.[18]

The sustained effort of prayer evangelism in a prayer room invites the Holy Spirit to do at least eight important things in a church in order for it to evangelize its community:

1. The Holy Spirit imparts compassion. As we pray, the love of God for a lost world is poured into our hearts. He is the agent of love. As we pray, the Holy Spirit imparts the love that transcends technique; He overcomes our apathy and coldness of heart; and He moves us to the self-sacrifice required to build a relationship with a lost person to secure them in Christ.

2. The Holy Spirit calls us to repentance. As intercessors pray in the prayer room, corporate repentance takes place as a work of the Spirit, beginning with the church first and then spreading outward to the community.

3. The Holy Spirit guides our outreach and gives us a relevant message for our community. When a church

prays continually in a corporate manner over its vision and outreach, the Spirit initiates mission. Divine alignment in evangelism is the work of the Holy Spirit in answer to prayer.

4. The Holy Spirit empowers Christians for witness.

5. The Holy Spirit grants laborers for the harvest.

6. The Holy Spirit gives means and resourceful ideas to the church's outreaches. New methods and approaches to evangelism are the work of the Spirit.

7. The Holy Spirit adds vitality and life to existing ministries in the local church. The Spirit empowers the life of the local church to make it attractive. Corporate intercession over a church's membership can invite the Holy Spirit to cleanse us of any and all attitudes that diminish our witness for Christ.

8. In answer to prayer, the Holy Spirit will give unity and a city-wide vision for the harvest.[19]

Implement, Maintain and Assess

Everyone who participates in prayer ministry needs to know the guidelines, rules and boundaries, and must be willing to submit to the leadership of the group. It's important that people understand that prayer is a discipline that can be learned. Training builds confidence and expertise in prayer. Dick Eastman's *The Hour That Changes the World* is an excellent teaching model. Each church needs to find what will work best for them.

As people pray the Scriptures, corporate prayer becomes alive and is saved from boredom. A prayer guide can be used to lead prayer through the Word, asking God to perform His Word in specific areas. The Word of God gives vocabulary to prayer and is the prayer language of the Father. Let the Word permeate your prayer ministry.[20]

As you recruit people to pray, it is helpful to set specific goals for recruitment, such as 20 hours of prayer each week, 40 hours of prayer each week, 144 hours of prayer each week or whatever is appropriate for your situation. Here are some guidelines for successful recruiting:

1. Try to offer a variety of prayer models to appeal to different people.

2. Make everything about your prayer ministry as first-class and attractive as possible.

3. The best place to recruit is from the pulpit. People support what the pastor supports.

4. Print the purpose of the prayer room in your bulletin or newsletter, and give updates on its development.

5. Make sure your prayer recruitment emphasis does not conflict with other major events in the church.

6. Approach groups in the church, such as youth, singles', women's and men's groups—make this a churchwide emphasis.

7. Put up a sign-up board in the foyer.

8. Be organized and state very clearly the ministry objectives and requirements, including the starting date and the date it will finish—term praying.

9. Make your prayer room part of the new member orientation.

10. Emphasize special considerations that may help people feel more comfortable with the idea of signing up for prayer.

11. Use alternates and day captains to improve participation and to establish accountability.

12. Give feedback to those who pray so they can be motivated by the answers. Publish the results of prayer in your church bulletin or newsletter, or make prayer announcements from the pulpit.

13. Appreciate those who pray in visible ways.[21]

It is very important to be alert and stand guard against the inevitable attacks of Satan. Five demonic attacks are listed below with an appropriate response through prayer:

1. *Satan wants to bring destruction*: Our response to this attack should be to pray God's protection over the prayer ministry. Take authority over Satan in the strong name of Jesus, binding him with the blood of our Lord.

2. *Satan cultivates indifference*: We can counter apathy when we ask God to raise up enough intercessors and reserves to fill each hour.

3. *Satan works through enshrinement*: We can combat pride when we pray that God will never let us become more impressed with the ministry than with Him. Ask God to help us to look only to Him, giving Him the glory.

4. *Satan wants to see carnal intercessors*: The solution to this subtle corruption is to pray that God will have full control over every intercessor's life.

5. *Satan encourages indiscretion*: Our defense is to pray that God will cause us to set a guard over our mouths. Nothing will destroy the intercessory prayer ministry as quickly as gossiping about people's problems and needs. Do not share these needs with anyone once you leave the prayer room unless you have permission to do so. This matter is critical. The effects are disastrous (see Prov. 16:28; 17:9; 18:8; 26:20,22).[22]

As you develop your prayer ministry, it is essential to be aware of the following obstacles to mobilizing corporate prayer in the church, in order to overcome them:

1. The Church has been inundated with Christian humanism (i.e., doing things for God in our own abilities).

2. Prayer is often human centered, not God centered. We tend to use prayer as a means to get what we want to further our own kingdoms—What will I get out of it?

3. Consistent, continual corporate prayer is difficult to establish because so much of our praying today is dependent on feelings. Prayer-room praying depends on a corporate mentality of discipline and commitment. Prayer is a choice, not a feeling. Prayer rooms are based on obedience, out of love for Christ.

4. Corporate prayer is work because it has been neglected for so many years. There is a huge void in the training of ministers in prayer.

5. Prayer rooms are slow to start because people are often afraid of group prayer. Fear of failure or discom-

fort, often based on past experiences, can be great hindrances to many people.

6. Prayer for the city in a prayer room is difficult to start because we live in an instant, fast-food society. We want formulas for quick results. Instead of just praying, we want to do something, even if it's wrong. We must not let the desire for quick results cause us to abort a season of prayer that is essential for spiritual awakening in our cities.

7. Prayer is hard to find when there is a lack of vision for church growth. With little vision, there can be little prayer. A vision to reach the city for Christ stretches us beyond ourselves and causes us to seek God.

8. There is resistance to prayer because the enemy hates sustained prayer and will throw every obstacle imaginable in the way of a prayer room.

9. Prayer rooms are hard to establish because churches are often too busy to pray.

10. Collective, consistent prayer is difficult when there is a lack of Christ-centeredness. The main reason we pray is the wonder and revelation of Jesus. You may need to pray for a return of His exaltedness to your church in order to pray rightly. The revelation of Jesus will cause people to want to simply come and sit in His presence. Without such a vision of Jesus Christ, prayer becomes a religious routine, void of intimacy and fulfillment.[23]

One of the Father's most important agendas is for us to spend time seeking Him for the lost and for ways to reach them. When God gives us a great task, He expects us to seek Him with all our heart and soul and strength before we endeavor to do that task. We must realize completely that His Spirit, not might or power, will accomplish this task.

One of the fastest ways to kill a prayer ministry is to allow it to become an end in itself. Once that happens, people will begin to lose interest and the ministry will starve for lack of commitment. The way to keep a prayer ministry going is to attach it to the Great Commission. Prayer is not an end in itself; it is a means to accomplishing the work of God. Remember, our ultimate goal is a harvest of souls, not just well-organized prayer ministries.[24]

Consider this testimony of Terry Teykl:

I remember during one of our first vigils, my time slot was 10:00 in the morning. You must understand that being a fledgling church, our office was a very obscure store front in a small strip of businesses. Yet while I was there praying alone, a young man came to the door wanting to know if someone could talk to him about how to become a Christian. I was astounded. It was our first profession of faith, and it appropriately happened while I was praying, not preaching. I was so moved by the experience that we planned another vigil for the next Saturday, and I signed up again, this time for 4:00 in the afternoon. Again, while I was praying, I heard a knock at the door only to discover another troubled young man who was looking for answers. He, too, accepted Christ, becoming our second profession of faith. For that to have happened once was almost unbelievable, but twice—I knew God was speaking to me. He showed me, "If you will find Me, others will find you." Prayer evangelism works. When we pray targeting the

Great Commission, people are drawn to Christ, not by
our sign or our building, but by the Holy Spirit.[25]

Note: The information contained in this chapter was adapted and *used by permission* from Terry Teykl. For further information by Terry Teykl on this subject of
prayer, you may write to Prayer Point Press, 2100 N. Carrolton Dr., Muncie, IN,
47304, or call (765) 759-0215 or (888) 656-6067.

Dutch Sheets

WATCHMAN PRAYER
STUDY GUIDE

The following study guide will help you become an effective watchman. You can use the guide individually, with a friend or in a small group.

If you are studying *Watchman Prayer* on your own or with a partner, consider starting a "watchman diary" in which you work through each chapter's reflection questions. Even if you do not have a partner for the study, find someone (a close friend or your spouse, for instance) to share your thoughts and prayers with as you progress. Writing and then talking about the growth you experience will strengthen you to move forward with confidence.

If you desire to discuss *Watchman Prayer* within a small group, the following guidelines will maximize your time with each other. In anticipation of your weekly meeting, be sure everyone has a copy of the book. Encourage group members to read the chapter that will be discussed at the meeting, and to write down questions or comments that come to them during the week. Bring your Bible to each study and invite group members to do the same. Each week, the group will pray as watchmen, and the Bible will be the primary text to help them discern what God is saying.

During the week, pray that the Holy Spirit will speak to each member of the group. In addition, pray that you will remain sensitive to the Spirit when the group comes together. When you meet, open each session with prayer, asking the Holy

Spirit to come and make His presence known and voice heard.

After prayer, ask each person to share his or her first impressions of that week's chapter. Work through the study guide together and encourage each group member to participate in the discussion. As the weeks progress, also take time to let each person share how he or she is learning to keep watch.

Finally, try to create an atmosphere that fosters trust within the group, freedom to pray and attention to the Holy Spirit's leading.

Chapter One
LOOKING FOR A FEW GOOD WATCHMEN

We love to watch things we enjoy. Football fans watch football. Parents ogle over newborn babies. Teenage boys delight in teenage girls. What about you? Are there things you would love to watch but simply don't have the time? How do you decide what to watch and what not to?

Becoming God's Watchman

- In what ways have you experienced the power of intercessory prayer?

- What would it take for intercessory prayer to become a lifestyle in your family?

Becoming a Lifestyle

Second Corinthians 2:11 states the basic principles of the necessity of having watchmen. After reviewing Dutch's teaching on page 402, consider the following questions:

- Why do you think people remain ignorant of Satan's activity?

- In what ways have you experienced Satan scheming to bring division or confusion in your family or church?

- How has Satan taken the advantage in your local community?

Even though Paul called the Corinthians to always be aware of the movements of Satan, he too had experiences in which he did not detect the work of Satan until it was too late.

- After reading 1 Thessalonians 2:18, think of a time you felt confident that God had called you to do something, but you experienced spiritual resistance.

- What would have been different if a watchman had been on duty?

Beginning with the Basics

Read the following verses slowly and reflect on the message of each passage:

> And pray in the Spirit on all occasions with all kinds of prayers and requests. With this in mind, be alert and always keep on praying for all the saints (Ephesians 6:18).

> Be self-controlled and alert. Your enemy the devil prowls around like a roaring lion looking for someone to devour (1 Peter 5:8).

> In order that Satan might not outwit us. For we are not unaware of his schemes (2 Corinthians 2:11).

Review the four principles of the Watchman anointing on pages 408-410 and answer the questions below.

- Describe a situation in which assuming God's protection from spiritual warfare could have disastrous results.

- When you assume the responsibility of living as a watchman in prayer, God's intent is to give you a "heads up" when Satan is on the move. What are your thoughts about this?

- Consider the image God paints of the watchman of Israel in Isaiah 56:10. If you were the commander of that watchman, what would be your response to the watchman who preferred to sleep and dream instead of keeping the city safe?

- Take a moment to consider how the Christian landscape across America has changed over the past 40 years. In what ways has Satan taken the bigger portion from the Body of Christ because we've been asleep on the job?

Chapter Two
GOD'S ALARM SYSTEM

In this chapter, we looked at the big picture: the broad concepts and definitions of a watchman. (If you prefer the forest and are not so concerned about the trees, this chapter was for you!) Before we jump into the details, take a moment to reflect on what you learned.

- In your own words, describe the primary roles of a watchman.

- Review the three Old Testament and two New Testament words that refer to the role of the watchman. How does the Holy Spirit enable a watchman to fulfill these roles?

- In Luke 21, Jesus warns His disciples about what will happen in the end times. Read verses 29-36 and examine how these words impact the need for watchmen today.

Watching for Wolves, Thieves and Enemy Assaults

The Holy Spirit raises up watchmen to protect the harvest. Consider pages 318-425 from your reading.

- Read John 10:7-14. In what ways have you seen a thief or a wolf attacking the flocks in your church or community in an attempt to stop God's work?

- Using Paul and Silas (Acts 16) as an example, what practical tools of prayer can you use as a watchman to protect the harvest that the Holy Spirit has given into your care?

Watchmen not only protect the harvest, but they also stand guard on the walls of the city.

- Why was it important for a watchman to watch for messengers? How did the watchman decide who to let in the city and who not to let in?

Satan's "odorless" activities will have a terrible impact on the work that God desires when we are not alert in prayer (consider the image of the school in London, Texas). In Acts 20:28-31, Paul warns the Ephesians that wolves will arise in the community of faith and speak perverse things to draw people away from God.

- Read Revelation 2 and describe how the Ephesians kept guard over the flock. What encouragement did the Lord give to those watchmen?

- How do these words from Corrie ten Boom encourage you to develop your abilities to serve as a watchman: *"It's a poor soldier indeed who does not recognize the enemy."*

The Many Kinds of Watchmen Today

We worship a huge God who calls people to huge assignments in prayer.

- As you read about the Holy Spirit working through Cindy Jacobs in Argentina, Peter Wagner in Turkey and "Margie" in Washington, DC, what is your impression? What stands out to you most?

- What are your thoughts about Chuck Pierce's prophetic vision over Houston and God calling intercessors to pray in anticipation of a flood?

- To whom has God called you to serve as a watchman?

Take time to pray and ask God where He has called you to serve.

CHAPTER THREE
LISTEN SLOWLY

Unlike so many parents with busy, hurried lives, your Father in heaven always has time to listen to your voice and hear your prayers. Do you believe that God is always ready to listen and visit with you? Take a moment and talk to Him right now. Tell Him about your day, your frustrations, your dreams and your concerns.

Pay Close Attention

- What emotions come to your mind when you consider talking to someone who has a very short attention span? What about someone who has all the time in the world and is attentive to the details of your concerns?

- How do the following verses paint a picture of God's attentiveness and desire to hear the prayers of His people?

  Psalm 34:15

  Malachi 3:16

- Read Proverbs 4:20-22. What are the benefits of listening closely to the voice of God?

Do You Hear What I Hear?

Are you a good listener? Tim Hansel's story of the American Indian in New York describes vividly how we listen to what's important to us in the moment. God calls us to keep His voice as our first priority.

- Read 1 Corinthians 7:35. What are the priorities in your life that make if difficult to give the Lord your full attention?

- Read Luke 10:38-42. What small changes can you make in your day that would create space to give the Lord your undivided attention?

Prayer Is a Two-Way Conversation

Young children are often more interested in what they can receive from a parent or grandparent than they are in the person. Likewise, we often settle for pennies (or half dollars) and miss out on the rich experience of developing a relationship with the One who is giving out the blessings.

- Have you graduated from simply receiving from God to knowing the heart of God? Do you know His face? His voice?

In order to effectively serve as a watchman, you must develop the ability to discern and know God's voice. It's a two-way street.

- What are the dangers of a watchman not learning to listen and know the voice of God?

- Read Cindy Jacobs's excerpt from *Possessing the Gates of the Enemy* on page 440. In your prayer life, have you allowed God to preempt your planned prayers in order to hear what he has to say? Why or why not?

As you consider the three ways the Lord alerts Cindy to pray for specific individuals, think about how you have experienced God giving direction to your prayers. God is calling you to work together with Him so that you experience synergism. We can't do it without Him. He won't do it without us. Before you come back for the next session, take time to listen in your prayers and allow God to direct your prayer ministry.

Chapter Four
WATCHMEN ARE GARDENERS

Through the last chapter, you began to develop the ability to listen closely. A watchman pays careful attention to the words spoken by our heavenly Father. Have you ever had the experience of a child paying too close attention to your words and actions?

- What are three concepts of a watchman that are discussed in this chapter?

Beware! Be Aware!

- Read Genesis 2:15-18 and describe Adam's role as a watchman in the Garden.

Dutch Sheets

- Adam and Eve were unaware of the serpent's ways. Can you identify three ways the serpent deceived them in Genesis 3:1-7?

- Dutch states, "The devil is after our 'gardens,' too—our families, homes, marriages, churches, cities, etc. Our responsibility is to keep the devil out" (p. 446). In what ways have you seen the devil trying to slither his way into the gardens that the Lord has given into your care?

The story of the Gibeonites serves as a warning to be aware of how the enemy will try to deceive you, and as a testimony to God's ability to reverse the subtleties of the devil and bring about something good.

- In what ways have you seen God redeem a situation that the devil meant for evil?

Stay Awake!

The tragic destruction at Pearl Harbor on December 7, 1941, could have been minimized if those in charge would have been alert and not underestimated the capabilities of the enemy.

- In what ways have you seen Christians neglect to listen and be aware of the devil's plans?

- What were the consequences for those ministries?

Observe, See and Behold

If you were with Jesus in the garden the night He was betrayed by Judas, do you think you would have been able to stay awake and watch when He was off praying so hard He sweated blood? The disciples were asked to serve on sentry duty, to watch the perimeter, but they failed miserably.

- How often do you think Christians do not see the approach of the enemy because they are busy with other priorities? "Continue in prayer, and watch in the same with thanksgiving" (Colossians 4:2).

As you pray this week, ask God to open your eyes to see how He is working and to observe possible approaches of the enemy. As He gives you insight, create a prayer covering over the area He has called you to watch.

- Have you ever had an experience similar to the speaker in Oregon when God called others to pray a cover over you? What happened?

Before moving on to the next chapter, make a plan for this week: When will you take time this week to remain awake, be alert and observe how God is working? How will you remain aware of the ways that the devil may be planning an attack in your garden?

CHAPTER FIVE
COVER ME! I'M GOING IN!

In chapter 4, you discovered three ways to create an effective prayer cover: *be aware, stay alert* and *observe*.

- In what ways did the Holy Spirit give you insights this week into the wily ways of the evil one?

If this is your first experience being aware of God's warnings, you might feel a little overwhelmed. Remember, God will fight for you. Your job is to create a prayer cover. Let's explore some other images of a watchman.

Protector

· Describe the four ways that the Holy Spirit uses the word *shamar* in Psalm 121.

· How do these images help you understand the watchman's protective role?

· Have you ever experienced a time similar to Janet's praying for Kevin, either as a young child or as a man (pages 456-457)? What happened?

Keeper

· As you have sought to serve as a watchman, what garden have you been assigned to keep the serpent from infiltrating?

· Have you determined to be tenaciously persistent in this task? Ask the Holy Spirit to come alongside you and help you develop the ability to never grow tired in this role of keeping the garden.

· What do you find encouraging about the example of Gordon Lindsay being willing to die for the sake of his dauther (pages 458-459)?

Guard

· Make a mental list of five people that God has assigned to you as their spiritual bodyguard. Ask God to give you wisdom to effectively pray for those persons.

· Describe a time when you felt a strong burden to pray for someone's protection similar to Barbara Wentroble's experience of praying for her husband (pages 460-461).

· What would have to change in your life to make you more available, sensitive and obedient to God's prompting to pray for others?

Doorkeepers and Gatekeepers

• As you consider the experience of Barbara Wentroble calling the pastor to guard the entrance of his church (pages 462-464), what do you find exciting about the possibility of serving as a gatekeeper? What do you find intimidating?

• Dutch states, "Sometimes we must be very aggressive our dealing with the enemy. Gordon Lindsay used to say every Christian should pray at least one violent prayer every day. He was, of course, speaking of spiritual warfare" (p. 464). What was the last violent prayer you prayed in order to protect your home from an invasion of the devil? How about for your city?

Think of ways this week that you can develop your faith, aggressive prayers and persistence, in order to keep watch over the gates to your gardens.

Preserver

• After reflecting on the incident of the freighter *Bright Field* (page 466), describe the role of being a preserver for a watchman

• Read Joshua 7 and discuss how Joshua could have kept the Israelites from the breakdown at Ai.

• In what ways do you sense the Holy Spirit calling you to preserve the good work happening in your family and church? What can you learn from 1 Corinthians 1:10-12 and 5:1?

Chapter Six
WATCHMAN—LAY SEIGE!

God's people have been laying siege to cities, villages and towns for thousands of years! The Holy Spirit has guided each of these successful conquests and will guide you as you serve as a watchman for your community. After reading Joshua 6:1-25, consider what role God played in laying siege to Jericho and what role the people of Israel played.

• How do those roles compare to what happened in Cali, Columbia; Almolonga, Guatemala; and in Hemet, California (pages 470-472)?

Review the following passages that describe how taking an offensive role (laying siege) to a city also involves watching.

Judges 1:24

2 Samuel 11:16

Jeremiah 4:17

Before moving on to explore specific strategies for taking your city, consider these five factors that have been proven to have an impact on stimulating revival. After reading the Scripture passage, develop one step you could take to help put these strategies into practice.

1. Persevering leadership (Nehemiah 6:1-16)

2. Fervent, united prayer (Jonah 3:5-10)

3. Social reconciliation (Matthew 5:23-24; 18:15-20)

4. Public power encounters (Acts 9:32-35)

5. Diagnostic research/spiritual mapping (Joshua 18:8-10)

If you are willing to obey God fully, walk in faith and never give up, you can have anything God wants you to have. And that absolutely includes revival in your local community (p. 473).

Deployment into Your City

Review the six strategies on pages 476-477 that will have a permanent spiritual impact on your community. Are these strategies being carried out in your community? What part have you taken to help develop this impact? Are you willing to start putting these strategies into place?

Consider the following possible realities that could pose a threat to spiritual revival in your community and make a note of the ones that apply. After taking an honest look at the reality of your situation, begin to pray that God would reveal to you how to combat these weaknesses.

- Disunity
- Apathy
- Prayerlessness
- Past Sins
- Pride
- Busyness
- Other: _____

As you read about the steps taken in Colorado Springs (page 480), what did you find encouraging? What would you like to begin to apply in your situation?

Making the Shift

- Describe the difference between *kairos* and *chronos* time.

- Can you think of a time in your life when God used a *chronos* season in order to bring about a *kairos* moment? What happened when you experienced this divine shift?

Only God knows how long the *chronos* season will last until you experience the *kairos* moment of great revival in your community.

As you pray over your community this week, ask God to give you a vision for that moment and the strength to continue laying siege until that moment arrives.

CHAPTER SEVEN

ARMED AND LOADED WITH PRAYER

We can either build prisons for our children to live in throughout their adult lives (and spend a lot of money on therapy!) or through prayer we can create pathways for the Holy Spirit to work so that our families will experience God's blessing for many generations.

- What type of spiritual impact did your parents have in your life? In what ways would you hope to replicate or change that impact in the lives of your children?

- Create a list of the people that live in your field. If you have children, include them, but also think about other immediate family members and distant relatives.

The following steps were developed by Quin Sherrer and used as she prayed for her son Keith and his spiritual health (pages 489-491). Choose one of the people you listed above and pray through these steps for the next three weeks.

1. *Be specific in your request.* What are you most concerned about?

2. *Pray Scripture passages out loud.* Ask God to give you a passage that applies to this situation. You may also want to pray the Scriptures on pages 491-492.

3. *Write down your prayers.* Find a journal and write down your prayers each day.

4. *Pray in accordance with God's will.* Take time to talk with a trusted friend and to search the Scriptures to be sure you are asking for God's will.

5. *Pray for your children's future.* What are God's plans for your family members? Pray for those!

It is essential for us to allow the Holy Spirit to give us the strategy needed at each specific moment. I always try to find the principles of God's Word that apply to my situation and then ask the Holy Spirit how to apply them in that particular instance. He is always faithful in doing this because He desires to see God's will accomplished even more than I do (pp. 102-103).

Ask God to reveal to you a strategy of prayer as you pray for those people in your garden.

Building the Wall

· What does *paga* mean?

· God has called you to build boundaries of protection around those you love. Read Ephesians 6:18. How does this verse instruct you to pray and build boundaries around those God has placed in your care?

· What insights do you gain from Beth Alves's testimony (page 497) or Shirley Dobson's experience (page 499) that help you understand Ephesians 6:18?

Moving Outside of the Garden

Commit to pray specifically this week for one of your spiritual leaders. As you do so, use the prayer guide given on page 504.

- Review the five guidelines for praying for your neighbors on page 505. Which of them can you begin to implement today?

- How does the story of Father Damien encourage you to exhibit the love of Christ to all those God has called you to pray for?

Chapter Eight
KEEPING WATCH OVER YOURSELF

As God fashions you into His watchman, the devil will try to slither his way into your heart to pull you away from hearing and following God's direction.

Watch over your heart with all diligence for from it flows springs of life (Proverbs 4:23).

- Why is it important that a watchman watch (*natsar*) over his own feelings, will and intellect?

For as he thinks within himself, so he is (Proverbs 23:7).

- Are there people that you associate with now, or are there activities that you participate in, that are shaping you into someone God would *not* want you to be?

- Describe the biblical understanding of a stronghold (page 511) and how strongholds become established in the life of a believer.

The weapons we fight with are not the weapons of this world. On the contrary, they have divine power to demolish strong-holds (2 Corinthians 10:4).

- What divine weapons have you been given to demolish strongholds in your life? Do you use them? Why or why not?

Many people have allowed in much unbiblical information be-
fore becoming Christians. Others have allowed great amounts
of perversion and unclean thinking to be engrained into their
souls. Still others have experienced great trauma, rejection or
other emotional wounds before coming to Christ (p. 513).

• Do you fall into any of these categories? As you reflect on
your past experiences, where do you see the greatest potential
for Satan to have established a stronghold?

The Liberating Power of God's Word

• What two choices must each person make in order to lay siege
to a stronghold?

• Have you struggled in your life to experience the power of
God's Word? How does understanding that we receive the
Word as a seed change the way you view the ability of the
Word to demolish strongholds?

• After reading Romans 12:2 and 2 Corinthians 3:18, describe a
time in which the Holy Spirit began a process of changing or
challenging an area of your life that was contrary to Scripture.

• In that process, how was God's Word constructive? How was
it destructive?

Read Hebrews 4:12-13 and answer the following questions:

• When have you experienced the piercing of God's Word to
bring healing to a specific area in your life?

• Has God's Word ever divided your soul and spirit in order to
give to each part of you what you need? What happened?

What strongholds exist in your life today? Take time each day to pray that God would reveal how your past is impacting your ability to minister today. Begin to apply God's Word to bring healing and hope.

CHAPTER NINE
THE WATCHMAN'S ALLY

The single greatest key to eternal success in any Christian endeavor is allowing the full work of the Holy Spirit in and through us (p. 525).

- Why do you think many individuals and ministries ignore or take for granted the work of the Holy Spirit?

- What about you? Has the Holy Spirit taken an active role in your walk with Christ? In what ways do you identify with the story of Herbert Jackson, the missionary who needed to connect his cable (pages 525-526)?

- Describe three to five ways that it is to your advantage to experience the presence of the Holy Spirit.

A Partner in Battle

- What two Greek words give a description of how the Holy Spirit helps us, and what do they mean?

- Review John 16:7 and Romans 8:26 and describe how the Holy Spirit comes alongside you in the battle.

- What words came to your mind as you read about the experience with Ceci and her cyst (pages 527-529)?

The Many Roles of the Holy Spirit

The Holy Spirit wants to commune with us. He has much to say if we learn to listen. He is the means to all revelation from God. He is the Teacher. He is a part of the Godhead we're to be in relationship with. Let Him fellowship and commune with you (p. 530).

- How is developing intimacy with the Holy Spirit a part of your regular daily routine?

- What do you do each day that isolates you from fellowship with the Holy Spirit?

- Read Proverbs 3:32 and Psalm 25:14. Think of two attitudes or actions you can change this week that will deepen your fellowship with the Holy Spirit.

Partnering, Distributing and Partaking

The Holy Spirit not only wants to have fellowship with you, but will become the ultimate prayer partner and give you the ability to pray for others in very specific ways.

- Has the Holy Spirit ever given you a special insight into someone's life in order to pray for them? What happened?

- Review Romans 1:11; 1 Timothy 4:14 and 2 Timothy 1:6. Who has God used to distribute His gifts to you in partnership with the Holy Spirit?

- The Holy Spirit will distribute information to you so that you can more effectively distribute His gifts through the Church. Are you open to partaking in what the Holy Spirit is offering? Why or why not?

The Holy Spirit is the ultimate counter-intelligence in giving you the ability to pray effectively. As a watchman, you've been given the tremendous opportunity to align yourself with the One who created the entire universe. Time spent with God is never wasted time. As you move into this week, make a commitment to develop your relationship with the Holy Spirit as you continue to serve as God's watchman.

CHAPTER TEN
WATCHMEN AREN'T WATCHDOGS

Unfortunately, it's not unusual for ministries who seek to develop an intimacy with the Holy Spirit to also attract people who become obsessed with demons, visions and prophetic words and confuse God's voice with their own imaginations or, even worse, fall prey to Satan's deceptions.

- Read 1 Thessalonians 5:19-21, and then make a list of some of the dangers of not examining what someone feels is a word from the Lord.

- What are the three major ways we can judge whether or not a revelation is from the Lord?

Let's take some time to dig deeper into these three major "acid tests" and develop some practical ways for you to use them.

Acid Tests

- Think of a time when either you or someone you knew felt as though the Holy Spirit had spoken a message that directly contradicted Scripture. How did you respond?

- Review the suggestions on pages 547-549 for how to discern the difference between a watchman and a watchdog when Scripture does not directly speak to the situation. Think of a recent situation in which you were cautioned about an individual and apply these suggestions.

- Create a "wise counsel" list. Ask God to give you the names of three or four people who you can turn to regularly to test how the Holy Spirit is speaking in your situation.

- Do you have a process in which you seek to confirm how the Holy Spirit is speaking? If so, what has been helpful and not helpful about this process in the past? If not, talk with some intercessors this week and ask if they would be willing to help you develop a process.

What Does This Mean?

- After you have confirmed that the revelation is from God, what three questions must you ask to find out what it means?

- Reflect on a time when the Holy Spirit gave you a vision and you needed help with its interpretation. What happened?

- Think about steps you can take when the Holy Spirit gives you a warning about a future event. What can you do to discern the timing of a particular vision?

The Final Step: How to Use the Information

In her book *Possessing the Gates of the Enemy*, Cindy Jacobs writes:

> *"Pray that God will teach you the proper time and place to sound the alarm. God reveals to intercessors the intimate needs of those for whom we intercede. This is a precious trust"* (p. 553).

Dutch Sheets

- Identify some pitfalls of breaking that trust by always sharing the information God has given to you with others.

- Consider the list of characteristics of the trusted intercessor on pages 554-555. How can you develop these characteristics in your pursuit of serving as God's watchman?

CHAPTER ELEVEN
ESTABLISHING A PRAYER MINISTRY

Now it's time to get things started in your church. Let's explore some of the essentials of a successful prayer ministry.

A Prayer Room

- Of the 10 reasons for establishing a prayer room given on pages 558-559, which are the most compelling for you?

- Make a list of the immediate obstacles that you sense in establishing a prayer room at your church.

- Pray specifically through this list, asking the Holy Spirit to provide a way for a prayer room to be established.

Next, let's explore some of the practical steps to establishing a prayer ministry.

Leadership

- How would you describe your pastor's support in pursuing a prayer ministry?

- Establish a time to meet with your pastor to talk about the idea of a prayer ministry. Before meeting, pray that God would give your pastor a vision for prayer.

- After reviewing the qualifications and responsibilities for a Prayer Coordinator on pages 562-563, brainstorm a list of people who might serve in this capacity. Ask God to prepare the right person for the role and to direct you to him or her.

Establishing and Maintaining

- What ministry in your church is of special interest to the congregation? Talk to the leaders of those ministries and ask for specific prayer requests.

- What can you implement at your church over the next three months to increase your congregation's interest in prayer?

- Review the guidelines for succesful recruiting on pages 569-570. Of these 13 suggestions, which would work the best in your church?

- As a watchman, it is your responsibility to be on guard, be aware and stand at the doorway of this ministry so that Satan will not impact your ministry. Review the five demonic attacks Satan tries to use to destroy a prayer ministry, and begin today to create a prayer cover.

- Of the 10 obstacles to mobilizing corporate prayer listed at the end of this chapter, which ones seem to fit your situation? Take time to pray against these obstacles.

Reaching the lost is why we pray. We want everyone to become a part of the Kingdom. As you close this study, ask God to show you how the Holy Spirit might use your prayer ministry to reach out to those who need to receive salvation.

ENDNOTES

Chapter One: Looking for a Few Good Watchmen

1. Dutch Sheets, *Intercessory Prayer* (Ventura, CA: Regal Books, 1996), pp. 233-236.
2. "Juvenile Crime Statistics," at Online Lawyer Source. http://www.onlinelawyer source.com/criminal_law/juvenile/statistics.html (accessed February 2008).
3. Julie Steenhuysen, "Suicides Rise Sharply in U.S. Youth, Studies Find," Reuters, September 6, 2007. http://www.reuters.com/article/domesticNews/idUSN06340 66420070906 (accessed February 2008).
4. "Fact File: Accessibility" at Common Sense About Kids and Guns. http://www.kids andguns.org/study/fact_file.asp#access (accessed February 2008).
5. "Number of Child Victims of Abuse and Neglect, 2005," from the National Data Analysis System at Child Welfare League of America. http://ndas.cwla.org/ data_stats/access/predefined/Report.asp?PageMode=1&%20ReportID=134&% 20GUID={43D5142B-E0A1-40F0-8133-2AF024D382F9}#Table (accessed February 2008). "Child Victims Who Died as a Result of Abuse/Neglect," from the NDAS at Child Welfare League of America. http://ndas.cwla.org/data_stats/access/pre defined/Report.asp?ReportID=350 (accessed February 2008).
6. "U.S. Teen Sexual Activity," Kaiser Family Foundation, January 2005. www.kff.org/ youthhivstds/upload/U-S-Teen-Sexual-Activity-Fact-Sheet.pdf (accessed February 2008).
7. "Abortion Surveillance—United States, 2000," Centers for Disease Control and Prevention, November 28, 2003. http://www.cdc.gov/mmwr/preview/mmwr html/ss5212a1.htm (accessed February 2008).
8. "Born Again Christians" statistics from The Barna Group. http://www.barna.org/ FlexPage.aspx?Page=Topic&TopicID=8 (accessed February 2008).
9. "Church Attendance" statistics from The Barna Group. http://www.barna.org/ FlexPage.aspx?Page=Topic&TopicID=10 (accessed February 2008).
10. "Researcher Predicts Mounting Challenges to Christian Church," *The Barna Update*, April 16, 2001. http://www.barna.org/FlexPage.aspx?Page=BarnaUpdate& BarnaUpdateID=88 (accessed February 2008).
11. "Beliefs: Trinity, Satan," statistics from The Barna Group. http://www.barna.org/ FlexPage.aspx?Page=Topic&TopicID=6 (accessed February 2007).
12. Ethelbert W. Bullinger, *A Critical Lexicon and Concordance to the English and Greek New Testament* (Grand Rapids, MI: Zondervan Publishing House, 1975), p. 400.
13. Spiros Zodhiates, *Hebrew-Greek Key Study Bible—New American Standard*, rev. ed. (Chattanooga, TN: AMG Publishers, 1990), p. 1797.
14. Spiros Zodhiates, *The Complete Word Study Dictionary* (Iowa Falls, IA: Word Bible Publishers, 1992), p. 1173.
15. James Strong, *The New Strong's Exhaustive Concordance of the Bible* (Nashville, TN: Thomas Nelson Publishers, 1990), ref. no. 4122.
16. Bullinger, *Critical Lexicon and Concordance*, p. 28.
17. Sheets, *Intercessory Prayer*, pp. 138-140.
18. Craig Brian Larson, *Choice Contemporary Stories and Illustrations for Preachers, Teachers and Writers* (Grand Rapids, MI: Baker Book House, 1998), p. 28.
19. Craig Brian Larson, *Illustrations for Preaching and Teaching* (Grand Rapids, MI: Baker Book House, 1993), p. 59.

20. Sheets, *Intercessory Prayer*, pp. 237, 238.

21. Ibid., p. 244.

22. "Youth Violence Facts at a Glance," Centers for Disease Control and Prevention, Summer 2007. http://www.cdc.gov/ncipc/dvp/YV_DataSheet.pdf (accessed February 2008).

23. "School Shooting: Notable Shootings," at Wikipedia.org. http://en.wikipedia.org/wiki/School_shooting#Notable_Shootings (accessed February 2008).

24. Solveig and Ken Henderson, "Abandoned to You, Jesus." Used by permission.

Chapter Two: God's Alarm System

1. James Strong, *The New Strong's Exhaustive Concordance of the Bible* (Nashville, TN: Thomas Nelson Publishers, 1990), ref. no. 4436.

2. Gordon Lindsay, *Acts in Action*, vol. 3 (Dallas, TX: Christ For The Nations, 1975), p. 93.

3. C. Peter Wagner, *Blazing the Way* (Ventura, CA: Regal Books, 1995), p. 76.

4. Edward K. Rowell, *Fresh Illustrations for Preaching and Teaching* (Grand Rapids, MI: Baker Book House, 1997), p. 103.

5. Corrie ten Boom, quoted in Elizabeth Alves, *Becoming a Prayer Warrior* (Ventura, CA: Regal Books, 1998), p. 97.

6. Rowell, *Fresh Illustrations for Preaching and Teaching*, p. 195.

7. Cindy Jacobs, "Healing and Deliverance Through Spiritual Warfare for the Nations," comp., John Sandford, *Healing the Nations* (Grand Rapids, MI: Chosen Books, 2000), pp. 202-212.

8. C. Peter Wagner, "Operation Queen's Palace—A Proposal for a Major International Prayer Journey and Prophetic Act" (paper for Global Harvest Ministries, Colorado Springs, CO, January 1998), n.p. See also "Celebration Ephesus News Release" issued by the World Prayer Center, Colorado Springs, CO, October 5, 1999.

9. Barbara Wentroble, *Prophetic Intercession* (Ventura, CA: Regal Books, 1999), p. 38.

10. Cindy Jacobs, *Possessing the Gates of the Enemy* (Tarrytown, NY: Chosen Books, 1991), pp. 59, 60.

11. Craig Brian Larson, *Illustrations for Preaching and Teaching* (Grand Rapids, MI: Baker Book House, 1993), p. 216.

Chapter Three: Listen Slowly

1. Spiros Zodhiates, *Hebrew-Greek Key Study Bible—New American Standard*, rev. ed. (Chattanooga, TN: AMG Publishers, 1990), p. 1773

2. Edward K. Rowell, *Fresh Illustrations for Preaching and Teaching* (Grand Rapids, MI: Baker Book House, 1997), p. 134

3. Zodhiates, *Hebrew-Greek Key Study Bible*, p. 1787

4. Craig Brian Larson, *Illustrations for Preaching and Teaching* (Grand Rapids, MI: Baker Book House, 1993), p. 102.

5. Ibid., p. 240.

6. Elizabeth Alves, *Becoming a Prayer Warrior* (Ventura, CA: Regal Books, 1998), p. 70.

7. James Strong, *The New Strong's Exhaustive Concordance of the Bible* (Nashville, TN: Thomas Nelson Publishers, 1990), ref. no. 2145.

8. Ibid., ref. no. 4332.

9. Craig Brian Larson, *Contemporary Illustrations for Preachers, Teachers and Writers* (Grand Rapids, MI: Baker Book House, 1996), p. 187.

10. Quin Sherrer and Ruthanne Garlock, *How to Pray for Your Family and Friends* (Ann Arbor, MI: Servant Publications, 1990), p. 24.

11. Cindy Jacobs, *Possessing the Gates of the Enemy* (Tarrytown, NY: Chosen Books, 1991), p. 75.

12. *New Webster's Dictionary and Thesaurus of the English Language*, s.v. "synergism."
13. Larson, *Illustrations for Preaching and Teaching*, p. 153.

Chapter Four: Watchmen Are Gardeners
 1. *New Webster's Dictionary and Thesaurus of the English Language*, s.v. "wary."
 2. Dutch Sheets, *Intercessory Prayer* (Ventura, CA: Regal Books, 1996), p. 244.
 3. Spiros Zodhiates, *Hebrew-Greek Key Study Bible—New American Standard*, rev. ed. (Chattanooga, TN: AMG Publishers, 1990), p. 1763.
 4. Edward K. Rowell, *Fresh Illustrations for Preaching and Teaching* (Grand Rapids, MI: Baker Book House, 1997), p. 146.
 5. Craig Brian Larson, *Illustrations for Preaching and Teaching* (Grand Rapids, MI: Baker Book House, 1993), p. 9.
 6. Ibid., p. 189.
 7. "Pearl Harbor Attack" *Encyclopedia Britannica*, 1972, vol. 17, pp. 507-508; *The American Nation* (New York: HarperCollins Publishers, 1991), pp. 797-798; Michael Portillo, "The Attack on Pearl Harbor," *Remembering Pearl Harbor*, April 10, 1997. http://brill.acomp.usf.edu/~mportill/assign/html (accessed April 2000).
 8. Zodhiates, *Hebrew-Greek Key Study Bible*, p. 1724.
 9. James Strong, *The New Strong's Exhaustive Concordance of the Bible* (Nashville, TN: Thomas Nelson Publishers, 1990), ref. no. 6544.

Chapter Five: Cover Me! I'm Going In!
 1. *The Consolidated Webster Encyclopedic Dictionary*, s.v. "protect."
 2. Quin Sherrer and Ruthanne Garlock, *A Woman's Guide to Spiritual Warfare* (Ann Arbor, MI: Servant Publications, 1991), pp. 214-215.
 3. Mrs. Gordon Lindsay, *My Diary Secrets* (Dallas, TX: Christ For The Nations, 1976), pp. 136-138.
 4. Barbara Wentroble, *Prophetic Intercession* (Ventura, CA: Regal Books, 1999), pp. 33-34.
 5. Elizabeth Alves, *Becoming a Prayer Warrior* (Ventura, CA: Regal Books, 1998), p. 57.
 6. Wentroble, *Prophetic Intercession*, pp. 59-60.
 7. Lindsay, *My Diary Secrets*, pp. 142-143.
 8. Craig Brian Larson, *Choice Contemporary Stories and Illustrations for Preachers, Teachers and Writers* (Grand Rapids, MI: Baker Books, 1998), p. 65.
 9. *The Consolidated Webster Encyclopedic Dictionary*, s.v. "preserve."

Chapter Six: Watchman—Lay Siege!
 1. George Otis, Jr., *Informed Intercession* (Ventura, CA: Regal Books, 1999), pp. 18-47.
 2. Spiros Zodhiates, *Hebrew-Greek Key Study Bible—New American Standard*, rev. ed. (Chattanooga, TN: AMG Publishers, 1990), p. 1752.
 3. James Strong, *The New Strong's Exhaustive Concordance of the Bible* (Nashville, TN: Thomas Nelson Publishers, 1990), ref. no. 6822.
 4. Zodhiates, *Hebrew-Greek Key Study Bible*, p. 1787.
 5. Otis, Jr., *Informed Intercession*, p. 56.
 6. C. Peter Wagner, *Warfare Prayer* (Ventura, CA: Regal Books, 1992), p. 163, 167, 169, 171-173.
 7. Ethelbert W. Bullinger, *A Critical Lexicon and Concordance to the English and Greek New Testament* (Grand Rapids, MI: Zondervan Publishing House, 1975), p. 804.
 8. Strong, *New Strong's Exhaustive Concordance of the Bible*, ref. no. 2657.
 9. Bob Beckett, *Commitment to Conquer* (Grand Rapids, MI: Chosen Books, 1997), p. 32.
10. Otis, Jr., *Informed Intercession*, n.p.
11. Bullinger, *A Critical Lexicon and Concordance to the English and Greek New Testament*, p. 804.
12. Zodhiates, *Hebrew-Greek Key Study Bible*, p. 1763.

Chapter Seven: Armed and Loaded with Prayer

1. Edward K. Rowell, *Fresh Illustrations for Preaching and Teaching* (Grand Rapids, MI: Baker Book House, 1997), p. 165.
2. Ibid., p. 68.
3. Jamie Buckingham, *The Nazarene* (Ann Arbor, MI: Servant Publications, 1991), p. 89.
4. Quin Sherrer and Ruthanne Garlock, *How to Pray for Your Family and Friends* (Ann Arbor, MI: Servant Publications, 1990), p. 79.
5. Craig Brian Larson, *Illustrations for Preaching and Teaching* (Grand Rapids, MI: Baker Book House, 1993), p. 219.
6. Quin Sherrer, *Good Night, Lord* (Ventura, CA: Regal Books, 2000), pp. 164-165.
7. Quin Sherrer, *How to Pray for Your Children* (Ventura, CA: Regal Books, 1998), p. 24.
8. Quin Sherrer and Ruthanne Garlock, *The Spiritual Warrior's Prayer Guide* (Ann Arbor, MI: Servant Publications, 1992), pp. 158-159.
9. Quin Sherrer and Ruthanne Garlock, *A Woman's Guide to Spiritual Warfare* (Ann Arbor, MI: Servant Publications, 1991), pp. 32-33.
10. Sherrer and Garlock, *How to Pray for Your Family and Friends*, pp. 43-44.
11. Ibid., pp. 34-35.
12. *The Spirit-Filled Bible—KJV* (Nashville, TN: Thomas Nelson Publishers, 1991), pp. 331-332.
13. Ethelbert W. Bullinger, *A Critical Lexicon and Concordance to the English and Greek New Testament* (Grand Rapids, MI: Zondervan Publishing House, 1975), p. 804.
14. Ibid.
15. Elizabeth Alves, *Becoming a Prayer Warrior* (Ventura, CA: Regal Books, 1998), pp. 29-30.
16. Cindy Jacobs, *The Voice of God* (Ventura, CA: Regal Books, 1995), pp. 176-178.
17. Mrs. Gordon Lindsay, *My Diary Secrets* (Dallas, TX: Christ For The Nations, 1976), pp. 181-183.
18. C. Peter Wagner, *Praying with Power* (Ventura, CA: Regal Books, 1997), pp. 57-58.
19. C. Peter Wagner, *Prayer Shield* (Ventura, CA: Regal Books, 1992), p. 177.
20. Sherrer and Garlock, *How to Pray for Your Family and Friends*, pp. 95-96.
21. Sherrer, *Good Night, Lord*, pp. 83-84.
22. Quin Sherrer and Ruthanne Garlock, *A Woman's Guide to Spirit-Filled Living* (Ann Arbor, MI: Servant Publications, 1996), pp. 227-228.
23. Rowell, *Fresh Illustrations for Preaching and Teaching*, p. 124.

Chapter Eight: Keeping Watch Over Yourself

1. James Strong, *The New Strong's Exhaustive Concordance of the Bible* (Nashville, TN: Thomas Nelson Publishers, 1990), ref. no. 3820.
2. Ibid., ref. no. 8176.
3. Daniel Goleman, "What's Your Emotional IQ?" *Readers Digest*, January 1996, p. 50.
4. Spiros Zodhiates, *The Complete Word Study Dictionary* (Iowa Falls, IA: Word Bible Publishers, 1992), p. 1393.
5. Craig Brian Larson, *Illustrations for Preaching and Teaching* (Grand Rapids, MI: Baker Book House, 1993), p. 47.
6. Strong, *New Strong's Exhaustive Concordance of the Bible*, ref. no. 2198.
7. Ibid., ref. no. 1756.
8. Ibid., ref. no. 1338.
9. Ibid., ref. no. 3311.
10. Ibid., ref. no. 2924.
11. Ibid., ref. no. 1580.

Chapter Nine: The Watchman's Ally

1. Spiros Zodhiates, *Hebrew-Greek Key Study Bible—New American Standard*, rev. ed. (Chattanooga, TN: AMG Publishers, 1990), p. 4851.
2. Craig Brian Larson, *Choice Contemporary Stories and Illustrations for Preachers, Teachers, and Writers* (Grand Rapids, MI: Baker Book House, 1998), p. 54.
3. Robert Heidler, *Experiencing the Spirit* (Ventura, CA: Regal Books, 1998), p. 35, citing Bill Bright.
4. Ibid.
5. Craig Brian Larson, *Illustrations for Preaching and Teaching* (Grand Rapids, MI: Baker Book House, 1993), p. 182.
6. James Strong, *The New Strong's Exhaustive Concordance of the Bible* (Nashville, TN: Thomas Nelson Publishers, 1990), ref. no. 3875.
7. Edward K. Rowell, *Fresh Illustrations for Preaching and Teaching* (Grand Rapids, MI: Baker Book House, 1997), p. 110.
8. Strong, *New Strong's Exhaustive Concordance of the Bible*, ref. no. 4878.
9. Rowell, *Fresh Illustrations for Preaching and Teaching*, p. 224.
10. Strong, *New Strong's Exhaustive Concordance of the Bible*, ref. no. 5475.
11. Larson, *Choice Contemporary Stories and Illustrations*, pp. 123-124.
12. Jane Hamon, *Dreams and Visions* (Santa Rosa Beach, FL: Christian International, 1997), pp. 98-99.
13. Quin Sherrer, *Listen, God Is Speaking to You* (Ann Arbor, MI: Servant Publications, 1999), pp. 148-149.
14. Bob Beckett, *Commitment to Conquer* (Grand Rapids, MI: Chosen Books, 1997), pp. 34-35.
15. Ibid., p. 35.
16. Larson, *Illustrations for Preaching and Teaching*, p. 83.

Chapter Ten: Watchmen Aren't Watchdogs

1. Bob Beckett, *Commitment to Conquer* (Grand Rapids, MI: Chosen Books, 1997), p. 151.
2. Mrs. Gordon Lindsay, *My Diary Secrets* (Dallas, TX: Christ For The Nations, 1976), pp. 192-193.
3. James Strong, *The New Strong's Exhaustive Concordance of the Bible* (Nashville, TN: Thomas Nelson Publishers, 1990), ref. no. 1381.
4. Elizabeth Alves, *Becoming a Prayer Warrior* (Ventura, CA: Regal Books, 1998), p. 73.
5. Edward K. Rowell, *Fresh Illustrations for Preaching and Teaching* (Grand Rapids, MI: Baker Book House, 1997), p. 26.
6. Cindy Jacobs, *Possessing the Gates of the Enemy* (Tarrytown, NY: Chosen Books, 1991), pp. 65-66.

Chapter Eleven: Establishing a Prayer Ministry

1. Terry Teykl, *Pray the Price* (Muncie, IN: Prayer Point Press, 1997), p. 134.
2. Ibid., pp. 134-138.
3. Terry Teykl, *Blueprint for the House of Prayer* (Muncie, IN: Prayer Point Press, 1997), p. 49. See also Teykl's *Making Room to Pray* (Muncie, IN: Prayer Point Press, 1993), pp. 60-68; and *Pray the Price*, pp. 130-133.
4. Teykl, *Blueprint for the House of Prayer*, pp. 48-49.
5. Teykl, *Mosquito on an Elephant's Rump* (Muncie, IN: Prayer Point Press, 2000), pp. 47-52.
6. Teykl, *How to Pray After You've Kicked the Dog* (Muncie, IN: Prayer Point Press, 1999), pp. 208-295.
7. Teykl, *Making Room to Pray*, p. 69. See also Teykl's *Pray the Price*, pp. 77-78.

8. Teykl, *Blueprint for the House of Prayer*, p. 33.
9. Ibid. See also Teykl's *Making Room to Pray*, pp. 77-78.
10. Teykl, *Pray the Price*, pp. 29-31.
11. Ibid., pp. 31-32.
12. Teykl, *Making Room to Pray*, pp. 92-93. See also Teykl's *Pray the Price*, p. 34.
13. Teykl, *Making Room to Pray*, p. 30.
14. Ibid., pp. 75-80.
15. Teykl, *Pray the Price*, pp. 35-36.
16. Teykl, *Blueprint for the House of Prayer*, p. 31.
17. Ibid., p. 25
18. Teykl, *Pray the Price*, pp. 38-44.
19. Teykl, *Making Room to Pray*, pp. 38-44.
20. Ibid., pp. 80-83, 93.
21. Teykl, *Making Room to Pray*, pp. 86-90. See also Teykl's *Pray the Price*, p. 43.
22. Teykl, *Blueprint for the House of Prayer*, p. 53.
23. Teykl, *Making Room to Pray*, pp. 95-100.
24. Ibid., pp. 12, 29. See also Teykl's *Pray the Price*, p. 103.
25. Teykl, *Pray the Price*, p. 47.

BIBLIOGRAPHY

Alves, Elizabeth. *Becoming a Prayer Warrior*. Ventura, CA: Regal Books, 1998.

Barna Research Online. "Angels Are In—Devil and Holy Spirit Are Out." April 29, 1997. http://www.barna.org/cgi-bin/Page Press Release.asp?PressReleaseID=3 (accessed April 2000).

———. "Annual Survey of America's Faith Shows No Significant Changes in Past Year." March 8, 1999. http://www.barna.org/ cgi-bin/PagePressRelease.asp? PressReleaseID=17 (accessed April 2000).

———. "Christianity Showing No Visible Signs of a Nationwide Revival." March 3, 1998. http://www.barna.org/cgi-bin/ PressRelease.asp?PressReleaseID=16 (accessed April 2000).

Beckett, Bob. *Commitment to Conquer*. Grand Rapids, MI: Chosen Books, 1997.

Buckingham, Jamie. *The Nazarene*. Ann Arbor, MI: Servant Publications, 1991.

Bullinger, Ethelbert W. *A Critical Lexicon and Concordance to the English and Greek New Testament*. Grand Rapids, MI: Zondervan Publishing House, 1975.

Goleman, Daniel. "What's Your Emotional IQ?" *Readers Digest*, January 1996.

Hamon, Jane. *Dreams and Visions*. Santa Rosa Beach, FL: Chris-tian International, 1997.

Heidler, Robert. *Experiencing the Spirit*. Ventura, CA: Regal Books, 1998.

Henderson, Solveig and Ken. "Abandoned to Jesus." n.p, n.d.

Jacobs, Cindy. "Healing and Deliverance Through Spiritual Warfare for the Nations." In *Healing the Nations*, comp. John Sanford (Grand Rapids, MI: Chosen Books, 2000).

———. *Possessing the Gates of the Enemy*. Tarrytown, NY: Chosen Books, 1991.

———. *The Voice of God*. Ventura, CA: Regal Books, 1995.

Larson, Craig Brian. *Choice Contemporary Stories and Illustrations for Preachers, Teachers and Writers*. Grand Rapids, MI: Baker Book House, 1998.

———. *Contemporary Illustrations for Preachers, Teachers and Writers*. Grand Rapids, MI: Baker Book House, 1996.

———. *Illustrations for Preaching and Teaching*. Grand Rapids, MI: Baker Book House, 1993.

Lindsay, Gordon. *Acts in Action*. Dallas, TX: Christ For The Nations, 1975.

Lindsay, Mrs. Gordon. *My Diary Secrets*. Dallas, TX: Christ For The Nations, 1976.

Otis, Jr., George. *Informed Intercession*. Ventura, CA: Regal Books, 1999.

Remembering Pearl Harbor. Portillo, Michael. "The Attack on Pearl Harbor." April 10, 1997. http://brill.acomp.usf.edu/ ~mportill/assign.html (accessed April 2000).

Rowell, Edward K. *Fresh Illustrations for Preaching and Teaching*. Grand Rapids, MI: Baker Book House, 1997.

Sheets, Dutch. *Intercessory Prayer*. Ventura, CA: Regal Books, 1996.

Sherrer, Quin. *Good Night, Lord*. Ventura, CA: Regal Books, 2000.

———. *How to Pray for Your Children*. Ventura, CA: Regal Books, 1998.

———. *Listen, God Is Speaking to You*. Ann Arbor, MI: Servant Publications, 1999.

Sherrer, Quin, and Ruthanne Garlock. *A Woman's Guide to Spirit-Filled Living*. Ann Arbor, MI: Servant Publications, 1996.

———. *A Woman's Guide to Spiritual Warfare*. Ann Arbor, MI: Servant Publications, 1991.

———. *How to Pray for Your Family and Friends*. Ann Arbor, MI: Servant Publications, 1990.

———. *The Spiritual Warrior's Prayer Guide*. Ann Arbor, MI: Servant Publications, 1992.

Stop the Violence, Face the Music. "Teens at Home." 2000. http:// www.stv.net/contents/stats/05.html (accessed April 2000).

———. "Teens at School." 2000. http://www.stv.net/contents/stats/ 04.html (accessed April 2000).

Strong, James. *The New Strong's Exhaustive Concordance of the Bible*. Nashville, TN: Thomas Nelson Publishers, 1990.

Teykl, Terry. *Blueprint for the House of Prayer*. Muncie, IN: Prayer Point Press, 1997.

———. *How to Pray After You've Kicked the Dog*. Muncie, IN: Prayer Point Press, 1999.

———. *Making Room to Pray*. Muncie, IN: Prayer Point Press, 1993.

———. *Mosquito on an Elephant's Rump: A Collection of Articles, Stories and Quotes*. Muncie, IN: Prayer Point Press, 2000.

———. *Pray the Price*. Muncie, IN: Prayer Point Press, 1997.

U.S. Department of Health and Human Services. Office of the Assistant Secretary for Planning and Evaluation. "A National Strategy to Prevent Teen Pregnancy, Annual Report 1997-98." June 1998. http://aspe.hhs.gov/hsp/teenp/97-98rpt.htm.

Wagner, C. Peter. *Blazing the Way.* Ventura, CA: Regal Books, 1995.

——. "Operation Queen's Palace—A Proposal for a Major International Prayer Journey and Prophetic Act." A paper for Global Harvest Ministries, Colorado Springs, CO, January 1998.

——. *Prayer Shield.* Ventura, CA: Regal Books, 1992.

——. *Praying with Power.* Ventura, CA: Regal Books, 1997.

——. *Warfare Prayer.* Ventura, CA: Regal Books, 1992.

Wentroble, Barbara. *Prophetic Intercession.* Ventura, CA: Regal Books, 1999.

Women's Wire. "Abortion's Unexpected Side Effects?" 1999. http:// www.women.com/ news/forums/backtalk/E0819 (accessed September 22, 1999).

World Prayer Center. "Celebration Ephesus News Release." Colorado Springs, CO (October 5, 1999).

Youth Culture Department. "Youth Culture Statistics." Focus on the Family, December 13, 1998.

Youthworker. Youth Specialties. "Youth Culture Update." November/December 1998. http://www.gospelcom.net/ys/free/stats (accessed April 2000).

Zodhiates, Spiros. *Hebrew-Greek Key Study Bible—New American Standard.* Rev. ed. Chattanooga, TN: AMG Publishers, 1990.

——. *The Complete Word Study Dictionary.* Iowa Falls, IA: Word Bible Publishers, 1992.

ABOUT THE AUTHOR

Dutch Sheets is an internationally recognized author, teacher and conference speaker. He travels extensively, ministering throughout the United States and in other nations, empowering believers for passionate prayer and societal transformation. Dutch has also pastored, taught in several colleges and seminaries, and served on the board of directors of numerous organizations.

Dutch is the author of 20 books, many of which have been translated into over 30 languages, including the bestseller *Intercessory Prayer*. His newest book, *Dream*, was released in April 2012.

Dutch's greatest passion is to see America experience a sweeping revival and return to its Godly heritage. He burns to see people find God's "dream" for them and tap into their destiny. Dutch is a messenger of hope for America, encouraging believers to contend for awakening in our day and reformation in our lifetime.

In 2012, Dutch was named Executive Director of Christ For The Nations Institute. Both Dutch and his wife, Ceci, are graduates of CFNI. They have been married for 35 years and have two grown daughters, a wonderful son-in-love, and an incredible grandson. They are residents of the Dallas area.

For more information about the Dutch Sheets Ministries, visit:

WWW.DUTCHSHEETS.ORG